India's Maladies

India's Maladies

Etiopathogenesis And Therapy

Sat Sharma

Copyright © Sat Sharma.

All rights reserved. No part of this book may be reproduced in any form or by any electronic or mechanical means, including information storage and retrieval systems, without permission in writing from the publisher, except by reviewers, who may quote brief passages in a review.

ISBN: 978-1-63684-577-7   (Paperback Edition)
ISBN: 978-1-63684-578-4   (Hardcover Edition)
ISBN: 978-1-63684-576-0   (E-book Edition)

Book Ordering Information

Phone Number: 315 288-7939 ext. 1000 or 347-901-4920
Email: info@globalsummithouse.com
Global Summit House
www.globalsummithouse.com

Printed in the United States of America

BOOKS BY DR. SAT D. SHARMA

1. INDIA MARCHING – REFLECTIONS FROM A NATIONALISTIC PERSPECTIVE
2. CORRUPT INEPT RUDDERLESS POLITIPOLITICIANS -- IMPEDIMENTS TO INDIA'S FORWARD MARCH
3. INDIA'S MALADIES – ETIOPATHOGENESIS AND THERAPY
4. HINDUSTAN'S FRAILTIES – ANALYSIS AND ALLEVIATION
5. HINDUSTAN: PAST, PRESENT, FUTURE [VOLUME I] – AN ORDINARY HINDUSTANI SPEAKS
6. HINDUSTAN: PAST, PRESENT, FUTURE [VOLUME II] – AN ORDINARY HINDUSTANI SPEAKS
7. WHAT AILS INDIA? ANTI-NATIONALS, SEDITIONISTS, SEPARATISTS, TRAITORS, More….
8. FRIENDS AND/OR FOES – INDIA, CHINA, AMERICA, PAKISTAN
9. THE TURBULENT TIMES – LIFE OF AN UNKNOWN HINDUSTANI
10. CROOKED HINDUSTANI POLITICIANS – BANE AND DISGRACE TO INDIA

DISCLAIMER

This Book is based on material collected from various sources and kinds of information – conventional, modern, technological, oral history or otherwise. Oral history is known to provide insight into the history that is obscure, forgotten willfully or genuinely, suppressed or distorted by rulers purposefully. No doubt Columbia University opened a separate department for Oral History. In any country there is no dearth of the patriots offering authentic peep into the past. Only issue(s): they must be located. With PM Modi being on the scene since 26th May 2014, their number is increasing as if they are coming out of hibernation! The objective of writing this book was to give a bird's eye view of the of the circumstances leading to the present scenario impacting my people and also to showcase some of the numerous burning problems we face today in Hindustan even 72 years after attaining 'independence' from Britain although the real freedom from mental slavery is yet to be attained.

Limitation of Liability/Disclaimer of Warranty: Whereas the author and publishers have used their best efforts in preparing the Text, they make no representation or warranties with respect to the accuracy and completeness of the contents of the Book and specifically disclaim any warranties of merchantability or fitness for any purpose.

ACKNOWLEDGEMENTS

I owe a deep sense of gratitude to numerous well-wishers and my all well-meaning friends who have ever been cajoling, challenging, coaxing and thereby amplifying to arouse a true sense of duty inside me to jot down something important or worthwhile for posterity. Nations are built over time. Unlike bulk of my compatriots, nationalism is my credo. To me, my country, India comes first and foremost. My only regret remains I started writing rather late in life during my 60s. They say better late than never. My motivation has ever been from my own biological daughter who left the motherland in her early 20s; and my godson living close by in the metropolis and financial capital of India – Bombay now known as Mumbai. And through them, their spouses and their children or my grandkids. I owe lot of gratitude to my friends and contemporaries for their sane advice, contribution and feedbacks from time to time.

Let me express my gratitude to my publishers, Global Summit House. It all started with a call from Ms. Jessica Santos, Marketing/Advertising Manager sometime during the Fall season in 2018. She spoke well and apprised me of republishing of books. Jessica prodded me to get book(s) republished through her organization. I chose to write afresh. And hence the time taken to complete the manuscript. I am grateful to Ms. Karen Smith and Ms. Andrea Gilberts for reminding me from time to time to complete my works. Last but not the least my thanks are due to Ms. Yvonne Johnson for helping me out to complete CORRECTIONS FORM.

CONTENTS

Books by Dr. Sat D. Sharma v
Disclaimer.. vii
Acknowledgements.. ix

1. Foreword... 1
2. Introduction... 45
3. The Basic Premise.. 70
4. Maladies Afflicting Hindustan And Remedies.........................199
5. Afterword 357

FOREWORD

Man keeps on learning till he is alive. Avid reading contemporary international news, books and literature has always kept me informed on the current happenings all around the universe. However, trying to indulge in dispassionate analysis, and reading in between the lines on mainstream and social media gives one an insight into the global 'climate' and environment. Sifting information to arrive at the truth remains a paramount necessity. MSM in India as its counterparts in America and some other democracies is anti-establishment. Both the media leave no opportunity in denigrating their Chief Executive. Making money at the cost of fooling generally gullible public is the norm for news and TV channels. The comparative degree of honesty and nationalism and patriotism is different in the oldest as compared to the largest democracy of the world. Our Indian medias are highly corrupt and perform antinational acts in the garb of 'freedom of speech and expression' aided and abetted by nonexistence of checks and balances or a defined 'Code of Conduct' and judicial inadequacies. Our courts take enormous time to decide their even simple cases so much so that a person may die awaiting the verdict. This makes India into a bizarre 'free for all' 'Demonocracy' where one can obtain any verdict to one's liking provided, he/she has the resources to influence or buy judgment of his liking.

Hindustan belongs to the oldest civilization of the world that has existed since tens of millennia BCE. Hinduism is the oldest religion. Its members or Hindus are stretching far and wide on the globe. The global perception and image about Hindustan are undergoing a sea change after the swearing in of Narendra Damodardas Modi as the prime minister on 26th May 2014. Even America starts valuing the importance: "It was my great honor to host a celebration of Diwali, the Hindu Festival of Lights, in the Roosevelt Room at the @Whitehouse this afternoon. I welcome very, very special people!" [*https://www.whitehouse.gov/briefings-statements/ remarks-president-trump-diwali- ceremonial-lighting-Diya/* …4:20 PM - Nov

13, 2018]. Many countries in the Far East attest to the fact that they are/were Hindus. One can find the evidence of this even today. Credit must be given to the largest Muslim country in the world for acknowledging that their ancestors were Hindus. Ramayana is played for a month once in a year in Bali; picture of Lord Ganesh appears on her currency notes; Garuda, the *Vahan* or the mode of transport of Lord Vishnu, is the national Airline. Ramayana and Mahabharata are two great Hindu epics. Lord Rama is the most revered earliest Hindu god. He was born on 11th January in the year 5132 BCE. And he was the 17th king in Suryavanshi Dynasty founded by *Rishi* Kashyap. Incidentally Kashmir is named after him. This dynasty can be traced down to Mahabharata. There were 51 generations. Ramayana was written by Rishi Valmiki in Rama's times and has been verified by Rama.

There have been concerted efforts *first* by the British historians to purposely ignore and denigrate the greatness of our culture and most ancient civilization. They were meticulously dishonest in systematically distorting/changing/meddling with our history. *First* effort was made by British historians: James Smith and Charles Grant when they were hired to write 'Syllabus of History' for Helisbury College. The British colonial masters were cruel, irrational, illogical and rarely followed the laws as practiced in their own country. There are tell-tale evidences of the White peoples' atrocities and excesses – mostly destructive or even inhuman acts like systematically annihilating the original natives in whichever country they colonized from Americas to Australia.

For many millennia, we Hindustanis have been best known for our culture, civilization, wisdom, tolerance and patience in assimilating thoughts of different saints and wisemen and everyone who sought shelter in the subcontinent. Brutal invaders were tamed on this pious soil. There have been many great Indian warriors in medieval times starting with the great Rajput Bappa Raval, the ancestor of great Sisodia kings Maharana Sanga and Maharana Pratap, who at age 18 not only defeated the first Muslim invader and looter Mohammad bin Qasim but pursued right up to his home Ghazni. Delhi king Prithviraj Chouhan who defeated Mohammad Ghouri 17 times. But (foolishly) showing magnanimity spared his life every time. Unfortunately, *this tolerance and compassion, one of the basic tenets of Hinduism, proved to be the undoing of this great culture, perhaps the best our world has seen.* The legendary Maharaja Ranjit Singh, recently voted as the greatest leader world has produced, is another classical example. greatest leader of all time in *BBC* poll. On 5th March

2020, *Yahoo News UK* reported: *'A Sikh warrior born in the 18th century has beaten Winston Churchill to be named the greatest leader of all time in a new poll.'* "Some 38% of the 5,000 people who voted in the *BBC World Histories magazine poll* said Maharajah Ranjit Singh, the founder of the Sikh Empire, was the greatest leader the world has ever known. Historian Matthew Lockwood, who nominated Singh, said of the leader: "Though certainly an imperialist, Ranjit Singh represented a different, more enlightened, more inclusive model of state-building, and a much-needed path towards unity and toleration. We could still benefit from his example." Arguing that Singh, who led Sikhs' troops against Afghan Ruler Shah Zaman, was "more than a mere conqueror", Lockwood added: "Singh was, almost uniquely, a unifier — a force for stability, prosperity and tolerance… He also went to great lengths to ensure religious freedom within his lands. "He patronized Hindu temples and Sufi shrines, attended Muslim and Hindu ceremonies, married Hindu and Muslim women, and even banned the slaughter of cows to protect the religious sensitivities of Hindus. [A classical TRUE real-life example of our greatest civilization] "His reign marked a golden age for Punjab and northwest India." Singh, who became the Maharajah of the Punjab in 1801, was born in 1780 and died in 1839. Matt Elton, editor of *BBC World Histories*, said: "Though perhaps not as familiar as some of the other names on the list, *Ranjit Singh's overwhelming success in our poll suggests that the qualities of his leadership continue to inspire people around the world in the 21st century*. And, at a time of global political tensions, it's telling that Singh's rule is interpreted as representing ideals of tolerance, freedom and cooperation." Results of *BBC World Histories Magazine* poll [Andy Wells, Freelance Writer]:

1. Maharaja Ranjit Singh, ruler of the Sikh empire 1801–39
2. Amílcar Cabral, 20th century African independence fighter
3. Winston Churchill, British prime minister 1940–45 and 1951–55
4. Abraham Lincoln, US president 1861–65
5. Elizabeth I, Queen of England 1558–1603

Gurudeva Rabindranath Tagore, too, spoke of how the Scythians, Huns, Pathans and Mughals have merged into one among the multitudes on the shores of India's oceans. Forcible *en-masse* conversions of this Hindu subcontinent into Islam or Christianity could never be accomplished despite the 800-year rule by Muslim invaders one after the other or by the 200-year occupation by Europeans. At least 100 million to maybe 200 million Hindus were massacred in Hindu genocide not reported by worthless historians who had/have sold their conscience for the sake of money and/or awards from anti-national anti-Hindu Congress party. The Muslims came from the Middle-East, Turkey and Central Asia; the last to come, Mughal dynasty effectively finished on 27th September 1857 with the arrest and exile of the 84-year old last nominal king Bahadur Shah Zafar to Rangoon (now Yangon) where he breathed his last longing to be buried in Hindustan. Today, his last surviving descendants live in penury – one of them was found in the eastern state of West Bengal. Muslim kings of Delhi were known for their anti-Hindu and anti-Sikh atrocities on a grand scale. Besides religious conversions into Islam, they abducted and raped innumerable girls and young Hindu women, destroyed at least 300,000 Hindu temples; set up mosques on the site of thousands of demolished Hindu temples. Shiva temple in Kashi, Ram Mandir in Ayodhya, Krishna's birthplace temple in Mathura and the repeatedly demolished Shiva temple at Somnath are classical examples of the tell-tale destruction. On Friday, 23rd November 2018, *The Indian Express* carried a story by Maulshree Seth: *'Demolish Delhi's Jama Masjid, hang me if idols are not found'*: "BJP MP Sakshi Maharaj said he be hanged if idols are not found below the staircase of Jama Masjid. Saying that he expects the government to bring a law for the construction of Ram Temple in Ayodhya (just like Somnath Temple in 1948) before the 2019 Lok Sabha election, Bhartiya Janata Party MP Sachidanand Hari Sakshi alias Sakshi Maharaj, in a controversial statement Friday, gave a call for the demolition of Jama Masjid in Delhi. In his address, the BJP MP from Unnao also said he be hanged if idols were not found below the staircase of Jama Masjid. He said that it was his first statement after he came to politics and he still stands by it. *"Main rajniti mein jab aya to mera pehla statement tha Mathura mein… Ayodhya, Mathura, Kashi ko chhodo… Delhi ki Jama Masjid todo, agar sidiyon mein murtiyan na mile to mujhe fansi pe latka dena… Aj bhi main kayam hun."*, [When I came to politics, my first statement was in Mathura. To leave Ayodhya, Mathura and Kashi aside and demolish Jama Masjid in Delhi and if idols are now found below the staircase then I should be hanged. I still stand by this statement], Maharaj said. He claimed that *Mughals played with the sentiments of Hindus and constructed over 30,000 mosques by demolishing Temples:* "Mugal kal mein Hinduon ke samman ke sath khilwad kiya gaya Mandir tode gaye, Masjiden banayi gayin, 30,000 *se zyada."* (During Mughal era, people played with the honor of Hindus and demolished temples and mosques were constructed, over 30,000). Stating that the BJP remains clear about the construction of the temple in Ayodhya, Sakshi Maharaj called on Congress president Rahul Gandhi, BSP chief Mayawati and SP president Akhilesh Yadav to make their stand clear on the longstanding burning issue of *Ram Mandir."*

On the same day, *Rediff.com News* published, *'Muslims ready to give up Babri claim, their leaders are not'*. "Syed Ghayorul Hasan Rizvi, chairman of the National Commission for Minorities, wants an out-of-court settlement in the Ram Janmabhoomi-Babri Masjid dispute and wants the Muslim community to be "large-hearted". Rizvi is making attempts to meet members of the All India Muslim Personal Law Board in Lucknow as well as Hindu leaders and find a way for an out-of-court settlement in the vexatious issue that is currently before the Supreme Court of India for a final settlement. The apex court last month posted the matter for hearing for the first week of January before an "appropriate bench" whose composition will be decided later. Speaking to *Rediff.com's* Syed Firdaus Ashraf, Rizvi stated that the Muslim community is willing to give up its claim on the Babri Masjid site, but community leaders are blocking the way for a settlement.

You have been saying that there must be an out-of-court settlement in the Ayodhya case. How is it possible given the hardened positions on all sides? I am saying an out-of-court settlement is necessary because whenever the verdict comes, one party wins and other will lose. Moreover, it is not necessary that even the Supreme Court's verdict will be accepted by everybody, just like what is happening in the case of Sabarimala. Therefore, I am saying the Ram mandir issue must be settled out of court.

But... (Interrupts) Muslims have this apprehension that 'What after Ram Mandir?' They are wondering that what is the guarantee that tomorrow they (Hindus will not target other masjids in Mathura and Kashi (Varanasi) too. This is a problem. And, therefore, I am saying that any solution that must come on this issue has to come out of peaceful talks.

Who takes the decision on behalf of the Muslims, that it is okay to build Ram Mandir at Babri site? The AIMPLB from one side and the RSS, the VHP, and the BJP from the other side will take the decision. Hashim Ansari's son (Iqbal Ansari) could have been fighting his case on an individual basis, but the decision from the Muslim side will have to be taken by Muslim Personal Law Board as the Sunni Waqf Board has the backing of the Personal Law Board. (Note: The late Hashim Ansari was the original litigant in the Ram Janmabhoomi-Babri Masjid case. Right now, the case fought in the Supreme Court by three main parties – the Sunni Waqf Board, the Nirmohi Akhara and the Hindu Mahasabha.) However, in November 2019, the SC decided in favor of Ram Mandir!

Talks of an out of the court settlement appeared earlier but no concrete result emerged. Several times this issue came almost to the verge of a solution, but something or the other came in the way of an out-of-court settlement. This time the situation is different. Today, the (communal) situation in the country is bad. The distance between Hindus and Muslims is increasing. This will stop only when good atmosphere will prevail in the country. Now, if an out-of-court settlement is reached in the Ram mandir issue, then there will be a cordial atmosphere in the country. Now, if an out-of-court settlement is reached in the Ram mandir issue, then there will be a cordial atmosphere in the country.

What happens to BJP MP's private bill on Ayodhya? 'Babri Masjid is not an ego issue for Muslims'

Who will take the decision on behalf of the Muslims, that it is okay to build a Ram temple at the Babri Masjid site? The All India Muslim Personal Law Board from one side and the RSS, the Vishwa Hindu Parishad, and the BJP from the other side will take the decision. Hashim Ansari's son (Iqbal Ansari) could have been fighting his case on an individual basis, but the decision from the Muslim side will have to be taken by Muslim Personal Law Board as the Sunni Waqf Board has the backing of the Personal Law Board. (Note: The late Hashim Ansari was the original litigant in the Ram Janmabhoomi-Babri Masjid case. Right now, the case is being fought in the SC by three main parties -- the Sunni Waqf Board, the Nirmohi Akhara and the Hindu Mahasabha.)

Did you speak to anyone from the Muslim Personal Law Board about this? I have spoken to one or two people from the Muslim Personal Law Board. I am in Lucknow right now. If some further development takes place, then I will inform you later. Talks of an out-of-court settlement have taken place earlier too, but no concrete result emerged. Several times this issue came almost to the verge of a solution, but something or the other came in the way of an out-of-court settlement. This time the situation is different. Today, the (communal) situation in the country is bad. The distance between Hindus and Muslims is increasing. This will stop only when good atmosphere will prevail in the country. Now, if an out-of-court settlement is reached in the Ram mandir issue, then there will be a cordial atmosphere in the country.

Do you think the Ram mandir issue is causing a rift between Hindus and Muslims? Ram mandir is such an issue that distances one community from another. The message that goes is that the Muslim community is fighting against the Ram mandir in Ayodhya. And it is only when the Muslim community withdraws from the case that the Ram mandir can be built. But the case is in the final stage of hearing in the Supreme Court. The Supreme Court too had said when Justice J S Khehar was the Chief Justice of India that they would like to have an out-of-court settlement and they are ready for it. But that did not work out then. Many learned people sat and tried to resolve this issue, but a solution did not come about. Now as time passes, things change and, therefore, I feel everyone must change, be it Hindus or Muslims. And, therefore, I am saying again that an out-of-court settlement is necessary in this case.

Do you feel the Muslim community is ready for a Ram mandir in Ayodhya? The Muslim community wants this issue to be resolved peacefully and they want to live peacefully.

Do you believe the Muslim community wants to give up its claim on the Babri masjid? The Muslim community is ready to give up the Babri masjid claim, but their leaders are not. You do a survey and find out the answer. Muslim leaders are not ready. *[Syed Firdaus Ashraf/Rediff.com]*

Well-known writer of Indian origin, Salman Rushdie once said, "*India's 'selfhood is so capacious, so elastic that it manages to accommodate one billion kinds of difference... it works because the individual sees his own nature writ large among the nature of the State.*" This milieu of peaceful co-existence, *Vasudevaih Kutumbkam*, has been continuously demolished by first INC and its dictator owners since 1917 when the first among the anti-national owners of the party, Gandhi joined hands with Ali brothers and Maulana Azad in the '*Khilafat Movement*' and conspired to help them send a group of 18,000 foolish anti-national Muslims to fight in favor of the dethroned Caliph of Turkey – both of Gandhi's nefarious actions were challenged and rebutted by his co-Muslim Jinnah – the Life President of Muslim League and 20-year senior to Gandhi in INC. Ottoman Empire was broken into pieces for her dismal defeat in WWI. That War finished the 900-year rule by the Caliph. Another Turk, Kamal at-Turk took over Turkey in 1922 and ushered in democracy! Half-Muslim Gandhi's wrong, harmful anti-India mal action produced no benefit to the Caliph who fled to Britain to save his life; but it did help FAKE Mahatma to establish as a pro-Muslim 'leader'. *With this, however, he started Islamization of INC.* That wrong process did not help the party se in the 1945-46 elections 85% Muslims voted for Jinnah's IUML. That was the biggest slap on the face of Gandhi. But the obstinate anti-Hindustani did not learn any lessons.

Gandhi nominated grossly undeserving Nehru – a fellow 'Muslim' – as the first PM of divided India at the expense of duly elected PM Sardar Patel. Surprisingly, one of the many silly reasons Gandhi gave was, "Jawahar speaks better English as compared to the Sardar." The AICC was opposed to Nehru's nomination but Gandhi acted as if he was the King and Hindustan was his property. Factually, Nehru was the second PM after *Netaji* Subhas Chandra Bose who became the First PM of undivided Hindustan on 21st October 1943 when he established the Provisional Government of Azad Hindustan in Rangoon that was immediately recognized by a dozen countries including Russia, Germany, Japan, Thailand, Philippines, and others. He installed his cabinet, issued the currency, postage stamps, planned the police set-up. Thus, he set the ball rolling for an effective and efficient administration. [News18]

On Subhas Chandra Bose's 123rd birth anniversary on 23rd January 2020, *Free Press Journal* published the following on the apostle of nationalism and the greatest patriot ever born in India. "Subhas Chandra Bose, popularly known as Netaji, has been at the forefront of many political debates on nationalism even after his death. Bose is also one of the most reputed freedom fighters of India with many conspiracy theories about his death and his relations with Gandhi and Nehru. Born in a Bengali family in Cuttack in Odisha, Bose was influenced by the freedom struggle movement from an early age. He kept track of the secret freedom movements and personalities in college and was assigned to do the same as part of his job at the INC. Bose started out as a radical leader of the INC's youth wing and later went on to become the party president in 1938 on a specific request from Gandhi – Nehru travelled by train from Zurich to Vienna where Bose was living in exile and personally conveyed the specific request and desire of 'his adopted father'. Bose was known for his tactics and radical approach towards attaining freedom, though the Gandhi-Nehru led Congress praised him, the party constantly maintained and often re-established its non-violent ideology. The patriot who said '*Tum Mujhe Khoon Do, Mai Tumhe Azadi Dunga*' [*You give me blood, I will give you Freedom*] inspired thousands of people to go beyond the obvious and sacrifice their lives for the freedom struggle.

Here are the 10 hair-raising quotes by him on Swaraj and patriotism:

1. "It doesn't matter who among us will live to see India free. It is enough that India shall be free and that we shall give our all to her free."
2. "Nationalism is inspired by the highest ideals of the human race, *Satyam* (truth), *Shivam* (God), *Sundaram* (beautiful)."
3. "No real change in history has ever been achieved by discussion."
4. "One individual may die for an idea, but that idea will, after his death, incarnate itself in a thousand lives."
5. "For an enslaved people, there can be no greater pride, no higher honor, than to be the first soldier in the army of liberation."
6. "India is calling. Blood is calling to blood. Get up, we have no time to lose. Take up your arms, the road to Delhi is the road to Freedom. *Chalo Dilli* [*March to Delhi*]!"
7. "Freedom is not given - it is taken."
8. "The secret of political bargaining is to look stronger than what you really are."
9. "It is our duty to pay for our liberty with our own blood. The freedom that we shall win through our sacrifice and exertion, we shall be able to preserve with our own strength."
10. "It is only on the basis of undiluted Nationalism and of perfect justice and impartiality that the Indian army of liberation can be built up."

As per INC Constitution, *Bose contested for Presidency of INC after his first one-year term.* Placing obstacle in the path of Bose, the pro-British 'anti-national' and least patriotic Gandhi nominated his candidate Pattabhi Sitaramayya to contest against him. Not only this, Gandhi announced he would leave politics if his candidate was defeated. *Pattabhi did lose but the CROOK and WORST LIAR Gandhi never honored his word as always and continued his dirty politics unabashed!* *In this like many other ways in the past and future, the FAKE Mahatma inflicted a colossal damage to my country. Thus, the degraded man changed the geography of Hindustan and tried his best to change its history as well.* His protégé Nehru outdid Gandhi by proving to the WORST Prime Minister and to be the core dirty anti-Hindu like his mentor Gandhi!

With the help of his comrades – Left Liberals and Pseudo-intellectuals Nehru changed the history of Freedom Struggle and He erased the roles of Netaji and 732,000 fanatic Freedom-Fighters who sacrificed their most precious life at the prime, mostly in their 20s. The 'Rascal' and 'Muslim' Nehru changed the complete narrative by giving credit to the INC who had done NOTHING at all to fight the Raj. In fact, Gandhi and Nehru were both paid British Agents who spied all their lives on the activities of the Greatest Leader that Hindustan has ever seen who single-handedly shook the foundations of the firmly established British Empire. India's independence acted as a trigger for disintegration of British colonialism. Within the next two decades practically all British colonies declared independence from Britain!

Least patriotic Muslim Nehru's anti-national acts and blunders are painstakingly set out in a book, *'97 Blunders of Nehru'*. A study of this book is an eye-opener for any patriotic Hindustani. Nehru matched his mentor and benefactor in inflicting colossal damage to Hindus, their culture, most ancient civilization as well as the geography and history of Hindustan. The Muslim duo of 'unwanted Bapu' and 'adopted son' disliked Hindus of the subcontinent to the core and their scriptures. They banned the teaching of Hindu religion and Bhagwadgita, the most important book Partition, a joint project of the 'Muslims' duo led to migration of 100 million Hindus and Muslims across the new arbitrary artificial border, mass-scale killings of 30 million Hindustanis, abduction/rape of at least 75,000 Hindu and Sikh girls and young women. For the sake of readers, few of his earliest BLUNDERS have also been discussed in, *'Jawaharlal Nehru: The Worst Prime Minister Ever'*, published by The Indian Interest @indianinterest on 20th March 2017. A brief overview of the immense irretrievable harm Muslim Nehru and his 'unwanted Bapu', half-Muslim Gandhi did to India's image, prestige and national interests following the latter's unpatriotic choice of pushing a totally undeserving naïve immature Nehru as the PM of newly 'independent' truncated Indian subcontinent. Unfortunately for new country, the most selfish self-centered unfit-for-highest-office Nehru (exactly like Gandhi himself) had unnecessarily long undesirable tenure. The highly selfish Nehru wanted to die in office as he perhaps thought he would become immortal that way and he did. Most of megalomaniac Nehru's BLUNDERS had far-reaching sinister consequences highly detrimental to country's interests. *The notable ones are*:

1] It is well-known that the immature and incompetent Nehru 'gifted' half of the princely state of Kashmir to Pakistan in 1948 and most foolishly took the matter of Pak invasion on Kashmir (and India) to the UNSC under a wrong section. That made Kashmir a disputed land. Kashmir, like the other 562 princely states earlier, had already ceded to India on 27th October 1947.

2] Subsequently, he 'gifted' 38,000 sq. km of Aksai Chin part of Kashmir province to China in 1962. Did the womanizer (like Gandhi) playboy Nehru consider Kashmir as his ancestral or father's personal property? Then, anti-Hindustan Nehru was stupid enough to bark on the floor of Parliament, "Not a single blade of grass grows in Aksai Chin. So, it is of no use to us."

3] Nehru had agreed to allow princely State of Hyderabad to accede to Pakistan and become South Pakistan. To appease the Muslims, Gandhi and Nehru had already created East and West Pakistan! Patel, as also the Minister for States ordered *Operation Polo* on the day Jinnah died in Karachi on 12th September 1948 without informing Nehru and brought the Muslim Nizam (king) to his knees. Nizam was preparing to flee to Pakistan, was arrested at the airport but Patel treated him fairly. He made Nizam to sign the Instrument of Accession to India like the 564 states had done earlier. That is why *Patel is known as the creator of the Unity of the country*. Accordingly, PM Modi very aptly laid the foundation stone in 2013 and then five years later, on Patel's birthday on 31st October, inaugurated the 'Statue of Unity', for the 2nd greatest Hindustani leader after *Netaji* Subhas Chandra Bose, on the famed Narmada in Gujarat. Incidentally, this statue is the highest in the world, more than twice the height of Statue of Liberty on Ellis island in America, erected, shipped and gifted by France!

4] No patriotic Hindustani can ever forget the folly of Nehru in hurling indignity upon the country as a result of 1962 Chinese invasion of NEFA (now Arunachal Pradesh) – worst debacle that was the handiwork of Communists Nehru as PM and his Communist pal Krishna Menon as Defense Minister. Later, this vacuum led to the formation of ULFA, BODO and other insurgent movements in the North-East. They don't want to stay with India, as the country did not help them when their people were mowed down by the PLA in 1962. The insurgency continues till date though on a low scale after over half a century of Sino-India one-sided war. My peers and seniors can never forget Nehru's slogan of

1950 used by him very often throughout the 1950s: *'Hindi-Chini Bhai Bhai'* (Indians and Chinese are brothers).

5] Sultan of Oman Said bin-Taimoor offered Gwadar port to India in 1958 for only $1 million. Anti-national Nehru declined the good offer against the interest of the country. Pakistan subsequently bought Gwadar. Today, it is a major strategically located port. China is investing billions of dollars in constructing the China-Pakistan Economic Corridor for its own benefit since it will drastically cut down the distance, time and money in transporting crude supplies from the Middle East.

6] In 1948, he 'rented' Coco island to Burma which stopped paying the 'rent' after 1949. Much later Burma gifted the island to China which has military presence there and is breathing into our neck. China uses the Coco island to spy over India.

7] Both the US and the USSR again offered a permanent seat in UNSC during 1955. The anti-national Nehru insisted that priority be given to China. Nehru left no stone unturned to get a Permanent Seat in UNSC to China at the EXPENSE of India. One cannot expect China to reciprocate since national interests are foremost to Chinese much unlike the infamous Gandhi-Nehru-Gandhi dynasty! This way, Nehru gave China the power to perpetually harm India on any issue as and when it wanted to do so. This process of antagonizing India's interests at the hands of China continues to date. Nehru-admirer and one of important Chamchas of Sania Antonia Maino, Shashi Throor admitted in 2004 that Nehru declined 'US offer of a Permanent seat of UNSC around 1953; and suggested that it be given to China'. On 18th March 2017, replying to @IndianInterest, Dr Rita Sehgal said, *"India needs to correct the (colossal) damage done by Nehru's dynasty. PM Modi is a ray of hope provided ALL TRUE Indians join hands."*

8] In 1959, the great Homi Bhabha, the legendary atomic scientist and the first Director of Bhabha Atomic Research Centre told Nehru, "We are 18 months away from making atomic bomb. We must go ahead and make it." Imagine if that happened India would have been only the 5th country after USSR, USA, UK and France; and thus, a member of the 'Big Five'. "I'll fly doves for peace rather than strengthen my country," was Nehru's dictum. Such was the skewed thinking of immature Nehru!

9] Much earlier in 1948 when the first British C-in-C of armed forces Field Marshal S Aikenhart came to meet him as the PM with a plan to modernize Indian army, Nehru threw the file at the General saying, "We need the police and NOT the army." Easily, one can imagine how the anti-Hindustan Gandhi was to nominate another anti-Hindustan co-Muslim as the second PM at the cost of Hindu Patel, the first PM of the divided Hindustan that the FAKE Pandit named India!

10] Soon after Partition, the Hindu country of Nepal wanted to join Partitioned India. But Nehru did not agree. PM Maitrika Prasad Koirala conveyed the same to Muslim Nehru who steadfastly refused and lost the opportunity for accession of this Himalayan kingdom within India.

11] Likewise, Baluchistan wanted to join the Indian Union. In 1946. Kalat (Baluchistan) king Ahmed Baloch expressed his desire to merge his country with India as a part of an earlier agreement between the two countries. That was during the days of British Raj. Nehru did not agree. The result: In April 1948, Pakistan forcibly occupied the huge landmass accounting for 46% of the area of present Pakistan. Or, in other words, today it is as big as the combined area of Pak's other three states namely Punjab, Sindh and NWFP.

12] Nehru gifted the most beautiful scenic Kabo valley Manipur (area 11,000+ sq. Km) to Burma. Did Nehru consider India as his property and the Indians his slaves, like the ousted colonial masters Britain whose agent Nehru was?

This obnoxious paradoxical job of giving importance to Muslims without doing any good for this community was close to their hearts. Willfully the downplaying of Hindus carried forward with élan in India by his 'descendants' in the Gandhi-Nehru-Gandhi dynasty was expected out of the Muslim dynasty in the INC and its later *avatar* masquerading as Hindus. Although Muslim, they were all cremated according to Vedic rites wasting tons of precious Sandalwood on. Congress(I) leaders who ruled the country for almost six decades. However, the party retained its pro-Muslim and anti-Hindu stance without materially helping the former community. This created a wedge between the two major communities in the country. They accomplished the absurd change in the geography and history of the subcontinent by creating a daughter country Pakistan losing one-third area of the original subcontinent. and with the help of their paid slave anti-national historians belonging to the Left Liberal category but having questionable integrity who have inborn hatred towards Hinduism. Even (Fake) Pandit Nehru, the first PM acted as a Muslim. Was he a Muslim and Fake Brahmin? *There are many anti-Hindu acts of his and his mentor or 'adopted father' – a FAKE Mahatma promising a strong anti-Hindu bias or even hatred. Creation of two Pakistans on each side of the country for Muslims is most significant of their classical nefarious anti-Hindu anti-India act essentially unpardonable. Insertion of Articles 370 in 1949 and 35A in 1954 both via unconstitutional Presidential order without ever seeking parliament's approval are a few of his most harrowing anti-national acts and BLUNDERING* repeatedly one after another Nehru was obsessed with and known for.

The famous French author and journalist Francois Gautier who chose to marry an Indian lady and adopted this country as his home lists INC #2 and Nehru #3 culprits in his book titled, '*World's 50 anti-Hindus*'. Incidentally, his infamous descendants namely: daughter Indira; her son Rajiv; daughter-in-law Sania Maino aka Sonia Gandhi together with children, Raul Vinci aka Rahul Gandhi & Bianca aka Priyanka – all find place in Gautier's book. Even Gandhi's name is there too! Thomas Babington Macaulay is at the top of the list. British introduced Macauley system of education in English by abolishing our multi-millennia old Gurukul system of Vedic education in Sanskrit. That was the only way they could wean their slave subjects from their roots! Another grossly abusive anti-Hindu act of Nehru was ban on the teaching of Bhagwadgita in even Hindu schools whereas Bible and Quran could be openly and freely taught in their schools. The list of his and his party's/Congress(I) successors' anti-Hindu acts is quite full. The latest anti-Hindu act by the accidental, dummy, unelected/unelectable Manmohan during his unceremonious and unnecessary ten-year rule thrust upon the country by Nehru's grand daughter-in-law needs mention. It was through an Affidavit filed to the Supreme Court in 2007. Existence of Lord Rama is a fiction and *Ram Setu* – the land bridge between India and Srilanka – is a fable. Thanks to NASA for providing scientific evidence for it. NASA attested to the existence of a continuous land bridge, now submerged in Straits waters of the Indian Ocean. Thus, NASA hit a hard slap on the face of Congress(I) and its Sonia-*Bhakts* (Mindless Worshippers). These are just a few notorious misdeeds due to purposeful distorted, skewed/bizarre thinking of the party *Bhakts* unable to fathom or question dynasticism! For one century now ever since 1917 when Gandhi supported Khilafat Movement rejected by even a Muslim Jinnah of a much bigger stature, the Congress party has been a privately-owned proprietary Company/Organization of Gandhi-Nehru-(Fake) Gandhi dynasty whose 'leaders' earned fame/notoriety, ill-gotten unaccounted wealth by always fooling the gullible, highly ignorant and unconcerned Indian masses.

Another aspect of destruction of our ancient culture is systematic clandestine theft and export of Indian idols from temples and historical sites by anti-nationals obviously with the connivance of unworthy politicians at the helm of affairs going on for a long time ever since the times of Congress PM Indira or maybe earlier. On 20th September 2018, *Rediff.com News* arrived a news item, '*The woman who nailed the idol thief*'. "The startling story of how a bitter ex-girlfriend helped capture artefacts raider Subhash Kapoor. The arrest of idol thief Subhash Chandra Kapoor, then 62, on October 30, 2011, at Frankfurt international airport, after Interpol issued a red corner alert, revealed something shocking to the world. It showed how a ring of fancily-turned out, high-flying antique dealers, like Kapoor, were stealing so many of India's historical treasures to send to art markets and museums in the West, while the guardians of these relics, be they temple caretakers or government officials, either turned a blind eye or secretly facilitated this illegal trade. The smooth, urbane Kapoor, India born but an American citizen, ran *Art of the Past*, a posh, spendy gallery at 1242 Madison Avenue in Manhattan, and belonged to a family of Indian art dealers. He was brought back to Chennai on 14th July 2012 to Puzhal Central Jail. Some years later he was transferred to the Trichy Central Prison in Tiruchirapalli, Tamil Nadu, as his trial proceeds. He faces trial eventually in the US too.

Kapoor was not the biggest of antiquity thieves. But his arrest was timely. It brought global awareness. Kapoor has till date been found allegedly responsible for the theft of 2,622 artefacts worth $107.6 million (approximately INR66.71 billion), according to *The New York Times*. A combination of factors led to Kapoor's lucky arrest. Very few know that it was a bitter ex-girlfriend named Grace Paramaspry Punusamy who helped set the ball rolling.

When the Brooklyn Museum in 2009 purchased a Chola-era Shiva and announced its arrival on its Web site, Punusamy, who knew way too much about Kapoor's pieces, writing under the handle Grace Paramaspry, started posting messages there, wondering about the piece's provenance (place of origin): Punusamy: 'Does this Siva has (sic) any history of passing through Mr. Subhash Kapoor in New York, any part of the provenance history from UK?' Brooklyn Museum curator Joan Cummins, not providing details of the Shiva's provenance, sidestepped the question with this lame answer: 'We know the Shiva's history since the late 1960s, and at that time it was not in the UK, nor did it come through Subhash Kapoor'. Punusamy's post caught the eye of an ICE (US Immigration and Customs Enforcement) officer named Brenton Easter and his team and they began their own course of action in building a case against Kapoor and his operation. She began to aid the Indian authorities too in their efforts to track down Kapoor, apparently even providing photographs and information on his movements, so he could be nabbed at Flugafen Frankfurt-am-Main in 2012.

S Vijay Kumar's book *The Idol Thief*, profiles Grace Punusamy and explains her connection with Subhash Kapoor and how she helped bring about his arrest. Singapore-based Kumar, who calls himself VJ and works in shipping, several years ago turned blogging into a special and very useful art, when he started keeping track, online, of idol thefts and the illicit artefacts trade. From his office/home desk chair, thousands of miles away, after diligently, laboriously scanning the Internet and newspaper reports, VJ would regularly post exhaustive details of the Indian artefacts and murtis that had been burgled and then catalogue when they reappeared in museums and auctions in other parts of the world. His efforts drew attention and eventually both American and Indian authorities reached out to VJ for his assistance in building a case against Kapoor.

An exclusive excerpt from S Vijay Kumar's The Idol Thief: The True Story Of The Looting Of India's Temples: A rather rundown shopping mall by Singapore's high standards, the Tanglin Shopping Centre on Tanglin Road, just off the high-end Orchard Road, holds within it a sprinkling of 'art galleries' selling a myriad art pieces, from modern Buddha faces in eclectic colors to Khmer funeral reliquary. They hardly seem to have any visitors except for the occasional 'foreign' tourist looking for a cheap memento. But art galleries the world over are similar -- they display a fraction of their actual stock, leaving the 'better' ones safe in their godowns for private viewings of their elite clients. One such gallery at the Tanglin Shopping Mall was Jazmin Asian Arts, run by Grace Paramaspry Punusamy who'd grown up in the island city-State, was the daughter of a Tamil father and a Chinese mother. She sold Kapoor's artefacts on consignment basis, and they began dating soon after they met in 1997. Kapoor had married Neeru in 1976 in India, shortly before the family emigrated to America. The couple had a daughter, Mamata Kapoor, but they had divorced in 1986 and had been living separately since then. Very scant details are available about the Grace-Subhash relationship, but they seem to have been quite a pair, embarking on many 'business development' trips into South-East Asia and creating a network of dealers and suppliers. In fact, Kapoor was so comfortable with Grace that he started using her as a cover for provenance paperwork which enabled him to create fake ownership records and helped to sell to prestigious museums -- paperwork signed by Grace for his artefacts. But some time in 2008, after nearly a decade together, Kapoor ended their relationship. During this time Kapoor had started a relationship with another woman, Selina Mohamed, in America, but it is not known if this was the reason for the split. What we do know is that Selina was also involved in Subhash's work. However, the parting was not peaceful, to say the least. They went to court in 2010 in Singapore to settle their business dealings. Kapoor won the case, displaying his shrewd business acumen and his relationship with dealers.

This is what The Straits Times had to say in March 2010: A Singaporean art dealer, who was in a relationship with an American art dealer, kept antiques worth hundreds of thousands of dollars after their affair soured two years ago. To get these back, Subhash Kapoor, 61, took her to the High Court and succeeded. Delivering his verdict on Thursday, Judicial Commissioner Steven Chong said he agreed with Paramaspry Punusamy's lawyer that the case should have never come to court as it really was about a break-up between two lovers. The judge also noted that while both parties were unable to produce much in documentation to prove ownership of the 19 contested antiques, Kapoor, 61, had called on three art traders from Bangkok to testify that they have sold some of the pieces to him. Paramaspry, 54, did not produce any witnesses during the three-day hearing heard last month. Ms. Punusamy, the proprietor of Jazmin Asian Arts at Tanglin Shopping Centre, was also ordered to pay costs for the proceedings. It is interesting to note a key finding by the judge that 'both parties were unable to produce much in documentation to prove ownership of the 19 contested antiques'. Though this was not front-page news in conservative Singapore, the Asian Civilizations Museum, which had done business with Subhash Kapoor's Art of the Past, would have surely followed this case keenly. Grace took the verdict badly. She had lost her case, money, artefacts and had also been publicly shamed. She was itching for retribution, hence her indiscreet and innuendo-laden comments on the Brooklyn Museum's Web site that had caught the attention of Indy (Easter) and his team. Grace would in due course reach out to Indian law enforcement agencies to nail Subhash Kapoor and extract her sweet revenge.

We turn again to an extract from the confession of Subhash Kapoor to piece together the story in his own words: 'My wife and I divorced in the year 1986-1987 in America and my wife is living separately now. My daughter Mamatha is presently 32 years old and she is living with her husband in New York... I could remember that the Chandrasekar bronze idol received from Sanjivi Ashokan was sold to (an) antique collector and now I believe it is in Brooklyn Museum...' 'I created false provenance documents for all these stolen idols received from Sanjivi Ashokan with the help of my long-time girlfriend Selena Mohammed, my employee Aaron Friedman and Jennifer Moore...' His confession also stated that he had been in a relationship with Selena for ten years and that 'she has the access for my office and residence'." [Excerpted from *'The Idol Thief: The True Story of The Looting of India's Temples* by S Vijay Kumar, with the kind permission of the publishers, Juggernaut. S Vijay Kumar]

Double whammy for some Hindustanis is they can't find fault with PM Modi but still oppose him. CA Vinod Arya tried to explain this in his blog: 'GOD SAVE OUR INDIA'. Hindustanis could tolerate 800 years of Muslim rule, 200 years of British Raj, 50 years of family rule (Congress party has been tolerating Gandhi-Nehru-Gandhi dynasty for 101 years), 10 years of Italian lady rule via proxy puppet but NOT 4.5 years of NDA rule! "Everyone agrees that Modi is NOT corrupt. If he fails to in his fight against corruption and black money, no PM of India will have the courage to take these issues again on his agenda for next 100 years. And corrupt politicians, bureaucrats, police, criminals, and businessmen will keep looting the masses as their birthright. So, it is the duty of every respectable citizen to stand in support of PM Modi and thwart the evil design of the corrupt people to incite violence and create anarchy. If we fail to discharge our duty today, our children and coming generations will NEVER forgive us, will hold us squarely responsible for NOT providing then a CLEAN Hindustan.

I am not in politics and as of now no plans to enter this dirty profession. But there will be dumb readers who consider this post politically motivated.

My apologies to those duffers in advance. I was wondering why there are some people against the Honorable PM Narendra D Modi. I noted that this started after Demonetization. Keeping that in mind, I was wondering which people would be affected by Demonetization. I was shocked to discover that here are people who will feel the impact more than anyone.

1] <u>*Educational Institutions*</u>. They used to get huge capitation fees in cash most of which was unaccounted.
2] <u>*Terror Organizations*</u>. Their funding is under heavy stress now.
3] <u>*Fake Currency Dealers*</u>. Those are in trouble because of Digital Economy.
4] <u>*Real Estate Mafia.*</u> We all know that a big chunk of payment used to be made in cash. Now the buggers find it difficult to account for unaccounted cash.
5] <u>*Hawala Dealers*</u>. With almost all deals with accounted money, they won't mind killing Modi.
6] <u>*Fake Trusts and Charities*</u>. These have been used for money laundering. Now, with ban on large donations by cash, they are unable to fulfill their agenda.
7] <u>*Politicians*</u>. Less said, better it is. Just look at NIL SCAM during his regime. This means that majority of politicians including some from BJP also are unhappy with Modi. They expected him to be a Maun Baba like his predecessor who would close his eyes to their corruption.
8] *Rich Agricultural landowners.* With subsidy directly going into their bank accounts, they are getting espoused.
9] *Film Industry.* It is well known that this industry used lots of black money except for a miniscule of genuine filmmakers.
10] *Betting in Sports and other areas.* We know gambling is banned except lotteries. Still there is a turnover of $150 billion. Hence bookies are affected. *Please note that these industries employ some of the most brilliant minds. They will leave no stone unturned that Modi does not get second term.* Now, it is for us the responsible citizens to decide whether we want to support the before-mentioned categories of Crooks or, to support ourselves and other honest compatriots!"

<u>*Our ancestors' wisdom left us with oceans of knowledge*</u>. It is a different story that we could never capitalize/build upon that for various reasons.

Foremost were ill-founded, illogical, irrational false divisions within the society. This unworthy 'virtue' rather vice was instrumental in bringing upon our downfall from the high pedestal of moral and physical strength and thereby security. Once Emperor Asoka reigned over most of the subcontinent and even beyond. Our inexorable wealth invited the wrath of numerous predators in the form of ill-cultured invaders, plunderers or traders-turned looters from Asia and Europe respectively. The strong character and strength that were our backbone or core strength for many thousand years got transformed into slavery, surrender and mental bankruptcy that continues to be passed on from one generation to the next through a dominant gene in the past 73 years since independence or precisely speaking *'Transfer of Power'* on midnight of 14/15 August 1947. *The white British rulers might have had possessed a few principles. But their brown 'Characterless' unprincipled crony Congress successors appear to possess none.* It may not be wrong to say that Gandhi and Nehru were the touts of the British Empire. That is why they received favorable treatment from the Raj and wrote books from jail. They never received a lathi blow whereas the hundreds of thousands of freedom fighters received harsh physical treatment and mental torture including many who were incarcerated in jails on the mainland or in exile in Andaman & Nicobar or Burma at the hands of the functionaries of the Raj. At least 730.000 freedom fighter fanatics sacrificed their lives for us to be free. For the first 67 years after departure of the whites, we saw PMs coming and going doing good to their families without doing benefit to the countrymen and even causing harm to the country. Were we allowed to even know those young revolutionaries who fought the Raj tooth and nail never afraid of the dire consequences? One such young lady was Bina Das. On 4th February 2020, The Indian Express brought out, 'Bina Das: 21-yr-old who shot Bengal Governor got Padma Shri, but died in penury', a story by Neha Banka. "This revolt laid the foundations of what came to be known as the *Chhatri Sangha*, a women student society that was semi-revolutionary in its activities. She was just 21. But Bina Das still opened fire on Bengal Governor Stanley Jackson in the convocation hall at Calcutta University. She was supposed to get her graduation degree the same day in 1932, at the same venue. Das served nine years of hard labor for her act which stemmed from a deep desire to see her homeland free from British occupation. But then not many know of Bina Das, one of the many women who were at the forefront of the freedom movement in Bengal. Her parents, *Beni Madhab Das and Sarala Devi, both* of whom were social workers and educationists, were deeply involved with the Brahmo Samaj. *The duo believed in giving their children, especially their daughters, freedom, education and instilling a quest for learning.* Uncommon traits in the early 1900s! Bina's mother Sarala Devi also ran a women's hostel named *Punya Ashram* in Calcutta that doubled as storage space for bombs and weapons the revolutionaries used. Several occupants of this hostel were revolutionaries themselves, belonging to various underground groups. Her parents' involvement in the freedom struggle was indirect and they focused on the upliftment of women and women's rights in Bengal. *But Beni Madhab Das, as a professor, served to inspire many of his students for the cause of India's freedom, the most notable being Subhas Chandra Bose.*

In her own memoir, translated from Bengali by Dhira Dhar, Das mentions how deeply "Subhas babu" was inspired by her father and was a regular visitor to her parents' home. Das' first meeting with Bose stands out in the memoir. She remembers her mother saying: "Subhas, my daughter is a great admirer of yours." Bose's political beliefs appealed to a young Das, serving to further her anti-British stance. In her memoir, Das "vividly" recalls an incident that occurred when she was still a school student. *"One day we heard… that the British Viceroy's wife was coming to visit our school. The day before that we were called from class to rehearse the program of welcome,"* wrote Das. *"We would have to carry baskets of flowers and scatter the flowers at her feet as she entered the premises. I was revolted by the idea and walked out of the rehearsal. The plan was so insulting. I sat quietly in the corner of the classroom with tears in my eyes. Two other girls also walked out and joined me."* According to her own writings, this incident held more significance than may appear. *"Much perturbed, we took a vow that we would sacrifice our lives for the freedom of the motherland. Later in life I often remembered this childish vow, and in moments of weakness it gave me strength and hardened my resolve."*

Bose continued to play the role of a mentor in Bina's life, especially when she joined Bethune College, under Calcutta University as a college student. The college library and books that urged theories of revolution and freedom further encouraged her beliefs and hopes for an independent India. Das, along with her group of fellow students, organized their first student protests against the Simon Commission that arrived in 1928 and faced threats from the college administration and the English principal if they did not apologize. In what may be called her first taste of victory against British oppression, the students' protesting the Simon Commission and refusal to submit to the college's demands, led to the "overbearing Englishwoman" resigning from service and leaving the institution. This revolt laid the foundations of what came to be known as the *Chhatri Sangha*, a women student society that was semi-revolutionary in its activities. Her sister Kalyani was the secretary of this organization. Like other revolutionary groups that came up across Bengal during the time, the members of the Chhatri Sangha were taught basic self-defense including *lathi lekha* where the women were taught to use batons. This student group also served to recruit other members and was helmed by noted revolutionaries like Dinesh Majumdar.

The full extent of Bose' role as a mentor and individual who deeply inspired Bina can only be understood through readings of her memoir. Their conversations and meetings as a college student involved reflection of their beliefs and discussions between the mentor and mentee on the future of their beloved motherland. *"How do you think our country will get freedom? Through violence or non-violence?"* asked the student. The teacher replied: *"You must want something madly before you can achieve it. Our nation must want freedom passionately. Then the question of violence or non-violence will not be important."* As the struggle for freedom adopted secrecy and began operation underground, Bina along with her contemporaries, women like Suhasini Ganguly, sisters Shanti and Neena Dasgupta, found themselves driven by slogans like, "*karenge ya marenge*"; we will do or die, one that finds specific mention in her memoir. *"The mantra inspired the boys and girls of Bengal long before it became a slogan in 1942."*

In the spring of 1932, she learned that the Governor of Bengal, Stanley Jackson, would attend the convocation ceremony at Calcutta University. Explaining her motivations in her memoir, Bina states quite simply, that it "would be a great occasion to register (her) protest against the empire". Das approached her friend Kamala Dasgupta, a revolutionary associated with the *Jugantar*, another revolutionary group, for weapons. After a volley of questions and answers, including attempts to enlighten Bina of the serious consequences of opening fire on the governor, Dasgupta agreed to supply the weapons Das needed to carry out her plans. At the convocation, Bina Das fired five shots at Jackson at close range, but was tackled and disarmed by Hassan Suhrawardy, the first Muslim Vice-Chancellor of Calcutta University. Bina was imprisoned and the British, having been so impressed by Suhrawardy's noble deed, awarded him a knighthood for the trouble. Newspaper back in England, devoted columns to the incident with headlines like "Calcutta Outrage; Stanley Jackson's Narrow Escape" in the *Glasgow Herald*. The February 8, 1932 edition of the Glasgow Herald devoted an entire newspaper length column to Bina Das opening fire on Stanley Jackson at Calcutta University.

Feminist author Radha Kumar, in her book *'The History of Doing'*, writes that Dasgupta collected funds from other group members and engaged a male comrade to purchase the gun. In her memoir, Bina explains the anxiety and hesitations she felt before the event that changed her life and the fears her parents had when she told them of her plans to open fire on the governor. Freedom fighters themselves who had instilled these very values in her from a young age, they understood her desire to devote her life to the cause of the freedom of the country. *"They knew their daughter would do anything for the country."* The February 15, 1932 edition included a small copy on Stanley Jackson surviving the gunfire at Calcutta University.

After her release from prison, she returned to a world she felt was different from one that she had been made to leave nearly a decade ago. She met her mentor, Bose, for the last time, only to never see him again. In the early 1940s, her work for the freedom movement once again led to her imprisonment in Presidency jail. She was released in 1945. Continuing her fight against the British, she witnessed more despair and bloodshed in the run-up to independence. In 1947, she married a fellow revolutionary, Jatish Chandra Bhaumik, a member of the *Jugantar* group.

Not much is known about Bina's life after India attained independence. In 1960, the Government of India awarded her the Padma Shri for her contributions in social work. *According to some reports, she died in destitution and poverty in December 1986, her body having been recovered from a ditch in Rishikesh, decomposed so severely that it took authorities weeks to identify.* Due to her revolutionary activities, the British authorities of Calcutta University had denied Bina Das her graduation degree, in a futile attempt to penalize and pressure her for her anti-British stance. About 81 years later, in 2012, the University of Calcutta posthumously awarded Das her pending Bachelor of Arts degree with second class Honors in English for the year 1931, that the British administrative authorities had withheld from her. "A second-class Honors degree is very prestigious because marks were allotted differently during that time," said Dr Soumitra Sarkar, Librarian of Calcutta University, who oversees university archives told indianexpress.com. *"Many freedom fighters graduated with similar marks from the university, but that is not a reflection of their academic abilities because the system was different then."*

Various pressures exerted by the British on Bina and her contemporaries failed to dissuade them in their cause. *Withholding her academic degree would possibly not have been of much concern to a woman who had dedicated her life to a nation and people who forgot her towards the end of her life.* But her hopes for her nation are clear in the opening sentences of her memoir. "The fifteenth of August (1947) is drawing near. Though our minds are filled with despair and heavy with despondency, though dark shades of doubt loom large, the thought that we are becoming free at last flashes like lightning through our thrilled souls. We have attained freedom. The British are leaving this country forever. Maybe, today we are unable to appreciate the significance of this event; but, in the course of time, true realization will dawn upon those, our future progeny, who will build a golden future for our nation on the foundation of this hard-earned freedom."

Fortunately for the hapless Indians starved of top-class leadership ever since so-called freedom or precisely for a century since *Lokmanya* Tilak's death on 1st August 1920, a phoenix rose from the ashes of those 'leaders or mad freedom fighters' in the form of the present PM Narendra Damodardas Modi who had developed into a strong truly nationalistic world leader in just his first four years. Unfortunately, *the value and true contribution of* Netaji *Bose were buried deep by his arch rivals Gandhi-Nehru who did their best for getting all the credit due to Bose who single-handedly masterminded the plan and achieved liberation from the reins of British slavery whose fervent stooges were the notorious 'father-son duo' of FAKE Mahatma and FAKE Pandit*! Modi understands the problems facing a common man and the needs of the country having seen abject poverty during his early days. He is trying his best to redeem our lost glory and prestige for which we Hindustanis were known for millennia! *The fifth world economy India should become 11th wealthiest country in the foreseeable future.*

<u>Today, India is world's 'largest' democracy though unwieldy.</u> Largest in sheer number of diverse people speaking at least 28 languages including alien English i.e. in quantity but NOT quality! Our colonial masters were the wiliest people who had deep-rooted plans for the destruction of any colony they ruled including this once great country after bitterly tasting The Great Revolt in the form of the *First War of Independence* in 1857 or what they call the Great Indian Mutiny. Being masters of 'Divide and

Rule' policy they knew that there were traitors who could be manipulated or purchased for a price. That time they made use of the vanquished army of minor prince Dalip Singh's defeated in the two Anglo-Sikh Wars in 1846 and 1849, more by intrigue than valor wherein the generals of late most powerful Maharaja Ranjit Singh i.e. Gulab Singh & company were purchased. The later was bequeathed the province of Kashmir for a certain sum of money. Earlier in 1757, Bengal's powerful king Nawab Siraj-ud-Daula's 50,000-strong army was vanquished by 10,000-strong (2,000 European whites and 8,000 Indian sepoys) British forces after former's general Mir Jaffer was purchased. Tipu Sultan of Mysore was likewise defeated with the help of Mir Qasim. Intrigue is the British trait finely tuned and used to the hilt by the most substandard politicians using FAKE religion and/or names to fool the stupid Hindustanis!

History tells us that many centuries ago, traitors like Jai Chand, the king of Kannauj colluded with Mohammed Ghori. In his 19th attempt, Ghori was able to defeat Delhi's king Prithvi Raj Chouhan. The benevolent or foolish Rajput King spared Ghori's life 18 times! *Khawaja* Chishti of Ajmer Dargah also helped Mohammed Ghori. *Khawaja* was instrumental in disrobing Queen Sanjukta to be raped by Ghori's soldiers as also handed over her two daughters to the victor as presents. Khawaja did not stop at that. He forcibly converted millions of Hindus to Islam. This is the general pattern in which Muslim invaders coming from Afghanistan or Central Asian countries acted. *Hindus have miserably failed to learn any lesson from history.* Today, antinational traitors exist in abundance thanks to a 'loose' and 'free-for-all' democracy; the so-called 'Freedom of Expression'; Media working in tandem for money and TRPs; Indifferent Courts at all levels; Pseudo-intellectuals; and Sickular political parties; and lack of political!

World's largest democracy cannot be compared with world's oldest democracy. And for that matter, with any of the established 'civilized' democracies of the world. A 22% Reservation for Scheduled Castes/Tribes for the initial ten years was introduced via the Constitution in the vain hope of uplifting them. The reservations continue indefinitely with the quantum capped at 50% by SC although various governments, the self-professed custodians of the public, were keen on enhancing those for the sake of their Vote Bank politics. A quick comparison between the largest and oldest world democracies with or without reservations respectively highlights the magnitude of advantage prevailing in those countries. For example, in America, the quantum of Indian Americans in various key institutions could be: 38% among doctors; 36% in NASA scientists; 34% of Microsoft employees; 28% of IBM staff; 27% of those working for Intel; and overall 37% of all scientists in the USA. That highlights the stark difference between a country offering job to the Deserving vis-à-vis its retrograde counterpart sticking to Reservations thus offering jobs to the Undeserving who have passed their examinations after obtaining dismally low performance!

The founding fathers of our Constitution were mostly poorly 'educated' so-called England-trained crony barrister-slaves fully subservient to the Raj and loyal to the white skin. Needless to say, a vast majority of the signatories to that document were of low caliber being mere matriculates who had willfully undergone three years' brain washing in London at the feet of their colonial masters. And sub-serving them by literally washing their plates after banquets twice a week during their 3-year 'training' at Lincoln's Inn London. They somehow or the other decided to copy the unwritten Constitution of their trainers ignoring certain gems from the Constitution of other countries especially that of America that they had studied. For some unexplained reasons, they took three long years to copy the 'Government of India Act 1935' that formed the backbone of the (useless meaningless) Document they wrote. The backbone or spine is broken badly by amendments at roughly twice in a year since its adoption on 26th January 1950. That event led to the ignominious change in nomenclature: Independence Day that has been celebrated since 26th January 1930, became Republic Day! Our Constitution proved to be an INADEQUATE document since it has been amended roughly 130 times or roughly two times a year since then. Constitution-makers' lack of wisdom and foresight is borne out by this!

Unfortunately, Hindustanis were/are NOT patriots and nowhere close to the class of Japanese, Germans, Swiss; or, like America's founding fathers like Benjamin Franklin, George Washington, John Adams, Thomas Jefferson, et al.; or, Europeans like Napoleon Bonaparte, Adolf Hitler, Eamon de Valera, Winston Churchill, Charles de Gaulle, Mussolini, Kamal at-Turk, et al. elsewhere in the civilized world. Contrarily, we in Hindustan had pigmies like 'Muslim' Gandhi – A Muslim by culture and European by upbringing, and an 'allegedly ba****d Muslim' Nehru born to a Muslim Prostitute Thussu Rehmatbai and her Paramour senior advocate Mubarak Ali. Motilal Nehru started as an errand boy under the same lawyer and by exploiting British law prevalent in the United

Provinces became a practicing lawyer, "Any matriculate could become a 'Vakil' by serving two years under an eminent Advocate or a Barrister!" *Our Gandhi and 'adopted son' Nehru were British agents par excellence.* On 9th January 2015, British brought back Gandhi after his failed 20-year sojourn in South Africa to sabotage the freedom movement spearheaded by the greatest Congress leader, *Lokmanya* Bal Gangadhar Tilak who was earlier exiled for six years in Mandalay for exhorting his compatriots and challenging the Raj with his vow, *"Freedom is my birthright and I will have it."*. The British-allotted job to FAKE Mahatma and FAKE Pandit was spying throughout their life-times over *Netaji* Subhas Chandra Bose – the only Indian leader and more popular than the fraud Gandhi-Nehru duo – and who fought the British on the Battle-front and the one from whom the Raj was mortally afraid.

<u>*Netaji is the ONLY leader instrumental in unshackling the stranglehold of the British Raj. He is the ONLY Indian leader who confronted the British on the battle front.*</u> *The ushering in of 'freedom' or 'transfer of power' which way you want to look at was capitalized by Gandhi-Nehru in the absence from scene of the firebrand real and the only leader India produced for the purpose.* This fact is finally fully and thoroughly documented through extensive research for many decades by eminent historian Dey – Professor of History at the prestigious University of Chicago – through a book released on 21st October 2018 by the INA Trust, on the 75th anniversary of the First Indian government of Free Undivided India in Rangoon; promptly recognized by a dozen countries which established their embassies as is the norm. The *book under discussion proves beyond an iota of doubt that INC or its dictator Gandhi, the FAKE Mahatma had any role whatsoever in Hindustan's freedom struggle*! That nails the bogeys and falsehoods created by the Congress party and the Left liberals and Pseudo-intellectuals distorting and falsifying the account of freedom struggle and falsely taking away all the credit from the MAN who accomplished that all important task! It is unfortunate (for the country) that the two faithful servants of the Raj spied over (till their respective death in 1948 and 1964) the activities of the greatest freedom fighter or in fact the firebrand leader *Netaji* whose efforts culminated in the eclipse of the British Raj forcing them to leave the shores of the subcontinent. Those two infamous men and their ilk were stooges of the British Empire and worked only to inherit power from the departing British. They or INC never fought for the freedom of the Subcontinent!

The infamous unpatriotic power-hungry duo did incalculable damage to the subcontinent by sheer loyalty to the Raj and acting on her whims and fancies. The two cronies *first* partitioned their motherland with the help of their cunning masters; then drastically distorted our independence struggle by relegating to the back pages of history the real 732,000 heroes who were instrumental in pushing out the British by sacrificing themselves in the prime of their lives. The two paid British agents had the temerity to mislabel our real/true freedom fighters as 'foolish revolutionaries' or even 'terrorists'. Their folly has been repeated by the successive Gandhi-Nehru-Gandhi dynasts. The twin British 'slaves' were doing it with the most selfish motive of undeservedly seating Nehru on the exalted position of Chief Executive or PM of partitioned India. The multi-millennia years old real name, Hindustan was abandoned. They foolishly thought that they will obliterate the time-honored name, Hindustan for all times to come.

The then British PM, Lord Clement Attlee made it clear during the debate in the British parliament on 'June 1946 India independence Bill': He said, "There are two reasons for us for abandoning the 'Crown of British Empire'. We have become bankrupt after WWII and don't have resources to run the large subcontinent; our own services are against us. He was referring to the erstwhile [Indian soldiers of the Royal British Indian army who unsuccessfully fought against Britain under the command of the charismatic *Netaji* who was the solitary truly patriotic Indian leader who, with the help of his 60,000-strong Indian National Army, raised from the deserters of the Royal British Indian Army and the POWs under the Japanese army, by Ras Behari Bose and himself, single-handedly fought our colonial masters on the battle-front with resolute single-minded devotion; 26,000 men and officers of the INA sacrificed their most precious lives in their prime to get rid of the vice-like grip of the British Empire. However, the self-serving, self-centered, totally selfish top Congress leaders or owners of the party, 'father' and 'adopted son' duo, played a deplorable dubious anti-national role. They etched their name making a mockery of the history and fooling the unconcerned slave and stupidest countrymen. Thus, they pushed the only true freedom fighter *Netaji* Subhas Chandra Bose into oblivion!

INC, later reduced to Congress (I) by the then PM Indira who this way put the final official seal of making the party a purely proprietary family-run concern, was anti-national right from its origin on 28th December 1885. The party was founded by a Scotsman, Allan Octavian Hume with express blessings of the then Viceroy Lord Dufferin. A Christian Womesh Chandra Bonnerjee was its first President. To acclaim undeserved acclaim, this party of 'crooks' relegated *Netaji* Subhas Chandra Bose to the nondescript back pages of history books. Bose's arch enemy, Communist Nehru persuaded/pressurized the Communist USSR leadership NOT to set him free but keep as a POW in Manchuria. Nehru was scared to hell that if Bose returned to India, Nehru will be thrown out from PM's chair! Instead Bose was taken to Siberia and tortured to death. Bose was the most popular Indian leader far ahead of the infamous duo in popularity. His return would have ended Nehru's undeserving prime minister-ship. In 1946, Sardar Patel was duly elected as PM with an overwhelming majority (winning 12 out of 15 votes; two went to Acharya Kriplani and none to Nehru. Maneuvering by the biggest crook Gandhi denied duly deserving Hindu Patel the honor of becoming the first post-independence Prime Minister! The beauty is the *FAKE* Mahatma was junked by FAKE Pandit as soon as his 'nomination' as would-be PM of divided India dominion. This notorious anti-national character has been the '*strength*' of different grades/shades of Congress leaders for one full century now ever since 1917 when Gandhi took over its reins!

It is *high time that our glorious history is reclaimed after all the willful inaccuracies and falsehoods are removed and/or rectified*! Unless the present generations of our citizens know how exactly the freedom was earned, they cannot appreciate its TRUE value. Rakesh Krishnan Simha is a journalist at New Zealand's leading media house. He mostly writes on defense and foreign affairs. His articles have been quoted extensively by universities and in books on diplomacy, counter- terrorism, warfare, and development of Indigent of the global south, and by international defense journals. Rakesh's work has been cited by leading think-tanks and organizations that include the Naval Postgraduate School, California; US Army War College, Pennsylvania; Carnegie Endowment for International Peace, Washington DC; State University of New Jersey; Institute of International and Strategic Relations, Paris; *BBC* Vietnam; Siberian Federal University, Krasnoyarsk; Centre for Air Power Studies, New Delhi; Institute for Defense Analyses, Virginia; International Center for Not-for-Profit Law, Washington DC; Stimson Centre, Washington DC; Foreign Policy Research Institute, Philadelphia; and Institute for Strategic, Political, Security and Economic Consultancy, Berlin. His articles have been published by the Centre for Land Warfare Studies, New Delhi; Foundation Institute for Eastern

Studies, Warsaw; and the Research Institute for European and American Studies, Greece, among others: *'Nexus in Lutyens: Meet the Forces that Conspire Against India'*, written on 12th July 2017 is the one that sheds light on one of the *Important* propagators of INDIA'S MALADIES: "Lutyens' Delhi is a snake pit. It is injecting poison into the country's body politic touching also upon Demography (Persecution & Proselytization).

<u>*Why are liberals, leftists and most mainstream journalists arrayed against progressive Indians?*</u> *Why are these groups so out of sync with the mood of the people? How could they rush to declare demonetization a failure, even as a billion ordinary citizens braved long queues and solidly backed the government? Why do they crank up the volume of protest when a Christian church is burgled and vandalized by criminals, but there is deafening silence when Muslim mobs destroy an entire Hindu town in Bengal? When Muslims are attacked for allegedly consuming beef, the cacophony of these groups doesn't end for weeks, but when six Hindu women are gunned down by Kashmiri terrorists during the Amarnath pilgrimage why do they dismiss it in a tweet? Why are they always on the side of forces inimical to India, such as fundamentalist Muslims, evangelistic Christians or communists who are in the pay of the Chinese? Why are they sympathetic to Pakistan, whose raison d'être is at worst the destruction of India or at best its Islamization?* You don't need to be on the inside track of politics or have exhaustive knowledge of the working of the news media to connect the dots. <u>Just follow the money – it's as simple as that</u>. They say Mumbai is India's financial capital where money is the great mover, but in real terms money is more important in the national capital. Here the working of the machinery is greased by cold cash, off-the-book perks, long-term sinecures and free junkets. Here, there is an incestuous relationship between disparate groups such as bureaucrats, journalists, fixers, so-called [pseudo]intellectuals and politicians who reside in an elite space known as Lutyens' Delhi.

<u>*Bishops all over the world have come up with harsh criticism for their sexual exploits.*</u> Books and books have been written on their notorious act. On 12th September 2018, *Rediff.com News* came up with, *'Bishop Mulakkal must be removed from his post'*. *"'The problem is not lack of evidence, but the unholy alliance between political parties and church authorities. If you are raising a voice against the priest, you and your family will suffer.' On* June 29, a nun from 'Missionaries of Jesus' filed a FIR alleging that Bishop Franco Mulakkal of the Roman Catholic diocese in Jalandhar had raped her a dozen times over a period of two years from May 2014, sending shockwaves through the

Catholic community. Following the nun's complaint, the Kottayam police registered a case and questioned the bishop. *Suspecting inaction in the matter, the nun petitioned the papal nuncio -- the Vatican's envoy -- in India to remove the bishop from his post and charging him with using political and money power to bury the case, as he has not been arrested.* Bishop Mulakkal dismissed the case against him and charged a group with conspiracy against the church. 'The nun is lying, made up the case against me because I had ordered action against her. The police have no evidence against me that's why they have not arrested me,' he told the media. While instructing the state government to file a progress report about the investigation into the rape, the Kerala high court on Monday, September 10, said no one is above the law. Meanwhile, Bishop Mulakkal has refused to step down from his post. *Even as the controversy snowballed over the police's perceived inaction in the matter, many nuns protested the bishop for the first time.* That opinion within the Catholic community stands sharply divided over the nun's complaint came to the fore when P C George, an Independent legislator in Kerala, kicked off a furor by his shocking comment about the nun. "With the help of financial power these people are destroying the entire administration of Kerala," advocate Indulekha Joseph -- vice chairperson, *Church Act Action Council* and one spearheading the protests against the bishop. [*Rediff.com*: *Syed Firdaus Ashraf*]

On 6th September 2019, *Rediff.com News* brought out, *'Demonetization gives Modi a powerful narrative for 2019'*. "'If the Modi government is successful in extraditing a high-profile fugitive such as Vijay Mallya or Nirav Modi before the 2019 election, the government will be able to link demonetization to this and turn it into a positive.' The source of political funding remains a shady and opaque element in Indian politics. Demonetization was an attack on black money, yet huge amounts of cash are spent in elections. The Karnataka assembly election in May was the most expensive in India. *Costs of Democracy,* edited by Devesh Kapur, director, Asia Programs, Johns Hopkins University, and Milan Vaishnav, director, South Asia Program, Carnegie Endowment for International Peace, is a scholarly investigation into how money flows into Indian democracy. *"Given the Modi government's uneven economic record, demonetization allowed them to change the narrative. It is no longer about growth, jobs, and investment. It is about launching the most ambitious attack on black money since Indian Independence," Milan Vaishnav tells Rediff.com's Archana Masih in an e-mail interview.*

PM Modi's demonetization was aimed at cracking down on black money, which is the main source of election funding. Yet in UP more cash was seized than the previous election and the Karnataka election in May was the most expensive in India in terms of money spent by political parties -- were there more losses than gains from demonetization? In my view, demonetization has not made a serious dent on illicit campaign cash. As you rightly point out, cash seizures in the 2017 UP election (which took place just months after demonetization) increased three-fold. The same was largely true of the other four states that went to the polls.

In speaking with politicians in India for the book, they privately suggested that demonetization could have a small short-term impact, but that parties and politicians are ingenious when it comes to laundering funds. Senior officials with the Election Commission of India have said as much. Money power -- and the use of illicit cash -- remains a principal concern for them.

The Reserve Bank revealed that 99% of the currency that was declared void has returned. The government's main contention was that demonetization would wipe out unaccounted wealth which has not happened. What was the point of this mammoth exercise then? I think the Modi government genuinely thought that a large proportion of outstanding currency would not come back into the system, which would allow the Reserve Bank of India to wipe those liabilities off their books and deliver a windfall to the government. The government, in turn, would issue a cash transfer to all households in India. In private conversations, senior economic officials have told me that they simply did not foresee the extent to which public sector bank managers would collude with those seeking to turn black money white. In my view, the Modi government was just flabbergasted as most analysts that nearly all the money came back.

Were the reasons for demonetization political rather economic? In your opinion, what were the political compulsions? Demonetization and the broader assault on 'black money' has given the Modi government a very powerful narrative with which they went to the polls in 2019 won with thumping majority. It is very hard for any political party to argue with steps taken against black money; it was Modi's 'either you're with us or against us' moment. Furthermore, given the Modi government's uneven economic record, demonetization allowed them to change the narrative.

It is no longer about growth, jobs, and investment. It is about launching the most ambitious attack on black money since Indian Independence.

Has this risk backfired? Frankly, as far as 2019 concerned, I think the net effect will be minimal.

Modi will get credit in some quarters for taking a bold gamble to squeeze the fat cats who amassed ill-gotten wealth. Others will mock him for unnecessarily damaging India's growth recovery and harming ordinary Indians for no reason. On average, I think these effects will probably cancel each other out. If the Modi government is successful in extraditing a high-profile fugitive such as Vijay Mallya or Nirav Modi before the 2019 election, the government will be able to link demonetization to this and turn it into a positive.

Have demonetization and GST dented Modi's popularity? Again, I think any negative effect is probably on the margins. The government is working overtime (through the GST Council) to iron out the most severe kinks in the GST system. It won't necessarily operate as a well-oiled machine by Spring 2019, but I think the worst will certainly be in the past. Indeed, the most recent GDP numbers suggest that the economy is in fact recovering from the twin shocks of demonetization and GST. I think where these two actions do damage is when it comes to Modi's perceived competence. Remember that was supposed to be the calling card of this administration. Whatever you might say about Modi and colleagues, they were supposed to be more competent that the UPA-2 regime. Modi was the 'CEO CM-turned-PM'. I still think the electorate is willing to give him the benefit of the doubt, but the implementation of demonetization and GST do not help in this regard. [*Archana Masih/Rediff.com*]

<u>A short history of Lutyens' Delhi</u>: In 1931 when the British moved India's capital from Kolkata to New Delhi, the city's central administrative area, with its wide avenues, extensive parks and imposing colonial homes was reserved for the empire's bureaucrats. This area came to be known as Lutyens' Delhi after its designer Edwin Lutyens. Many of these administrators were little men – colonialists who descended on India with utter contempt for the people they were going to rule over, not serve. Their only qualification was white skin. In keeping with the general caliber of Englishmen and Scots of those days, they were men of questionable intellect and average to poor skills. However, they were paid obscene amounts of money. Each of these bureaucrats had at least a dozen Indian servants, some had up to 30.

When the British hastily retreated in 1947, their rapacious administrators were replaced by a class of Indians derisively described as Macaulayites – Indians only in name but who were otherwise disconnected from Indian culture and thought. These Indians had inherited all the biases that the British rulers harbored towards Indians. They were the product of Thomas Macaulay's English Education Act of 1835 whose sole purpose was to create a class of people who would assist the British in administering India. In almost every country when oppressive rulers or colonizers were overthrown by freedom fighters or revolutionaries, the entire country went through the wringer. The old ways of governance were replaced by the new. This was true of the US in 1776 after the war of independence, in Russia after the 1917 revolution, in China after the 1949 revolution and in Vietnam in 1975 after the Viet Cong defeated the Americans.

In contrast, *nothing changed in India after the hasty British retreat*. It was a smooth transition from colonial looters to Congress carpetbaggers. The bureaucracy, which facilitated British loot, now joined the political class in looting 'nominally free' Indians. When the Congress introduced socialism-style permits for operating industries, the middlemen moved in. These fixers were soon joined by journalists who realized that their easy access to the political leadership and the bureaucracy could be monetized. The nexus between these groups is so profitable (as I will elaborate further in gory detail) that it is now a virtual cartel. Just like the Sicilian mafia tried to eliminate honest judges and policemen who came after it, the Lutyens mafia will target anyone who tries to stop its freeloading. That is why it is targeting the current political leadership, particularly PM Modi, who threatens to end the deeply entrenched loot-culture of Lutyens' Delhi.

The *award wapsi* (returns) drama, beef festivals, the constant drone about intolerance and the manufacturing of fake news to make the current BJP government look like a failure are all a synchronized act by deeply entrenched Lutyens' Delhi groups who have been effectively checkmated by Modi and now are desperate to make a comeback. Their 70-year long ride on the gravy train has ended and they want it to continue. They will even seek the support of the foreign media, intelligence agencies, NGOs and religious outfits to keep India down. In the following story, you will see how Lutyens' Delhi operates and why it needs to be checked and neutralized and the nexus completely broken if India is to rise. For, their interests are diametrically opposite to India's. Only by keeping India weak, struggling (if not poor) and in a state of chaos can they continue to leech off the ineffectual nation state.

Diplomatic impunity: This event took place sometime in the latter half of 2001 at a leading New Delhi-based newspaper. It was a slow night and nothing newsworthy had arrived from the state bureaus. I was the chief copy editor and along with other senior editors, I was scanning the wires for a lead story for the following day's paper. The reality of the news business is that most nights there is nothing interesting happening nationwide, so the media must spin, or spice up, the news. But that night, we didn't have to resort to spin as the ceasefire broke down on the Line of Control in J&K and the guns opened from both sides. However, trading projectiles across the LoC wasn't news. What got our attention was *CNN* anchor Christiane Amanpour – the well-known India-hater reporting live from PoJK. What shocked me and the rest of the journalists on duty was, like a typical American, her completely one-sided reporting – practically frothing at the mouth, alleging that Indian cannons were laying waste to peaceful villages in PoJK. Although she was presenting the news as a massive human rights violation, all that the *CNN* crew could broadcast as evidence was footage of a couple of huts with their roofs blown away, the odd crater and a dead buffalo. Amanpour's neutrality – and her standard of journalism – can be judged by the fact that she was flying in a Pakistan Army helicopter accompanied by Pakistan military officers.

And *now we come to the devious part*. After he watched the footage the resident editor (who takes the executive decision) said: "*Splash it on the front page. Let's expose CNN.*" For journalists like me – used to seeing news stories get smothered because of various lobbies at work – this was great news. We decided to give the story a six-column display that would take up most of the top half of the front page. I'd never seen such an expose of the western media in a leading newspaper, so this was going to set one hell of an example, I thought. I had even come up with a headline for the story: "*CNN* goes ballistic on India at LoC". With barely an hour to go for the presses to start rolling, the Resident Editor came rushing into the news desk. "Pull the story, find something else," he said. You can imagine my disappointment when I heard this. "Why can't we run the story?" I asked. The resident editor said: "We got a call from Blackwill. He has requested us to not publish the story." He was referring to American ambassador Robert Blackwill. It is not known whether the envoy himself had called up the resident editor or if he had directly called the owners of the paper.

Now the thing to note is *how on earth did the Americans come to know that our newspaper was going to press with the CNN story*? A good guess is they were monitoring the India media in real time via electronic methods. American whistleblower Edward Snowden who defected to Russia revealed in 2013 that India is the fifth most penetrated country by American intelligence agencies. NSA and CIA operatives may have tipped Blackwill off about the PR disaster that was about to hit the US in India. However, a more plausible explanation is that they had an inside man. The one journalist that fit the bill is a senior editor who still works there. He was educated in the US and had even worked at American media outlets. He had become a sort of fixer for the owners by ensuring their family members were always granted American tourist or business visas. This was not a job he enjoyed much, but several times I had heard him speak over the phone, asking that so and so relative's visas be expedited. What aroused my suspicion was that he hung around till late even when his page had gone to press? And his presence was NOT required. He could be seen slowly walking the long aisles, a mobile phone glued to his ear. He would frequently come to the production area, looking at the various screens as he walked past. This editor also ensured that nothing too critical was written against the US. In 2011 when an American diplomat disgusted the entire country when she told a group of students in Chennai that after a long train journey her skin became "dark and dirty like the Tamils", this editor defended the US diplomat in his blog, saying she did not really mean it. That was a good hint he was a flak for the Americans. So, here you have a journalist who was clearly operating against India's interests by working for a foreign power. He fits the description of presstitutes, as described by former army chief and current junior external affairs minister V.K. Singh.

Pakistan fixation: By nature, *Indian liberals and leftists are anti-India and anti-Hindu*. They conflate caste oppression with Hinduism and are therefore predisposed to hate Hindus. Also, because they are conditioned by Macaulayite education to believe their own country's religion and culture are inferior to the West's, they suffer from a deep inferiority complex. They, therefore, disown India. But what explains their affinity for the Islamic madhouse that masquerades as a nation? Pakistan is an Islamic state where Marxism and atheism are considered blasphemous. Indian leftists and the so-called intellectuals will be dragged out and lynched on the streets of Islamabad, Lahore and Peshawar. In India, they misuse free speech by attacking Hindu gods and religion, and yet they get away with it. In Pakistan that would not be possible. Shah Rukh Khan and Aamir Khan claim India is intolerant, yet they prosper and thrive in India. Frankly, if they move to Pakistan (and perhaps they should give it a try) and say Pakistan is intolerant, they wouldn't last more than a few hours.

There is *no real mystery to the Indian liberal's Pakistan fixation*. It's again about money and junkets. The 2003-04 India-Pakistan cricket series provides an excellent example. No cricket series had been played between the two sides since 1999, and the Kargil War was fresh in people's mind. The nation did not want any sporting contact with Pakistan, but those who had a vested interest in the resumption of cricket matches were parroting the usual line: 'Cricket should not become a victim of politics', or 'cricket unites peoples'. The debate whether India should tour Pakistan was being played out in the media. At the Delhi-based newspaper where I worked, there was a discussion on what line we should take. The associate editor – the journalist who decided what news went on which page and was also responsible for copy editing, headlines and photo selection – led the voices who said India must tour. I argued *why we must not by presenting these arguments*: Pakistan is an artificial country of incompatible ethnic groups that virulently hate each other. The only time these Punjabis, Pathans, Seraikis and Sindhis come together is when the Pakistan cricket team plays India. Cricket acts like the glue that periodically makes disintegrating Pakistan stick together. Indians, therefore, must not do anything that stops the disintegrating process. Therefore, we must not play cricket with Pakistan.

Pakistani cricketers come to India and are hosted, wined and dined by celebrities. The Pakistanis begin to believe they are superstars, without whom cricket would not sell in India. A similar claim was made by Pakistani artists. According to Hindi movie playback singer Abhijeet, Pakistani artists used to brag that "without us your movies will not sell". Pakistani artists have the same mentality of hardcore Islamists who have a sense of entitlement. They believe they can enjoy Indian hospitality, earn megabucks in India and then snub India because a Muslim is entitled to take anything from a Hindu. Indian starlets try and hook up with some of the cricketers to boost their careers. The delusional Pakistanis then go around claiming that Indian women like Pakistani men. This is highly insulting for any self-respecting Indian. Of late, Pakistani cricketers have taken to "thank the almighty Allah" in post-match interviews. They also offer namaz on the cricket grounds, injecting an unhealthy dose of fundamentalism into sport. Since my arguments were well presented and solid, the associate editor got up and walked away, saying, "No we must play cricket with them." Further meetings were held that day to decide the paper's policy on whether we should pitch for resuming cricket or not. I was not invited to these meetings. By evening, the line taken was 'India must play Pakistan'.

Now here's where it gets interesting. The associate editor wrote the main front-page story, arguing the case for playing Pakistan. A few weeks later when the Indian cricket team toured Pakistan, the newspaper sent a sports reporter to cover the matches. Joining him was the associate editor, who was feted like royalty by the Pakistanis. Over a period of more than a month, this journalist filed several pieces about how great the Pakistanis were. The paper had daily fixed allowance for journalists travelling overseas. It was US$150 for South Asian countries. I heard from a very reliable source in the administration department that the total amount was so high that the accounts department did not clear the bill because they believed these expenses had been incurred on a frivolous tour. The matter went to the owners before the bill was cleared.

Pakistan, easy cash and Indian journalists were also the subjects of an FBI investigation. In 2011 when the FBI busted an ISI front in the United States, they discovered that the man running the racket, Ghulam Nabi Fai, had funneled $4 million from the ISI to influence American opinion on Kashmir. The FBI recorded 4,000 emails and phone calls from his Pakistani handlers. According to the FBI, of the statements Fai made 80% were provided by the ISI for him to repeat and disseminate verbatim. The other 20% were Fai's own ideas, but which were pre-approved by the ISI. In other words, he was a 100% Pakistani spy.

And *guess who were among his guest list*: retired justice Rajinder Sachar (who headed a committee, which falsely claimed Indian Muslims faced discrimination in all aspects of life); Gautam Navlakha (editor of the communist rag *Economic and Political Weekly*); Dileep Padgaonkar (former editor of *the Times of India*); Harish Khare (the media adviser to the previous prime minister); Ved Bhasin (editor, *Kashmir Times*); Harinder Baweja (former India Today journalist) and Praful Bidwai (experienced columnist with communist leanings). *Think about it.* When Indian liberals and media figures attend conclaves where the agenda is India's exit from Kashmir, you think they are doing it for free?

Episode Tharoor: Because they all feed from the same trough, members of the Lutyens' club solidly support each other, cutting across ideological and party lines. This is best illustrated by how they closed ranks to try and protect Shashi Tharoor. The former diplomat and Congress politician may or may not be involved in his wife Sunanda Pushkar's murder, but everyone agrees that the Delhi Police botched the investigation at the behest of someone powerful. It was classic O.J. Simpson style reprieve – there was plenty of circumstantial evidence to book Tharoor, but the police closed his file without pursuing any of the leads.

Sunanda Pushkar and Shashi Tharoor-The law is very clear – any mysterious death of a woman within seven years of her marriage needs to be investigated by the anti-dowry cell. That wasn't applied to Tharoor. But, for the Lutyens cabal, the possible murder of a woman is irrelevant. In their view, the law should be bent to favor one of them. Leading the mob against *Republic TV* was columnist and longtime BJP supporter Tavleen Singh. The veteran writer switched sides the moment *Republic TV* produced evidence that someone had indeed interfered in the police investigation. Writing in *the Indian Express*, she describes the channel's investigation as "a media lynching". She even lies that *Republic TV* journalists were not attacked, whereas the visuals show Tharoor's goons aggressively pushing and shoving them. Tavleen admits in her column that Tharoor is a "Lutyens' darling", meaning that he was one of their star members. A breach cannot be allowed. If a celebrity member is questioned and investigated, let alone booked or jailed like a criminal, it would be the beginning of the end for other law breakers as well. Powerful clubs do not operate like that; they nip such moves in the bud. Which is why Tavleen was quickly joined by Sadananda Dhime, a pro-Congress journalist and secular apologist (translation: opportunist), who tweeted Tavleen's words to give her hatchet job more traction.

Another example is the March 2002 suicide of Natasha Singh, the estranged daughter-in-law of then external affairs minister Natwar Singh. Just two months later Natwar's daughter Ritu Singh committed suicide. Both deaths were highly suspicious and were extensively covered by the Delhi media. Except by *Hindustan Times* – the city's largest circulation daily. HT did not cover the suicides even as a matter of record. The reason for blanking out the suicides was that the HT is a highly pro-Congress paper and Natwar Singh was a Gandhi-family loyalist. Once again, *the ranks closed to shield a member.*

Supari (hit job) journalism: In May 2017, a leading Delhi newspaper produced a report that said 60% of the toilets built under the *Swachch*

Bharat scheme lacked water and were non-functional. An insider at the paper told me that the report was published despite a senior editor asking the reporter to provide more information about his claims. The story had several serious flaws:

1) Why was 2015 data being used to write a story in 2017?
2) Some of the toilets may not yet have received water supply, but perhaps were about to.
3) What were the chief reasons for the lack of water supply?
4) The water supply may have been denied by vested interests to make the initiative fail.

However, without addressing any of the above issues, the team that was anchoring the story sent it for publication. This led to a huge confrontation – between the more balanced editors and a new anti-Modi team that is creating news tailored to fit their agenda. "They are spinning journalism," the insider told me. "A narrative is being built that Modi is not an effective PM." The *insider*, who is a senior editor at the paper, said secular, leftist, Christian, Muslim and plain opportunist journalists have formed networks and WhatsApp groups where the constant refrain is how to spin a news event to make Modi look bad. Once upon a time, members of this group jealously guarded their sources and tips, today they are cutting across media loyalties, constantly sharing bits of information with each other, in the hope that something that could connect Modi to a scam could crop up. A typical example is the train murder near Ballabhgarh Railway Station, where the first take was that the stabbing was a result of a scuffle between two groups. As more details trickled in, the headlines and news reports were quickly changed to reflect the fact that the dead man was a Muslim and the other party was Hindu. Within hours the narrative was changed to show that the Muslim man was murdered because he was allegedly carrying beef.

This is a classic hatchet job, with low risks. As the news business is not an exact science, you can always allege something loudly, make your target (the Modi government) look guilty, and then retract silently if you are outed as a liar. Meanwhile, the international media (or more accurately, the India-hating media of the English-speaking countries) picks up these scraps of misinformation and soon you have usual villains such as The Economist, Washington Post and New York Times proclaiming that India is descending into fascism. The Indian secular media, which contributed the original lie, now quotes the western media to buttress their claims that India is indeed intolerant. That India's name is sullied, and Indian men are now labelled rapists and killers are of no concern to the Indian media.

<u>Says the media insider</u>: "The seculars or Sickulars as known in India do not want secularism. They are least bothered about the welfare of Muslims. They just want to eat kebabs and drink whisky at Khan Market. They want their perks back, so they can breathe easy and go back to their offices and file their unreadable stories, which have little to no readership anyway. Web stats don't lie – many of these journalists are the living dead because nobody clicks on their stories."

So, doesn't it bother these secular journalists at all that they have such abysmal readership. The insider explains: "Their only readers are the NGOs and foreign journalists. Even their families would not read their articles if they paid them. They are that bad – besides being fake. The public knows it and they are tired of us. Our credibility is near zero. But these secular journalists keep getting paid because they perform a useful hatchet job for their owners. Plus, the odd NGO will quote their story and thereby boost their ego. It is the classic tyranny of low expectations. Throw in a few free foreign trips per year and they are happy like a Larry."

<u>Why is the media going after Modi</u>? There are two reasons. One, the current government has decided to treat journalists for what we are – journalists. No more, no less. Many undeserved perks have been taken away. For instance, Modi has ended the practice of the PM taking the media along on a free junket on his overseas trips. Rajiv Gandhi may have popularized this practice, but Vajpayee and Manmohan also massaged the egos of the political journalists by taking them along on official trips. *Senior editors based in Delhi were used to grandiosely by-lining their stories*: 'From the Prime Minister's Aircraft'. Or even 'Somewhere in the Skies Over Washington DC'. It didn't matter that the copy itself was an anticlimax. Poorly worded, equally bad analysis and most likely recycled from a report written at a similar junket two years ago.

Being denied VIP treatment is something the Lutyens' media cannot swallow. They may come from ordinary middle-class homes, but as journalists, they are used to be being treated as guests at the reasonably high table, wining and dining in the company of celebrities, industrialists and politicians. *Modi has taken away this perk*. This is the chief reason why this supari or vendetta journalism has replaced normal reporting.

On a side note, *one* of the little-known facts about the media is the *enormous number of junkets* that journalists are used to. Most of these go to business journalists, but the others get a good number too. In 2001 when I joined a leading Delhi-based newspaper, within the space of three months, I was offered a two-day junket to Malaysia and a seven-day trip to Russia, all expenses paid plus US$250 a day allowance. This was followed by a five-day Konkan Railway sponsored stay in Goa. *And I was not even kosher – meaning that I was not a leftist, secular, smelly, unkempt journalist.* I did not try and curry favor with a business house or political party. And yet I got picked for these rewards. The point is that if you blend in with the presstitutes, the rewards are greater. The *second* – but equally important – reason why the media is going after Modi is that many members of the media moonlight as fixers, and once again the Prime Minister has taken away that handy second income. Among the first things he did after moving into the PM's Office was to ban his cabinet ministers from meeting people they should not. There was one instance where a certain minister, who was meeting an industrialist, got a call on his mobile from Modi, who demanded what he was discussing with the industrialist at a five-star hotel. The minister freaked and scooted back to his office. Therefore, with ministers – and bureaucrats – being under the Intelligence Bureau's scanner, the media fixer's hands are tied, and his role greatly curtailed.

The *Radiia tapes scandal* of 2010 showed the country how leading journalists such as Barkha Dutt (*NDTV*), Vir Sanghvi (*Hindustan Times*) and Shankar Ayyar (*India Today*) were acting as fixers for the rich and powerful. For instance, Dutt and Sanghvi canvassed for DMK party politician A. Raja to be appointed telecom minister. According to a government auditor, Raja caused a $40 billion scam because of his illegal spectrum sale. Assuming an extremely conservative kickback of 1%, can you imagine the payoff for the media fixer?

Endgame: Lutyens' Delhi is a snake pit. It is injecting poison into the country's body politic. Its shrill denouncement of Modi is not just jarring, but also diverting attention from vital governance. Its actions send the government into defensive or firefighting mode. No government deserves to be treated in such manner. *A remedy is to go on the offensive.* The Congress is feared by Lutyens' Delhi because it is vindictive. Late PM Indira was a vindictive person. So is her daughter-in-law, the Italian-born Sonia Gandhi. Modi should emulate them and drill some fear into the hearts of his opponents. Each one of them must have a skeleton in their closet. They must have stashed ill-gotten wealth in a *benami* account. They must have spoken with some Pakistani terrorist. They could be cheating on their spouses. You don't need the IB to go after them. A private detective agency will give you all the dirt.

Modi *must use Machiavellian tactics to neutralize enemies*. He should stop being goody two shoes because the *Award Wapsi* gang and *supari* journalists are not impressed by kindness. They will not reciprocate. Their agenda is to make him fail. Or, at least make him look like a failure. If they keep on throwing dirt at him unchecked, the danger is some of it could stick. India cannot afford a return of the Gandhis in 2019 or even 2024. *The country needs a long innings from Modi to make India strong and rich again.* If the Lutyens nexus tries to stop him, he must stop them, *Mr. PM don't say you weren't waned in his first 54 months so far.*" [Courtesy: *IndiaFacts*]

Modi is a non-sense man. His only interest and passion and single-minded devotion to the cause of nation are country's welfare. Otherwise, why should he work for 18-20 hours a day non-stop without taking a single day's leave during his first 54 months so far. It is quite natural that the corrupt antinational in politics and media are hell-scared of him and working against him to safeguard their own skin. There has been a chorus from the anti-national and corrupt politicians as well as media who falsely regard 'Demonetization' was a failure and a cause for slowdown of Indian economy. Immature Congress (I) President Raul Vinci is used to barking in any country he goes to. Now the cat is out of the bag. On Tuesday, the 4th September 2018, *Rediff.com Business* published, *'Rajan's policies and not Demonetization that slowed down economic growth'*. "NITI Aayog's Rajiv Kumar accused former PM Manmohan and senior Congress leader P Chidambaram of creating a 'false narrative' He said on Monday that the economic slowdown in the immediate six quarters in the aftermath of demonetization was because of the revised scheme for identifying banking non-performing assets (NPAs), initiated by Raghuram Rajan when he was the governor of the Reserve Bank of India (RBI). Kumar accused former prime minister Manmohan and senior Congress(I) leader P Chidambaram of creating a "false narrative" that demonetization led to the economic slowdown. The Narendra Modi government has faced much flak from the Opposition after the RBI's annual report for 2016-17 revealed that 99.3 per cent of the demonetized currency came back to the banking system.

In an interview to *ANI*, Kumar said: "The declining trend for the last six quarters starting 2015-16 when the growth rate was as high was 9.2%, was not a result of demonetization." The growth was declining because of the rising NPAs in the banking sector. Kumar said: "When this (Narendra Modi) government came to office, that figure was about Rs 4 trillion. It rose to Rs 10.5 trillion by the middle of 2017. Because under the previous RBI governor Raghuram Rajan, they had instituted a new mechanism to identify stressed NPAs. "This continuously began to rise, after which the banking sector stalled credit disbursal to the industry. "In some cases, like that of the MSME (micro, small and medium enterprises) industry, credit actually shrank. It was a negative growth in some years." On Sunday, Congress leader P Chidambaram had countered the PM's statement that loans given under UPA have turned bad. "How many of those loans (given under UPA) were renewed or rolled over (that is 'evergreened') under NDA? Why were those loans not recalled?" Chidambaram had asked. On Monday, Kumar said there was "no evidence" to show direct link between economic slowdown and demonetization, and the decline being simply in continuation of a trend and not because of the shock of demonetization as has been claimed. *[Archis Mohan in New Delhi: Business Standard]*

There are media houses in the West which would not like India to come up. Hence, they must oppose him. Notable among prominent among those are: *New York Times, Washington Post, Wall Street Journal, Economist* – all in America; *The Times, The Guardian*, etc. in Britain; *La Monde* in France and *Der Spiegel* in Germany, to name important ones. To distort and mispresent Indian news to show India in a bad color is their pastime. Recent example is a headline on p.6 of *New York Times* on 20th July 2018: 'Repeatedly gang-raped at age 11, and then blamed for it, in India'. The American President, being a businessman and NOT a crooked politician is opposed by 55 American media houses: only two i.e. *Fox news* and *The Independent* support him *by Not giving Fake but genuine news*. American economy is booming and dollar reigning supreme among world currencies. Trump has been in office for merely 20 months until now.

INTRODUCTION

It may be of interest to everyone among my compatriots as to remember that a country first known as *Bharat* and later *Hindustan* came to be called *India* although the Indus no longer flows through it albeit a small area of the extreme north. Of course, more than Britain Nehru played his sinister game. We will have to go back to early 1947. 'Muslim' Nehru, heading pre-partition provisional government of British India, called kings and nawabs of princely states and AICC members to rename the partitioned subcontinent yet to be born. The consensus was on *Bharat* (pronounced as *Bhaarat*), the original name of the land after the first Hindu king Bharat son of legendary Dushyant and Shakuntala from times immemorial. Anti-Hindu megalomaniac Nehru opined that this name would depict our backwardness. He insisted on India as the nae for divided sub-continent although the Indus flowed over a small northern part in the then princely state of Kashmir that had still not acceded to India. Moreover, he said that if the old name Hindustan stays it will remind us of our rich history like *Ramayana, Mahabharata, Bhagwadgita, Koutilya Shastra*, etc. He was preparing the ground to spell out his own selfish motive: *"If it is named India, people will remember me; and my coming generations will be able to rule over it"*, as if the country was his personal property. His burning desire to establish a dynastic rule in the so-called democracy was evident. [Source-https://dainikakhbar.com/nehru-to-congress-bharat-to-india]

Like other countries, we have our own national anthem – *Jana Gana Mana*...... and national song *Vande Mataram*. The former is the Hindi translation of the first of the four stanzas of Bengali poem by (Sir) Rabindra Nath Tagore and was first adopted on 24th January 1950 or over 29 months after India became a dominion of Britain. Tagore composed this poem solely as a salutation to George V, the King of England and Emperor of India, on his maiden visit when he set his foot on the specially erected *Gateway of India* in Bombay in May 1911. Vande Matram is also a poem but in two languages, Bengali and Sanskrit, composed by another famous Bengali Bankim Chandra Chattopadhyay in 1870s. Ever since then, it has been sung by revolutionaries, Hindus, Sikhs and Muslims alike, during their very long armed struggle against the British slavery and the attendant oppression by the Raj. Thus, it is older than the INC. However, the Congress leaders from pro-Muslim Gandhi and his protégé 'Muslim' Nehru not only disliked but also undermined it. Such has been the sentiment of anti-nationalism among their patriarch Gandhi and 'beloved' Nehru and their crony followers. With appeasement in mind, they polluted the minds of the Muslims and induced a sense of deep hatred for the national song. *Vande Matram* also spoken as *Bande Matram* in Urdu and Punjabi was freely and volitionally sung by all the freedom fighters including the Muslims during their struggle during the times of pre-independence British India. As a matter of fact, its namesake Urdu newspaper, '*The Daily Bande Matram*' was bring regularly published from Lahore, the capital of the big province of Punjab, since 1920. Such high had been the addiction and sentiment to *Vande Matram*! How is it the Muslims in independent India don't do it now? So much so Hamid Ansari, a Muslim nominee of Congress-I, who relinquished the office of Vice President after unprecedented two terms (of five years) on 10th August 2017, also belongs to the same category: *He is Muslim only and NOT a nationalist Indian*. It is an irony in independent Hindustan that such ordinary substandard men from Gandhi and Nehru onwards have occupied such high or even higher Constitutional places!

It may not be wrong to say that Congress along with its offshoots like NCP, TMC, etc. along with crony/like-minded regional parties behave and act in a manner inimical to the interests of their motherland! The antinational parties are embroiled in non-stop mud-slinging efforts to malign the high-performing NDA governments at the Centre and 19 states by falsely creating stories from thin air. The pattern is the same followed to malign the high-performing Vajpayee government in 2004. But this time around, the 'attacks' are more sinister maybe on the advice of defamed Cambridge Analytica. Government-to-government Rafale Deal is a case in point. Earlier, all the anti-nationals got together to file Mercy Petition to save the life of Ajmal Kasab, the sole survivor among 10 Pakistani terrorists responsible for 26/11 Mumbai terror attack. PM Manmohan knew in advance of the Mumbai terror attack. He did not take precautionary measures to thwart that. On the contrary, he had plans to kill all the terrorists involved thus leaving behind no evidence. A book blaming RSS for the terror attack was written down in advance, kept ready to be released after the attack to finish the most patriotic Non-political outfit to serve Congress(I) ulterior motive. To Manmohan government's misfortune, Thanks to the extreme bravery of Mumbai police ASI Tukaram Omble who grappled with Ajmal Kasab despite 23 bullet injuries and apprehended him alive. Thus, shameless dumb anti-national Manmohan's plan under orders from his Italian boss Sania Antonia Maino met its Waterloo.

That was the worst in our history killing 166 persons including 18 foreign nationals. It is beyond comprehension that 203 antinational individuals signed the mercy petition to the save the life of Pakistani Kasab who was convicted following the due course of law for years. His death penalty was ratified by the Supreme Court and Mercy Petition to the Indian President Pranab Mukherjee was already rejected long back. The list of these *dirty 203* includes persons like Harsh Mander and Aruna Roy who are very close to the Italian Sania Antonia Maino having served in her unconstitutional NAC advising and overseeing the working of the dummy puppet worst ever PM Manmohan who possessed all the 'good qualities' to qualify as the foremost Chamcha of Sania. The 'Qualities' common to all key members and office bearers of Congress(I) include: *Swami bhakti, Kushamad, Chaaplusi,* Liar to the core, 'good false story-creators/tellers, etc. Others who signed the mercy petition include lawyers Vrinda Grover, Abdul Wahab Khan plus many; Meeenal Baghel, Editor Mumbai Mirror and other co-editors from different publications; Aakar Patel, India Head of anti-India Amnesty International; Journalists: Shyam Vij, V Venkatesan, and many others; Anusha Rizvi, independent film-maker, plus some other film-makers; Mahmood Farooqui: historian, artist, film-maker; Colin Gonsalves, senior advocate SC; Dr. Madhav Thambisetty, professor of medicine, brother S Thambisetty, professor LSE; Gautam Babbar possibly related to the unprincipled UP Congress-I Chief and actor Raj Babbar, working for the UN; Nandita Das, actress and some others; Sankar Sen, IPS retired; Dr. Akhil Katyal and a number of his colleagues from Delhi University; Anjali Dave and many colleagues, TISR Mumbai; Madhu Sarin, psychoanalyst; Padmini Mirchandani, publisher; Amrita Shodhan, School of African and Asian Studies, UK; etc. It is surprising that women outnumbered men in signing the petition.

Hindustan is the only country in the world to offer a philosophy for inward digression. We Hindustanis, undoubtedly, belong to one of the earliest civilizations of the world having practiced Hinduism, the oldest living religion, for many millennia. This liberal religion gave birth to at least three more religions on the subcontinent. It also allowed at least four more alien religions, namely Christians, Jews, Muslims and Zoroastrians in alphabetical order, the freedom to practice their rituals unhindered and live peacefully, with no strings attached. In fact, the last-named religion (known as Irani in Hindustan) has more inhabitants living here than in the rest of the world put together. Very recently, Pakistan – the daughter country of Hindustan – reinstated three non-Islamic national holidays namely Holi, Diwali and Christmas Day after a gap of many decades. Consequently, the 'Festival of Colours' or Holi was celebrated from that year with great fervour and fanfare in many parts of Pakistan. One of the important places for the celebrations and rejoicing we saw, in video clippings, was the 10,000-year old Hindu temple, duly renovated for the purpose by authorities, in the famous beautiful city of Lahore, the capital of the West Punjab. Thus, Hinduism must have existed since at least those times!

Hindustan was a big country to start with as is apparent from the Empire of King Asoka, a few centuries before the birth of Christ. It is a myth created by slave-minded left-liberal historians that the British united the small states into one country. Another wrong statement made often is that the southern part is different from the northern. This untruth is broken by an article: *'In Revisiting history: A Harappa in Tamil Nadu'*, appearing on 14th June 2016 in *Rediff.com News*. "A major excavation by the Archaeological Survey of India of a Sangam era settlement is making big news with its amazing discoveries. About 12 km from Madurai on the highway to Rameswaram, a large coconut field on the banks of the Vaigai river in Keezhadi village of Sivaganga district is being excavated, where Roman artefacts and vessels with writings in the Brahmi script have been discovered. Brahmi is the earliest script which the Tamils used during the Sangam period from the 3rd century BC to the 3rd century AD. There were three dynasties during this period: The Cheras, the Cholas and the Pandyas who traded with the Romans. After the 6th century AD, the *Grantha* script replaced Brahmi. In the 13th century AD, this area was called Kunti Devi Chaturvedi Mangalam and there are no records from before that period. This area is spread over about 80 acres and covers a radius of about 3.5 km. Since the ASI, to seek permission for the excavation, had to give the owners of the land a written assurance that they will get it back in the same condition, ASI staff refill the digs after photographing and collecting the artefacts.

The *first* survey in the area commenced in 2013, the excavation was conducted in 2015 and again in 2016. The ASI plans another excavation next year, but that would have to be sanctioned by the Survey's headquarters in New Delhi. Students from Chennai University and the Krishna Arts College helped the ASI in the current round of digs. In the *present* phase of excavation -- apart from the Roman artefacts and vessels with Brahmi text -- relics confirming the presence of handicrafts like weaving, shipbuilding, metal working, carpentry, rope-making, ornament-making, making of ivory products, tanning etc during the Sangam period have been found. Nails and other iron and ivory products have been found, which confirm the presence of this town during the Sangam period. Structures built with bricks and mortar have also been unearthed.

A team of ASI experts -- including Superintendent K Amarnath Ramakrishna, Assistant Archaeologists Rajesh and Veeraraghavan -- is involved in the excavation work, which began on January 18 and is likely to continue till September. The ASI officials say the settlement was more than 2,000 years old, and dates to the Sangam era. So far, about 3,000 ancient artefacts, including a signet made of clay with an ornamental design, have been excavated.

As per the ASI officials, the ancient settlement had an underground drainage system which was on par with the Harappan system. The sewage drains had been laid with baked clay pipelines, which are still visible. The drainage system was the same as the one found in Harappa. Apart from signets, arrows, weapons made of iron and copper, rare ornaments have been found, ASI Superintendent Ramakrishna said. "It is very rare to find the constructions intact. The findings threw more light on the Sangakaala (Sangam era) Tamil civilization," he added. This town was a residential area, Assistant Archaeologist Rajesh said, and they have discovered brick buildings in it, which were very rare during that time.

The ASI team surveyed the banks of the Vaigai in 2013-2014, checked out 293 sites for excavation, and chose the present site. As many as 43 excavations were conducted last year and 1,800 artefacts found. This year, 53 excavations have been conducted and 3,000 items discovered and preserved. Among the artefacts were semi-precious stones, glass, shells, burnt bricks, tusk, and iron. Products used by people in their day-to-day lives were recovered.

There were plenty of small water tanks made of bricks and mud. The water tanks were fed through well-laid channels, which are still present. Though most of the place looks residential, some business centres were also found. They have found roof tiles and nails which suggest that the buildings were storied. Vessels with names written in the Brahmi script have been found, names like 'Sattan', 'Thisan', 'Chandan', 'Inavadan', 'Muyan' and 'Udhiran'. "The date we are looking at is between the 3rd century BC and the 3rd century AD, which was the Sangam period. Carbon dating is still to be done," Rajesh said. This is the second phase of excavation the ASI and the team has sought permission for another one. There has been no important excavation in south Tamil Nadu, so we want to do this extensively. The history of this area has not been properly understood. In the third phase, we will learn more." [A. Ganesh Nadar, *Rediff.com*]

There are quite some commonalities with our northern neighbour, China being quite an old civilization, culturally speaking, since there have been inter-person exchanges right from the earliest times. Many similarities do exist even now. On 11th May 2016, *Rediff.com News* published a related article, *'Human beauty and cruelty go hand in hand'*. "If Han Kang wrote only about cruelty and suffering, readers might respect her writings and her conscience, but her novels would not be as loved as they are by readers across the world, says Nilanjana Roy.

The Tiananmen massacre is better known than the Gwangju Uprising in South Korea, where hundreds of students were killed in May 1980 for protesting the imposition of martial law. May is an ominous month for students. In 1989, thousands of them spent the month marching and gathering in Tiananmen Square in Beijing, after the death of the liberal reformer Hu Yaobang. The answer to their demands for democratic reform and more freedoms came on May 20, when martial law was declared in Beijing. Citizens joined the students' protest; they gathered around the foam-and-papier-mâché statue of the *Goddess of Democracy* on May 29 and 30.

In June, as everyone knows, their urgent pleas for democracy and freedoms were answered by gunfire. A tank pushed at the *Goddess*, and she was soon reduced to rubble. "That night, looking around at all those bodies crammed into the gym hall, you thought to yourself how like a convention it seemed, a mass rally of corpses who were all there by pre-arrangement…" thinks one of Han Kang's characters in her third novel, *Human Acts*.

Kang is an extraordinary writer; her voice in this novel and the previous two, *The Vegetarian* and *Convalescence*, is pitched at a haunting murmur that rises above more direct, politically strident novels. She lives and teaches in Seoul. Her family moved out of Gwangju "purely by chance" when she was 10, escaping the massacre. "That fact became a kind of survivor's guilt, and troubled my family for a long time," she told *The White Review* in an interview. Each generation of students -- anywhere in the world -- finds their way to the writers who speak most truly for them. Kang's writing, subtle, steeped in violence but also in humanity, profoundly honest, is intensely universal, but she is also one of the few contemporary Asian writers whose work connects so directly with this generation of students, in India as much as anywhere else. She writes of violence with the easy familiarity that is the hallmark of authors who have grown up in times of uneasiness, disruptions and censorship, and who have faced the duplicity and brutality of unjust regimes. Her approach is the opposite of violence porn. Both *Game of Thrones* and *Daesh*, to compare completely different things, a TV show and a militant army, treat violence as a spectacle. They carefully choreograph acts of great inhumanity as performances intended to elicit either shock (but shock that reels the viewer in, wanting more) or fear (but fear that cannot look away in case the viewer is next).

In the 'Vegetarian and in Human Acts', Kang does not write about violence as a subject as much as she bears witness. *The Vegetarian* features a woman about whom her husband says she is ordinary, nothing special, though he notes disapprovingly that for all her featurelessness, she prefers not to wear bras, saying that she dislikes feeling constricted. One day, she decides that she will not eat, serve or keep meat in her house. This spirals into a frightening, guerrilla war between her and her family. She takes a knife to her wrist when they try to make her eat meat, forcing it into her mouth, and the narrative circles back to a time when a dog was tortured by a family member.

Kang makes a basic truth elementally clear: violence is not even about the infliction of pain as much as it is about overriding the will and desires of another living being, about teaching them a lesson. When a state commits violence, when a government persecutes the young and along with them, crushes the more vulnerable members of its society, when a nation meets student protests and hunger strikes with hectoring, accusations and force, it is laying bare its deepest terrors. hat such a state finds most frightening is the idea that its citizens might prize free will more highly than the will of the regime; that they might enjoy and care for freedoms more than obedience.

Kang offers a disconcerting and useful way to frame the aggressive demands for nationalism in a time of oppression: "That afternoon there were several positive identifications, and there ended up being several different shrouding ceremonies going on at the same time, at various places along the corridor. The national anthem rang out like a circular refrain, one verse clashing with another against the constant background of weeping, and you listened with bated breath to the subtle dissonance this created. As though this, finally, might help you understand what the nation was." If Kang wrote only about cruelty and suffering, readers might respect her writings and her conscience, but her novels, in Deborah Smith's intelligent translation, would not be as loved as they are by readers across the world. Her other great gift is to understand that, as she says, human beauty and human cruelty go hand in hand -- in times of the worst crackdowns, there are still acts of kindness and caring, and these acts have as much weight and meaning as does the torture, the censorship, the imprisonments and the open killings.

Human Acts, for instance, begins with a 15-year-old searching for his friend among the bodies of the massacred, brought to the municipal gym. He finds horror, and mutilation, and the ineradicable smell of death. But he also joins Eun-Sook, a high school student in her final year, and Seon-ju, a machinist at a dressmaker, helping them to clean up and tally the corpses. It is grim work, but as you spend more time with the dead, Kang lets you see the living souls behind them, the precious ordinariness of their lives before the massacre. [Nilanjana Roy]

<u>What has happened during the recent times</u>? The two countries moved apart from their long-time similarities. China, with the whole-hearted efforts on Reforms and Capitalism, became the second most powerful economy of the world. India, with first PM Nehru's fallacious ill-founded faith in Communism as well as its 'misguided' economic system and in non-alignment, lagged far behind. In 1991, another Congress PM PV Narasimha Rao gave a clarion call for economic liberalization and moving on to Capitalist economy, undoing Nehru's socialist ideology that has been blindly followed for 44 years. However, the new process was implemented in fits and starts as the Communist ideology of keeping every citizen poor was involuntarily ingrained at the back of every prime minister's mind. *China started reforms just dozen years ahead of India but went the full hog relentlessly.* The results are for the whole world to see! Other successive prime ministers, on the contrary, almost wasted the next 23 years as well (making into first 67 years after independence) for one flimsy reason or the other. Now, with the most dynamic, hardest working, incorruptible, well-meaning staunchly nationalistic Prime Minister endowed with realistic thinking and mind-set having the single aim of improving the lot of common man and thereby that of the country, at the helm for the last four years, we

can surely expect positive results. Unfortunately, there exist many failed parties that are vestiges of the British Raj. Those are strongly opposed to Modi due to their natural fear that all the anti-nationals – parties and persons – are going to be exposed brutally in public for their wrongdoings or acts of omission and commission. Their false halo, of being pro-poor, they have assiduously worked around them over the decades, is going to be torn apart into shreds. To the chagrin of the expectant hapless masses, the utterances and actions of all these anti-national political parties, blocking Rajya Sabha proceedings on one excuse or the other, are not allowing full blast of the much-needed reforms to usher in various fields including the two most important namely GST and Land Act to be enacted. This ploy is to demean Modi in their vain hope that that is going to bring down the Modi government, the first with absolute majority in Lok Sabha after a gap of 30 years. That unholy nexus between unscrupulous politicians and their captive anti-national media persons, working in unison, continues even today. They have already amassed huge ill-gotten wealth. And hence, they are not bothered whether the country and its citizenry go to hell. They fail or don't want to understand that all their mal actions are dragging any progress and thus preventing Hindustan to occupy its real well-deserved place in the comity of nations! Outsiders appreciate this more. The then British PM David Cameron rates his Indian counterpart very high at the top of rankings of the present heads of State. And he believes India can overtake even the USA if a decade of free hand is given to PM Narendra Modi!

In less than five years of gaining independence, a great Indian articulated the problems faced by the nascent nation pertaining to those undesirable and unwanted inhabitants who believed in breaking but NOT making India great once again. Shyama Prasad Mukherjee stood for integrity of Bharat or Hindustan or India. And, he laid down his most valuable life fighting against permit system in J&K unlike the then selfish, self-centred undeserving prime minister who live only to die in office without doing anything substantial for his motherland in 17 long years he stuck to the chair gifted by his benefactor unwanted *Bapu*. Mukherjee's *balidaan divas* (Day of Sacrifice) was 23rd June 1953. He once said: *"We live in an age where the dire need for 'paraakram '[in English: 'hard labour, ceaseless exertion, courage and valour'] in all spheres of activity affecting the public wheel, is more imperative than ever! The menace of invasion from without is within the bounds of possibility. Disruptive forces are at work within the country. A nation can only save it by its own energy. But energy and strength hardly come to a people that do not enjoy the blessings of unity and freedom"*. Alas! That sort of unity does exist even today after seven decades since independence. *We failed miserably to get rid or even rein in anti-national elements and traitors scattered here and there in this vast country.* Instead our governments created equitable conditions for them to proliferate. The not-so-nationalistic Congress party firmly believed in the British dogma of 'Divide and Rule' so much so it went overboard to perfect different refined nuances of this nefarious game to keep the people fighting among them all the time. Speaking, it got 'Divide and lose' during their long misrule of the country – running the central government for 80%r cent of the time since independence. Hence everybody now aspires for *'Achhe Din'* or 'Good Times'. But we everyone among us will have to contribute towards that goal. The most important first step is following the law of the land.

Introspection into our deficiencies created during the past 67 years especially the gross misrule in the previous decade under the worthless puppet Congress PM Manmohan is quite justified before we inspire for better times. *'India's systemic flaws, a big barrier to growth'*, by Shyam Ponappa appeared in *Rediff.com Business* on the 6th November 2014. "Apart from inadequate infrastructure, which must be well-orchestrated to achieve supportive ecosystems for investment and operations, the tax-claims fallout continues to undermine growth prospects. On the face of it, several developments augur well for the economy. But major systemic flaws persist that must be overcome. Some gains have resulted from PM Modi's direct selling and 'heavy lifting', as in eliciting Japanese investments. Others, such as a dropping in petroleum and commodity prices, are attributable to extraneous factors. The positive developments that seem to be coalescing into a glow on the economic horizon include: The revival of stalled projects; A reduction in raw material costs, with oil prices now well under $90 a barrel; Significant investments from Japan's SoftBank in Snapdeal and Ola; other significant investments and announcements in e-commerce, for example, Flipkart and Amazon; The implementation of electronic toll collection (ETC) on our highways Introduced between Ahmedabad and Vadodara on National Highway-8 (NH-8) in 2013, the ETC became available last week between Delhi and Mumbai on the NH-8. It is expected to be available on all national highways in the next two months. Vehicles with prepaid tags can drive through without slowing down, whereas until now, all vehicles had to stop to pay tolls. The productivity gains will be enormous, with fuel savings across toll stations estimated at rupees 60,000 crore or 600 billion. But all is not entirely well.

The fiscal deficit is at 80% of what was budgeted for the full year; there was a decline in projects completed in the September quarter; and there is uncertainty about growth rates. *The real issue, though, is that major systemic flaws persist, resulting in growing economic and operating constraints.* There are the problems of retrospective tax claims, of coal allocation and of spectrum allocation. In the societal dimension, there are continuing indications of disharmony, resulting in wariness and insecurity about whether we have a unifying or divisive top leadership, let alone rank and file.

Proceeding with business as usual with the present ineffective ways will lead to continuing and increasingly overwhelming detrimental effects. Each of these areas needs breakthroughs to achieve convergent, synergistic results. Over 60% of stalled projects tracked by the Performance Management Group in the Cabinet secretariat are power projects, held up because coal is not available. Coal-mining rights must be auctioned on the lines of spectrum. *What are the likely outcomes?* The government was jubilant about funds collected from the auctions creating enormous capital and operating constraints for the communications sector because the INR1.05 lakh crore (1.05 trillion) bid for spectrum became unavailable for network construction and operations, and the limited bandwidth available to each operator adds to costs and restricts delivery capability. Growth in network capacity has deteriorated to the point where we have higher levels of dropped calls in metros, with continuing poor broadband access countrywide.

The effects on productivity are ruinous. What can we expect from mining rights auctions? If the results are as for the spectrum auctions, we'll have high treasury collections, high life-cycle project costs affecting critical inputs like electricity, steel & aluminium, and a reduction in investment in mining operations and downstream manufacturing. These are logical outcomes: the consequence of higher costs is either higher prices, or financial under-recovery leading to collapse, and capital used for auctions is unavailable for investment. Instead, what we really want from the mining allocation is inexpensive electricity and efficient production of industrial materials, such as steel and aluminium.

The financial insolvency of our state electricity boards reflects the magnitude of the problem. Even the story of Gujarat's electricity distribution raises questions for the rest: Gujarat's average farm tariff is under rupee 1 a unit, compared with a non-farm tariff of rupees 4-5. The high cost of providing these connections is unviable with the low revenue of 56 paise a unit. Therefore, there is a backlog of about 400,000 farmers waiting for connections despite Gujarat's "surplus" of over 2,000 megawatts. Distributing electricity at such low rates is simply unsustainable, and the situation is much worse in states providing free electricity.

A possible way to approach this is to appoint two or three individuals with the integrity and competence to work with the government, industry and experts to develop an allocation plan. If this "beauty-parade" approach seems too utopian or academic for India, please be aware that this is precisely how land acquisition was done for the Calcutta Metro around 1982 after years of delay, and for part of the Bangalore Metro in 2006.

The spectrum constraints, meanwhile, show in the high levels of dropped calls because of congested lines, and the slow rollout of networks into rural areas. This slowness is because of the unfavourable economics: of high cost and difficult execution, with lower revenue potential. What we want from spectrum allocation is access to broadband networks at prices that will result in productivity gains. Instead, we have neither adequate broadband networks, nor sufficiently widespread access for productivity. A better solution is pooled networks with mandatory shared access on payment, with the government getting a share of revenues. Apart from inadequate infrastructure, logistics, finance and regulations, all of which must be well-orchestrated to achieve supportive ecosystems for investment and operations, the tax-claims fallout continues to undermine growth prospects. While the Vodafone problem may be resolved, the closure of Nokia's manufacturing facility in Chennai because of tax claims undercuts all the sales talk.

Each sector needs a supportive ecosystem, integrated with the rest. Above all, social disharmony seriously affects our capacity for collective action. Social coherence is essential for constructive development. The leadership's effectiveness in reaching out and inspiring constructive aspirations can help to harmonize and channel citizens towards desirable common goals. Such collective initiatives would reduce our fractiousness and infighting, making win-win outcomes more possible. The solutions in all these areas need to be path-breaking, based on integrity, trust and bold, collaborative action. We *must* learn these ways." [Source: *Business Standard*]

On 1st September 2018, *Rediff.com. Business* published, '*Piyush Goyal bats for team India*'. "'When all the states compete to try and achieve aspirational goals and bold targets, that's when truly the potential of India will be unleashed,' asserts Union Minister Piyush Goyal. I remember Virat

Kohli mentioning 'No cricket team in the world depends on one or two players; it's always the team that plays to win.' And in some sense that has been the approach of PM Narendra Modi when he got around to building trust between the Union government and the state governments and truly bring about a federal system where the states have an equal voice along with the Centre in policy making, in execution of policies, in reaching the benefits of development to the last man at the bottom of the pyramid. In fact, if one looks at the successful launch and implementation of the Goods and Services Tax, the GST, I believe there can be no better example of true federalism, cooperative and collaborative federalism at play than the finalization of thousands of items - GST rates, the finalization of the procedures and processes that would be implemented along with the GST and the entire process being run through complete unanimity. Not a single decision of the GST Council over so many meetings in the last few years has seen even one voice of dissent while implementing the GST.

We saw the 14th Finance Commission being accepted by the Government of India by which we were able to have a larger share of the devolution of funds from the Centre to the states being untied finances. Earlier, 32% of the total devolution of funds used to go through an untied mean and the rest were through specific projects. PM Modi recognizing that different states have different development imperatives, different need for funds, it is best that we increase the allocation of funds which is untied from 32% to 42% as recommended by the 14th Finance Commission. And we were able to give states more voice and more power to implement the projects which are suitable for them. On a lighter note, as the states are competing to grow, competing to perform, competing to meet the aspirations of the people in each state, we now have a story where states are competing with one other.

So, when PM Modi was in Uttar Pradesh, he excited or ignited their interest to try and achieve a trillion dollar-economy ahead of Maharashtra. And actually, when all the states compete among themselves to try and achieve aspirational goals and bold targets, that's when truly the potential of India will be unleashed and we will be able to see all round development and growth across different regions in the country. All the schemes of the central government, by and large, get implemented through the states. So be it the effort to take electricity to every home in this country in the next nine months. Within the next nine months, every home in the country, every willing consumer will get the benefit of electricity. After all, that program cannot be successful without the active involvement and participation of the states. And in that, every state has its own challenges. Maharashtra has a challenge to reach electricity to remote tribal areas, deep in the jungles, in the forests, sometimes left-wing extremists affected areas. It's a difficult proposition. Uttarakhand has a problem of taking electricity to remote homes. It's a unique situation. Sushil Modi inherited from earlier times, a situation where more than half the population of Bihar did not have electricity in their homes, but they have taken up the challenge in right earnest and I dare say, the most successful rural electrification program to reach power to every home would be carried out in Bihar, given the enthusiasm and the active involvement of the political leadership and the bureaucracy working together to give this basic amenity to every citizen of Bihar. And a very-very active program on mission mode, I can see before my eyes being carried out in Bihar.

This kind of cooperation where the Centre supports finances, the states actively implement the Centre's programs is the way forward to reach development to every citizen. We are shortly going to launch the *Ayushman Bharat* program where we hope to give free medical treatment worth almost $8,000 per year to every family living below a certain threshold of income, which will cover nearly 500 million people in the country. Now, *500 million people getting the benefit of Medicare -- sometimes called ModiCare in India now -- is truly transformational in terms of the future of these children, the future of these families.* Very often, many of us are aware families have got into distress largely because of debt taken during an illness in the family.

All these projects, be it our projects to take the railways into the nook and corner of the country, be it our effort to revive the discoms in the different states, be it the effort to take rural road connectivity to every home cannot be a success unless there was active participation of all the states. And truly, this country today is demonstrating to the world the true meaning of federalism, the true meaning of working in partnership between the central government and the state governments, working as a team, working as a team to win, working as a team where the nation comes first, working as a team to meet the aspirational goal that by 2022, when India will be celebrating 75 years of Independence, every citizen in this country should have a roof on his head, with clean drinking water and electricity 24x7, a good toilet in his home, good healthcare and educational facilities in the vicinity, good transport and road access to the village and home. And to meet that aspiration, to meet that goal, to meet that target in a short span of time, I think all of us in government at the Centre and the states, are equally committed.

We are all passionate about the job that we have on hand. We are working together through different fora, through different means where we have the NITI Aayog giving us logistic support, where we have organizations like the department of industrial policy and Promotion and the Invest India organizations working to bring industrialisation to different parts of the country. We are working on getting ease of doing business, cleanliness, getting the different states to work, both in collaboration and competition. *I think that truly will be the game changing program that we have launched over the last four years to bring about change in the lives of a billion plus people, a better future for the children of our country, a better future for the planet and India's contribution to make the planet a better place to live in.*" [Edited excerpts from Union Minister Piyush Goyal's speech at a discussion with chief ministers on the *'Vision of infrastructure development in India'* in Mumbai, June 25, 2018.] [Source: *Business Standard*]

On 26th July 2016, *Rediff.com News* had an article, *'Want Achhe Din? Implement these taxes!'*. "From curbing population to dealing with speedsters, presenting a list of need-of-the-hour-taxes, we hope, our ministers take note of. We Indians are already paying 33% income tax. Add to it 15% service tax inclusive of Swachh Bharat Cess and the latest Krishi Kalyan Cess at 0.5% each. Welcome to India, the land where you pay more for every rupee earned and spent. Dear Prime Minister, while it's a great way to involve taxpayers in your governance, we think you missed some more important taxes. Including these new taxes in budget will aid the government and the *Janata* towards the dream of *Achhe Din*. So, here's our *Wishlist*:

1] *Population tax*: India is sitting at 1.3 billion people and that figure looks like it will soon touch the sky. We moved from *hum do hamare do* to *hum do, hamara ek* almost a decade ago, but that doesn't seem to be helping much. In a country where a new-born is viewed as *'Bhagwaan ki dua'*, perhaps levying a tax could dissuade couples, young and old, to maybe think of contraception?

2] *Gutka tax*: In India, spitting should be a skill worth qualifying for the Olympics. Almost everyone is skilled at it; there are some who can aim at the wall from the bus and train windows. In 2015, the *Indian Express* reported how Western Railway spends close to INR35 million cleaning up paan and gutka stains on railway platforms. If that figure is anything to go by, multiply it by the number of railway stations and the walls in the country. Do the math. Meanwhile, can we have a gutka tax please? The Swachh Bharat Cess doesn't really cover gutka, or can it?

3] *Profanity tax*: Blame it on new age Hindi films or popular item songs, profanity is the new cool. Words like b*******, m******** have found a plum place in daily conversations. Since the Censor Board can't be everywhere, how about a tax (more like a fine) to fight profanity? Perhaps, every service provider could have an app that would identify cuss words. You will be charged a premium per abuse at the end of every month.

4] *Littering tax*: Some of us think the world is our restroom and any place outside our home is a free to use garbage can. So much so, we even let our kids grow up believing that littering in public places is the most convenient thing to do. Well, how about making them pay a tax for it?

5] *Honking tax*: Ask anyone who has travelled out of India what is the one thing they hate the most and pat comes the reply -- honking! How many times have you yelled at the person honking behind you to stop doing it and thought if there was a way to stop it? Well, if there was a way the CCTV cameras on roads counted the number of times you honked and taxed you for it! Maybe that would be some lesson to use the horn more responsibly.

6] *Tobacco tax*: Written on the pack, yet people ignore the warning. There are hundreds of people getting away with smoking in public places. Kids, pregnant women and elderly passively inhale the smoke. As per the 2012 data, nearly 600,000 people died due to passive smoking of which 165,000 were kids. Don't you think it would make sense to tax those who smoke in public?

7] *Jumping signals and speeding tax*: In India, there is an unwritten traffic rule which many of us follow: Jump a signal if no one is watching or reprimanding you. Well, what if your actions were being monitored and you get a tax slip at the next fuel station for your impatience? There should be some way to stop the speedsters, shouldn't it?

8] *Junk food tax*: According a 2015 World Health Organization study, India has the third-highest number of obese and overweight people, of which 11% are adolescents. The increased consumption of junk food is to be partly blamed -- the pizzas, the burgers, colas and what not. Kerala has already introduced a tax on junk food. How about making it a national junk food tax? That way parents and kids would junk Junk Food.

9] *Cutting trees tax*: We complain about the poor monsoon, scarcity of water and fresh air and pollution without looking around and noting that trees cut for our concrete civilisation? By charging people who cut trees, we can at least try to restore the man-nature balance.

10] *Queue breaking tax*: Sometimes you wonder if there could have been a law to prohibit people from breaking the queue. You'll find these queue breakers everywhere -- at railway stations, movie theatres, historical sites, places of worship. They are impatient, restless and anxious to get ahead of everyone, sometimes creating a stampede-like situation. How do we get the point across to these adult kids? Tax them!

11] *Plastic tax*: It doesn't matter we are charged a premium for plastic bags; we still can't do without them. 'Thaili do na bhaiyya, (Brother, give me a plastic bag),' we insist almost shamelessly. As per a 2015 Central Pollution Control Board survey, 60 cities produce 15,342 tons of plastic waste every day. India ranks 12th in the world for dumping plastic in the ocean. From bottles to plastic bags and what not, we dump everything with the simple reason that the ocean eats up everything. The only way to condition these irresponsible humans is by taxing them for every bit of plastic they use and carelessly dump."[*Divya Nair/Rediff.com*] As a matter of fact, *we Hindustanis are slow learners and averse/resentful to any change. Our citizens find it difficult to shed 'slave' mentality. We need constant prodding on maintaining even civic sense for which the governments use repeated TV advertisements to teach the use of toilets after Modi, in his very first year, laid emphasis on the construction of toilets.*

In our type of sham democracy, it is free for all. There is no restraint on criticism of any person on earth. On 31st May 2016, *Rediff.com News* published an article, '*Modi and the art of event diplomacy*', that is quite interesting. "PM Modi's decision to visit Afghanistan on June 4 is inexplicable. He had visited Afghanistan in December. Of course, a prime minister can visit a country as many times as he wants to. But he must know that he can't go everywhere and pay another visit to a neighbouring country as strategically important as Afghanistan just because a major project in Afghanistan, funded and built by India is ready to be operational. Modi will visit Afghanistan for a few hours on June 4. He will travel to Herat province in western Afghanistan to inaugurate the Salma dam project, which is finally ready after missing several deadlines. Everyone familiar with India's strategic affairs will appreciate the importance of the Salma dam project and appreciate that India is finally ready to deliver the finished project to the Afghans, a project that may win many friends in that landlocked country. But Modi should realize that the success of foreign policy is not predicated on the number of visits an Indian prime minister undertakes to a country, no matter how sensitive and important that country is for Indian national interests. After all, the Salma dam, constructed by the Indians at a budget of almost $275 million (about INR18.5 billion) will produce only 42 MW electricity. By comparison, the peak daily power consumption in Delhi is over 5,000 MW. Granted that for a country like Afghanistan, which has been ravaged by bloody internal strife and political instability for close to 40 years, 42 MW power is significant and crucial. But then the Indian PM is not required to visit Afghanistan for this purpose alone as it dilutes the significance of the visit. Modi could have, and should have, entrusted this job to any of his Cabinet colleagues. External Affairs Minister Sushma Swaraj would be most ideal for the purpose and if she was unavailable on health grounds then the power minister or water resources minister could have done the honours. *Modi's decision to do it himself shows his penchant for indulging in event diplomacy.*

Afghanistan is not a part of the Indian Union which presents the prime minister with a ribbon-cutting opportunity or where the prime minister stands to gain electorally and politically by inaugurating a developmental project. It shows that Modi the politician does not want to let go any opportunity to visit a neighbouring country to make a song and dance about the dam project the construction of which was begun by the UPA government in right earnest a decade ago. Moreover, Iran has always looked at the Salma dam project with suspicion as the Iranians somehow believe that the dam will reduce the river water flow into Iran.

From June 4, Modi was on a five-nation trip, the other countries being Qatar, Switzerland, the USA and Mexico in that order. He visited a sixth nation in June when he travelled to Uzbekistan to attend the Shanghai Cooperation Organisation summit on June 21-22. He could have easily kept this number to five by sending a Cabinet colleague to Herat. After all, he was in Afghanistan in December to inaugurate the Afghan parliament building, another construction project funded and handled by India. Afghanistan became 2nd South Asian country which Modi visited twice. Nepal is the other one. Look at the current state of India-Nepal relations! Nepal continues to poke a finger in India's eye even after Modi pampered it. The moral of the story is simple. Prime ministerial visits to a country are not directly proportional to the state of bilateral relations. [Rajeev Sharma, an independent journalist and strategic analyst, tweets @Kishkindha]

On 8th June, Modi addressed America's joint Congress session where he was warmly applauded throughout his 50-minute extempore speech in English. On 9th June, *Rediff.com News* reported it under, *'Modi hit the ball out of the park'*. "Republican Congressman Ed Royce, chairman of the United States House of Representatives Foreign Affairs Committee, and the driving force behind urging Speaker Paul Ryan to invite PM Modi to address a joint meeting of the US Congress, says Modi hit the ball right out of the park during his Capitol Hill speech. In an exclusive interview with Aziz Haniffa/*Rediff.com*, immediately after he hosted a reception for Modi, along with other senior members of the House Foreign Affairs Committee and the Senate Foreign Relations Committee, Royce said: *"It was both an honour to serve on the Escort Committee that welcomed and then accompanied the prime minister on the House floor, and to host the reception afterwards with members of the key foreign policy committees in Congress."* Asked what he believed were the highs of Modi's speech, the lawmaker, who has struck up a close friendship with the prime minister from the time the latter was Gujarat chief minister, said, "He finished with a strong argument using Walt Whitman's comments about a new symphony here. The symphony has changed. The relationship is going to be obviously much deeper. Our partnership is going to be much stronger, and so, he hit on these issues -- whether it's a nuclear power, or a space exploration, or defence or trade or renewable energy -- we are going to build a very strong partnership based on our many shared values," Royce said. "I believe that that theme resonates, and the prime minister offered a very thoughtful and compelling address about how we can continue working together to promote peace and prosperity," he added. While concluding his speech, Modi referred to poet Walt Whitman's line. "The orchestra have sufficiently tuned their instruments, the baton has given the signal," he said, quoting from Whitman's iconic poem *'Leaves of Grass'*. Then he added, "And there is a new symphony in play."

Royce acknowledged that the prime minister's tough remarks on terrorism -- much of it fomented from across the border in Pakistan -- and Modi's naming the Lashkar-e-Taiba would help bring about "much greater understanding" in the US Congress. "I believe there is much greater understanding in Congress post 9/11 of the arguments that the prime minister was making," Royce observed. "In the past, when this discussion (on terrorism) has come up, prior to the attack in New York, it was difficult, probably for some members of Congress to comprehend what India was going through with the terrorist attacks in India. But now, people understand, and I think that was an important message, because counterterrorism and intelligence sharing cooperation is going to be such a big part of our joint efforts going forward," he said.

Recalling his earlier interview with *Rediff.com* on the eve of Modi's fourth visit to the US, Royce said Modi's address to Congress would afford him a tremendous opportunity to not just speak to members of Congress but to America also. Now he has most definitely made use of that opportunity. "A joint meeting of Congress," he said, "is a unique opportunity to address the American people and their representatives. I believe he was so effective in speaking not just to Americans, but to the world. PM's address was an important sign of the special US-India relationship." "I had spoken to the prime minister about this issue when I had a bipartisan delegation to New Delhi last year, and I don't think he could have been more effective. He really hit the ball out of the park. That speech he delivered had a profound impact on my colleagues," said Royce. He acknowledged how Modi's speech played even better because it was laced with humour and contained many laugh lines that elicited peals of appreciative laughter. "It was a case of him being comfortable in being able to use humour with an American audience and the humour was effective," Royce said.

Over the years, Royce said, he had listened to several addresses by world leaders and others to a joint meeting of the US Congress, and Modi's speech was right up there with the best of them.

"It was and I believe this address will have a stabilizing effect as the two democracies -- India and the United States -- on the world stage, have an important responsibility to help bring stability and peace. And, he referred to that," he said.

During his speech Modi referred to the role that the United States and India must play and how US-India defence trade has strengthened India's role as a provider of security in the Indian Ocean region. "So, when he speaks to the issue of India's air force evacuating Americans and Indians and other nationals from Yemen, and about the relief efforts, whether it is for Nepal or Sri Lanka, Americans understand that India was using American-manufactured C-130s (Hercules) and C-17s (Globe master III) on this mission," he said. "The points or the arguments he (Modi) was making before Congress resonated very strongly with the members and I think also with the American people as he referred to the role America played during D-Day -- in terms of protecting freedom in Europe," Royce observed.

At the reception, he hosted after Modi finished his speech, Royce recalled his first meeting with Modi 15 years ago. "When we first met, PM Modi was the chief minister of Gujarat and at that point, an earthquake had levelled Bhuj. I remember, we flew in with USAID (United States Agency for International Development) the day after the quake and my memory is of the chief minister bringing order out of the chaos. I remember the leadership. I remember his efforts on the ground, directing and setting an example. As we watched the enormity of that perseverance and that entrepreneurial spirit of the people in Gujarat, what struck me was that the reforms you were bringing then as the chief minister. They were bringing a situation where we saw 10 percent economic growth per year. It looked as if this was the type of leadership that India could use. Today, US-India cooperation is better than ever. We have seen the navy-to-navy exchanges. We have seen the cooperation on counterterrorism. We have seen efforts now that you've put forward to build up what we're doing on space cooperation. And on so many different fronts that set this foundation, these two great democracies are intent on seeing the same values," Royce told more than 500 people, including several hundred members of the Indian-American community present at the reception. "We understand that India is in a tough neighbourhood, but we also understand that with your words here today, that you have, with that symphony that you spoke of, set a new note." [*Aziz Haniffa* in Washington, DC]

An outsider's view on *'What does India need to do'*? On 7*th* July 2016, *Rediff.com News* published an interview with Joseph Stiglitz: *'India has an image problem: Nobel laureate'*. "Joseph Stiglitz says: India should not be bothered on inflation and instead focus on rapid growth. *At a time when the National Democratic Alliance government at the Centre is going all out to improve the country's image globally, Nobel laureate and economist Joseph E Stiglitz on Wednesday said there is a lot of improvement needed on that front.* Stiglitz, who was in Bengaluru to give a lecture on "*Global* *inequality – causes and consequences,*" said India's image has taken a beating globally, especially because of Modi government's policy to crackdown on non-governmental organizations (NGOs) and students of JNU. Stiglitz, Professor of Economics at Columbia University, who received Nobel prize in 2001, noted: "India should be aware that it has an image problem abroad. It should be a matter of concern that NGO's are subjected to a condition that makes it difficult for them to operate. This has got a lot of attention abroad. There are very few governments that have made it difficult for NGOs to operate. Also, very few countries, mainly authoritarian ones, have engaged in the harassment of students in universities. These two events have had a strong effect on public opinion abroad.

It puts (India) in the club of countries such as Egypt, Russia and Turkey. Most people in India will not want to be in this group. These events also have been in the spotlight and have influenced foreign investors," he added. Stiglitz said with India growing in the global economy, this was not how it should be portraying itself. Speaking about the state of Indian economy, Stiglitz said the country should look at a high rate of growth and give lesser importance to inflation. "When there is high level of unemployment, inequality thrives. India should make sure that the overall economy grows at a rapid rate. That means, not getting overly obsessed about inflation. Excessive focus on inflation almost inevitably leads to higher unemployment levels and lower growth." Stiglitz applauded the National Rural Employment Guarantee Act (NREGA). "The NREGA is one of the most important programmes ever introduced. It is the single most innovative programme from India, which is a lesson for the rest of the world. However, to make sure there is no inequality, the government should look at the continuation and strengthening of the programme," he added. [*Apurva Venkat* in Bengaluru. Source: *Business Standard*]

<u>An Indian American living in USA observed,</u> "Now onwards MODI is not only a surname but also a qualification: *Master of Developing India*." She went on to add, "Five days, five countries. Landing at 2am. Meetings starting at 8am. Flying out if the afternoons. Sleeping during flights. Eating during flights, *yet smiling all the times,* Commitment, energy 100% at age 65! Oration on point Bullseyes. Business as usual. Bingo. As we Indians watched his speech to American Congress, we awed and swayed by his punch in oratory skills. It had substance, promise, signals to Congressmen, it had diplomatic friendly overtones, veiled warnings to China and Pakistan without naming them, it had history, geography,

culture, science, defence and trade partnership offer with mutual respect, and rare but true sprinkling with some sense of humour which went down very well in Congress. More than an hour of extempore excellent speech. Eight standing ovations by complete US Congress house; 66 spontaneous applauses (for the information of cynics of Modi they were unsponsored). Later US Congressmen/women could be seen breaking lines to meet him, shake his hand, or get his autograph. *That's just great and splendid.*

I mean.... In our lifetime, we have not seen any Indian leader get so much of attention, respect and honour in USA and the world. Most PMs have been seen coming with begging bowls. Here comes a Game-Changer, NaMo. Bashing of Indians stopped in Australia after stern signals sent by our foreign minister Sushma Swaraj last year. This (NDA) government has spine and muscle and now presenting this 65-year Superman from India. May he live long and take India to *Param Vaibhav* (Extreme Glory)! This Narendra Damodardas Modi-the World Boss. JAI HIND."

<u>Non-Performing assets</u> (NPA) kept on escalating year after year during a 10-year long misrule of UPA under a Cambridge and Oxford-educated 'financial wizard' PM Manmohan and his finance ministers namely Pranab Mukherjee and P Chidambaram. It is debatable if Manmohan and his assistants had any worthwhile knowledge on finance! The trio created a mess. A few notable uncalled for and shameful misdeeds: buying crude from Iran in debt of $500 billion; and using part of the following financial year's budget. This produced a precarious 'Balance of Payments' situation for the successor NDA government. A multi-pronged effort was embarked upon by Modi government. Public Sector banks reeling under the unbearable burden of NPAs were sternly warned to recover or else quit. Finance

On 30th August 2018, *Yahoo Finance* published, *'How India's Debt Recovery Is Spurring Record M&A'* by Anton Antony and Rajesh Kumar Singh. "India's banks have stepped up a drive to sell the assets of companies that can't repay their debts. A deadline set by the central bank to restructure an estimated 3.6 trillion rupees ($51 billion) of stressed loans expired on 27th August, driving at least a dozen companies into bankruptcy proceedings. Many of the other indebted companies are finding buyers, adding to already record levels of mergers and acquisitions in Asia's third-largest economy this year. Purchasers of stressed assets have included ArcelorMittal, the world's biggest steelmaker, billionaire Anil Agarwal's giant Vedanta Resources and Tata Group, the South Asian nation's largest conglomerate.

1. ***How much is at stake?*** India has the worst bad-loan ratio after Italy among the world's 20 largest economies, with state-run banks responsible for nearly 90% of the $210 billion in loans where payments are in arrears. For PM Modi, getting rid of the soured debt is crucial to reviving Asia's third-largest economy and meeting his election pledge of adding millions of jobs before his party seeks re-election in 2019. His government's separate plan to inject 2.1 trillion rupees into state-owned banks should give the lenders enough capital to write off bad loans weighing down their balance sheets.
2. **What does the bankruptcy law have to do with this?** The Insolvency and Bankruptcy Code, India's first consolidated bankruptcy law, was passed in 2016, overwriting a patchwork of laws that in some cases dated back a century. One of Parliament's primary aims was to give state banks a tool to resolve the growing problem of bad debts. Among other steps, the law created a new class of insolvency professionals to help steer the liquidation process.
3. ***What made India overhaul the bankruptcy law?*** The inability to shut loss-making companies and collect on dues had locked up funds at banks and damped lending and investment. Indian insolvencies took longer to resolve than in any other major economy; only in Brazil did creditors typically recover less. Overall, India was #103 in the World Bank's 2017 ranking of how nations handle insolvencies, just behind Nicaragua.
4. ***Why does India have many bad debts?*** Most of the companies that found themselves in a hole were hobbled by loans taken in 2007-08 (during UPA regime), which became difficult to service as demand cooled. Some borrowers found it even harder to repay when the government tightened various regulations, the courts cancelled coal mining licenses and gas supplies dwindled, real-estate prices fell, and interest rates rose. *Making matters worse, there was a belief among some Indians that they could walk away from their debts without facing consequences.*
5. ***What else is happening?*** RBI last year pushed lenders to take about 40 large defaulters to bankruptcy court. This February, the regulator laid out stringent new rules for resolving the loans of companies that missed payments by even a single day, allowing 180

days for a restructuring. Delinquent loans that can't be resolved must then be taken to insolvency court within 15 days. More than $50 billion in loans that were already in default when the rules came into force ran out of time on 27th August, leading to a rush of deal-making -- and bankruptcy pleas.

6. ***Who has been hardest hit?*** The power sector: India's largest bank identified 34 stressed coal-fired projects with a combined capacity of 40 gigawatts and about 1.8 trillion rupees in dues. Their troubles began when India de-licensed private investments in thermal power generation in 2003, drawing in new money, without investing in the supporting infrastructure, such as fuel supplies, railway networks to ship coal and transmission lines. The most enduring problem though has been the financially weak distribution companies, which weren't able to buy and carry the new power generated to consumers. Plants were under-utilized, and several projects stalled due to a lack of funds or difficulties in getting land and environmental approvals.

7. ***How does the insolvency process work?*** A creditor to a company that has defaulted on its payments files an insolvency plea to the National Company Law Tribunal to recover its dues. The Tribunal hears arguments. If it is satisfied that the dues cannot be paid, it suspends the defaulting company's board, determines the quantum of claims to be recovered and appoints an independent insolvency resolution professional. That professional invites restructuring plans from bidders, who can submit their bids within 180 days, extendable by another 90 days. If the submitted plans are not approved by many creditors, the Tribunal declares the company bankrupt and starts the process for liquidation of assets.

8. ***Which industries are seeing successful resolutions?*** The steel sector has been the biggest success so far in the bankruptcy resolution process. In May, Tata Steel Limited bought Bhushan Steel Limited for about 364 billion rupees, paying about 63$ of the 560 billion rupees claimed by creditors. Billionaire Agarwal bought the assets of Electro steel Steels Ltd., while the country's top mill JSW Steel Ltd. and partner Aion Capital Partners purchased Monnet Ispat & Energy Ltd.

THE BASIC PREMISE

We live in an amusing rather *funny* land mass known by many names: *Bharat, Hindustan, India*, and so on I remember reading a magazine, *'Mother India'* as a young school-going boy. Its well-known author used a cliché, *'India that is Bharat'*. The Muslim countries, and Urdu as well as Arabic newspapers still refer to the country as Hindustan or Hind respectively. Many lies are spread in Tamil Nadu that Hinduism is a foreign religion. But many proofs have squashed the bogus Aryan invasion theory invented by British evangelists for mass conversions. Sage Agastya was the founder of the oldest language in the world. The oldest book in Sangam literature Aggatiyam was written by the sage himself. And the game British evangelist Bishop Robert Caldwell who was the pioneer of Aryan invasion theory and spread lies and canards that Hinduism is a foreign religion. Many most important aspects of our history have been thus changed first by the British, and then by their stooge Nehru through his band of the 'left-liberal' historians who flourished on public 'tax payers' money changed history books at the instance/instructions of this allegedly 'ba****d' Muslim *aka* fake Pt. Nehru who not only usurped the position of first PM of independent India at the expense of 14-year senior duly elected PM, Sardar Patel but committed fatal blunders repeatedly not once but over 90 times during his longest stint as the chief executive! That anti-national idiot Nehru was a key player in Partitioning the great Subcontinent, took the country backwards, made Hindustan lose hundreds of thousands of square miles of its territory and created a deep Hindu-Muslim divide by largest scale riots. Nehru obliquely admitted his folly at the time of Partition leading to exodus of tens of millions across both sides of the new artificial borders. He ruefully said, "*The history of India has been one of assimilation and synthesis of the various elements that have come in… it is perhaps because we tried to go against the trend of the country's history that we are faced with this* (the communal carnage)."

On 23rd October 2018, *Rediff.com News'* article, *'Hinduism is inclusive, assimilative and based on dialogue'*, makes an absorbing reading. "'It is exceptionally important for Hindus to once again get in touch with the foundation of Hinduism.' 'Aggressive evangelists are reducing Hinduism to its lowest common denominator.' And national spokesperson of the Janata Dal-United, is a scholar and among the rarest of rare politicians who can discuss Hinduism threadbare and at length. His latest book *'Adi Shankaracharya -- Hinduism's Greatest Thinker'*, examines the legacy of the 8th century Hindu seer who revived Hinduism after the rise of Buddhism and Jainism established four mutts (monasteries) across India in Dwarka (Gujarat), Jagannath Pura (Odisha), Sringeri (Karnataka) and Joshimath (Uttarakhand).

"Hinduism as a religion cannot be separated from Hinduism as a philosophy and if you are unaware of that philosophy, you will fall prey to Hinduism as a practice as defined by these people who know nothing about Hindu philosophy," Varma tells Rediff.com's Syed Firdaus Ashraf. A rationalist writing a book on Adi Shankaracharya, an icon of Hinduism -- what triggered this? There is rarely a philosophical discourse or thesis which is based on such a rational structure of thought. In other words, this is not mythology, not obscurantism, not a chauvinistic glorification of the past, but it is the exposition of one of the finest minds developing a rigorous structure of philosophical thought based on reason and logic. On the eclectic Upanishadic insight of 4,000 years ago, which is why if I am a rationalist on television today, I have a direct correspondence with the rationalism that is an aspect of Hindu philosophy.

Adi Shankaracharya left his widowed mother, which to many could come across as not being responsible towards her. *What about the dharma to take care of his mother? What does Hinduism say about it?* I think that he was torn between his duties as the only child towards his widowed mother and (spiritual urge), he did not take a unilateral decision to leave her. He waited to have her permission, as described in the book, which she gives. And this aspect of his duties to his mother has to be balanced or seen in the perspective of a very strong desire for mumutsa (yearning to find the truth and for liberation) which was a very strong intimation, if not resolve within, to become a sanyasin. He left his mother after her permission and went with the promise that he will be with her and especially at the time when she needs him, and he does come when she is bedridden. In a sense, he balances what he felt to be his duty with the much stronger urge to pursue a larger quest of what is the absolute truth. In which human relations do become to some manner subordinate.

To a layman, what is the Advaita doctrine and why is it so important for the Hindu way of life? Essentially, Advaita is about not the search for God, but for the search of absolute truth. Therefore, it is nothing short of a miracle that Shankaracharya's philosophy and the *Upanishads* have a concept of what is the ultimate cosmic reality which is not confined to attributes which are familiar to the human category. It is about the entity that is Brahman: which is attribute-less omnipotent omniscient as also a *drishti* (vision) unseen and beyond thought, pure intelligence, undifferentiated consciousness, and all pervasive. *Therefore, that is remarkable.* From that derives an entire structure of philosophical thought that if *Brahmaand* (universe) is suffused by this entity called Brahman, which is pure consciousness and which by inference is bliss, an awareness which you are entitled to if you experience it through Brahm Anubhav (experience of the Absolute), then everything else follows in terms of what is this empirical world, who am I? Therefore, the four Mahavakhyas of the Upanishads, Tat Vam Asi, you are that and not what you think what you are. Pragyanam Brahman, Aham Atman Brahman and Aham Brahmasmi. On that basis you build a philosophical thought. I want to add to this what happens is that the Hindu religion is a way of life. In other words, it has no one pope, no one church, no one prescribed text, no one prescriptive ritual and no mandatory congregations. But it is a way of life, that is the strength of the religion which is why it is sanatan anaadi anant (life is cyclical). Hinduism is dialogic. Hinduism is inclusive, assimilative and based on dialogues described as *Shastras*, the ability to debate and listen to contrary viewpoints and to argue what you believe It is not evangelical that is being propagated today. Therefore, it is exceptionally important for Hindus to once again get in touch with the foundation of Hinduism. *That is why I wrote this book.*

You have mentioned very little about the Avarna sect in your book. Why is it so? And how did this section of society remain a part of Hinduism? Why did they agree to be the lowest strata of Hinduism when Buddhism and Jainism were then gaining ground in India? In fact, it is precisely the nature of Hinduism that it could allow religions like Buddhism and Jainism, which have great areas of overlap with Hinduism, to develop as different strands of thought without necessarily any violent conflict in the evolution of such a development. It is a mythology that Adi Shankaracharya although differed with Buddhism in certain aspects. I do not believe in the hagiographical biography of Shankaracharya that he was an avatar of Shiva to destroy Buddhism. There was at best a dialogue when Buddhism was already in decline. The principle dialogue which changed the course of Hinduism was with Mandan Mishra, who believed in Karam Kaand as against Adi Shankaracharya who believed in Gyan Marg and that dialogue took place through process of shastras (or debate). As regard to the lower castes, there is no doubt Hinduism in due course developed a very oppressive system where the Brahminical order prevailed. But credit must be given to Shankaracharya when he said that all are equal and emanations of the same *Brahman*. There is a famous story that he came across a *Chandaal* in Varanasi where he says you are my guru. He negates it and says go beyond jaati and caste as they have no consequences. I am neither a believer in the varna system nor teerth. *An excerpt from Pavan K Varma's book: 'When Adi Shankaracharya met the chandaal.* He was not a social reformer but a philosopher. He could conclude that certain rituals or exclusionist sects of Hinduism had no place in his structure of thoughts'.

<u>Why was Buddhism on the decline during his time</u>? One reason is perhaps, that there was some level of deterioration both in the intellectual calibre and practice of Buddhism in the monasteries themselves as established. Therefore, for whatever reason Buddhism having reached a certain apogee in the time of Ashoka, subsequently went through a relative decline. Shankaracharya is credited with the revival of Hinduism because he once again took Hinduism and linked it to its deep philosophical foundation beyond merely somewhat degenerated ritualism to which it had descended. He said Ishwar, Bhakti, atmasamarpan and yoga, all of them are valid if they are done without thought of reward because they prepare you for that higher knowledge which is called Paramvidya, which takes you towards Brahman or allows you to experience it. *In that sense he was a great synthesiser and he revived Hinduism.* It is said Zoroastrianism as a religion was not organised and therefore it could not hold its believers, especially after the battle of Qadisiyyah when Muslims defeated the Sassanid empire.

<u>Would Hinduism have gone the Zoroastrian way</u>? I think Adi Shankaracharya's contribution in providing for Hinduism is the rigorously reasoned philosophical foundation and of reviving once again the spirit in which Hinduism first evolved from the time of the Upanishads. The Brahma Sutras and Bhagwadgita are the foundational text of Hinduism and that contribution can never be underestimated. The tragedy is that

most Hindus are today adrift from their own philosophical underpinnings. If you ask a normally practising Hindu, who is Adi Shankaracharya, he may say, I know, but ask him when he was born, what he wrote, what are the six systems of Hindu philosophy, what is the Charvaka school? How many Upanishads are there? People don't know. *These are the real treasures of Hinduism.* And it is in this absence of that knowledge that we have these aggressive evangelists whose aggression is in direct correspondence with their ignorance of Hinduism. They are reducing Hinduism to its lowest common denominator. And you cannot fight them until you go back and immerse yourself into philosophical richness of Hinduism.

<u>Which language did Shankaracharya speak while convincing people to establish the four mutts?</u> Prakrit had taken strong root in India replacing Sanskrit at that time. I think it must have been a combination of Malayalam and Sanskrit. What is significant is that he was a travelling philosopher who did not stay in one place. He moved from Kaladi where he was born and took samadhi in Kedarnath. Sringeri one mutt, Puri another mutt, Dwarka another mutt and Joshimath and this is the civilisational map of India. And he undertook this journey not once, but thrice. I would assume that apart from local languages, Sanskrit must have been known across India.

Do you think these did mutts help establish an organized religion, like in Islam where people look in the direction of Mecca to pray? Is that the brilliant understanding of Shankaracharya that the mutts were important to give Hindu religion a sense of direction if it had to survive in the 8th century? I feel Adi Shankaracharya was influenced by the creation in Buddhism of monasteries to train and develop the philosophical thought and practice of Buddhism. I think that must have been an influencer, which is why he thought to create institutions where some of these great learnings could be preserved in an institutional manner, not through memory but in an institutional manner. Therefore, he set up Sringeri, Dwarka, Puri and Joshimath.

Why do Marxist historians say Hinduism is a Brahminical religion, that Brahminvad has captured it? I think to some extent the manner in which Hinduism is practised, or the inequities inflicted in the name of Hinduism by the relatively privileged higher castes, especially against the lowest rung of the social ladder, which includes the Dalits, was definitely a condemnable development. And it is for this reason that very often Leftists or critics throw the baby out with the bath water. They say everything in Hinduism is a perpetuation only of an inequitable Brahminical order, whereas the truth is while that indeed it was present, it needs to be confronted, fought and defeated. There was equally in Hinduism an emphatic acceptance of equality. If *Brahman* is attribute less as in you and me or anyone, the human categories of hierarchy have no meaning.

How did the caste structure in Hinduism get such a grip on the religion even though Shankaracharya spoke against it? It did because inequity, inequality and injustice continued until those who are the victims or being exploited get a voice of their own. I give credit for the faults that our democracy may have that these equations have begun to change because of the empowerment of democracy. One interesting thing one encounters in your book is that *'scientific nature was natural to Hinduism'*. How then did blind beliefs creep into Hindu society? No religion is monolithic, and it can happen that within a religion which is also a way of life practices that develop not necessarily having the sanction of the philosophy of that religion. But it reflects the human tendency to perpetuate inequity and use religion to sanctify or validate. It is possible. Hinduism as a religion cannot be separated from Hinduism as a philosophy and if you are unaware of that philosophy, you will fall prey to Hinduism as a practice as defined by these people who know nothing about Hindu philosophy. There was never a revolt by the castes in Hinduism.

Why haven't the lower castes never violently revolted against such an oppressive regime for years? Not only did Adi Shankaracharya not validate the caste system, he spoke against it. Anyway, to support the human category of hierarchy would be a direct negation of his postulation of Brahman. But why did Hindu society not change radically? This is one question all Hindus need to ask themselves. And today it is changing in some manner because of democratic empowerment. Therefore, in a state like Uttar Pradesh you had a Dalit chief minister. It comes with democracy. Have you started believing in the Mundaka Upanishad which says 'The universe comes forth from and will return to *Brahman!* Verily, all is Brahman'. I genuinely believe the cycle of time is beyond human imagination. In one chapter I speak of the co-relation between science and certain attributes of Brahman, be it infinity, be it intelligence, be it attribute lessness, be it consciousness, be it the nature of reality (*mayavad*). And above all, be it the fact that in each of us there is that uncalled Atman which is the same as Brahman. All of these have been proven by science today. This has been proved in the laboratories of Harvard. The statements of Nobel Laureates, physicists, neurology and even in cosmology agree to it.

If there was a big bang that started it all, then why can't there be a big crunch? And if there is a big crunch, why can't be there be a big bang again? Therefore, the cycle of time is *'eternal',* and I think that it is borne out by science. [*Syed Firdaus Ashraf/Rediff.com*]

It is worth etching on our minds as well as hearts and remembering for all times to come what President Donald Trump said recently: "*Loyalty to our nation* demands loyalty to one another. *Love for America requires* love for all its people. When we open our hearts to patriotism, there is no room for prejudice, no place for bigotry, and no tolerance for hate. The American Legion embodies the spirit of patriotism and that is the source of our strength and the best hope for the future. The dishonest *Fake* News Media is out of control! They won't talk about the things that matter to the American people, like the TREMENDOUS economic success we've had since I took office. Big things are happening!" A top five-cable network, Fox News Channel has been the most-watched news channel in the country for 17 consecutive years. According to a 2018 Research Intelligencer study by Brand Keys, FOX News ranks as the second most trusted television brand in the country. Additionally, a *Suffolk University/USA Today* survey states Fox News is the most trusted source for television news or commentary in the country, while a 2017 Gallup/Knight Foundation survey found that among Americans who could name an objective news source, FOX News is the top-cited outlet. FNC is available in nearly 90 million homes and dominates the cable news landscape while routinely notching the top ten programs in the genre. Earlier, American President Ronald Reagan said: "If Fascism ever comes to America, it will be in the form of Liberalism." *Exactly, today the same applies to us FULLY. We ought to substitute the word 'India' for America'.* However, it is intriguing that world's richest and one of the most advanced countries in the world could not produce a woman president in its 130-year history. This time there were record number of women in reckoning, however only two white women remain in the contest for electing the Democratic contender to contest Republican Trump for his second term! Elizabeth Warren who was reportedly doing well in the running dropped out of the race due to misogyny. It is tragic that such attitude still exists in America even in the 21st century. Some Democrats said sexism led to Elizabeth Warren's failed presidential bid, reaction from Scott Bolden, former D.C. Democratic Party chairman.

In recent times, some say or feel that *India* lives in cities and *Bharat* in villages! Thanks to the extreme degree of politicization, we the citizens of this once great country are deeply and finely divided in thought and action. There are many interesting *paradoxes* in our day to day lives:

One, among the three anti-nationals/terrorists: L-e-T activist and a trained human-bomber Ishrat Jehan is *Behan* (sister); Terrorists-cum-traitor Dawood Ibrahim, the financier of terrorist attacks or Yakub Memon, the Mastermind of 1992 multiple Bombay blasts is *Bhai* (brother); and Sinister plotter of December 2001 Parliament House attack Afzal Guru is *Beta* (son); and likewise, Traitor-separatist Kanhaiya Kumar also is a *beta*; but strangely Bharat is not their *Mata* (Mother)! Isn't that bewitching, insulting, humiliating, disrespectful and disgraceful?

Two, a huge country with 1,652 spoken dialects is united by an alien language, English – yet another evidence of slavery passed down the generations by a dominant gene.

Three, national Animal-endangered, national Language-not spoken or respected by everyone, national Pledge-unintended, national Anthem-praise for our erstwhile ruling Emperor and Monarch of England, national River-highly polluted.

Four, on paper, we call ours a 'secular' country but on every damn form used for official work we are supposed to write our religion but NOT Indian.

Five, everything run by the government is bad but NOT the government jobs that are the first preference of all and sundry.

Six, parents want their children to stand out in a crowd but make/expect them to do what everybody else is doing.

Seven, every Indian mother wants her daughter to control her husband but her son to control his wife.

Eight, seeing a cop makes us nervous rather than make us feel safe.

Nine, we often say *'Atithi devo bhava'* (Guest is god) but don't allow visitors' parking in residential premises.

Ten, we are always in a hurry but never on time.

Eleven, our holy places are very interesting – the rich beg inside and the poor outside. I should stop at that since 11 is considered an *auspicious* number in my country!

"We are so liberal or secular that our rulers come from Italy and voters from Bangladesh", said Kiran Bedi some years ago. She happens to be country's first woman IPS officer who conducted herself with élan throughout her chequered career and was few years ago appointed Lt. Governor of

Pondicherry whose name French has been changed to Tamil, Puducherry. We Indians have *many* traits in our character, all of those may not be practiced together in many countries that have progressed. But maybe they are derided upon instead. To name just the *important* ones. We are: "*basically dishonest; essentially law-breakers; hardly nationalistic or patriotic except in times of war or national calamity of a grave dimension or cricket/hockey match against our 'arch enemy' Pakistan; not responsible nor accountable at all; insensitive to the needs of others, more so towards those of females and the elderly; more involved/wedded to our region, religion, community, caste or even sub-caste rather than to our motherland; culturally neither become Westernized nor remain Indian, amply elaborated by 'Trishanku' (a Hindu term for unstable, hanging in the air); and so on'.*" I am inclined to go by Naim Naqmi's words, "*Indians do often behave one moment like poles apart and the next like real brothers. We are moody, mercurial, often prejudiced but usually benign, tolerant and secular.*" Having been benign and tolerant has been our greatest drawbacks for which we have/are presently continuing to be paying heavily as we have been doing all along and in future will continue to do so since we are averse to change. In short, we have lost the ethical, moral and other important values enshrined in our civilization that were still intact not long ago i.e. prior to the British onslaught on our culture and economy.

In 1830, Lord Macaulay travelled far and wide on the subcontinent. He observed tremendous *bonhomie* among its inhabitants. During his address to the British parliament on 1st February 1831, he passionately pleaded to place Sanskrit – the language of our civilization, culture and heritage – in oblivion by changing the educational system from Sanskrit as the medium of instruction to English. Hence the Raj introduced educational system named after him. That started the decline which the British faithfully monitored and accelerated to its infamous 'Divide and Rule' policy. What was most shameful was to follow as its parting shot: 'Transfer of Power' its stooges who continued the British Anti-Hindu and pro-Muslim tirade that led to the present dismal situation. Human life has totally lost its value. Our moral fabric has thinned beyond recognition. Today, if you have the power or the tacit support of anti-national pseudo-secular pseudo-intellectuals sponsored by similar politicians belonging to the Congress (I) and her crony Left and Left-of-Center parties, you feel you can do anything you wish to. *Might is right in its meaning and spirit.* That's the Rule that counts. There is no empathy, sympathy, kindness or respect for our age-old traditions and values. This hypothesis was amply proven by genocide of thousands of innocent Sikhs ordered by top Congress leaders of the capital i.e. HKL Bhagat, Jagdish Tytler and Sajjan Kumar presumably at the behest of Indira's son Rajiv who was hastily sworn in as the PM by prime Chamcha of the deceased namely Gyani Zail Singh who happened to be the President of India. Strangely the Delhi Police remained an onlooker or even helper in the ghastly act. No action has been taken against the culprits even after 34 years. *This is a classic example of non-accountability of the politicians and executive*!

This unsavory blot in the history of independent Hindustan was recapitulated in an article, *"1984 is a symptom of a bigger disease"*, that appeared in the e=paper, *Live Mint* on 27th August 2018. *"The lack of political and institutional accountability for the anti-Sikh riots is the norm.* Congress chief Rahul's defense of his party's role in the 1984 anti-Sikh riots in his London School of Economics talk the other day is brazen and ahistorical. His party's defense of him goes further yet, descending into bathos. Party luminaries such as P Chidambaram, the *charge-sheeted and on bail* former UPA minister and close aide of Congress (I) owner Sonia, and Punjab CM Capt. Amarinder Singh do him no favor by suggesting that his youth (he was 14 years old)-at the time of the riots absolves him of responsibility for what he says today. Such arguments diminish him further. They should not come as a surprise, however. The *Indian state has a long and troubling history of failing to fix political and institutional accountability for riots and mass killings.*

Claims that the Congress (I) party had nothing to do with the frenzy of violence targeting Sikhs after Indira's assassination are hokum. *Ten* commissions have been formed in the decades since then. *Majority of them have found the state machinery and police to have either been complicit or having played an enabling role for the rioters*. Many of the commissions, most notably the Nanavati Commission, have pointed to the likely involvement of local Congress leaders and workers, incl. late HKL Bhagat, Jagdish Tytler and Sajjan Kumar. Yet, little action has been taken.

It is a familiar story. In the wake of the 1969 Gujarat riots, the Justice Jaganmohan Reddy Commission of Inquiry found police complicity. No action was taken by the state's Congress government led by Hitendra Desai. In Mumbai's Worli riots in 1974, Shiv Sena supporters took on the Dalit Panthers with, by all accounts, police backing. Nothing much came of the judicial inquiry led by SB Bhasme. The Justice Saxena Commission report on the 1980 Moradabad riots in Uttar Pradesh was quietly brushed under the carpet.

The Tiwari Commission report on 1983 Nellie massacre in Assam under Congress (I) was never made public to begin with. The work done by the commission of inquiry set up after the 1989 Bhagalpur violence in Bihar came to little despite its indictment of the police under superintendent of police KS Dwivedi. Justice BN Srikrishna Commission report on riots that swept Mumbai from December 1992 to January 1993 indicted the Shiv Sena and several policemen but was roundly ignored by state government. As for the 2002 Gujarat riots following the Godhra train burning alive of 59 Hindu Kar Sewaks incl. women and children, despite former BJP minister Maya Kodnani's conviction in 2012, the response has been lacking on multiple fronts—from credibility and timeliness of inquiries to convictions. There are *several common elements to these and the hundreds of other riots* that have taken place over the decades. *First*, political rhetoric attempts to paint the violence as a spontaneous upsurge of common sentiment and resentment. *The corollary, of course, is that politicians can't be held responsible for failing to stop the violence, or for inciting it*, depending on where they stand. This is specious. Time and again, effective deployment of Central forces has stopped the violence when the police have failed to do so. Journalist Shekhar Gupta's eyewitness account testifies to this in 1984 Sikh genocide, for instance (goo.gl/tts4Ld). This points to the role of the police on the ground and the political establishment directing it—either in enabling the violence, or, by failing to respond adequately, allowing it.

Second, political incentives in India work against the logic of the social contract. Maintaining law and order doesn't always provide the greatest electoral rewards. In their 2016 paper, *'Do Parties Matter for Ethnic Violence? Evidence from India'*, Gareth Nellis, Michael Weaver and Steven C Rosenzweig put this in empirical context. Based on Election Commission of India data and the 1950-1995 dataset on Hindu-Muslim violence in India prepared by Ashutosh Varshney and Steven Wilkinson, they look at the effect of local Congress incumbency on the probability of riots breaking out. The results are flattering for the Congress—but their dampening effect is roughly proportional to the size of the Muslim population. In other words, how much of an effort the Congress—or, undoubtedly, any other party—makes to maintain law and order is tied directly to polarized voter behavior, not constitutional norms. This should not come as a surprise to even a casual observer of Indian politics.

Third, India is a weak state with compromised institutions. This is apparent at every stage of a riot and its aftermath. It starts with the police who lack institutional support and structures for functioning effectively—or resisting political pressure to do otherwise. The lack of sanction for any number of policemen indicted by the various commissions, meanwhile, establishes the low cost of doing business with the political establishment. It continues with the commissions themselves: often, their reports gestate for so long that they lose relevance and the probability of meaningful evidence fades. CBI further muddies the waters. Its susceptibility to political pressure means that when it stepped in, its findings lacked credibility. This weakness on the part of a state ties into electoral incentives. As political scientist Milan Vaishnav argued, in the absence of a strong state, the criminality of a politician—in other words, the kind of local strongman who is often in the thick of riots—becomes a qualifying factor rather than a disqualifier. Pushing back against the rot in the system will require immense political wherewithal and courage. Based on the reactions and counter-reactions to Rahul's statements, these are in short supply."

The following day, *Rediff.com News* published, "***Is Rahul illiterate***? 'Can he remain ignorant by saying he was 13 years old? That means Rahul must not talk on any subject in this country that precedes his adulthood! He should remain unaware of history and knowledge of anything that has happened.' Congress President dug into a hole by asserting in London that the Congress party was not involved in the October 31-November 4, 1984 countrywide anti-Sikh genocide in the wake of then PM Indira's assassination by her own Sikh bodyguards. At 24th August meeting with British MPs in London, Rahul described the violence as a 'very painful tragedy' but 'insisted' that the Congress was not 'involved'. [Like the first dictator of INC namely a FAKE Mahatma, Rahul – a FAKE Gandhi is a perpetual liar concocting false stories. Is that under the diktat of Cambridge Analytica, the British company already charge-sheeted in own country, engaged by his mother Sania Antonia. Like the blind Dhritrashtra in Mahabharata, she appears to be blinded by love for her good-for-nothing son]. Senior Sonia-Bhakt P Chidambaram tried to stem the damage from Rahul's statement by saying, 'We are not saying the Congress is absolved. The Congress was in office in 1984, nobody is denying that. A very terrible thing happened for which ex-PM Manmohan has apologized in Parliament. Now you can't hold Rahul responsible for that, he was 13 or 14 years of age. SAD described Rahul's statement as 'rubbing salt into the wounds' of the Sikh community while its ally, the BJP, said the Congress president was trying to wash his party's hands off its alleged culpability in the riots. Even as a controversy swirls over Rahul's statement, Hartosh Singh Bal, political editor, *Caravan* magazine, spoke to *Rediff.com's* Syed Firdaus Ashraf about the 1984 riots on which he has written extensively including an essay in the book '*1984: In Memory and Imagination -- Personal Essays and Stories on the 1984 Anti-Sikh Riots*'.

"For a generation which has little idea about the 1984 riots, can you tell us how far the Congress party was involved in it in which 2,733 Sikhs were killed? Let me correct the terminology. *The 1984 riots were not a riot as two communities were not clashing, but it was a massacre of Sikhs*. They were being pulled out and killed. There was no resistance from their side and there was no counter-violence. The actual numbers were 3,000 Sikhs died in Delhi alone. Across the country there were 7,000 deaths. This figure is from the sources which has been verified and tallied. The massacre was not in Delhi alone, but spread across other states like UP, MP, Haryana and Bihar. It was widespread. I have written in *Caravan* about it. Persons like HS Phoolka and Manoj Mitra have written about it and they have documented this. In each pocket of the city prominent Congress leaders led mobs. These leaders include Sajjan Kumar, Jagdish Tytler and Kamal Nath. My own report, and I have testimony from a senior bureaucrat who said that coordination of this violence was being done by Arun Nehru, PM Rajiv's cousin and right-hand man. During this period, he was reporting to Rajiv on a regular basis minute to minute and there is no way Rajiv could be unaware of this organized implementation of violence by his senior party member.

What do you make of Rahul's statement that Congressmen were not involved in the massacre, or Chidambaram's point that he was just 13 years old at that time? Rahul was not born in 1947, so is he unaware of what happened in 1947? Does every politician only rely on eyewitness testimony? He can't read, or is he illiterate? Has he not read or heard anything that continuously figures in contemporary politics, that continuous questions are asked to him all the time? Can he remain ignorant of that by saying he was 13 years old and in school? That means basically Rahul must not talk on any subject in this country that precedes his adulthood. He should remain unaware of history and knowledge of anything that has happened. Rahul must not talk about the Babri Masjid too. He must not talk about the Gujarat riots. How old was he then? He was too old to remember what happened in Gujarat, but too young to remember what happened in 1984.

The then PM Rajiv Khan did make a statement, 'Bada ped girta hai toh dharti kampati hai (when a big tree falls the earth shakes) Rajiv in a public speech justified the 1984 violence by saying when a big tree falls the earth shakes, as if the assassination of Indira was a justification for the violence that followed. Subsequently, when the Congress party went to the elections it was on a communal platform. In some ways it was a model for the 2014 election fought by Modi. What Modi did with the Muslim community in terms of communal bigotry, Rajiv Gandhi did with the Sikh community.

No Congressman has been convicted yet for the violence... Obviously, they won't be convicted. They (Congress governments) set up the inquiry commissions. They handpicked the people who led those inquiry commissions. They ensured no procedure was followed. They allowed no police investigation. Ranganath Mishra, head of the first inquiry commission, was later rewarded by the Congress party with a Rajya Sabha seat, that too a Congress seat. No norms of commission were followed. Innumerable commissions were set up and the Congress ensured that none of them functioned, the legal processes did not happen. The legal processes were directed, controlled and manipulated by the Congress, so obviously there would be no results.

Nine commissions of inquiry were set up to probe the massacre of 1984: Commissions of inquiry here are meant to suppress the truth rather than reveal it. They serve political ends to justify. It is like what has happened with the SIT Report on Modi. You read the report, it is meant to bury Modi and not to examine his culpability. This is what the nine commissions of inquiry (probing the 1984 riots) were about. Every trick Modi has played, the Congress has played before. That is where Modi has learnt his tricks on how to subvert and manipulate the truth.

You have written that Girilal Jain, the then editor-in-chief of 'The Times of India', rationalized the violence, saying the Hindu cup of patience had come full to the brim. Is that why Sikhs were being targeted? When communal bigotry is given official sanction, as was the case with the Congress, you have enough endorsers where people come out of their little holes in the ground and express their bigotry in public. This is what Girilal Jain did. This is what pro-Modi editors are doing today and so are TV anchors. The same hatred, the vitriol that was coming out against the

Sikhs, the same kind of hatred is coming out from the journalists (now) who have no self-respect but cater to the whims and fancies of the government.

As mourners filed past Indira's body on TV, slogans like 'Khoon ka badla khoon se' were heard. Was that telecast permitted or done intentionally? It was the most absurd thing to do. I can find no other equivalent of it in the use of public media or an act of violence to provoke reactions. The only comparable example would be again to take the bodies of those killed in Godhra and march them around in Ahmedabad happened 18 years later. As I write, every action has been preceded by the same kind of idiocy by the Congress – an antinational party right from its birth on 28 December 1885! *Deliberate manipulation of public opinion is not idiocy? It was deliberate.*

Dummy PM Manmohan did apologize in 2005. He spoke 21 years after the crime. Government must regret for any violence under its watch. But the Congress party NEVER admitted culpability or apologized for its own involvement in the violence? Give me a single instance. People keep saying Sonia did, but she didn't. *Not for a moment did Sonia apologize for the 1984 massacre of Sikhs. She never has, the Congress party never has.*

Why are the FAKE Gandhis not apologizing for the violence when (their Prime CHAMCHA Manmohan already has? Manmohan did it on behalf of the government and not the party. The FAKE Gandhis cannot do so because the culpability is personal." [Syed Firdaus Ashraf/Rediff.com]

Undoubtedly, *Bhagwadgita* is the greatest treatise on philosophy of human life *enunciated in just 45 minutes* by Lord Krishna on the battlefront at Kurukshetra and recorded by Maharishi Veda Vyasa. Lord Krishna spoke out on this philosophy just before the commencement of the epic Mahabharata – a War between the real cousins, Kauravas and Pandavas, approximately seven millennia ago and *recorded* by *Maharishi* Veda Vyasa. It has 18 *Adhyayaas* (chapters). Eighteen lessons we can learn from it are as follows:

Chapter 1: *Wrong thinking* is the only problem in life.
Chapter 2: *Right knowledge* is the ultimate solution to all our problems.
Chapter 3: *Selflessness* is the only way to progress and prosperity.
Chapter 4: Every act can be an *act of prayer*.
Chapter 5: *Renounce the ego* of individuality and rejoice in the Bliss of Infinity.
Chapter 6: Connect to the *Higher Consciousness* Daily.
Chapter 7: *Live what you learn*.
Chapter 8: *Never give up* on yourself.

Chapter 9: *Value your blessings.*
Chapter 10: *See divinity* all around.
Chapter 11: *Have enough strength to see the Truth* as it is.
Chapter 12: Absorb your *mind in the Higher.*
Chapter 13: *Detach from Maya (Worldly pleasures and allurements)* and *Attach to the Divine.*
Chapter 14: *Live a lifestyle that matches your vision.*
Chapter 15: *Give priority to Divinity.*
Chapter 16: *Being good* is a reward in it.
Chapter 17: *Choosing the right over the pleasant is a sign of power*; and
Chapter 18: *Let Go ... Let's move to Union with God.*

We may leave that aside for the present and try to know more about the land and its people. Shocking scientific *inventions by ancient Hindu saints have been made obscure to any reader because the past millennium existed to annihilate Hinduism and the Hindus, and anything they had or did.* During the growth of our ancient civilizations, ancient technology was the result of incredible advances in engineering. These advances in technology stimulated societies to adopt new ways of living and governance. However, many ancient inventions were forgotten, lost to the pages of history, only to be re-invented by different names and terminology millennia later.

Here are the best examples: The land of Bharat is known to be the abode of saints and gods. It is filled with various types of unexplainable things. During the ancient times, various saints after doing years of hard meditation, their work and with their patience found the secrets hidden in the Vedas. These inventions later came to be known as modern science. Some of the saints came out with such amazing inventions that shocked the kings of those times as well. That is universal. *John Dalton (1766 – 1844),* an English chemist and physicist, is the man credited today with the development of atomic theory. However, a theory of atoms was actually formulated 2,500 years before Dalton by an Indian sage and philosopher, Acharya Kanad. He was born in 600 BCE in Prabhas Kshetra (near Dwaraka) in Gujarat, India. His real name was Kashyap. It was he who originated the idea that 'anu' (atom) was an indestructible particle of matter. An interesting story states that this theory occurred to him while he was walking with food in his hand. As he nibbled at the food, throwing away the small particles, it occurred to him that he could not divide the food into further parts and thus the idea of a matter which cannot be divided further came into existence. He called that indivisible matter anu, i.e. molecule, which was misinterpreted as atom. He also stated that anu can have two states: Absolute rest and a State of motion.

Newton's Law, 1200 Years before Newton: "Objects fall on the earth due to a force of attraction by the earth. Therefore, the earth, planets, constellations, moon and sun are held in orbit due to this attraction." The meaning of these lines is parallel to that of Newton's Law of Gravity. But these lines are not the first to have been said by the British physcist. They are told by an Indian – in 'Surya Siddhanta', circa 400-500 AD, the ancient Hindu astronomer Bhaskaracharya states that. Approximately 1200 years later (1687 AD), Sir Isaac Newton rediscovered this phenomenon and named it the 'Law of Gravity'. *Cambridge University accepted that Newton stole it from Vedas.*

Acharya Charaka has been crowned as the Father of Indian Medicine. His renowned work, the Charaka Samhita, is considered as an encyclopedia of Ayurveda. His principles, diagnoses, and cures retain their potency and truth even after a couple of millenniums. When the science of anatomy was confused with different theories in Europe, Acharya Charaka revealed through his innate genius and inquiries the facts on human anatomy, embryology, pharmacology, blood circulation and diseases like diabetes, tuberculosis, heart disease, etc. In the Charaka Samhita, he has described the medicinal qualities and functions of 100,000 herbal plants. He has emphasized the influence of diet and activity on mind and body. He has proved that the correlation of spirituality and physical health contributed greatly to diagnostic and curative sciences. He has also prescribed and ethical charter for medical practitioners two centuries prior to the Hippocrates Oath. Through his genius and intuition, Acharya Charaka forever remains etched in the annals of medical history as one of the greatest and noblest of rishi-scientists.

Sage Bharadwaj: In 1875, the Vymaanika-Shaastra, a 4th century BCE text written by *Maharshi* Bhardwaj, was discovered in a temple in India. The book dealt with the operation of ancient *vimanas* (aircrafts) and included information on steering, precautions for long flights, protection of the airships from storms and lightning, and how to switch the drive to solar energy, or some other "free energy" source. *Vimanas* were said to take off vertically or dirigible. Bharadwaj the Wise refers to no less than 70 authorities and 10 experts of air travel in antiquity.

Rishi Kanva: He described the science of wind in Rigveda sections 8/41/6 in *Jagati meter* of God wind. Sage Kashyapa described the features and properties of this in Rigveda 9/64/26 in the hymns of God *Pavamana Soma* in Gayatri. Great Rishi Kanva, waa a descendent of Sage Angirasa. He looked after Shakuntala when she was abandoned by her mother and father (*Rishi* Vishwamitra). He also brought up her son Bharat, after whom my country is named.

Sage Kapil Muni, Author of the '*Sankhya Darshan*'. Kapil muni was born equipped with rare intellect, dispassion and spiritual powers. He authored *Sankhya Darshan* that defined the term *Dhyaan* or Meditation as 'the state of mind when remains without any subjectivity/objectivity i.e. without any thought (when the mind is away from worldly objects)'. He teaches that there is an unbroken continuity from the lowest inorganic to the highest organic forms. The source of world according to him is *Prakriti* (fundamental nature).

How the Universe was created? There are twenty-five principles responsible for the manifestation of the Creation (*Samasara*), out of which *Purusha* and *Prakriti* are eternal and independent of each other. Kapil did not deny the reality of personal God or *Maheshwara*. Yet his assertion was that, *no arguments can irrefutably establish God's reality*. Therefore, in his model of creation the *Purusha* (Spirit) and *Prakriti* (Matter) are held solely responsible for creation, without acknowledging an Almighty and intelligent Creator, the God.

Patanjali, The father of Yoga: The Science of Yoga is one of several unique contributions of India to the world. It seeks to discover and realize the ultimate Reality through yogic practices. Acharya Patanjali, prescribed the control of *prana* (life breath) as the means to control the body, mind and soul. This subsequently rewards one with good health and inner happiness. His 84 yogic postures effectively enhance the efficiency of the respiratory, circulatory, nervous, digestive and endocrine systems and many other organs of the body. Thanks to the efforts of our PM Modi, the United Nations finally accepted to celebrate the World Yoga Day on 26th June.

Aryabhata was a master Astronomer and Mathematician, born in 476 CE in Kusumpur (Bihar). In 499 CE, he wrote a text on astronomy and an unparalleled treatise on mathematics called "Aryabhatiyam" He formulated the process of calculating the motion of planets and the time of eclipses. Aryabhata was the first to proclaim that the earth is round, it rotates on its axis, orbits the sun and is suspended in space - 1,000 years before Copernicus published his heliocentric theory. Recently, Aryabhata's bust has been installed at UNESCO headquarters in Paris.

Sushruta, Born to sage Vishwamitra, is the father of surgery. Around 2600 years ago, he and health scientists of his time conducted complicated surgeries like Cesareans, cataract, artificial limbs, Rhinoplasty (restoration of a damaged nose), 12 types of fractures, 6 types of dislocations, urinary stones and even plastic surgery and brain surgery. Usage of anesthesia was well known in ancient India. Sushruta is the author of the book "*Sushruta Samhita*", in which he describes over 300 surgical procedures and 125 surgical instruments.

Bhaskaracharya calculated the time taken by the earth to orbit the sun in 5th century AD, hundreds of years before the astronomer Smart; Time taken by earth to orbit the sun: 365.258756484 days. Born in the obscure village of Vijjadit (now Jalgaon) in Maharastra, Bhaskaracharya's mathematical works called "*Lilavati*" and "*Bijaganita*" are considered to be unparalleled. In his treatise '*Siddhant Shiromani*', he writes on planetary positions, eclipses, cosmography, mathematical techniques and astronomical equipment. In the '*Surya Siddhant*' he makes a note on the force of *Surya* or the Sun.

Varahamihir's book '*Panch Siddhant*' noted that the moon and planets are lustrous not because of their own light but due to sunlight. In the "*Bruhad Samhita*" and "*Bruhad Jatak*", he revealed his discoveries in domains of geography, constellation, science, botany and animal science. In his treatise on botanical science, he presents cures for various diseases afflicting plants and trees.

The galaxy is oval, Earth is spherical: Yajur Vedic verse: '*Brahmaanda vyapta deha bhasitha himaruja...*' describing Lord Shiva as the one who is spread out in *Brahmaanda* (Universe). *Anda* means an egg depicting the shape of the galaxy. It was the middle east Europians and Greeks who wrongly believed that earth was flat. But Indians, since long have always known that it was spherical. In many scriptures, the word *Bhoogola* is used. *Bhoo* means Earth, *Gola* is round.

Existence of Atomic and Sub-atomic particles: The world accounts discovery of atoms and sub atomic particles to Western scientists who coined these words and theories only in the early 17th century. An excerpt from *Lalita Sahasranama*, told by Hayagreeva to Agasthya *muni*, dating back to the distant ages in the past, describes the Goddess as the super consciousness/*Brahman* that pervades even the sub-atomic particles within matter. *"Paranjyotih parandhamah paramanuh paratpara."* The word *"anuvu"* means atom. *Paramanu* (*Param* meaning smallest) is sub-atomic particle, finer than the finest of atom, meaning electrons and the others.

Ancient times and nuclear weapons: Radiation still so intense, the area is highly dangerous! A heavy layer of radioactive ash in Rajasthan, India, covers a three-square mile area, ten miles west of Jodhpur. For some time it has been established that there is a very high rate of birth defects and cancer in the area under construction. Scientists have unearthed an ancient city where evidence shows an atomic blast dating back thousands of years, from 8,000 to 12,000 years, destroying everything most of the buildings and probably a half-million people.

The *Mahabharata* clearly describes a catastrophic blast that rocked the continent. "A single projectile charged with all the power in the Universe... An incandescent column of smoke and flame as bright as 10,000 suns, rose in all its splendor...it was an unknown weapon, an iron thunderbolt, a gigantic messenger of death which reduced to ashes an entire race." Historian Kisari Mohan Ganguli says that Indian sacred writings are full of such descriptions.

Ancient ultrasound machines? Using a variety of complicated instruments, gynecologists have gradually come to know how the embryo grows during the period of pregnancy. But the Shrimad Bhagavatam, 3rd canto, 30th chapter, gives a vivid description of the growth of the embryo in the mother's womb. If we compare the information given therein with the information given in a standard textbook such as the embryology section of Gray's Anatomy, there are striking similarities in the information obtained from the two sources.

Ancient science knows more than modern science? The Vedas claim that there are living entities everywhere - even in fire. Modern science, however, presumed that no life could exist in fire. This presumption is in fact the basis for the process of sterilization. But recent advancements in the field of medicine have shown that microbes called 'fire bacteria' survive even in fire.

The incredible powers of the ancient Siddhars! Siddhars are a type of saint in India who are said to have had many powers and achieved a 'god-like' state through specific secret practices that were known only to them. These powers spanned from controlling time and space, to transforming the body, manipulating matter at the molecular level and achieving immortality. The Siddhars were followers of the God Shiva and according to different texts there were 18 of them. Their teachings and findings were written in the form of poems in the Tamil language.

Who were Siddhars? There is a debate as to who was the first Siddhar. Some legends talk about Sri Pathanjali, who was considered to be an incarnation of Adiseshan, the celestial five-headed snake associated with God Vishnu. But the prevailing tradition refers to Agasthya (or Agasthyar) as the first Siddhar, one of the seven sages (or Saptarshis) as mentioned in the Vedic texts, and he was the son of the god Brahma of the Hindu creation story.

Siddhars or scientists? Agathiyar is considered to be the author of a lot of the first Siddhar literature and he was supposed to have lived in the 7th century BC. About 96 books are attributed to him and that includes writings in alchemy, medicine and spirituality. Apart from the legends that exist, the beginnings of the Siddhars' are lost in time.

Ashta Siddhis of Siddhars: The powers that the Siddhars possessed were separated in categories. The main category included 8 powers called ashta siddhis: To become tiny as the atom within the atom (Anima); To become big in unshakeable proportions (Mahima); To become as light as vapour in levitation (Laghima); To become as heavy as the mountain (Garima); To enter into other bodies in transmigration (Prapti); To be in all things, omni-pervasive (Prakamya); To be lord of all creation in omnipotence (Isatvam); To be everywhere in omnipresence (Vasitvam).

Ten Siddhis of Siddhars: There are ten secondary siddhis as described in Bhagavata Purana that include the following: Being undisturbed by hunger, thirst, and other bodily appetites; Hearing things far away; Seeing things far away; Moving the body wherever thought goes (teleportation/astral projection); Assuming any form desired; Entering the bodies of others; Dying when one desires; Witnessing and participating in the past times of the gods; Perfect accomplishment of one's determination; Orders or commands being unimpeded.

Ancient science and Siddhars: A famous *Siddhar* was Tirumular, who was a Tamil mystic and writer of 6th century AD and was also one of the 18 Siddhars according to the *Tamil Siddha* tradition. His main work is named "*Tirumantiram*", a 3,000 verse text, which is the foundation of the Southern Shaiva Siddharta School of philosophy. Another Siddhar, Bhogar (Bhoganathar), who lived between the 3rd and 5th century AD is said to have discovered the elixir of immortality – one his main works is the Pharmacognosy.

The mystery remains...! Due to the closely-guarded nature of the Siddhar records, the original knowledge of this enigmatic group of saints has remained shrouded in secrecy. The question remains whether their powers were real and, if so, how they managed to attain them. Manipulating space, time and matter would require knowledge far.

Politics must have been as old a profession as prostitution and hence there are lot many similarities between the two. *Soliciting* is the first common factor in both like selling your body. Since my childhood, I have been conditioned to watch the goings on in our politics since my *Nanaji* (maternal grandfather) happened to be a freedom fighter and a pragmatic individual. Immediate post-independence days were different. There was a talk of the freedom struggle all around. The sentiment of nationalism was very high. Still, there was a sane talk on the quality of INC leadership which was not seen in good light. There were rumblings on the ugly deeds of the top leadership provided by the triumvirate: Gandhi, Patel and Nehru. Famous quotation, *'Politics is the last refuge of scoundrels'*, had entered the discussion table. This has been so beautifully endorsed in my country. The quality of politics has gone down a lot since then but that of the politicians plummeted to abysmal lows. The only motive is: *'To get votes'* by fooling the gullible, mostly uninterested, insensitive Hindustanis not worried at all about their motherland. To a question, *'Has the level of Indian politics gone down significantly ever since Sonia Gandhi took charge of the Congress?'*, Maheswara Sastry M answered, *'Same law for everybody'*, sounded interesting. "While PM Modi is foolish in working for all sections of the society, Sonia of Congress wants to adopt election winning strategy by taking care of certain segments. I think Congress is smart to milk certain vote bank. Sonia and Rahul know what is known as survival tactic as it matters least whether you win with votes from all segments of the society or just from two or three groups. After all, vote is a vote whether you obtain by developing the society or by any means. *Campaigns of disinformation on Indian society losing secular nature, pseudo-intellectuals and 'sickularists', award wapsi, JNU row, Dadri lynching, Osmania university episode and unfounded campaign against Hindutva and RSS are the major part of the election strategy.* Congress disappearing fast across India, retained Karnataka. The following data gives each reader complete understanding of what Congress is up to. Any good citizen is for the growth of all segments of the society including SCs, STs and OBCs. However, if the process eliminates merit, the disparities remain which is contrary to the aim of developing a society for homogeneity. Kindly read each of the following to understand the sinister design of Congress and its leaders.

In 2014: Karnataka CM Siddaramaiah came out with an 'innovative' policy to empower *Dalits* in the state of reservation for the community in liquor (excise) license. The state government secretly issued a notification enabling scheduled caste and scheduled tribe members to easily obtain licenses to open and operate a bar.

Sixteen months ago: Congress party has always tried to portray itself as "SECULAR" in front of the people of the nation and has always termed itself as a party which thinks for all irrespective of caste and religion. But a recent Incident has once again unmasked the communal face of this 131-year old political party. *Financial Assistance is being provided for Muslims and Christians to study in abroad using public funds by Karnataka Congress CM Siddaramaiah.*

About 12 months ago: Siddaramaiah-led Congress government in Karnataka took quota politics to a different level. The state announced a 20% reservation for Scheduled Castes (SCs) and 5% for Scheduled Tribes (STs) in the award of contracts to maintain shoe stands in 34,543 temples which fall under the government's purview.

Today: In a new populist move, Karnataka government decided to introduce reservation in public tender works. A total of 24.10% of the public works under INR5 million would be reserved for SC/STs. Karnataka Law, Parliamentary Affairs and Higher Education Minister TB Jayachandra said a suitable amendment to the Karnataka Transparency in Public Procurement Act, 1999 would be brought in to provide reservation to the SC/STs in tenders in that category. He said that 17.15% of the tenders would be reserved for the SCs and 6.95% for the STs – based on the population of the two communities. Jayachandra said the government would come out with a list of the departments that would provide reservation for the SC/STs in the tendering process. According to a report published in the *Deccan Herald*, these works would be directly allotted to the SC/STs and they would not have to go through the tendering process. The only clause is that the work should not exceed INR5 million. In a new populist move, Karnataka government has decided to introduce reservation in public tender works. A total of 24.10% of the public works under INR5 million would be reserved for the SC/STs." *Such a decision appears arbitrary and discriminatory in view of the fact that our Constitution stipulates equality to all its citizens.*

The so called 'grand old party' is on a ventilator for quite some time now. Congress (I) has no Indian who can lead the party. Hence, they depend upon Italian-born sparsely educated white lady who is unfamiliar with Indian civilization, culture and history. Even her trusted *chamchas* do not feed her the reality about the public perception on/about the jaded party. *'They are misleading Sonia and Rahul'*, was the title of article in *Rediff. com News* on 26th May 2016. "'If the leadership gets wrong information, what results you can expect?' Rashmi Sehgal reports for *Rediff.com* Should Congress stalwarts Ghulam Nabi Azad, Digvijay Singh, Ambika Soni, Ahmed Patel and a host of others be forced to take a sabbatical? This is the opinion of former Union minister Kishore Chandra Deo who has demanded the time has come for "15 to 20 Congress leaders to be sent on a forced holiday." Deo did not spell out the names, but it was obvious his ire was directed at leaders who have been at the helm of affairs and who he believes been consistently giving wrong advice to Congress President Sonia Gandhi and Vice-President Rahul Gandhi, thereby bringing the party to this pass. "These leaders play a game of musical chairs in senior positions at the AICC (All India Congress Committee) or as PCC (Pradesh Congress Committee) and have gone on to become Union ministers when the party had catapulted to power," says Deo, a five-time MP. "They are misleading both Sonia and Rahul. If the leadership gets wrong information, what results you can expect?" asked Deo.

For the *first* time, a leader from the south demanded to break the stranglehold of the Congress old guard to make way for a team of talented and credible youngsters who can make their way up within the party echelons. "Indira gave Devaraj Urns and J Vengal Rao the opportunity to become chief ministers of Karnataka and Andhra Pradesh respectively even though they were not known leaders," says Deo. "They proved their mettle and continue to be remembered in their states till today." "There is no dearth of talent in the Congress," emphasizes Deo. He scoffs at the idea of 'major surgery' suggested by Digvijay Singh, insisting that all "defeated chief ministers should have been sent back to their states to revive the party at the grassroots level. The party has already done too much introspection and now needs to go in for action."

His views are seconded by Dr. M Shashidhar Reddy, former chairman of the National Disaster Management Authority and former Andhra Pradesh CM Marri Chenna Reddy's son who insists the time has come for a major party reshuffle. "The existing general secretaries need to be dropped. They have been consistently providing wrong inputs and even the best computer will go wrong if it receives wrong data," said Dr. Reddy. Party veteran Kamal Nath also called for a reorganization of the party, demanding a new AICC, a new team of general secretaries and a fresh team of state leaders to revive the party. "Congress got more (assembly) seats if we combine all states. In recent elections, we got 140 seats while the BJP got jut 64," said Kamal Nath,

Former Information and Broadcasting minister Manish Tewari endorses this view. "We lost Assam because of anti-incumbency; the Kerala elections follow a cyclical pattern. In Tamil Nadu, the vote percentage of the alliance (DMK-Congress) did not fructify, but in West Bengal we have emerged as the principal opposition. The results followed expected lines though they were a disappointment," explains Tewari. The clamor for greater accountability by Congress leaders is matched with the demand to come up with a long-term strategic vision document on both how to revive the party at both the central and state levels and then to implement it. "We need to think through very carefully what is our trajectory for the next 36 months and who will carry this narrative through before discussing personalities," says Tewari. "The key is what will this narrative be. Will the narrative be an extension of the UPA (United Progressive Alliance) philosophy or will we come up with an alternative narrative?" asks Tewari. "Ultimately, if there is dysfunctionality at the party hierarchy, it needs to be corrected."

Congress spokesperson Tom Vadakkan admits a major obstacle in the party functioning has been infighting between different groups within each state. He cites the example of how Kerala state Congress President VM Sudheeran had pushed for prohibition without consulting other senior leaders. "CM's views were the diametrically opposite of the state president. No doubt, drinking must be controlled and is bad for health," says Vadakkan, adding, "Sadly, Kerala has more bars than schools. In one street, there will be six bars and one school, but the CM could have tackled the situation in a different manner. The liquor lobby in Kerala was the main factor behind our defeat in the state. The problem with the party is that it follows an extremely democratic style of functioning. If a request comes from the state, it is considered and followed through even when the Congress president is not too enthusiastic about it."

With the threat of a Congress-mukt India, party realizes that the moment of reckoning has arrived. Today the NDA rules 20 states and the Congress only four. If Congress fails to pull up its socks, Deo warns the nation will witness the further mushrooming of regional parties. He cites the example of AAP capturing power in Delhi and believes such a phenomenon may be witnessed in another 15 to 20 states with no established regional parties. Absence of strong central leadership can prove detrimental. Congress leaders believe another key area lies in winning the battle of perception where BJP is way ahead of the Congress. A failed economy, a poor foreign policy and a complete fiasco in handling the drought situation that has hit half the country has not stopped the BJP from tom-toming its victories, Congress leaders say, reflecting how successful the ruling party is in the art of media management. [Rashme Sehgal]

On 6th June 2016, *'Like Queen Elizabeth, Sonia Gandhi should continue'*, was the title of an article appearing on *Rediff.com News*. "'Bringing Rahul in now would be like throwing petrol on the flames consuming the Congress,' says Aakar Patel. Once again, there are reports on Rahul Gandhi taking over the Congress leadership. He is 48 and has been in active politics for over a decade. As per the wishes of his supporters in the party, he became President in December 2017. His mother made way for him by abdicating the 'throne'. There are *two* things that were thought to be the reason for seeking the change. *First*, that it is inevitable that at some point the older must make way for the younger. So, it made sense for her heir to be anointed. The *second*, less transparent reason, is that she has been keeping indifferent health. It has been reported in the past that Sonia has required some medical treatment at the Memorial Sloan Kettering Hospital New York.

<u>*Why then was the rush to elevate Rahul*</u>? One could be internal pressure. Congressmen who are alarmed at the rapid decay of the party want to see some change in direction. Unless something drastic and dramatic is not done, the party will die very soon. The Congress has fallen from 205 Lok Sabha seats to 44. The 150 Congressmen who are not in the Lok Sabha each spent a few crores (ten million=one crore) of rupees in a losing election. Many have invested decades of their life in the party. They have a personal stake in it and its collapse will mean that their investment and their future is lost. It could be that some or many of them are anxious and are seeking clarity about the party's leadership. Losing power at the Centre and in almost all major states means that the party is struggling to raise money. That is another reason for seeking urgent change.

The question is whether such a change will benefit the Congress. Sonia's record in leading the party has been quite good. She took over the party at a time like the present times. The Congress had been in power twice under a non-Gandhi PM and had been involved in many scams/scandals. Its earlier PM Narasimha Rao was accused in a case and had to appear in court. The BJP's rise to power happened in the same period and its charismatic and respected leader Vajpayee became prime minister, winning a plurality (though not a majority) in three elections. It was in this period, when the BJP was the dominant party and the Congress was losing, that Sonia took charge. She revived her party and, once (through coalition) she could bring the Congress back to power in 2004. She lost the last election miserably, but she has experience of what is needed to nurse a wounded Congress back to health. *Does Rahul?* No.

Noises in favor of Rahul began during Manmohan's second term. His elevation to party vice-president clarified the future. *For whatever reason, he was not able to perform.* Congress(I) lost many states in his period. Then, when he was shown as its leader in the 2014 campaign, suffered a terrible beating. *Rahul has so far lost 26 successive elections that is like a Guinness Book record*! Many have noticed his lack of focus, lack of energy and lack of enthusiasm. He is two decades younger than PM Modi but almost seems out of date compared to the latter. Sonia is now 72. If she had no health problem, was likely to be active for a few years. Unfortunately, she has a serious disease for which she often goes to New York for treatment and follow-up *She also had a credibility that her son lacks.* Despite her thick accent, when she makes a statement on an important issue, it is more likely to receive attention than her som. When Rajiv was struggling, in the late 1980s, Arun Shourie came to our college in Baroda and made a pitch for the alliance of the BJP and VP Singh to take over. When one's house was on fire, Shourie said, one did not look for *Ganga Jal* to douse the flames. One student in the audience got up and told Shourie that one did not throw petrol on the fire either. *It seems to me that bringing Rahul in now would be like throwing petrol on the flames consuming Congress."* [Aakar Patel is Executive Director, Amnesty International India-an anti-India and anti-Modi outfit. The views expressed here are his own].

History must be repeatedly examined, re-examined, and examined again and again to arrive at the factual happenings in the past. That alone can form the basis of an understanding. That alone can bring a strong bonding with one's motherland. Unless the youth who are the future custodians and the backbone of any country know the truth about their land of birth, they are not expected to understand what is expected out of them to know the needs and nuances of their populace. Our history has, unfortunately, been heavily tinkered with by the foreign rulers of the millennium before independence. Obviously, they wanted us to look silly and useless thereby obliterating all the greatness of our oldest civilization and many a time changing the facts on our legion achievements. Nehru and his favorite Left Liberals did not stop short in distorting our recent history even more in a shameful way to prove that INC brought about independence when it had hardly any role in that. *The fact of the matter is freedom was earned by the collective efforts of the revolutionaries on the Indian soil plus those operating from foreign lands; Netaji Subhas Chandra Bose-the only Indian leader who confronted the Raj on the battle-front with his 60,000 men and officers comprising of thousands of deserters and POWs of the Royal British Indian Army; and the 30,000 Indian sailors at Bombay, Karachi and Vishakhapatnam ports who refused to work under the whites.* Hence, the *British had no alternative but to leave*!

Emperor Chandragupta Maurya had established a vast empire. He vanquished invading Selucus, the erstwhile general of Alexander. Alexander's life was spared by Porus with not much losses bur Selucus had to pay heavily for his misadventure including his daughter was to be offered to the Indian king. His grandson Emperor Asoka is rated one of the three greatest generals of the world after Alexander and before Napoleon Bonaparte. The biggest strategic blunder in Indian history was the conversion of Asoka to Buddhism. The Mauryan dynasty was the first major empire in India and at its peak the territory occupied by Asoka could rival or even exceed the future British Indian Empire in size. At that point of history, most of the contemporary civilizations were graduating from being City States to Empires, with a corresponding increase in wealth and fighting capability e.g. the Roman Empire and the Chinese Kingdoms (Mongols). The Magadha Empire founded under the tutelage of *Acharya* Chanakya was also destined to consolidate the Indian economy and make the country a fighting force to reckon with. We had managed to stop the Greeks and driven them off from our western borders (present Afghanistan). The Indian economy of that time comprises ~30-40% of the World economy, with a corresponding share in World trade. Our philosophy and way of life had spread far and wide to Indochina and the Indonesian islands in Indian ocean. However, the conversion of

Asoka to Buddhism and abjuring of further violence and expansion lead to the decline of the Mauryan dynasty and subsequent Indian capabilities. The children of Asoka spread out to preach and spread Buddhism rather than continuing the dynasty and consolidating the Empire. At the same time, Europe was consolidating under the Romans and even though there were subsequent divisions within the various states in Europe, they could absorb the unified spirit and laws of the Roman empire and continue forward, leading to their subsequent domination of the World. The Indian sub-continent that could have consolidated under the Mauryan rule was, however, fragmented, and left open for attack.

While the civilizing influence of the Mauryan dynasty lead to a philosophical and scientific revolution in Ancient India, the corresponding military benefits were lost. We were never able to regain the consolidating force of the Magadha empire, forever fragmenting the India polity into multiple small states that continued to be small prey for subsequent attackers. Whether it was the Slave Dynasty, the Mughals (successors of the Mongols corrupted to Mughals) or the British (successors of the Roman Empire), everyone managed to capture India by dividing us as we lost forever the *'Akhand Bharat'* (United India) spirit espoused by Chanakya. I would say that while we might have lost many subsequent wars due to technical blunders as has been pointed out by several authors, this small and disregarded change in the religious persuasion of one person was perhaps our greatest strategic defeat and changed the entire discourse of Indian history.

Emperor Asoka won the Kalinga battle. But after conversion to Buddhism, India lost its bite in coming wars against invaders. We could never unite against our enemies. It can be argued that the Buddhist philosophy had a strong positive impact on our society and significantly increased our world-wide influence. Perhaps, we are a happier and more tolerant nation as compared to other societies consequently due to Buddhist teachings of forgiveness. However, the converse is also true that we are repeatedly taken for granted by attackers, terrorists and criminals because of the same. Further, speaking in militaristic terms and subsequent loot and enslavement of India by repeated invaders, the above blunder was perhaps the biggest historical blunder in India.

Here comes the role of our unconcerned and uninformed youth towards our real history. On 12th September 2018, *Express News Service*, Ahmedabad brought out an interesting write-up, *'Rahul Gandhi 'mansik* *rogi'*, *born with silver spoon, says BJYM General Secretary'*. "The way these creepers were spreading in the country, the day Narendra Modi took governance in his hands, there has not been a single terrorist incident in the country." Abhijeet Mishra, national general secretary of BJYM, the youth wing of BJP, said that the biggest challenge today in the country was the 'azadi gang', which is emerging with its *Kendra Bindu* (centre-point) as Jawaharlal Nehru University (JNU). He was speaking at the 'Vijay divas' celebrations, the event organized by BJYM to commemorate the 125th year of Swami Vivekananda's speech at the World Parliament of Religion in Chicago. Mishra also called Congress president Rahul Gandhi 'mansik rogi' (mental patient) and went on to suggest that the youth today instead of idolizing the Khans (Salman, Aamir and Shahrukh) and members of the 'azadi gang' should idolize leaders like Bhagat Singh, Chandrashekhar Azad and Guru Gobind Singh. Addressing members of BJYM from Gujarat on 'Vijay divas', Mishra said that a few who come out of it (JNU) demand azadi (freedom), sometimes for Kashmir, and asked the audience to join him in a slogan he said was inspired from them only. *But for them, I want you to say that we are working on how to give them freedom.* Please sing azadi after me: *Hum de ke rahenge, Azadi… Kasab ko de di, Azadi… Afzal ko de di, Azadi… Burhan ko de di, Azadi…. Saddam ko de di, Azadi… Tariq ko de di, Azadi,* he led the chant. As the crowd repeated "azadi", Mishra stated that at times such slogans of Yuva Morcha shook up the Opposition too: [Freedom to Hafiz (Saeed), Dawood (Ibrahim), Umar (Khalid), Leftists, Terrorists, Naxals, Anti-nationalists… Freedom… now to Bangladesh… to Baluchistan… to Sindh… We will give freedom… Whoever wants freedom we will give now]. Attributing peace in country to PM Modi's efforts, Mishra said, "*The way these creepers were spreading in the country, the day Modi took governance in his hands, there has not been a single terrorist incident in the country.* Wherever there was Naxalism and terrorism, it has been restricted. Today terrorism has been limited to four-five districts of Jammu and Kashmir. Naxalism in a few districts of the country."

The past millennium was a period of turmoil for Hindustan or the Indian subcontinent as it was known when foreigners' invasions by 'uncouth' and 'uncivilized' Arabs or Mughals and 'cultured' Europeans kept us busy fighting against the aliens. Still there have been thinkers and philosophers starting with Chaitanya *Mahaprabhu* in the 17th century and going down to *Swami* Vivekananda towards the end of the 19th. The

20th century could not produce any worthwhile selfless single political leader but for the whole lot of great young revolutionaries like Bhagat Singh, Chandrashekhar Azad, Ram Prasad 'Bismil', Ashfaqullah Khan, Udham Singh, Kartar Singh Sarabha, and their likes. A mere 47 years from 1856 to 1903 produced very few outstanding and intelligent political like *Lokmanya* Bal Gangadhar Tilak, Mohammed Ali Jinnah, *Netaji* Subhas Chandra Bose and Shyama Prasad Mukherjee in INC. Unfortunately, they were strongly resisted by the run-of-the-mill cunning power-hungry 'leaders' and hence not allowed to come to center-stage and perform to their capabilities. The *reason* was very simple: Mediocre and highly selfish Gandhi, the tallest among the pygmies (who always tried his best to overshadow everyone else in INC and was amply supported by his prime *chamchas* or sycophants including Nehru, Patel, Maulana Azad, Rajendra Prasad), was scared to hell by the fact that those geniuses would easily overshadow him – the *fake not so highly nationalistic* and very wrongly called a *Mahatma* (a great soul). Classically *narrow-minded, petty, self-centered, extremely selfish and stubborn politicians like the most eulogized Gandhi and his protégé Nehru did incalculable harm to the cause of their motherland.* They were instrumental in inflicting heaviest body blow to the *geography* of the subcontinent by imposing Partition taking the excuse of flimsy, untenable *'Two Nation Theory'* in which its author Jinnah had little faith; and Hindustan's *culture or soul* by Islamization of the pure Hindu civilization. *Worse than that, they did the severest damage to all the generations to be born in the country by simply distorting and falsifying our recent history only to glorify their useless party that hardly played any role in country's freedom struggle.* That was a joint project of their Leftist INC, in collusion with like-minded Communists. Gandhi's double standards and *Ahimsa* cost the country tremendously in general but the Hindus (as well as the Sikhs, Baluchs and Pathans) and very small minority two (now three) countries for them!

Nisid Hajari's article, *'Nehru was as much to blame as Jinnah for Partition',* appeared in *Rediff.com News* on 28th January 2016. "'Nehru had multiple chances to make compromises that would have preserved a united India. And he chose NOT to... There was particularly mutual dislike between Nehru and Jinnah. Probably their personalities were so different... They were though very similar in some ways. They were complete opposites in many other ways. Nisid, who wrote *Midnight's Furies: The Deadly Legacy of India's Partition* -- which won the 2016 William E

Colby Award – spoke with Vaihayasi Pande Daniel [of *Rediff.com*]. Nisid spent a decade overseeing *Newsweek's* coverage of post 9/11 Afghanistan. As the foreign editor and with subcontinental roots, he was often asked to interpret Pakistan's role in the crisis. "I kept getting a lot of interest from people. And questions. 'Why does Pakistan do this? Why? And I kept saying there is this story (of Partition) you don't know," recalls Nisid, who is currently based in Singapore, whose Gujarati Hindu parents grew up in Mumbai. Those perplexing riddles seeded the idea of doing a book on Partition – It grew out of the work I was doing.

Nisid felt there was a direct connect between a string of incidents in Pakistan's often murky present and its blood-soaked, tumultuous birth in the monsoon of 1947. That cause and effect was something the world now might be rather interested in since it was no longer just a regional tale for Indian and Pakistani school textbooks. It was the 70-year-old chapter of history, he believed, that was responsible for the buildup of an explosive situation that has the potential to rewrite world events, quite comparable to Gavrilo Princip shooting Archduke and Duchess Franz Ferdinand in Sarajevo on 28th June 1914, or the never ending, bitter Palestine-Israel conflict, or Kim Jong-un building a rogue empire. When *Newsweek* changed ownership in 2013, Nisid was looking for a change. He decided to take two years off from nine-to-five journalism (if there is such a thing) to write a book on Partition. He spent the next 18 months hopping between the cavernous archives, on three continents, digging up as many key documents, accounts and records of the turning points that led to Partition. Those crucial footnotes of history -- letters, diaries, telegrams and memoirs -- were gleaned to construct, and flesh out, new profiles of the main players of Partition to bring them back to life. Over finally what turned out to be three years, he constructed, what he felt was, a fresh perspective on Partition, taking time to re-evaluate historical roles, snipping and weeding out redundant biases. In the bargain, offering coverage befitting of what he considers to be a landmark happening in the history of the 20th century.

'*Midnight's Furies: The Deadly Legacy of India's Partition*' was published by Houghton Mifflin Harcourt in June 2015. '*History ought to be examined, and re-examined, threadbare, before nations have the capacity to move on*', is Nisid's contention. Only then maybe Partition and its overstaying ghosts can be laid to rest, eventually maybe, optimistically, leading to better relations between India and Pakistan. "The only persons this current situation serves are the Pakistani army and Indian television channels," says Nisid, who now works with Bloomberg in Singapore. In his previous stint at *Newsweek*, he spent 10 years in New York. He has also lived in Seattle, Hong Kong, New Delhi and London. Nisid has been surprised by the praise *Midnight's Furies* received from Indian intellectuals, who picked up his book, not thinking they would be reading anything new and told him they ended up learning a lot. He received some criticism too -- on Twitter of a different kind from people who had clearly never read his book and believed him to be Muslim -- for what they felt was his going easy on the British over their role in Partition.

Nisid Hajari was in India for a rapid two-city book tour in July 2015 and spoke to Vaihayasi Pande Daniel/Rediff.com about *Midnight's Furies* and *Partition*. *In your book, you came up with a lot to incriminate Jinnah. And plenty to blame Nehru for too.* You seemed to have found Jinnah a troubling, polarizing, egotistic character, known for his vindictiveness and his negligence of the human cost. That leads to the most important question those of us in India have: Who would you apportion the blame, chiefly, for the perilous path the subcontinent took in 1947? It would be hard to assign a number or figure, percentage wise. I thought Nehru and the Congress leaders were equally to blame. Actually speaking, I hope it comes across, that I had a bit more sympathy for Jinnah then most Indian accounts of Partition generally have.

But through your book, Nehru sounds much more charming, giving us insight into the Peter Pan side of the statesman that Jinnah often spoke bitterly about saying, 'Peter Pan who never learns or unlearns anything.' Personality-wise, Nehru was more charming than Jinnah; even Jinnah's friends would admit that. But in terms of who is responsible for the mistakes -- and ruining the chance of political compromise -- I think, in that case Nehru was at least as much to blame as Jinnah. *Jinnah was arguing the case like the lawyer he was. Nehru had multiple chances to make compromises, that would have preserved a united India, and he chose not to.* He may have been more charming personally. Personally, he might have been the person you wanted to have dinner with! He was a flighty, impractical, emotional politician, who was operating at some level of high principle, that was not very pragmatic. *I think Jinnah had very good reasons not to trust Nehru and the Congress and that is Nehru's fault. Nevertheless, do you think that Jinnah was aware that his politics was akin to riding a tiger, which he would eventually not be able to get off?* I am not sure any of them were. They were all doing it. Gandhi and Nehru, as well. There was as much vicious anti-Muslim behavior going on, as the opposite. And these people were followers of the Congress. Gandhi didn't realize it. There was (for instance) that scene of Noakhali (the riots in October-November 1946, in Chittagong district in un-partitioned Bengal in which 5,000 Hindus were killed) in the book. *Gandhi did not understand that some of the things he was saying there were inciting Hindus to go kill Muslims. In Bihar?* Exactly, in Bihar (riots broke out in Chhapra and Saran districts in late October 1946, as a reprisal for the Noakhali riots, killing anywhere upwards of 5,000 Muslims; the death toll figures varied widely).

At the very, very top level, all these people -- Nehru, Jinnah and Gandhi -- were so distant from their followers. They were in Delhi. They were just in drawing rooms, with each other, negotiating and they were so used to the kind of rhetoric you would use in a courtroom. The things they would say, the things they would write in the press. I don't think they quite realized the impact those words would have at the ground level. In that case, I would hold all of them guilty.

So, they were all guilty of riding that tiger? They all didn't understand that the negotiations they were doing -- the kind of brinksmanship, the hardline positions they were taking, all part of negotiations -- were happening against the backdrop of these increasing tensions all around the country. They were too focused on what was happening in their little room and didn't understand this was having an impact elsewhere.

You describe that Nehru admitted that when discussing the Partition of the Punjab, for instance, they had NOT gone into any great depth about how it would happen eventually. So, Nehru's wrongdoing was not just alienating his rival Jinnah but also not understanding the nitty-gritty of how Partition would unfold? They were all, perhaps, guilty of being vague about the details?

Impractical. About the ground realities? Yes, yes. About the mechanics. None of them were administrators. None of them had ever held executive positions. They were all trained as lawyers and had become politicians. So, if you asked Nehru: 'Okay you want to split the Punjab -- how are you going to divide the education part of that?' he would have had no idea. (Or about) the police force, the administration. All stuff that the British had handled till that point... They again didn't understand the reality of the impact of the things they were doing.

So, in your view, would you equally apportion the blame? You wouldn't say perhaps Jinnah was more to blame? And, also do you think if the Congress knew about Jinnah's poor health, the formation of Pakistan could have been avoided? This has come up all the time. His illness (Jinnah was suffering from tuberculosis since the 1930s). He wasn't hiding anything. He had been a sick man for many years. And in 1946-1947 he wasn't anymore sick than any other time. His disease didn't get too serious until 1948. In 1947, he had to take a whole month off, and recuperate in some village outside Karachi. The year before, he had done something similar.

But wouldn't it have made a difference if people knew? Impossible to say. Let's say he had died in 1947. Who is to say that whoever came after him, in the Muslim League, wouldn't have been more radical? How do you know, somehow, that this would have been better for India?

Let me give another analogy. Supposing you are having a child and you know you are not going to be around, sometime after the child is born. You are frail. You would think a little more about how things would happen in your absence? Pakistan, in a sense, was Jinnah's child. There was nothing to suggest that he thought he was about to die. Perhaps he thought he was going to live long and continue to lead Pakistan. *Even in the pictures taken on Pakistan's Independence Day he looked very frail.* **H**e was a sickly man. But a lot of sickly people think that they are healthy.

As described in your account, in the days after Independence, as Nehru and Patel grappled with controlling the rioting, one might feel that Patel understood the reality better. He seemed to have his finger on the pulse, even if he was a hardliner. Yet at the same time, one had to admire Nehru's dashing spirit in trying to go out there and discipline mobs single-handedly, in a sort of romantic Lochinvar style. Or, was it more for show? Has your research shown he was really that kind of man? That was his genuine personality. I don't think he was showing off for anyone. That captures both what's admirable and frustrating about him. It is admirable, that in a cinematic sense, he would risk his life. *It was also exactly the wrong thing for a leader to do.* A leader, to effectively control the riots, should delegate and order the army to go there. This is what frustrated Jinnah no end. He is sitting in Karachi, while these riots are happening. He's getting biased reports, but he is (*still*) getting reports of what is happening. Jinnah is sitting and thinking: Why cannot Nehru and Patel? They have this powerful army, police, a government in place -- why can't they control this? It is because instead of trying to control it Nehru was running around... *Looking for his father's pistol to fight the rioters with?* Exactly! *But that sort of vignettes you don't have about Jinnah?* Right, right. He was a different kind of man.

What did you like best about Jinnah? The way people have treated Jinnah in modern Indian accounts is just to demonize him. The inherent assumption is that demanding Pakistan was the wrong thing to do. I tried to come at the subject with an open mind. Maybe partitioning was the wrong thing to do, maybe it was right, but Jinnah at least had legitimate support for his demands. He'd just had to prove that democratically, through provincial elections. And *it was a demand, that up until the very last minute, he was willing to negotiate.*

Until the spring of 1946 he was still willing to accept a united India, under the right political conditions. If you just look at that, then there is no reason to demonize him. He was a leader, leading his people. He happened to do it in a way that a lot of people found abrasive, and Nehru particularly loathed Jinnah. You are a lawyer arguing a case. You should be able to do it in whatever way that is appropriate.

Jinnah was on the political scene first, even long before Gandhi. Nehru came along later and both sort of stole Jinnah's position. Was Nehru's primacy in the Congress under Gandhi responsible for making Jinnah more bitter that his ambitions had been thwarted? He (*Nehru*) had a great deal to do with it. Jinnah was also frustrated by Gandhi, Patel and all the Congress leaders. But there was a mutual dislike between Nehru and Jinnah. Probably their personalities were so different. I don't think they could really understand each other and what (*each was*) trying to do. They were very similar in some ways. They were complete opposites in many other ways.

Of the three leaders you portray -- Gandhi, Nehru and Jinnah -- Pakistan's future Quaid-e-Azam is the most fascinating, in that what could have made an alcohol-drinking, (reportedly) pork-eating man take the right turn that he did? Well, he kept on drinking alcohol. I don't know if he kept on eating pork or not. In his personal life, I don't think he changed that much. He became more of an Islamic, Muslim figure. He did this on purpose to broaden out his appeal.

A fascinating man? Fascinating he was! Extremely frustrating to research. Unlike Gandhi and Nehru -- who wrote everything down and it has all been collected; there are letters and diaries, a ton of material to work with -- with Jinnah that just wasn't what he did. He just didn't write. His letters are all very formal, business like. He kept no diaries. He kept people away from him. There was nobody close to him who could write a memoir and say this is what Jinnah was like when no one else was around. Even his dentist sister (*Fatima Jinnah*), her book (*My Brother*) about him is written... everything written about him is such a hagiography, that no real picture of the man comes out. I did the best I could, but it was very hard as a researcher... *So, you there was a lot more to the man, but not enough material available to construct a kinder or more fascinating view?* Yes. He is clearly a complex figure. Getting at the heart of that complexity is difficult.

In one of the reviews of your book I read that it remained unclear how much Jinnah really wanted Partition. Or, whether he pursued the idea more as a tactic to increase Muslim clout within a larger India? Also, in your view, what could have been done to avoid Partition? This is the famous debate -- whether Jinnah was demanding Pakistan merely as a bargaining chip, or not. No one knows the truth. My best guess is that it started out as a bargaining chip, and at some point, probably very late in the process, probably as late as 1946, it became something more. After WWII, the demand for Pakistan became more widely popular than maybe even Jinnah might have imagined it would. And he was both pushing the demand and being carried along.

Up until the spring of 1946, a political compromise that would have preserved a united India, was still possible. The Congress -- Nehru in particular -- would have granted Muslim areas that (eventually) became Pakistan more autonomy and accept a weaker Central government.

Abandoning that compromise was the fatal mistake. Nehru couldn't just dismiss this demand as illegitimate and say they weren't going to deal with it. He had to accommodate it somehow. And as the larger, more powerful party it was their responsibility to accommodate it. You don't ask the weaker party to make the concessions. One had to be generous.

Nehru for his own reasons chose not to. I think that was the last real chance to avoid Partition. Maybe it could have still happened later, no one knows, but at that point it was really possible to preserve a united India."

MK Bhadrakumar's blog on *Indian Punchline*, 'NSA Doval has struck gold', appearing in *Rediff.com News* throws insight on tenacious Indo-Pakistan relations made more complex by Pak's Western close friends like America and Britain to start with and now China. "Pakistan's policy is highly accident prone. Let me strike when the iron is still hot. But what needs to sink in is that slowly, steadily, a meaningful engagement between Delhi and Islamabad seems only way out. Of course, it faces the risk of sniper fire not only from right-wing nationalists (who are in unholy alliance on this turf with the political opposition), but also from within our establishment. The sharp remark by Foreign Secretary S Jaishankar and Pakistani High Commissioner Abdul Basit's prompt clarification last week testify to how the bureaucracy is indulging in vanities without knowing what is happening. Basit obviously knew much more than he was willing to admit. These are early days but sharing of intelligence by Pakistan's NSA Lt Gen Naseer Janjua with our NSA Ajit Doval regarding the strong likelihood of a major terrorist strike in India suggests that a critical mass is possibly developing in their mutual engagement. If so, it could presage a breakthrough that has only few precedents in the tortuous India-Pakistan discourse.

Doval's strength is that he is PM Narendra Modi's trusted aide on foreign and security policy front, while Pakistan's interest would lie in developing a matrix of mutual understanding with him precisely for that reason. It could be that the Pakistani side is testing the waters — how far Doval is willing to take a walk into the night with his counterpart. On the other hand, paradoxically, this is an instance where we can only sincerely hope that Lt Gen Janjua raised a false alarm. Nonetheless, it is significant that Lt Gen Janjua appears to have named the L-e-T and J-e-M. A strong case can now be built to mount a crackdown on these terrorist groups. Is the crunch time coming for the jihadi leadership? Equally, we need to appreciate this stunning development against the backdrop of a much bigger canvas, which is strongly suggestive of a clean break in Pakistani policies, both internal and external – execution of Mumtaz Qadri, which is undoubtedly a brave and audacious decision by the civilian and political leadership of Pakistan (here), as well as the signs of a profound shift in the Pakistani strategy towards Afghanistan [see my article in *Asia Times* entitled *Pakistan shifts its Afghan strategy: To what end?*]

Unfortunately, the stereotyped mindset prevalent among the Indian pundits blocks new thinking. Besides, there is also the pro-American lobby in India, which will inevitably try to ascribe the credit for all that is happening to the US 'pressure' working on Pakistan. But that is sheer baloney, because the US is barely able to look after its own self-interests in the AfPak.

Suffice it to say, what we are seeing here is no effect of some American magic formula. These are hard-headed Pakistan-led, Pakistan-owned decisions and moves. And a hardcore realist like Doval surely would be willing to see it that way. Of course, the dictum should nonetheless be 'Trust but verify' — always, always, always.

Which brings us to the efficacy of the entire approach PM Modi has wisely taken by putting Doval in sole charge and taking the India-Pakistan engagement off the radar of public view and perceptions. Clearly, this sequestered approach must be continued and taken to its logical conclusion. Let the foreign-policy bureaucracy be brought in laterally to dabble in 'dialogue' in due course, if need be. There is no hurry on that score.

One can only hope that Modi resorts to the same thoughtful, practical approach to reset the Sino-Indian ties. Too many cooks spoil the broth – even if they claim to be professional cooks with previous experience in making Peking Duck."

In August 2018, former cricketer Imran Khan's won the rigged Pakistan elections under the tutelage of army. Although his party did not get absolute majority, he was able to form government. Like his civilian predecessors he is under the thumb of army. Can he come out? Doesn't seem likely! On 5th September 2018, *Rediff.com News* published a news item, '*Imran appears very meek and almost unhappy*.' "Imran and his government have obviously agreed to be subservient to the military establishment.' 'How can we expect him to take a stand on anything?' The autobiography of British-Pakistani broadcast journalist Reham Khan has made more news for its controversial revelations about former husband and present Pakistan PM Imran Khan than about Reham Khan's own journey after walking out of an abusive first marriage with three children and no job. The initial questions sent to Reham Khan for this interview were returned because it was felt that they were mostly about Imran Khan. Some additional questions were asked for. Yet when Reham finally replied, she did not evade any Imran-related question. A journalist herself, she does understand that every question deserves an answer. Libya-born Khan, who was married at 19, worked with the *BBC* in England and returned to Pakistan in 2013 continuing with television journalism. It was in the course of her broadcast work that she first met Imran Khan. The couple wed in January 2015, eight months later, they were divorced. The book has been in the eye of the storm for the accusations of sex, drugs, illegitimate children and corruption. Her critics say the book aims to malign Imran Khan. Cricket legend Wasim Akram sent Reham a legal notice. No publisher wants to risk helping with the book in Pakistan, says Reham.

In an e-mail interview from England, she tells *Rediff.com's Archana Masih* that since Imran Khan's swearing-in, as the days go by, his every blunder is proving that every word in her book is a hundred percent true.

How has life changed for you after the release of your book? Do you plan to return to Pakistan?

The only change is that must be away from Pakistan at the minute and it is a serious disruption to my social causes as well as difficult for me as I miss Pakistan desperately. I only came away because it was clear that they would stoop to any level to stop the book from coming out. No publisher wanted to risk helping with the book and even printers refused as they feared their personal safety. A fascist individual and regime thrive on this perception of fear they build up. Everyone knew in Pakistan that the military establishment was going to bring in Imran as PM and people did not want to risk the wrath of this powerful lobby.

I am in love with Pakistan. How can I be kept away?

You were recently heckled in a London park when with your son, you maintained your calm through it -- how much do negative responses like this incident affect you, and your children? It doesn't affect me or my daughters as much. Sahir is naturally the eldest and his cultural values of protecting women kicks in at times. It can make him angry sometimes, but generally we laugh off as stupidity. We know that these are isolated incidents by people entrusted with this task of stalking me. Majority of Pakistanis both home and overseas are loving and respectful.

What is the worst thing -- anyone has said/done -- to you because of the book? And what are the positives that have emerged because of the book? Again, the paid propaganda lobbyists and party position holders say awful things, but it is predictable now. They are on direct instruction from Imran, use swear words and resort to character assassination on social and national media.

The accusations are so bizarre that it is almost funny. So, it is all awful, but honestly (it) doesn't bother me one bit. What used to affect me after my divorce was: the man I loved had gone out of the way to spread lies about me to save his public image. That hurt for a bit. He told his mouthpieces to say that I was trying to kill him by arsenic poisoning. For a woman, who lovingly gets up in the middle of the night to make food for her husband to be maligned by the same man by saying this was naturally shocking, but I got over it. My feedback has been largely extremely positive and supportive from people who have read the book. I have melted some hard cynics, it seems. My friend was seeing an ophthalmologist the other day and when she told him her ethnicity, he started telling her how he was surprised at the courage of a Pakistani woman called Reham Khan. I am frequently given such encouraging messages from random strangers.

Now that Imran Khan is prime minister, do you feel that in spite of the scandalous revelations about him in your book, the people of Pakistan did not care or believe these personal scandals, putting their hope instead in Imran for a 'Naya Pakistan'. That in the people's court, he is the winner? The people have not elected him or selected him. He was chosen by the military establishment and he got here by rigging the system. We all know this. Not only the journalists or politicians, but the public too. The book is more of a 'I told you so' about different issues I have encountered. *Imran is also a major issue now that he is in the PM's seat. As the days go by his every blunder is proving that every word in my book is a hundred percent true.*

He has made some populist proclamations in his victory speech -- he said he will not stay in the official PM's home and opted for a simple oath ceremony -- this is a welcome change, isn't it? Will it especially resonate with the youth? These optics can only fool a few. His attempt at a cosmetic camouflage of a feeble government is the butt of jokes and memes. From official pictures appears he is in the official residence. The oath taking was bog standard fare and Pakistan's problems cannot be fixed by serving tea and biscuits. His daily trips back and forth to his own home in a helicopter is another example of fake rhetoric. The party people are following in the footsteps of the leader and as political upstarts they are blatantly misusing and abusing power and VVIP protocol. *Bureaucrats, police officers and general public are being insulted daily.* He and his government have obviously agreed to be subservient to the military establishment and we saw evidence of their friendship in the recently hyped unusually long eight =hour meeting. People like me who can read his body language are noticing that he appears to be very meek and almost unhappy looking. The cult is brainwashed and so his tactics may work on them but not for very long.

You see our biggest challenge in Pakistan is the fact that 64% of our population is under 30 and are largely jobless. Imran had made ridiculous claims in his election campaign of providing 10 m jobs etc. In his first speech after taking the oath there was no plan given for job creation or an economic recovery. There was no mention of tackling extremism or terrorism either. In the first week in office two major lies came to the forefront; *one,* the offer of talks by India and the other was the diplomatic *faux pas* with the US. This demonstrates a party and leader that has no clue about the basics of running a government. I, of course, have inside info about how Imran had no interest in poverty alleviation or tackling the rights of the minorities and curbing extremism when he got power in one province in the last five years.

The lack of performance in Khyber Pukhtunkhwa is well documented and visible. His position on the Taliban and the use of religion for vote bank appeasement has already resulted in the US cancelling aid to Pakistan. The record on militants is pushing Pakistan into isolation and it is all because no democratic leader has been allowed to stay put in Pakistan.

Imran got to this chair just like (Muhammad Khan) Junejo and (Mir Zafarullah Khan) Jamali before him did. on anything *How can we expect him to take a stand?"*

On 23rd March 2016, an interesting article titled, *'The end of civilization as we know it? Not really',* appeared on *Rediff.com News*: "Ever pragmatic, the Americans are convinced that the future is in the Indo-Pacific. 'This is a new Indo-Pacific century and India has to decide whether it has eyes on the prize', says Rajeev Srinivasan. The headlines were dramatic and the prognoses gloomy. In separate stories in two of the few Western journals that I read consistently, the *Financial Times* and *The Economist,* there was a palpable sense of *fin-de-siècle* (end of the century) pessimism as though an era were ending. Parallels were made with the 1930s which, according to their lights, was the worst of times, because of the rise of the Nazis and the Fascists, the most abominable villains ever in the history of the world. The fact is that for an impartial observer, it is not obvious that they, villainous as though they undoubtedly were, are the worst of the worst. For that dubious honor, there are many claimants. The Khmer Rouge in Cambodia, who wiped out roughly a seventh of their fellow citizens. The Communists who have killed, all told, a hundred million people. I am sure you can think of others.

A fair case can be made that the very worst rulers in history were the British Empire, who, in their heyday casually exterminated at least 30 million people (see the riveting account in *Late Victorian Holocausts: El Nino and the making of the Third World*) and caused the permanent impoverishment of a billion people through loot and de-industrialization.

By my rough calculations, they looted $10 trillion from India alone. You can debate if the British were the very worst, but there is a correlation between colonization and prosperity. Britain went from being a small economic power, with about 2% of global GDP in the 1750s, to a superpower, with about 18% by 1900. Some will point out other colonizing powers such as Spain and Portugal (despite the vast riches of Latin America that they looted) did not do so well and will point to the Industrial Revolution as a reason.

But there is a plausible argument that it was the loot from Bengal that formed the venture capital that led to the Industrial Revolution. William Digby (*Prosperous British India: A Revelation from Official Records*) quoting Brooks Adams suggested that the Industrial Revolution (circa 1760) could not have happened in Britain had it not been for the loot that came in from India. It is indeed a curious coincidence: *The Battle of Plassey* (1757); the *flying shuttle* (1760); the *spinning jenny* (1764); the *power-loom* (1765); the *steam engine* (1768).

The fact is that, today, the momentum from that colonial loot has come to an end, and Britain is finding it increasingly difficult to justify having a place at the top table. This is leading to neurotic behavior: for example, the threat of 'Brexit', that is, of Britain leaving the European Union. To an outsider, this sounds like madness, because the European Union (despite its many problems), as a unified single market, is far more viable as a single economic unit than individual European nations. Britain, to put it unkindly, has no future.

Even America, which has always had a 'special relationship' with Britain, is no longer quite so keen. *Ever pragmatic, the Americans (except for Atlantic holdouts) are convinced that the future is in the Indo-Pacific.* he very logic of Barack Obama's 'pivot to Asia' -- even though it was half-hearted -- was an implicit acknowledgement of this fact. I suspect that the angst exhibited by the British journalists is based on this realization of increasing irrelevance. Especially if Scotland decides to secede, 'Great' Britain will be 'Little' Britain, and the days of living off old glory will come to an end. As it is, Britain has no sustainable competitive advantage or core competence: There is nothing they produce that anybody else really wants, except for their banking, journalism, the odd Burberry or two, and Scotch whiskey (which, of course, is in jeopardy if the Scots take off).

On the other hand, there is the realization that long-held myths propagated by the West that they are the very culmination of history, may well be off base. There was *The End of History* by Francis Fukuyama which many took to mean that the Anglo-American model, in the post-Cold-War era, had finally won against all alternatives. Fukuyama himself claims that he was misunderstood, but that hubris remains. The irony is that the Communists also had similar millennial views about history and how their worldview was the ultimate in the evolution of societies; we know what happened when the Soviet empire disintegrated. It did appear that the Anglo-Americans had won a final solution.

The Anglo-American worldview was all-conquering at that time, having seen off its only competition. Their mythology was partly that of a 'shining city on a hill,' partly the political ideal of a representative democracy; partly the economic ideas of the Washington Consensus; partly seductive ideas about 'life, liberty and the pursuit of happiness,' and partly cultural memes about blue jeans, the open road, Coca-Cola, Hollywood, rock music, and Silicon Valley.

These ideas were marketed to the rest of us, to the extent that there are many who believe this ideal, dream-like society is the norm that everyone should aspire to. (I did too, in my youth, before I spent decades there and acquired a more nuanced, balanced perspective.) Indeed, there is the 'Good Life in the West' for many, but not all people. The fact that much of it is unsustainable based on environmental impact is a detail.

There is also the sad fact that there is a 'Deep State' that controls those in the West. Dwight Eisenhower called it the military-industrial complex, but we now know that is the military-industrial-media-church complex. Noam Chomsky wrote of how it 'manufactures consent.' Recently, Pat Buchanan *echoed the sentiment (external link)* when he said: 'We talk about the 'deep State' in Turkey and Egypt, the unseen regimes that exist beneath the public regime and rule the nation no matter the president or prime minister? What about the 'deep State' that rules us, of which we caught a glimpse at Sea Island?

Whatever you think of Donald Trump, Buchanan was suggesting, the Deep State is going to ensure he will not win. This Deep State is the one that is in jeopardy now. Its mythology is that there is democracy; in fact, the people are deceived into thinking they have a voice. People think they are free; in fact, the US is a highly regulated country.

The Economist had *an interesting story (external link)* about why it and all the other media were wrong about Trump: They depended on a 2008 book, *The Party Decides*, which suggested that party insiders think elections are too important to be left to the people, and therefore they are 'using their influence over the media, fundraising... to guide voters towards preferred candidate.'

In other words, Big Brother is watching you. What did you dream? It's alright, we told you what to dream. That could be Pink Floyd or the dystopian Blade Runner. Thus, the enormous *schadenfreude* from the Chinese and the Russians at this display of dysfunctional politics in the West: Trump and Hillary Clinton, both not exactly the most desirable candidates in the US, and an extreme leftist named Jeremy Corbyn leading the Labor Party in the UK. Add to this the chaos in Europe, and you can pretty much hear the power of the old order crumbling.

That is painful for the Deep State and its acolytes, including many in India. But it is hardly the end of the world. It just shows that we are far from the end of history. European domination of the world, although it looked pretty much like Manifest Destiny, is only a blip in the relentless march of time. The moving finger writes, and having writ, moves on. Like Ozymandias's vanities, the *ancient regime* of the West is collapsing, that's about it. There is a new Indo-Pacific century, and India will have to decide whether it has its eyes on the prize. It is there for India to lose."

Donald Trump, with possibly Newt Gingrich as his running mate may be taken the future President of America. MK Bhadrakumar's blog on Saturday, the 30th April 2016, *'What is there in Donald Trump for India'* on *Indian Punchline* is worth noting. "Surely, it is about time to seriously take Donald Trump as the front runner in the US presidential election. The Indian media, including some experienced reporters in the US, have so far treated Trump as a macabre joke. But such an approach is no longer tenable.

<u>What is there in a Trump presidency for India?</u> The question is assuming urgency. Again, we are faltering, looking for an odd remark of his at an odd town hall meeting in Indianapolis in a disparaging way about Pakistan to rush into a facile conclusion that Trump presidency is just what the doctor prescribed for India. Such off-the-cuff remarks that politicians everywhere are wont to make while on campaign trail do not necessarily translate as policies when they hold the levers of power. [*Times of India, Hindu*] Fortunately, however, Trump has put his foreign policy vision together, finally, in a major speech he made at the Center for the National Interest in Washington. The stunning thing is that in the entire speech he never once mentioned Pakistan or India. Yes, there was a deafening silence. Trump's priorities are *three*: *one*, the fight against radical Islam and terrorism;

two, reset of ties with Russia and China; and, *three*, his thesis of 'America First' in anything and everything. India is a stakeholder in all these three templates of Trump's foreign-policy vision, although he does not visualize a specific role a such for India. To be sure, India's vital interests will be affected if Trump stuck to what he has outlined last Tuesday.

So, what does Trump say? First, he underscores his determination to hunt down extremist Islamist groups, and he is not only open to taking help from all quarters willing to join the fight but deploy US military if need arises. In both his prioritization of the fight ahead and his optimism about taking it to a successful conclusion in a near future, he is akin to Russian President Vladimir Putin. Conceivably, he will be open to taking Russian help – unlike President Barack Obama who puts caveats. If such US-Russia cooperation ensues, it could have positive impact on Syria, Iraq and Afghanistan. However, quintessentially, Trump's vision is one-dimensional and is somewhat naïve insofar as he is unable or unwilling (or both) to co-relate terrorism with the underlying contradictions in regional politics in the Middle Eastern societies and in the US' regional policies historically. The good part is that Trump will be wary of starting any new Middle Eastern wars or of making unilateralist interventions. (He was and still is harshly critical of the US invasion of Iraq.)

On the *second* template – US' relations with Russia and China – India has much to guard against. On Russia, Trump seeks détente as Henry Kissinger would have advised him or late Nixon by balancing interests. The possibility of a New Cold War becomes distinctly less under Trump. And in turn India's close relations with Russia which is an important aspect of its 'strategic autonomy' become sustainable and will not come under pressure from Washington as is happening lately. Trump's approach to China, however, is highly ambivalent, from an Indian perspective. The hardliners in Indian foreign and security establishments have reason to worry. In his entire speech, Trump failed to mention the tensions in South China Sea or the US' rebalance in Asia.

Draw your own conclusions. Was it a deliberate omission? Or, strategic ambiguity? India, of course, is saddled with a *Joint Vision Statement* (by PM Narendra Modi and President Obama) issued January 2016 during the US president's state visit to India, which has complicated the India-China normalization process. In his speech (under discussion), Trump eschewed threats or harsh criticism directed against China and its policies. His focus is on China's cooperation in tackling the North Korea problem and, most importantly, on how far the US can have a balanced trade relationship with China. China's massive trade balance vis-a-vis US infuriates him. Plainly put, he seeks a reset with China whereby the US drives a much harder bargain with China on the economic issues with the aim of persuading/ cajoling/arm twisting Beijing to recycle some of its massive earnings and reserves accumulated through trade with America.

Trump acknowledges that the US and China have "serious differences" but he goes on to say that the two countries are not destined to be adversaries, and it is possible to "seek common ground based on shared interests". This translates in practice as one of Washington negotiating with China from a position of strength because of its superiority in comprehensive national power (including military power) so that the US can "find a better friend in China". The high probability is that the Chinese who are in the long game will be savvy enough to compromise and work out a new type of relationship. At the very minimum, India must put on hold the so-called 'foundational agreements' with the US until the post-Obama era sails into view and the strategic ambiguity clears up. To be sure, the Asia-Pacific may hear an entirely different American symphony by the end of next year if Trump gets elected as president.

Put differently, Trump alerted us to the India-centric agenda we should coolly and calculatedly define during Modi's forthcoming visit to Washington in June. For a change, Modi must pin down Obama and insistently demand what America can do for India rather than the other way around, as the US lobbyists in India have advocated. Modi is accountable to his country, and that includes constituencies other than the US lobbyists and American think tankers merchandising dreams.

This brings us to the *third* template of Trump's foreign-policy agenda – 'America First'. In a nutshell, Trump's top priority will be on rebuilding the US economy and military. He will be careful about husbanding resources and in ensuring that the US' foreign policy moves are cost-effective and 'self-accounting'. Plainly put, for example, instead of advocating an open-ended US involvement in the Afghan war, if India so keenly seeks such an American role in the Hindu Kush, what it should also do is to loosen its purse strings and show readiness to bankroll it. For Trump, a self-made billionaire, money doesn't grow on trees. And be it NATO or any other alliance system, the US' partners must be willing to put money on the table. Equally, for revamping and rebuilding the American economy and military, Trump needs money – and lots and lots of it. So, we (US) are also going to have to change our trade, immigration and economic policies to make our economy strong again – and to put Americans first again. This will ensure that our own workers, right here in America, get the jobs and higher pay that will grow our tax revenue and increase our economic might as a nation. *Got it? No free ride, no trade concessions, no easing of visa restrictions – and, most important, no 'Make in India'.*"

The festive occasion of Deepavali is currently gripping people across India and beyond. The *Festival of Lights* is being celebrated with joy and fervor by people from all walks of life. During such a jubilant atmosphere, can the able politicians be left behind in their revelry? After all, they are often perceived as the lifeline of the nation. PM Modi spent the most auspicious day with the armed forces and Indo-Tibetan Border Security Forces as he usually does every year. Modi's attempts to improve relations with our tough northern neighbor (and the 2nd strongest both financially and militarily) China appear to bear fruit after all. On the auspicious Deepavali Day on Wednesday, the 7th November 2018, *Hindustan Times* reported a very important and significant development: *'Hotline linking India, China military headquarters on the Cards'*. "New Delhi and Beijing will consider linking up military headquarters and regional commands with hotlines during the Defense Secretary level dialogue next Tuesday to prevent any adventurism along the 3,488 Km Line of Actual Control (LAC) between the two Asian giants, people familiar with the matter said. The issue could be discussed in the two-day dialogue Defense Secretary Sanjay Mitra is to hold with Lt General Shao Yuanming, the deputy chief of Joint Staff department, central military commission of Peoples Liberation Army (PLA) on November 13 and 14. Specifically, in addition to the hotline between the two countries' military headquarters, diplomats based in New Delhi and Beijing added, there is the possibility of a hotline between PLA Commander of Western Theater covering Tibet Autonomous Region and Xinjiang, and a designated Indian Army Commander. The two hotlines will address requirements of both countries: New Delhi wanted direct contact between the heads of military operations at the headquarters and Beijing, dedicated communication between heads of regional commands as there is no centralized military operations at the PLA headquarters. India's problem in having a dedicated hotline between regional commands is that it does not have theater commands concept in its military. In PLA, the Western Theater commanders manage both the Tibet and Xinjiang regions bordering India, while the Indian Army's Northern, Central and Eastern Army commanders manage the LAC.

Former Foreign Secretary Kanwal Sibal said that military hotlines will be helpful if they are between the highest military levels on both sides as PLA formations in Tibet should get instructions from PLA Beijing headquarters to maintain peace and tranquility in the LAC. According to senior government officials, the two defenses will finalize the bilateral military cooperation agenda for 2019, including bilateral military exercises and exchanges. India and China will be holding the "hand-in-hand" military exercise in Chengdu region next month with Special Representative dialogue on boundary issue scheduled on November 23, 24, and 25. The exercise – there have been six editions so far – was put on hold in 2017 on account of Doklam fiasco: India hosted the annual exercise in 2016.

The officials, who spoke on condition of anonymity said India is unhappy at China's support for Pakistan's shallow overtures to New Delhi. On November 4, a joint statement on PM Imran Khan's visit to Beijing said: " China appreciates Pakistan's quest for peace through dialogue, cooperation and negotiation, on the bases of mutual respect and equality and supports Pakistan's efforts for improvement of Pakistan-India relations and for settlement of outstanding disputes between the two countries." The Chinese endorsement of Khan comes at a time when the Pakistan Army is routinely indulging in cross-border firing in support of terrorist infiltration into J&K. On the bilateral front, the incidents of transgressions across the LAC have recorded a low this year with armies on both sides ready to discuss the issues rather than adopt an aggressive posture on the borders. Hindustan Times reported in June that the number was 20% down from last year."

America has all along (since 1950) been toeing British line inimical to India's interests that fueled her animosity towards Hindustan. As a part of Anglo-American conspiracy, America has been continuously protecting, financing and furthering Pakistani interests more than Britain knowing full well that Pakistan was always at fault right from its inception. As we look back in reading *'NOW DE-CLASSIFIED FILES of US, during 1971 INDO-PAK WAR'*, it is worth appreciating our own performance as INDIAN ARMED FORCES vis-a-vis Tele-conversation between (the then) US PRESIDENT Nixon and SECRETARY OF STATE Kissinger...

"In December 1971, India won a famous decisive victory over Pakistan due to our brilliant soldiers, an unwavering political leadership and strong diplomatic support from Moscow. It resulted in the breakup of Pakistan and the birth of Bangladesh. But *lesser known fact is the power play of Russia (then USSR) that prevented a joint British-American attack on India.*

Washington DC, 3rd December 1971, 10:45am: President Nixon is on the phone with Secretary of State Henry Kissinger, hours after Pakistan launched simultaneous attacks on six Indian airfields, a reckless act that prompted India to declare war:

Nixon: So West Pakistan giving trouble there?

Kissinger: If they lose half of their country without fighting, they will be destroyed. They may also be destroyed by fighting but they will go down fighting.

Nixon: The Pakistan thing makes your heart sick. For them to be done so by the Indians and after we have warned the bitch (reference to Indian PM Indira). Tell them that when India talks about West Pakistan attacking them it's like Russia claiming to be attacked by Finland.

Washington, December 10, 1971, 10:51 am: A week later the war is not going very well for Pakistan, as Indian armor scythes through East Pakistan and the Pakistan Air Force is blown out of the subcontinent's sky. Meanwhile, the Pakistani military in the West is demoralized and on the verge of collapse as the Indian Army and Air Force attack round the clock.

Nixon: Our desire is to save West Pakistan. That's all.

Kissinger: That's right. That is exactly right.

Nixon: All right. Keep those carriers moving now.

Kissinger: The carriers – everything is moving. Four Jordanian planes have already moved to Pakistan, 22 more are coming. We're talking to the Saudis, the Turks, we've now found they are willing to give five. So, we're going to keep that moving until there's a settlement.

Nixon: Could you tell the Chinese it would be very helpful if they could move some forces or threaten to move some forces?

Kissinger: Absolutely.

Nixon: They've got to threaten or, they've got to move, one of the two. You know what I mean?

Kissinger: Yeah.

Nixon: How about getting the French to sell some planes to the Pakistan?

Kissinger: Yeah. They're already doing it.

Nixon: This should have been done long ago. The Chinese have not warned the Indians.

Kissinger: Oh, yeah.

Nixon: All they've got to do is move something. Move a division. You know, move some trucks. Fly some planes, some symbolic act. We're not doing a goddamn thing, Henry, you know that.

Kissinger: Yeah.

Nixon: But these Indians are cowards. Right?

Kissinger: Right. But with Russian backing. You see, the Russians have sent notes to Iran, Turkey, and to a lot of countries threatening them. The Russians have played a miserable game.

If the two American leaders were calling Indians cowards, a few months earlier the Indians were a different breed altogether.

This phone call is from May 1971.

Nixon: The Indians need - what they need really is a -

Kissinger: They're such bastards ....

Nixon: A mass famine. But they aren't going to get that...But if they're not going to have a famine, the last thing they need is another war. Let the goddamn Indians fight a war.

Kissinger: They are the most aggressive goddamn people around there.

The 1971 war was modern India's finest hour, in military terms. The clinical professionalism of the Indian army, navy and air force; a charismatic brass led by the legendary Field Marshal Sam Manekshaw; and ceaseless international lobbying by the political leadership worked brilliantly to a famous victory. After two weeks of vicious land, air and sea battles, nearly 100,000 Pakistani soldiers surrendered before India's rampaging army - largest such capitulation since General Paulus' 1943 Stalingrad surrender. However, it could all have come unstuck without help from veto-wielding Moscow with which New Delhi had the foresight to sign a security treaty in 1970.

As Nixon's conversations with the wily Kissinger show, the forces arrayed against India were formidable. The Pakistani military was being bolstered by fighter aircrafts from Jordan, Iran, Turkey and France. Moral and military support was amply provided by the US, China and the UK. Though not mentioned in these conversations, the UAE sent in half a squadron of fighter aircrafts and Indonesia dispatched at least one naval vessel to fight alongside the Pakistani Navy. However, *Russia's entry thwarted scenario that could have led to multiple pincer movements against India.* Russian naval experts were incognito keeping a stern eye on the movement of US 7th Fleet Enterprise along with a nuclear-powered fighter naval ship. Few months after the landmark victory, a Punjabi Brigadier traveling with me in Dakshin Express from Hyderabad to New Delhi told me that Russia provided with maps of the Enterprise and told us to attack its most vulnerable segment to sink it and also the US prestige for all times to come. Hence after crossing the Straits of Malacca the 7th Fleet turned southwards in the opposite direction. Possibly the Americans got wind of the Russian strategy and preferred to run away from the theater of Indo-Pak War! In a nutshell this is the American bravery. They had almost lost to the Communist fighters in the Vietnam War and were on the run after heavy losses. Hence another loss in a quick gap would have finished America's position as the perceived *numero uno* armed forces!

Superpowers Face-Off: On December 10, even as Nixon and Kissinger were frothing at the mouth, Indian intelligence intercepted an American message, indicating that the US' 7th Fleet was steaming into the war zone. It was then stationed in the Gulf of Tonkin, was led by the 75,000-ton nuclear powered aircraft carrier, the *USS Enterprise*. As the world's largest warship, it carried more than 70 fighters and bombers. It also included the guided missile cruiser *USS King*, guided missile destroyers *USS Decatur*, Parsons and Tartar Sam, and a large amphibious assault ship *USS Tripoli*. Standing between the Indian cities and the American ships was the Indian Navy's Eastern Fleet led by the 20,000-ton aircraft carrier, *Vikrant*, with barely 20 light-fighter aircrafts. When asked if India's Eastern Fleet would take on the 7th Fleet, the Flag Officer Commanding-in-Chief, Vice Admiral N. Krishnan, said: "Just give us the orders." The Indian Air Force, having wiped out the Pakistani Air Force within the first week of the war, was reported to be on alert for any possible intervention by aircraft from the Enterprise. Meanwhile, *Soviet intelligence reported that a British naval group led by the aircraft carrier Eagle had moved closer to India's territorial waters. This was perhaps one of the most ironic paradoxical events in modern history where the Western world's two leading democracies were threatening the world's largest democracy only to protect the perpetrators of the largest genocide since the Holocaust in Nazi Germany.*

However, *India did not panic*. It quietly sent Moscow a request to activate a secret provision of the Indo-Soviet security treaty, under which Russia was bound to defend India in case of any external aggression. The British and the Americans had planned a coordinated pincer to intimidate India: while the British ships in the Arabian Sea would target India's western coast, the Americans would make a dash into the Bay of Bengal in the east where 100,000 Pakistani troops were caught between the advancing Indian troops and the sea. To counter this two-pronged British-American threat, Russia dispatched a nuclear-armed flotilla from Vladivostok on December 13 under the overall command of Admiral Vladimir Kruglyakov, the Commander of the 10th Operative Battle Group (Pacific Fleet). Though the Russian fleet comprised a good number of nuclear-armed ships and atomic submarines, their missiles were of limited range (less than 300 km). Hence to effectively counter the British and American fleets the Russian commanders had to undertake the risk of encircling them to bring them within their target. This they did with military precision. In an interview to a Russian TV program after retirement, Admiral Kruglyakov, who commanded the Pacific Fleet from 1970 to 1975, recalled that Moscow ordered the Russian ships to prevent the Americans and British from getting closer to "Indian military objects". The genial Kruglyakov added: "The Chief Commander's order was that our submarines should surface when the Americans appear. It was done to demonstrate to them that we had nuclear submarines in the Indian Ocean. So, when our subs surfaced, they recognized us. In the way of the American Navy stood the Soviet cruisers, destroyers and atomic submarines equipped with anti-ship missiles. We encircled them and trained our missiles at *the Enterprise*. We blocked them and did not allow them to close in on Karachi, Chittagong or Dhaka." At this point, the Russians intercepted a communication from the commander of the British carrier battle group, Admiral Dimon Gordon, to the 7th Fleet commander: "Sir, we are too late. There are the Russian atomic submarines here, and a big collection of battleships." The British ships fled towards Madagascar while the larger US task force stopped and turned south before entering the Bay of Bengal.

The Russian maneuvers clearly helped prevent a direct clash between India and the US-UK combine. Newly declassified documents reveal: Indian PM went ahead with her plan to liberate Bangladesh despite inputs that the Americans had kept three battalions of Marines on standby to deter India and that the American aircraft carrier *USS Enterprise* had orders to target the Indian Army which had broken through the Pakistani Army's defenses and was thundering down the highway to the gates of Lahore, West Pakistan's second largest city. According to a six-page note prepared by India's foreign ministry, "The bomber force aboard the *Enterprise* had the US President's authority to undertake bombing of the Indian Army's communications, if necessary."

China in the Box: Despite Kissinger's goading and desperate Pakistani calls for help, the Chinese did nothing. US diplomatic documents reveal that Indira knew the Soviets had factored in the possibility of Chinese intervention. According to a cable referring to an Indian cabinet meeting held on December 10, "If the Chinese were to become directly involved in the conflict, Indira said, the Chinese know that the Soviet Union would act in the Sinkiang region. Soviet air support may be made available to India at that time." Interestingly, while the cable is declassified, the source and extensive details of the Indian PM's briefing remain classified. "He is a reliable source" is all that the document says. There was very clearly our cabinet level mole the Americans were getting their information from. [Cold be Jagjivan Ram, YB Chavan or somebody else!]

Cold Warriors: Another telephonic conversation between the scheming American duo reveals a lot about the mindset of those at the highest echelons of American decision making:

Kissinger: And the point you made yesterday is we must continue to squeeze the Indians even when this thing is settled.

Nixon: We've got to go for rehabilitation. I mean, Jesus Christ, they've bombed - I want all the war damage; I want to help Pakistan on the war damage in Karachi and other areas, see?

Kissinger: Yeah.

Nixon: I don't want the Indians to be happy. I want a public relations program to piss on them.

Kissinger: Yeah.

Nixon: I want to piss on them for their responsibility. Get a White paper out. Put down, White paper. White paper. Understand that?

Kissinger: Oh, yeah.

Nixon: I don't mean for just your reading. But a White paper on this.

Kissinger: No, no, I know.

Nixon: I want the Indians blamed for this; you know what I mean? We can't let these goddamn, sanctimonious Indians get away with this. They've pissed on us on Vietnam for 5 years, Henry.

Kissinger: Yeah.

Nixon: Aren't the Indians killing a lot of these people?

Kissinger: Well, we don't know the facts yet. But I'm sure they're not as stupid as the West Pakistanis - they don't let the press in. But the idiot Pakistanis have the press all over their place!"

PM Indira perceived as a strong leader disappointed with Shimla Agreement. On 2nd July 2016, *Rediff.com News* published an eye-opening article: *'Secured in Dhaka but squandered in Shimla'*. "Indira, it appears, did not consult her Cabinet colleagues, or the diplomats, or the civil servants when she decided to sign the agreement at Shimla. We ruefully recall Bhutto's perfidy and the Indian PM's gullibility,' says Lt General Ashok Joshi (Retd.). The blitzkrieg by India that brought about the spectacular victory on 16th December 1971 was a rare event in post-Independence history. The military campaign lasting no more than 14 days produced decisive results on the battlefield. Such was the impact of the speed of operations that a stunned Pakistani military leadership surrendered to the numerically smaller Indian contingents at Dhaka. The surrender ceremony, which included a guard of honor to the winning commander, was promptly organized by the Pakistan military. Over 90,000 Pakistan POWs were in the bag. Indian military operations liberated the eastern wing of Pakistan from the brutal repression by the Pakistan army and assisted Bangladesh in securing freedom. The prestige of the Pakistan military was in the dumps. The undertaking of a military campaign by India to liberate the oppressed and persecuted Bengalis in the eastern wing of Pakistan had not been a facile decision on its part. The refugees started trickling into India from East Pakistan from end-March 1971. Soon, the trickle turned into raging torrents of hundreds of thousands, and eventually of millions. Several hundred thousand Bengalis had been massacred by the Pakistan army. No wonder that the dispossessed and the hunted turned to India for succor. Finding food, shelter and minimal medical help for this sea of humanity was a Herculean task for India, itself a developing nation. But it shared with the refugees the half loaf that it had."

The US, normally at the forefront of humanitarian causes, was preoccupied with building a friendly relationship with China. The move was based on enduring geopolitical factors that would confer major advantage on the US in the ongoing Cold War. The initiative had come at the highest level and President Nixon and Secretary of State Kissinger had decided to open this new front in the Cold War with Pakistan's assistance. This would have outflanked the Soviet Union. Pakistan military was active in helping the US establish a friendly relationship with China. Such was the obsession of the Nixon-Kissinger duo with their new Cold War maneuver that they had become unmindful of public opinion in the US. Their obligation to the Pakistan military made them turn a blind eye to the reign of terror unleashed by the Pakistan army. Many eyewitness accounts of Pakistan atrocities in the eastern wing appeared in the US media. The Blood Telegram tells the story of the duo's insensitivity in vivid detail. The US exerted considerable pressure on PM Indira to desist from any military action against Pakistan. Indira showed great fortitude and courage in withstanding this pressure. She entered in a 'Treaty of friendship and cooperation with the Soviet Union' in August 1971 and turned the tables on Pakistan. Her foresight paid rich dividends, and when the US decided to send the *USS Enterprise* into the Bay of Bengal with a view to browbeating India, Soviet submarines nullified the effect by trailing the task force. Indian military's swift and decisive operations left the US with no choice. The happy enmeshing of military and political objectives by India continued. It was a wise decision to commence the reinduction of the Indian armed forces from Bangladesh as early as March 2, 1972. This harmonized the national interests of India and Bangladesh. *The pursuit of political objectives by India after the military victory was not so sure footed. The Indian military had created a unique opportunity that was waiting to be exploited. The victory against Pakistan had been won at considerable human cost -- over 3,840 soldiers killed and about 2,500 wounded. The sad truth is that India failed to make use of the unique opportunity that was ripe for exploitation.* The very large number of Pakistan POWs in Indian custody yielded a great leverage to India and it would have been unwise not to utilize it and settle Kashmir imbroglio. It is true that India could not have retained the Pakistan prisoners indefinitely; it did not have to.

Some of the leverage could have been used up to get back Indians captured by Pakistan. This aspect had obviously not been thought out and there are reports even now that 54 Indian military men were left to rot in Pakistan jails. India had the choice of appointing a judicial commission with members from India and Bangladesh to record evidence to expose the role of senior Pakistan military officers in atrocities committed against the Bengalis. The guilty-mostly senior Pakistan army officers could have been detained but released a large majority of POWs.

The genocide in Bangladesh was the handiwork of the Pakistan generals who were racists to the core. They were waiting for an opportunity to sort out the contentious Bengalis who had the temerity to ask for greater share of power and resources. They had no time for the 'small and dark' people from the eastern wing, particularly so if they were Hindus. They decided to teach a lesson to the unruly in the East and eliminate the

Hindus. These aspects of the stark reality could have been culled from the available evidence which was waiting to be formally brought on record. This was a unique opportunity for India to place before the common man in the subcontinent, the problems created by Pakistan military leadership for the entire subcontinent, not excluding their own country. Unlike in most other countries where the armed forces are raised and maintained for protecting national interests and assets, *Pakistani military had appropriated a country for itself. It ruled out the possibility of peaceful coexistence with India and created a myth that hostility to India was a pre-condition for the very survival of Pakistan.*

Next, it tried to appropriate the leadership of the Islamic world by pretending that it is an extension of the Middle East into the subcontinent. Thus, it justified a fat military budget to an impoverished under-developed country. This was also an opportunity for India to persuade Pakistan to accept the ceasefire line (CFL) in J&K as the *de facto* international border or better still forget Pak claim on Kashmir. The Pakistan military has looked upon the CFL as eminently violable. Most of the wars between the countries can be traced to this conviction. Six months were to lapse before the talks to normalize the relationship between the two countries were held at Shimla in July 1972. Pakistani objective was clear and simple -- to take back the prisoners. India had been informed that Bhutto had vowed to sleep on the ground for so long as the Pakistan prisoners were in Indian custody. This dramatic gesture was principally aimed at the home constituency. The agreement that was on the anvil at Shimla reflected the fulfillment of all the requirements of Pakistan. *There was nothing in it for India except Pakistan promises of goodwill and good neighborliness.* It offered to allow India and Pakistan to retain the territory across the CFL that they had captured in December 1971. This conferred no advantage on either side. [Apparently the 'shrewd' Indira was fooled to the hint. A short real incident: Services of the most eminent Cardiologist from North India, Prof JN Berry's (of PGIMER Chandigarh) were sought for when Bhutto feigned a heart attack. My teacher ordered me to accompany him as a Resident. The 18-year old beautiful daughter Benazir was her father's side. Prof Berry, speaking chaste Punjabi exited her from medical examination of her father who was told in clear language that he must stop his drama. Bhutto fell on the feet of the Professor asking for help to salvage his prestige back home. Prof Berry told him to do the same on the feet of Indian PM advising him that his sincere begging may melt the shrewd lady's heart. That is what happened. *Indira acted in a highly stupid manner. She squandered every gain and turned a facile victory into stark defeat].*

On the other hand, Pakistan was to get back all the prisoners without any enforceable commitment on its part. Bhutto was unwilling to include in the agreement the one single Indian demand that the de facto CFL would be recognized by both countries as the international border. There were some internal contradictions too in the draft agreement as it was; What it said in the preamble that 'the two countries (would) put an end to the conflict and confrontation that have hitherto marred their relations' was negated in Paragraph 3 (ii) by saying that the agreement about the withdrawal of the troops across the new ceasefire line would be 'without prejudice to the recognized position of either side.'

This created room for Pakistan to air its unchanging argument that the Kashmir dispute was to be resolved by plebiscite, and further that Kashmir was a part of the unfinished agenda of Partition. This being the case, Indira was not willing to sign the agreement. The Shimla talks had virtually broken down. This meant that Bhutto would have had to return empty handed, without securing any agreement about the repatriation of Pakistan prisoners.

At this stage, Bhutto pleaded with Indira that he needed time to prepare Pakistan for acceptance of the CFL as the *de facto* international border although he had no reservations on that score. To achieve the common purpose, India should help Bhutto in building up his image in Pakistan. To this common end, he requested her to sign the agreement although the written word was at variance with his verbal assurance. *'Aap mujh pe bharosa kijiye* (Trust me)' and stupid Indira believed him. She decided to sign the agreement. This decision was taken at the eleventh hour when the talks had broken down and the bags had been packed.

In the early hours of the morning, some unpacking had to be done to get the agreement ready for signatures because by then even the typewriters and stamps had been packed. It is believed that, the stamp could not be found even after much searching, and the agreement does not bear the stamp impression. Bhutto had his way and except for a promise he conceded nothing.

India lost opportunities by signing the Shimla Agreement on July 2, 1972. On that day, India agreed to repatriate Pakistan POWs without any pre-condition or any written assurance from Pakistan. It is believed by some that the release of Pakistan prisoners was agreed to in return for the recognition of Bangladesh by Pakistan. If so, there is no such mention in the agreement. The recognition ultimately came about in 1974. The linkage between the release of prisoners and the recognition of Bangladesh by Pakistan is a highly tenuous proposition. It appears PM Indira did not consult her Cabinet colleagues or the diplomats or the civil servants when she decided to sign the agreement at Shimla. The question of consulting the military leadership just did not arise. General (later Field Marshal) Sam Manekshaw, the army chief, had certainly not been consulted. There may have been a reason for it. After the victory at Dhaka, his image had been built up by the media in the popular mind. This was clearly not acceptable to the political leadership or the bureaucracy. Possibly Bangladesh should also have been consulted before releasing the prisoners since the *Mukti Bahini* had played its part in bringing the Pakistan army to its knees.

Bhutto returned victorious. He set about training terrorists to operate in India and building Pakistan's nuclear bomb. Very little that is tangible is left of the talks at Shimla. We ruefully recall Bhutto's perfidy and the Indian prime minister's gullibility. It now seems that what was won at Dhaka was squandered away in Shimla. [Lieutenant General Ashok Joshi (Retd.)]

Forty-Five years after Shimla Agreement, on 11th May 2016, *Rediff. com News* published an article, *'India' out, 'South Asia' in. How academics ill serve US'*. "South Asian studies' academics in the US would do well to introspect how they wittingly or unwittingly become part of Pakistan's proxy war in wielding influence over academics and policy, says Sankrant Sanu. In the early 2000s, I tracked the activities of an organization called the *Kashmir American Council*, started by Ghulam Nabi Fai. KAC conferences regularly included prominent Indian Leftists in the US such as Angana Chatterjee who would excoriate India for 'human rights violations' in Kashmir. According to The Atlantic (external link), Chatterjee was among 20 special guests that Fai flew, all expenses paid, to a five-star conference in Uruguay about 'human rights' in Kashmir. Later Fai was exposed as being a front for Pakistan's spy agency and pleaded guilty (external link) to receiving millions of dollars of illicit ISI funding for his US lobbying efforts. While Chatterjee and others denied knowing about Fai's ISI links, the issues that the Fai episode raised go beyond that. Of concern remains the fact that the anti-India work of certain scholars neatly align with Pakistan's advocacy agenda whether direct funding from Pakistan was being received.

Another Indian origin 'radical' academic Kamala Visweswaran has been leading the fight to erase references to India (external link) and replace these with 'South Asia' from textbooks in California. How does this relate, if at all, to the issues raised by the Fai episode? For this, we must look at *two* aspects: *One*, at the goals of Pakistan's multimillion-dollar advocacy campaigns in the US, and *two*, how the work of some Indian Marxist academics in 'South Asian studies', whether by accident or by design, actively support those goals.

Unlike India, Pakistan is a client State heavily dependent on funding, particularly from the US, for its defense needs. It also is, as C Christine Fair points out, a revisionist State (external link), one that seeks to change the *status quo* in Kashmir. Being that, it is hampered in its goals by the fact that India is much bigger economically, militarily and geographically than Pakistan. Thus, it sees influencing government and academia in the US as critical to both a continuing flow of funds as well as leverage over India while such influence is of relatively lower importance for the India.

Practically, Pakistan's goals in influencing public opinions, particularly in think-tanks and academia include 1]. Continued hyphenation of the India-Pakistan relationship with Kashmir as the outstanding issue needing resolution; 2]. To project Indian Kashmir as 'occupied territory' and highlight 'human rights' issues there while keeping its occupation and abuses in Pakistan occupied Kashmir, Gilgit-Baltistan out of the discourse; 3]. Hurt India's soft power and rising economic power that it sees as a threat to its territorial ambitions; 4]. Keep the independence movement in Baluchistan and its widespread human rights abuses there out of view; 5]. Create a narrative of India as a source of terrorism to counter the well-documented reality of Pakistan's support for 'non-State' terrorist actors; and finally, 6]. Promote a 'there was no India' narrative to help in a goal to create a 'national history that seeks to claim Pakistan's pre-Islamic past to compete with India's historic antiquity' (Ayesha Jalal, *Conjuring Pakistan: History as Official Imagining*, International Journal of Middle East Studies, 27, (1995), 73 to 89, here (external link).

Given this, Visweswaran's work could be an example of the confluence of some South Asian academics' work and activism with the Pakistani establishment goals. This individual confluence may be coincidental. Our idea is not to single out Visweswaran as an individual but use her work as an illustration of a larger malaise, of the rot in 'South Asian' academics and throw light on other academic signatories of these petitions. Visweswaran is the queen of petitions, a *petitionista* par excellence. In February 2016, she petitioned for the erasure of references to India in California textbooks, to be replaced by 'South Asia.' Earlier, in 2015, she was part of the petition urging Silicon Valley companies to boycott PM Narendra Modi's visit and to not work with India (external link). She was part of earlier petitions to prevent Modi as Gujarat's chief minister to come to the US. Visweswaran has also been actively involved with FOIL (Forum of *Inquilabi* Leftists) and the related FOSA (Forum of South Asia), self-described 'radical activist' organizations whose members support various violent insurgencies in India, including those by ultra-left 'Maoists.'

Interestingly, the Fai-linked Angana Chatterjee has also been active in these two radical left organizations. It is not to mean that Visweswaran is funded by ISI nor are we even implying it. But we do point out that her positions have been consistently aligned with the goals of the Pakistan establishment. Her petitions against Silicon Valley's economic collaboration with India attack India's economic interests. Her California textbooks petition, for instance, reveals explicit awareness of the Pakistani agenda. The proposed edits suggest multiple insertions of the term 'Pakistan', and the agenda of replacing India with 'South Asia' is stated at the outset.

This is an ahistorical stance, since variations of the term 'India' have been vogue to refer to this region from before the time of the Greek traveler Megasthenes's work *Indica* in the 3rd and 4th centuries BC while both 'Pakistan' and 'South Asia' are 20th century creations with no historic precedence. If it is argued that the boundaries of modern India are somewhat reduced, it's worth a mention that the term 'India' also referred to present-day Bangladesh, but Visweswaran's recommendations do not include a single reference to that term.

The Mauryan empire, for instance, had its capital Pataliputra in modern-day Bihar and included most of present-day Bangladesh. Yet, even when referring to the Mauryan empire, Visweswaran does not bring up Bangladesh, keeping a persistent focus towards the inclusion of the term Pakistan. Visweswaran's proposed edits (external link) claim to be countering changes by imagined 'Hindu nationalists' in the US. Commenting on a previous set of changes, the document states: 'Indeed, apparently responding to pressure from Hindu nationalist and community organizations, several deleterious changes have been made... '

<u>What drives these changes</u>? To understand Visweswaran's motivations there are also possibilities of sympathies beyond links to Pakistan. For

instance, in a passage dealing with the most significant event in the US in the 21st century, the bombing of the World Trade Centre on September 11, 2001, Visweswaran recommends the following change: 'On p. 498 we recommend that the sentences, "Anti-Western violence perpetrated by the followers of a fundamentalist version of Islam has contributed to the appearance of deep conflict between the Islamic and Western worlds, especially since 9/11. Students should learn about the roots of modern Islamic extremism by reading a variety of sources from Egyptian writers and the Muslim Brotherhood," for example be changed to, "Anti-Western violence has contributed to the appearance of deep conflict between the West and other parts of the world. Students should learn about the roots of modern religious extremism by reading a variety of sources from Christian, Jewish, Islamic, Hindu and Buddhist nationalist texts."

So, 9/11 must be erased and the 'appearance of deep conflict between the Islamic and Western worlds' must somehow allude to 'Hindu and Buddhist Texts'. While Visweswaran repeatedly points out others' motivations in the proposed textbook edits, she appears completely oblivious to documented advocacy by the Pakistani establishment in the US. 'South Asian studies' academics would do well to introspect how they wittingly or unwittingly become part of Pakistan's proxy war in wielding influence over academics and policy in the United States." [Sankrant Sanu is a former Microsoft manager and an IITian. The views expressed are personal]

An internationally acclaimed author, Dr. Taslima Nasreen has written 40 books in Bengali, which includes poetry, essays, novels and autobiography series. Her works have been translated in 30 different languages. Some of her books are banned in Bangladesh. Because of her thoughts and ideas, she has been banned, blacklisted and banished from Bengal, both from Bangladesh and West Bengal part of India. She has been prevented by the authorities from returning to her country since 1994, and to West Bengal since 2007. She states candidly: "No individual or organization or state follow Islam as accurately as ISIS or Islamic State. Prophet Muhammad killed non-Muslim men and used their girls and women as sex slaves. ISIS guys did the same. They killed Yazidi men and held Yazidi girls and women as sex slaves. Islam always advise Muslims to do everything what Muhammad the prophet did. Even though Muslim men love the Prophet, it is extremely rare that they marry 13 times or marry a 6-year-old girl or their daughter in law. It is ISIS that shows the courage to behave like true Muslims and adapt the character of the prophet. The prophet loved swords or knives to kill people, IS does the same. The prophet treated women as sex slaves, ISIS does the same. The prophet occupied land by arms and violence, ISIS does the same. The prophet destroyed non-Muslims' temples and sculptures, IS does the same." "ISIS could not pose a real challenge to India despite its spreading tentacles among anti-Muslims. A report titled, *'ISIS's plan to terrorize India'*, by *Sumitha Narayanan Kutty* on behalf of *The National Interest* appeared in *Yahoo News* on 20th July 2016. "The attack in Dhaka earlier this month and the news of twenty-odd "missing" Indians who possibly joined Islamic State have sparked a vigorous discussion on India's preparedness to take on the threat posed by ISIS. These incidents have led to more questions than answers on the group's presence, appeal and capabilities in the Indian subcontinent. This piece is a preliminary attempt to engage with some critical questions that shape how Indian security and intelligence agencies assess and address this threat in the short-to-medium term. What place does India have in Islamic State's operational strategy? Where do competing regional organizations targeting India, like Al-Qaeda in Indian Subcontinent (AQIS) and L-e-T, lie in IS's universe of friends and foes? And how significant are the linkages between IS and India's most important homegrown terror outfit, the Indian Mujahideen (IM), today? In 2017, ISIS was thrown out of its capital Raqqa by Syrian army. Then other places were liberated. Even in Iraq ISIS lost Mosul it occupied in 2014 and practically lost all territories. It exists now in cyberspace, making efforts to recruit some Sunni Muslim Jihadists. On 27th August 2018, The Wall Street Journal gave an apt and topical headline on p. A9: 'Battered on Battlefield, ISIS Alive Online'. Under Virtual World, Real extremists, the paper gave a distribution of the internet reach of ISIS within the same news item. Number of Users, by region; Africa 206, Southeast Asia 180, Iraq and Syria 159, South Asia 106, Middle East 66, Central and South America 48, Europe 46, Turkey 24, North America 23, East and Central Asia 9, Australia 1, Unknown 131.

'*Go Big but Stay Home*': With the group taking heavy losses in its own territories in Iraq and Syria, its spokesperson Abu Muhammad al-Adnani's message in May encouraged "lone wolves" to pursue targets within their home countries. The call was not for all believers to head over to the expanding "*khilafah*" (caliphate) as per usual but urge them to prove their allegiance by staying exactly where they were and inflict pain locally. The spate of attacks since June, namely in Istanbul, Dhaka and Medina, are in sync with this shift in narrative. As Islamic State gets more and more desperate, we will see more such attacks.

Is India ready to manage this shift? The approach now greatly depends on (1) our understanding of IS's operational strategy for India, (2) whether L-e-T and AQIS are competitors or collaborators with Islamic State, and (3) in what ways India's most active, indigenous terror group—the IM—is contributing to Islamic State's agenda.

India in ISIS's Operations Manual: At the global level, IS's message concerning India focuses on Kashmir. Probing deeper by examining the recruitment video targeting India and interviews with its regional leaders in its mouthpiece Dabiq, ISIS makes threats against Indian PM Modi, and declarations to avenge atrocities against Muslims in Mumbai, Gujarat and Assam, along with highlighting the group's all-encompassing hatred for the "cow-worshipping, pagan" Hindus.

As a territorial entity, Islamic State organizes its domain under "*wilayat*" or administrative divisions. So far, the group has declared one such division in the Indian subcontinent—Wilayat Khurasan, consisting of Afghanistan and Pakistan. Apart from this provincial unit, the group's magazine Dabiq regularly features operations and fighters from a second area, simply termed Bengal (i.e., Bangladesh) often branded "the Khilafah's soldiers in Bengal." There is no specific mention of a separate administrative unit or chieftain operating from within India.

Thus, in ISIS's scheme of things, India lies vulnerably sandwiched between Wilayat Khurasan in the west and Bengal's fighters in the east. Such a scenario facilitates guerilla attacks inside India from both sides. In an interview to Dabiq in April, the "*Amir*" (chief) of the Bengal faction laid out his two-step strategy for India. The first stage would require both Wilayat Khurasan and the fighters in Bengal to create "a condition of *tawahhush* [fear and chaos]" with the help of "existing local mujahidin." The second stage would involve gaining territorial control of India, but only after "first getting rid of the 'Pakistani' and 'Afghani' regimes" to exploit their conventional capabilities. Now, the second and final phase seems a very, very tall order. However, the first one—colluding with local elements to create chaos—is quietly underway. Before exploring these indigenous elements, it will prove useful to study Islamic State's attitude towards two major South Asian terrorist groups that target India: L-e-T and AQIS.

Contempt for AQIS and L-e-T: It is well-established that there is no love lost between Islamic State and Al Qaeda. Its leader Ayman al-Zawahiri is firmly branded "a leader with no real authority" in the pages of Dabiq. As one expert recently commented, Islamic State's "special ire for Muslims" is what sets it starkly apart from its competition. Ironically, its closest competitor shares this sentiment. A senior AQ operative in an interview to the AQIS magazine Resurgence (summer 2015 edition) slammed Islamic State for "being built on falsehood . . . working for its own interests at the expense of the greater interest of the Ummah."

The subcontinental manifestation of AQIS is also viewed by Islamic State as colluding with Pakistan. As seen in Dabiq: "In India, they [AQ] are the allies of the nationalist Kashmir factions whose advances and withdrawals are only by the order of the apostate Pakistani army." It is also important to note that unlike L-e-T, AQIS has yet to prove itself a credible threat in India. Hence, unlike in the Middle East or Afghanistan, plans to manipulate the rivalry between ISIS and AQ is not an idea worth investing in just yet. When it comes to L-e-T, ISIS also demonstrates strong contempt for the group and its handlers, Pakistani army and its ISI. In an interview with Dabiq, the chief of Wilayat Khurasan minces no words in criticizing the "apostate factions and agents" of Pakistan. Mentioning L-e-T by name, he then shares his disapproval of how the group's members "proceed in accordance with the orders of the Pakistani intelligence." The Kashmir-focused group's lack of control over any territory is also viewed as a huge negative by Islamic State. It would be worth examining how and, more significantly, where this rivalry between ISIS and L-e-T could play out. Some discussions predict its likelihood in parts of eastern Afghanistan.

An ISIS Feeder Group: Indian Mujahideen–Linked Faction. Returning our attention to the indigenous terrorist elements most active within India, IM has topped this list ever since its rise to notoriety in 2008 with a slew of strikes across the country. The trajectory of this local entity, it now seems, is directly linked to the future of Islamic State in India. IM is proving to be a successful feeder for Islamic State. More specifically, a certain splinter group of the organization: Ansar ut-Tawhid fi Bilad al-Hind (Supporters of Monotheism in the Land of India), or AuT.

This faction broke away from IM due to its growing frustration with its bosses (the Bhatkal brothers, Riyaz and Yasin) and their Pakistani handlers in the ISI. Eager to gain combat experience, its members left Pakistan for Afghanistan, ultimately reaching Islamic State. Their story was confirmed by one of the Indian fighters featured in the propaganda video. The leader of the group, Shafi Armar (alias Yusuf al-Hindi), was based within Islamic

State and, until his alleged death by a U.S. airstrike in April, led not only the recruitment of Indian fighters but also directed attacks within India through local modules. This second stream of local operatives organized themselves as Junud-ul-Khalifa-e-Hind (Soldiers of the Indian Caliphate), or JKH. This group was set up under Armar's orders once it became increasingly difficult for large groups of Indian fighters to travel to Iraq and Syria unidentified. Mapping this local landscape leaves us with a few questions. For instance, who are the key figures guiding Indian recruits since Armar's alleged death in April? Secondly, how complete was AuT's falling-out with the Pakistani intelligence service? Would an "alliance of convenience" still prove useful to the India-based JKH?

The Threat Is Local. Now, the counter-war in India must be prioritized against IS-the ideology, rather than IS-the territorial entity. This demands a quick shift in the strategies already employed by security agencies in Indian states as well as the central government. The principal focus should revolve less around the few "misguided" citizens who primarily engage online and proceed to the Middle East, and more strongly around the Indian operatives who choose to hang behind, using existing virtual and offline networks to create chaos in the homeland.

A secondary focus should remain on intercepting those returning from the "Khilafah," better trained to orchestrate an attack inside India. In the sole propaganda video that Islamic State has released targeting India, one of the six featured jihadists vowed to return to avenge atrocities committed against Muslims. As IS loses territory in Iraq and Syria, desperate fighters returning home to continue the struggle is a very real possibility.

In time, this would also indicate a change in the dominant profile of the average ISIS recruit inside India—not the youngster plotting to head abroad, inspired by the caliphate's way of life, but the one who is willing to do the groundwork and the heavy lifting to execute its ideology within India. This recruit is willing to patiently organize, plan and execute targeted strikes with a resolve more tenacious than the former. And these ISIS-inspired recruits continue to rely on local networks to survey targets and access weaponry and explosives. The focus very much remains on disrupting these networks while probing and mending grievances at home.

It is thus essential that we should not be swayed by Islamic State's penchant for the spectacular and its seemingly unstoppable global rhetoric. The threat in India remains very much local, and its networks familiar." [Sumitha Narayanan Kutty is an Associate Research Fellow with the South

Asia Program at the S. Rajaratnam School of International Studies (RSIS), Singapore]

An interesting development took place as a preparation to Indian PM's scheduled US visit. When the US officially announced that PM Modi would meet President Obama at the White house on 7th June to review bilateral progress in defense, security and energy, US lawmakers on 19th May approved amendments to a defense bill seeking to bring India on par with its NATO allies for sale of defense equipment and technology transfer, reported Chidanand Rajghatta. The move comes even as the lawmakers voted to increase curbs on military assistance for Pakistan, including blocking $450 million in aid, unless certain conditions are met. *They moved to codify US's 'Asia pivot', a strategy that includes strengthening New Delhi's military muscle, by easing terms for sale of defense equipment & technology transfer, implicitly aimed at countering China's expansionism.*

On 17th June 2016, *Rediff.com News* reported, '*India has many countries seeking defense equipment: minister.* "The matured indigenous military technology of India has drawn the global attention with Countries from both East and West seeking to import military equipment, Defense Minister Manohar Parrikar today said. Speaking to reporters after the inaugural fight of India-made HTT-40 trainer aircraft at HAL airport here, he, however, said: "The country was bound by its own norms and the international understanding on defense exports that will be based on exchange only with 'legitimate and permitted countries' as per international convention. Our Act-East policy has seen many countries on this side of the world show interest in varying degrees to purchase our missiles and other (defense) equipment. But we also see interest from the Westside also. They (countries to the West of India) have also shown interest for buying military equipment including missiles from India. I cannot disclose the details for strategic reasons." Citing example rising military related exports Mr. Parrikar said: "Vietnam government had issued an order to private sector L&T to import offshore patrol vessels worth USD 100 million. Our military exports have improved. The near-term goal is to double it to two billion dollars." The minister, however, stressed, "The Indian government will act in most responsible manner while exporting military hardware. It will be to legitimate and permitted countries under various international laws. India is in final stages to forge agreements to develop technology within to manufacture aircraft carriers. But, transfer of technologies by the partner countries is not to the expected level and manufacture of engine for the aircraft carrier is still not worked out."

Our history is witness to the existence of ignominious and unfortunate problem that every person living on the subcontinent always has/had his/her price and is, was and perhaps will be available for sale. It is disgusting to know that there was mole(s) in PM Indira's cabinet from the late 1960s onwards as disclosed in a write-up titled, *'India Could Have Split West Pakistan in 1971'*, by Anuj Dhar on 17th December 2016: "Declassified US records show that India's objectives during the 1971 Indo-Pak war were greatly curtailed following an instance of high treason committed by a member of Indira's government. Exactly 45 years ago, Pakistani Lt Gen AAK Niazi surrendered to Lt Gen JS Aurora of the Indian Army and the *Mukti Bahini* in what was then East Pakistan. But did you know that India's war objectives in 1971 were greatly curtailed following an instance of high treason committed by a member of Indira Gandhi's government? This person, whose identity is most likely known to our government, betrayed India's "war objectives" to the Central Intelligence Agency in December 1971, prompting the US to arm-twist India into ending the war much sooner than it would have if there was no such betrayal. In other words, the *Vijay Diwas* (Victory Day) marking the victory in East Pakistan was never meant to fall on 16th December.

In the run-up to the 1971 India-Pakistan war, *The New York Times* first hinted at the presence of a CIA agent in the Indian government. By December that year, *The Washington Post* had reported that US President Richard Nixon's south Asia policy was being guided by "reports from a source close to Mrs. Gandhi". Records declassified a few years ago show that a dramatic turnaround came on 6th December when a CIA operative leaked out India's "war objectives" to the agency. Then PM Indira had informed her top ministers in a meeting that, apart from liberating Bangladesh, India intended to take over a strategically important part of Pakistan-occupied Jammu Kashmir (PoJK) and go for total annihilation of Pakistan's armed forces so that Pakistan "never attempts to challenge India in the future".

When he came to know of the CIA report, a furious Nixon blurted out that "this woman (Indira Gandhi) suckered us", for he was under the impression that in their last interaction at Washington, Mrs. Gandhi had promised him that India wouldn't attack East Pakistan—not to speak of targeting West Pakistan and PoJK. The CIA went on to assess that fulfillment of India's "war objectives" might lead to "the emergence of centrifugal forces which could shatter West Pakistan into as many as three or four separate countries".

As a direct result of the operative's information, the Nixon administration went on an overdrive to save West Pakistan from a massive Indian assault. Records very clearly demonstrate that Nixon then threatened the USSR with a "major confrontation", should the Soviets fail to stop the Indians from penetrating West Pakistan. Kissinger secretly met China's Permanent Representative at the UN to apprise him of the CIA operative's report and rub it in that India's plan for Pakistan with Soviet backing could turn out to be a "dress rehearsal" of what they might do to China.

All this led to the USSR's first Deputy Foreign Minister Vasily Kuznetsov visiting New Delhi and telling India "to confine their objectives to East Pakistan" and "not to try and take any part of West Pakistan, including Azad Kashmir, as Moscow was concerned about the possibility of a great power confrontation over the subcontinent". Kuznetsov also extracted a guarantee from PM Indira that India would not attack West Pakistan. This decision was promptly conveyed to Nixon.

On 16th December 1971 when Nixon was told that India had declared a ceasefire, he exulted: "We have made it…it's the Russians working for us." Secretary of State Henry Kissinger congratulated him for saving West Pakistan—India's primary target, as per the operative's report to the CIA. In subsequent years, it was disclosed that former PM Morarji Desai, and two deputy PMs—Jagjivan Ram and YB Chavan — were alleged to be the CIA Operatives active during the 1971 war. However, all such charges lacked substantiation; there was no confirmation whether such an operative ever existed. As such, no constructive discussion on the issue ever took off. This changed after the release of unassailable US records making it clear that the CIA had a "reliable" source (pimp) operating from inside the Indian cabinet in 1971.

In declassified records, the name of the operative has been censored because the CIA Director has "statutory obligations to protect from disclosure (the agency's) intelligence sources". Naming the operative even after so many years will obviously adversely impact the Indo-US relations and hit the agency's prospects of recruiting new informants.

The question now arises: Does India know who that traitor was that leaked out 1971 war plan? Former joint director of the Intelligence Bureau Late Malloy Krishna Dhar, no relation of this writer, told me yes. However, my efforts to get that name officially out failed. In 2010, I asked the PMO whether the office had received inputs from the R&AW about the identity of the minister who was said to have leaked information to the CIA during the 1971 war. I was informed that the inputs from R&AW were exempt from disclosure under the RTI Act. To me, it would mean that somewhere in the R&AW archives are lying details of the Indian version of *Tinker Tailor Soldier Spy*. And ours was for real."

Historians purchased by the unholy Congress party, in their strong biases and prejudices and the moneys they got, aided abetted and supported by Leftists, distorted the modern history for personal benefits tried their best '*to make this party that did practically nothing towards the independence of India*' into the only player to have won freedom by Gandhi's *ahimsa* (non-violence). That is too far from the truth. It was the consistent relentless pressure exerted by young unselfish revolutionaries, culminated by the revolt of army men to form *Netaji's* INA who fought the British in the north-east and the March 1946 revolt by 30,000 Indian sailors at Bombay and Vishakhapatnam – a fact admitted in the British parliament by PM Clement Attlee – that proved to be the last nail in the coffin of British Raj. Plainly stated, its stupid stooge Nehru played into their hands from whom we had snatched our freedom with great sacrifices spanning over nine decades from the 'First War of Independence'. *The credit of winning freedom goes to the one and only Netaji Subhas Chandra Bose*, the greatest leader of 20th century and the only one to fight the British on the battlefront. Netaji towered over the pygmies who clandestinely ruled over the masses and the country. Bose was far more popular than Gandhi and Nehru, the two paid British agents of the Crown and slaves of the Raj, put together! The duo continued to spy over Netaji till they were dead in 1948 and 1964 respectively, Of course, approximately.732,000 brave Hindustanis sacrificed themselves in the prime of their lives if we start from those martyred in the '*First War of Independence*' in 1857-58. Or even earlier, the Maratha uprising against the British in 1812. Congress's undeserved self-aggrandizement relegated our freedom fighters (young revolutionaries within/outside the subcontinent) whose efforts led to throwing the British out and steer the subcontinent clear of the yoke of slavery, to the back pages of history or at best mostly and preferably ignored them. "*The most important catalyst that made the British quit India was the threat of violence, i.e. 'forceful Himsa' (Violence) and NOT the Gandhian benign or innocuous 'Ahimsa' (non-violence)*," opined Swaminathan Aiyar. Rightly so, Congress had lost steam and was in shambles. It needs to be understood that the failed and *aborted 'Quit India'* movement, planned by Gandhi at Wardha, led to widespread violence (*Hamas*) and destruction. Before it started, Gandhi and his *chamchas* (members of AICC and prominent followers), as all the important functionaries of Congress were imprisoned. *Netaji* wrote to Gandhi in end-December 1939, *"It is high time the Congress does something for the freedom of India."*

The Congress movement, if at all there was one, had petered out five years before the British left the Indian shores. The whole leadership including the dictator Gandhi were in jail and out of limelight. The so-called 'Quit India' movement was crushed with a heavy hand. Raj brought in white soldiers from Britain, Canada and New Zealand. <u>Then what suddenly compelled the British to move out</u>? Sir Clement Attlee, during his visit to Calcutta in 1949, was asked by the former CJ Calcutta HC, PB Chakraborty the reasons prompting his Government to grant independence to India. *Attlee admitted that the most important reason was the erosion of loyalty to the Crown among personnel of Indian Army and Navy because of the glory of military activism preached by Netaji Subhas Chandra Bose.* Upon being *questioned about the effect, if any of the agitation led by Gandhi on the decision of the British to quit India, Sir Atlee's reply in a wry tone was that it was 'minimal', if at all.* There have been numerous revolutionaries right from the days of *'Gadr Party'* on the west coast of America and Canada in 1890 who contributed their might in their own ways. The lives of many were cut short by the Raj. There were some who survived British onslaught, one of them being VD Savarkar *aka Swatantryaveer* Savarkar was a man of enlightenment with a modern bent of mind who recognized the positive spin offs, the benefits to humanity in the advancement of the knowledge base of mankind while valuing the heritage bequeathed to us by ancestors. He said, *"I dislike any restrictions on the innovative spirit of the human mind. That is because modern progress and modern culture have emerged out of innovation. The very essence of the progress made by humanity over the past many years in science and knowledge can be found in contemporary cinema. There is no better example of the use of modern technology than the movies, and that is why I will never back any restrictions on them."* His prescience was truly remarkable, *"I doubt the theatre can compete with the movies. It will barely survive in a corner just as the folk arts barely survive in our villages today. But its best days are behind it."*

Look what the classically double-faced Gandhi said on Veer Savarkar way back in 1921, *"He is clever. He is brave. The evil, in its hidden form of the present system of Government, he saw much earlier than I did. He is in the Andaman for having loved India too well. Under a just government, he would be occupying a high post."* Was the Nehru Government just? Then, why did his untruthful protégé and crook Nehru try to falsely implicate *Veer* Savarkar in Gandhi murder case? The Punjab High Court rebutted megalomaniac Nehru; acquitting Savarkar of the false charges. Today, the *fake* Gandhis – Sonia and Rahul, sparsely educated foreigners of Italian descent not conversant with Indian history – are insulting *Veer* Savarkar, one of the greatest freedom fighters who had many useful contributions while working in Britain and India – the most significant was his efforts on recruitment of Hindus into the British Indian Army that reduced the percentage of Muslims in the army from 70 at the beginning of WWII to 30 at the end! *One can conclude that the Congress cornered glory at the cost of revolutionaries but dropped them like hot potatoes.* For Congress, there were only two leaders: pro-Muslim Gandhi and his protégé 'Muslim' Nehru and hence their anti-Hindu (and anti-Sikh policy) and tirade. Obviously, there was a non-publicized secret agreement between the two crooks to make the latter as the first post-independence prime minister come what may. Gandhi and Nehru went to the farthest extreme and Partitioned the subcontinent. This was avoidable. Jinnah could have been Governor General and Nehru PM!

<u>Our glorious history has been neutralized.</u> An outstanding Emperor Asoka of ancient India was the most illustrious and most compassionate ruler. Historians all over the world prefix 'Great' before his name. He had many *firsts* to his name: His sign *'Asoka Wheel'* adorns the center of our national flag; Indian government is run with his symbol *'Four-faced lion'*; Greatest peace-time bravery award is named *'Ashok Chakra'*; He ruled over the biggest empire ever, *'Akhand Bharat'* (Unbroken India) that includes present day Bangladesh, Nepal, India, Pakistan and Afghanistan and nobody before or after him could emulate him; During his tenure, intellectuals of highest character lived in India and historians all over world call it the 'Golden Period', and India was a world leader, a 'Golden Sparrow' and its public was prosperous and united with no fissures or differences among them; His ministers worked for the benefit of mankind and even the animals as killing of animals was banned; and so on. It is tragic that birth anniversary of the greatest ever Indian Emperor in neither known nor celebrated whereas the country observes unnecessary national holidays for the birth of pygmies. *Isn't it a matter shame that my compatriots*

don't know the true history behind attaining independence from Britain nor do they want to learn the real stuff? The tragedy is they don't observe a holiday to celebrate the Birth Anniversary of this greatest Monarch Asoka when there are plenty of holidays earmarked for all and sundry whose contribution was NOT that significant!

In our local parleys why do we use a phrase: *'Jo Jeeta wohi Sikandar'* (Winner is Alexander)? Why it is not *'Jo Jeeta wohi Chandragupta'* (Winner is Chandragupta)? The fact is Alexander could not cross the Jhelum, was defeated for the first time in his life by Porus that made him retreat along with his army to his capital, Babylon where he died on his bed in his palace at the young age of 33 years – the mental shock of his first ever defeat could have been a possible factor. After his death, his general, Selucus took over and ventured an attack once again on Hindustan. He was so handsomely defeated that besides gifting war material, he had to offer the hand of his daughter to Chandragupta Maurya, the Indian Emperor and the grandfather of Emperor Asoka.

Why alien Mughal King of Delhi, Akbar is Great and NOT our own Maharana Pratap, King of Mewar? After Akbar manipulated a division among Rajput kings and took *Raja* Maan Singh's help in defeating Pratap in the Haldighati battle, Pratap reassembled his Rajput army, took back practically the whole of his land from Akbar. Then why have we forgotten the great warrior *Maharana* Pratap who in several battles brought to knees mighty Akbar's armies? On the other hand, we are eulogizing the communal Akbar who had kept nearly 5,000 Hindu women in his harem and who had debarred the marriage of his own sisters and daughters. Akbar changed the name of famous city of Prayag into Allahabad that the present Government must rectify along with many other such anomalies!

Famous Rajput King, Sawai Jai Singh was the architect of great buildings including Agra's famous *Tejo Mahalaya* falsely renamed Taj Mahal, and the Red Fort in Agra and Hawa Mahal in Jaipur. Why another alien Mughal king, Shah Jehan is 'credited' with the construction of Taj Mahal, the 7th man-made wonder which had existed many centuries before Shah Jehan lived? History tells us a lot about Hindu genocide and other atrocities by the Muslim rulers of Delhi including the Mughals from Babar down to Aurangzeb killing/enslaving maybe 100 million Hindu men and raping millions of young Hindu women! They desecrated and destroyed hundreds of thousands of Hindu temples including the most important ones at Ayodhya (Rama's), Kashi now known as Varanasi

(Shiva's) and Vrindavan also called Mathura (Krishana's); defiled hundreds of thousands of Hindu women; and converted innumerable numbers of Hindus into Islam. The Mughals also tortured and killed the Sikh Gurus Arjun Dev and Teg Bahadur and the four sons of the last Guru Gobind Singh including two of his very young sons around whom wall was erected thus suffocating them to death! As a Punjabi, I am aware of the other stories of hurling untold miseries and atrocities on the warrior clan of the Sikhs in the Punjab.

The bravery of Marathas, King Shivaji and Peshwas especially Bajirao II have been conveniently forgotten under the hidden agenda of the pro-Muslim and anti-Hindu (and anti-Sikh) Congress but the wicked and terrorist King Aurangzeb, who mercilessly killed his scholar and brave older brother and heir to the throne Dara Shikoh who translated the Upanishads and other Hindu scriptures from Sanskrit to Persian as well as kept his father King Shahjehan along with his older sister seven years in prison till he died, is remembered. We witnessed too much of arrogance, fuss and unnecessary resistance from Indian Muslims as well as our pseudo-intellectuals, *'sickular'* Congressmen/women and our anti-national media personalities when the name of Aurangzeb Road in New Delhi was changed in the name of the illustrious former President of India, APJ Abdul Kalam-another Muslim. *Are these Muslims faithful to India?* Can they be called patriots? *Are the Indian Muslim descendants of the Mughal?* No, the fact is 99% are converts from Hinduism. Saudi Arabian intellectual Muhammed al-Arifi said, *"Only Arab Muslims are the real ones, rest are all converted from other religions and are considered inferior (to the Arabs)."*

We have been made to forget and ignore great statesmen like *Acharya* Chanakya and great reformers like Swami Vivekananda and made to remember the anti-Hindu (and anti-Sikh) third-rate pygmies who enjoyed their lives and wrote books in British prisons including undeserving men like Nehru are praised to the hilt and his benefactor Gandhi labelled Mahatma, (wrongly) bestowed upon by *Gurudeva* Tagore and 'Father of Nation' by Nehru who also forbade the study of Bhagwadgita-one of the greatest books on philosophy of life but allowed the study of Quran and Bible in Muslim and Christian schools respectively! Why Nehru, on attaining Dominion status within the British Empire, was made *the undeserving* first PM over duly democratically elected real statesman and much senior Patel? These are some of the ironies and misdeeds of our Congress leaders who established a dynastic rule in a democracy! Besides all their wrongdoing to their motherland and the citizenry of Hindustan, the falsification of the true account of freedom struggle need to be rectified. History must be examined, reexamined again and again if we want to know our true worth to make us proud of our motherland and if we want to progress. Congress, being an organization set up by a Scotsman with the express sanction by the Viceroy Lord Dufferin with a Christian first President had to be always subservient to the British Raj and to be ever slave to the white skin – the last-named trait has not been abandoned even today. A white Italian lady is owning the defunct party in the capacity of a 'Life President' and who is 'blind' like Dhritrashtra of Mahabharata trying her best to make her unworthy 48-year old son to ascend the 'ancestral throne'! *Unless our youth constituting 65% of our population are made aware of their culture, civilization, roots and the past, they will never understand our greatness and work for making their country into a duly deserved 'Great Nation'.* Granted the current generation of India's students and youth are not as fortunate as their counterparts in the decades of the not so distant past. During the 1920s they had Bhagat Singh (1908-1931) and Chandrashekhar (1908-1931); during the 1930-1940s they had Bose (1897-?) and Patel; (1875-1950) and after Independence, during the 1960s and 1970s, they had Ram Manohar Lohia (1910-1967) and Jayaprakash Narayan (1902-1979). Lohia fought Nehru's autocracy, ambiguity and bigotry. JP and JB Kripalani fought Indira's dictatorship and notorious Emergency imposed on June 26, 1975.

What about today? *Rediff.com News* brought out, '*What draws today's young men to the Ayodhya campaign?*' by Ritwik Sharma. "More than 25 years after the Babri Masjid was destroyed, another generation proclaims its commitment to building a Ram temple. A saffron-robed crowd begins to disperse at the end of a two-day meeting of Hindu religious leaders at the swanky Talkatora Stadium, a facility named after a Mughal-era garden in the heart of Delhi. The conclave on November 3 and 4 threw the might of sadhus behind the BJP government and called for an ordinance to compel the building of a Rama temple in Ayodhya, Uttar Pradesh. I spent two days at the event trying to find answers to some questions:

What does Ayodhya mean for young RSS members who grew up in a liberalized economy after the demolition of the Babri Masjid nearly 26 years ago? What is it about Hindutva that brings young men -- I can spot virtually no women here other than the odd sadhvi on the dais -- to events such as these?

What is it about their life experiences that draw them to this 'movement'? I sit back in my chair to listen to Ashok Kumar. If the sadhus earn Kumar's disapproval for failing to detach themselves from material possessions in the manner appropriate to the ascetic, a man called Ravi Prakash wins his admiration. Kumar considers Prakash his mentor. Ravi Prakash is the founder of a voluntary organization called the Samarpan Foundation Trust which has been providing free medical treatment to leprosy patients for a decade at Tahirpur in Delhi's Dilshad Garden. Ashok Kumar, a final-year student of nursing at a college in Partappur near Meerut, is one of the children of patients from the cluster of leprosy colonies in the area. His father, a leprosy patient who volunteered at the Tahirpur trust, died in a road accident in 2012. His mother, a heart patient, stays home, while his younger brother studies at a higher secondary school in Kaithal, Haryana. "He has been serving people for so long, but he still hasn't bought a car. He says, 'If I take a car, it will deprive a child's fees'," Kumar says of Prakash, who has served as an RSS Zilla Pracharak (full-time district-level worker) in parts of eastern UP and Uttarakhand. Kumar rides about 40 km on his bike to college every day. In his batch, he says, there are nearly 30 children of leprosy patients whose education is being funded by the trust. He leaves by 7 in the morning, attends classes and rides home by 3.30 pm. From 4 to 7 pm, he works as part of the trust's management. Nearly 150 patients, mainly from the leprosy colonies, visit the centre every day where four volunteers and a doctor dress their wounds and administer medicines. "The government has done nothing for the patients," he says, showing me photos of patients on his iPhone 6S to suggest how negligence for even a couple of days can result in maggot-infested limbs. Kumar, who belongs to the sizeable Dalit sub-caste of Pasi, says he didn't face casteism. At the trust-run hostel where he studied, children perform a morning *havan* (sacred fire ritual) and read the Bhagavad Gita in the evenings. We didn't feel we were from the scheduled castes as we participated in cultural events." He feels obligated to continue at the medical centre in Tahirpur. He loves to play cricket but spends more time listening to singers Arijit Singh and Atif Aslam on Coke Studio by logging on to the Wynk music app on his iPhone. The crime saga Gangs of Wasseypur is his favorite film, as is one of its actors, Nawazuddin Siddiqui, whose rags-to-riches story inspires him. Dressed in a checked shirt, jeans and shoes with red threads tied to his wrist like an amulet and an orange sash with 'United Hindu Front' printed in black around his neck, Kumar is conspicuous in his role of karyakarta (worker) at the conclave. He was among those tasked with registering the thousands of participants and recording their personal details "so that when the mandir is made, we can summon them if required". We have interacted for several hours, and by now I understand that I am not going to be given easy answers to the questions I set out with. Kumar's life has been complicated, and so are his politics. He has been made the head of a BJP unit at his colony but is at the conclave in the capacity of a volunteer of an NGO called Mission Modi Again PM, which "conveys the prime minister's welfare schemes to people at the grassroots". He stresses, "Modiji alone is working. In his speeches, he can talk for hours at a stretch, which is also hard work. I don't support those under him." To iterate that political support can't be blind, he explains that corrupt practices of leaders at the municipality denied his father, a sweeper, a permanent position. "No wonder now both the ward councilor and the legislator in our constituency are from the Aam Aadmi Party." Kumar plays multiple, overlapping, even confusing roles. Not unlike the mingling of disparate elements at the conclave, where the Akhil Bhartiya Sant Samiti -- an umbrella body of priests, gurus and monks -- occupied centre stage. And although the Samiti's resolution put pressure on the Centre to push for the construction of the temple -- and even pitched for re-election of the Narendra Modi government. Not all the clergy's voices were political or partisan.

On day one of the meet, former BJP MP and *Ram Janambhoomi Nyas* member Ram Vilas Vedanti caused a stir when he suggested a mosque could be built in Lucknow if the temple was constructed in Ayodhya. His remarks were met with indignant retorts from the dais. But back to my new-found friend, Kumar confesses to have never understood the long-pending Babri Masjid-Ram Janmabhoomi dispute but recognizes that it's a perennial election-time issue. "There's a Constitution, the court and an administration. If something is done by force, people from other communities won't stay quiet. Putting pressure here won't make a difference," he says. He admits to a growing tension in the run-up to elections in a few states and to the Lok Sabha. "Agar Baat community pe aa jati hai, hamein toh Hindu ke saath hi khada hona padega, ya toh danda leke ya shaant hoke (If it comes down to a question of faith, I have to stand with Hindus, whether with a stick in hand or quietly)."

Chandrakant Bairagi, 25, and Raj Kumar, 26, from Mandla and Jabalpur, respectively, in Madhya Pradesh, have recently moved to the national capital and are staying at the quarters of Faggan Singh Kulaste, the BJP MP from their constituency. The civil engineers are enrolled at a coaching institute in Delhi's Mukherjee Nagar to prepare for recruitment exams for the posts of assistant and junior engineers. Both claimed to be *Kabirpanthi*, members of a religious community that follows the teachings of Kabir. They are disciples of Mahant Mohan Das, a *Kabirpanthi* guru who works for the poor and is also an Ayurvedic doctor. I glean two interesting facts from them: That their mahant is linked to the RSS and its affiliate, the Vishwa Hindu Parishad despite being a votary of Kabir's syncretic teachings; and that "he is with whichever party is in power". "Guruji told me the aim of this meeting is Hindu unity," Bairagi, a lean youth in a black shirt and jeans, says earnestly. His presence here is, at once, based on a lack of faith in the political system as well as a conviction of the need for a political push. Thus: "Only when saints unite and work together will something happen for the country, because political parties pay little attention to people after coming to power." And: "The aim of this *sammelan* is to push for building the Ram mandir. Because then in the forthcoming elections in MP, Chhattisgarh and Rajasthan, the ruling governments will have a strong chance of winning." The duo went to RSS schools and later attended VHP *shakhas* where they were taught of the need to "protect Hinduism". They believe in their guru's dictum that one can discover divinity by serving the poor. They met him at a *Satsang* (spiritual discourse) four years ago. *A sense of duty, to attend and organize, is instilled in them.* Says Bairagi, "If Mohan Bhagwat (the RSS chief) comes to a program, we have to go and listen to him." Both Bairagi and Raj Kumar come from middle-income families. Bairagi's father is a forest ranger, and he has two younger siblings and a mother at home. Raj Kumar's father is an assistant sub-inspector. "His job is good, but the family is big," he smiles, adding that it includes his mother, two sisters and a brother. They graduated from colleges in Jabalpur and Bhopal under a state technology university. During their brief time in Delhi, they have been impressed by the city and have formed a positive opinion of the AAP and its leader Arvind Kejriwal. "We want neither the BJP nor the Congress to come to power in Madhya Pradesh, but a new party and leader who is from among the people," says Bairagi.

Raj Kumar, a bespectacled man with an already receding hairline and beard, jokes, "*Pehle thhe Diggy raja, abhi Shivraj mama. Mama khud hain ki hamein bana rahe hain, woh bhagwan jaane* (Earlier there was Diggy

Raja [former chief minister Digvijay Singh], then Shivraj Uncle [current CM Shivraj Singh Chouhan]. Only God knows whether he is pulling a fast one on himself or us)." More seriously, he says the sordid Vyapam scam involving government recruitment and admissions in educational institutions has ruined people's lives. With the BJP government at the Centre, too, Kumar says houses and toilets are being built, but there is no employment generation. "I will vote NOTA next year," he says. I lead the discussion back to the agenda of the day: The Ram temple. Raj Kumar suggests that a hospital be built rather than a temple. "There is no shortage of temples in India. But people don't visit them. Will they visit a Ram mandir? They will. As a formality," he asserts. A discussion ensues between the two friends. Bairagi feels Ayodhya ought to mean for Hinduism what Mecca means to Islam. There should be no communal disharmony, he reasons, as it is bad for the economy and everyone stands to lose. But, if a Statue of Unity could make it to the record books and instill pride, there is no harm in building another statue or a temple. Kumar agrees, "When the mandir is built, it will suppress Muslims, which is only fair. Their numbers are increasing." Before rushing off, Bairagi fires a parting shot. "News will flash that there was a *sammelan* on the Ram mandir. Those believing in Hindutva will think Hindus are backing the BJP. So, they will vote for the BJP." I leave too, with a notebook full of quotable quotes. Did I receive answers? I'm not sure. Sometimes, it seems, questions lead only to more questions. [Ritwik Sharma in New Delhi. Source: *Business Standard*]

Congress, many a time, highlights British contribution towards India's modernizing. The historical facts point in the opposite direction. Recently, the 400th anniversary of the beginning of the British colonial rule in India was celebrated in London with a debate on whether British rule did good to India. The person invited from India to speak on this subject was Shashi Tharoor. *With facts and figures, Tharoor argued that British rule did more harm to India than good.* And in the final voting, Tharoor's arguments won. On returning from London, Tharoor shared that experience with *Manorama Online*. A speech that you made recently in London was very remarkable. It is said that it opened the eyes of many British people. *Could you elucidate?*

"This year marks the 400th anniversary of the British presence in India. It was in 1614 that Sir Thomas Roe came to the court of Emperor Jahangir as the first ambassador of King James I. They have also directly ruled India for 200 years. Many believe that their rule was very good for

India. The topic of the debate held in the chamber of the Supreme Court in London was this: *Under British rule, India gained more than Britain.* Three people spoke in favor of the subject and three spoke against it. That's how they made the panel. I spoke against it. Besides me, there were two British writers on our side. At the beginning of the debate, they took a vote. Most of the audience was British. Because of that, in the first vote, most votes were cast in favor of the subject. However, in the final voting, after our counterarguments, we got more votes. A big chunk of the British who voted in favor of the topic first, supported us in the end. If you ask what we did, we presented some facts and figures there. At the time when the British came to India, the GDP of India was 23% of the global GDP. Which means India was a rich country. However, when the British left India, our GDP had fallen to merely 4%. What was the reason? The British industrialized their country by de-industrializing India. That destroyed India.

For 2,000 years, i.e. from the Roman era, we were exporters of the best textiles. The best textile industry in the world cotton, muslin, linen, etc. was in India. a. By destroying it, they relocated the industry to Britain. The British industrial revolution started from there. After coming here, the British destroyed our industry. The best weavers of the world were in Bengal. To prevent them from weaving again, the British cut the thumbs of many of them. Then they took the art of weaving and the looms to Britain. They took our raw material too. Then they started making the products there and exported them to India. Thus, the industry here was completely relocated there. I highlighted all these things in my speech.

We were a very big exporting country at that time. Our share was 27% of the global exports. Under British rule, this fell to merely 2%. In addition to that, the cruelty that they showed to India was very big. Because of that cruelty, 27.5 million people lost their lives. They starved so many Indians to death. They exported all the grains produced here to Britain and ended the availability of food here. That caused the Bengal famine and the deaths from starvation in India's history.

Though many others had ruled India before the British arrived, deaths from starvation had never been widely reported. Ours was never a starved country. However, the British knowingly made it into one. That is the truth. In Bengal alone, 40 lakh people died. It was the time of the Second World War. All the food made here was forcibly exported for British soldiers and others. Nothing was available here. Then Winston Churchill was the British PM. When some good British people told Churchill that it was famine in India and people were dying in hordes, what was his reply? His sarcastic reaction was that if Indians were starving to death, why wasn't Gandhi dying with them. We were ruled by such people then. The truth is that those rulers had so much racial hatred. What is their claim? They claim that India never had political unity, and it was because of their ability that many local kingdoms were united to form a big country like India. These claims do not stand the test of history. The historical fact is that even much before that those who ruled here, and the people here had the concept of a big country called India.

Long before the British arrived, a cultural unity called India or Bharat existed here. Not only that, it is history that many kings waged wars and made conquests to transform India into a big country. Asoka, Vikramaditya and few others like Maharana Pratap, Chhatrapati Shivaji, Maharani Lakshmibai are some examples. They all have tried to unify India from the north to the south and from the west to the east. Adi Shankaracharya, who was born in the 7th century in Kerala, travelled all the way to Kashmir and established monasteries from Dwarika in the west to Puri in the east. The thought that India is one big country was there in the minds of the people here a thousand or even two thousand years ago. The argument that the British united India through modern transport facilities and communication is not right. The argument that the British themselves were needed to unite India is beyond reason. What was the condition of Italy 150 years ago? Then Italy was made up of about 25 local kingdoms. Did Britain unite them? No, it was spearheaded by their nationalist leaders like Garibaldi. Don't you remember the Garibaldi March? That was for the unification of Italy. The division of Bengal was part of the British policy of divide and rule, making Hindus and Muslims to fight each other. One million people died and about 17.5 million lost their homes, hearths and wealth.

Another thing they claim is the railways. It is said that the railway united India. Did they make rail facilities for Indians? No, it was for their needs, to transport goods. In the beginning, they had not considered passenger trains. Railway was necessary to take raw materials for British industrialization from different corners of India to the ports for shipping. There is railway in places where the British have not ruled. If there is money, all such things can be brought. Who made profit from the railway here? Wasn't it the British? Do you know how British investors were brought to establish railway in India? The East India Company had offered twice the profit for investing in Indian railway compared with the investment in shares in London. Thus, they collected money, and the British companies that invested made huge profits. That is the historical truth. To build one kilometer of railway line in India, they had calculated twice the amount spent in America and Canada. As per that they collected taxes also from Indians. That is how railway came to India to serve the British. It was not meant to improve the lives of Indians.

Then, there is the English language. Whatever, they taught us English was to serve them. They did not teach every Indian. *What did Macaulay say?* To serve their needs, they needed some Indians who could speak English. They gave the opportunity to study English to many Indian clerks who served as intermediaries of British governors. However, the ability of our freedom fighters and our 'leaders' was that they were able to make that language popular and turn it into a weapon in the fight against the British. *I will agree about cricket, which they taught us. However, we defeated them recently at Lord's, the Mecca of cricket."*

The situation in the country is to the contrary! Our great kings/fighters/people who fought the tyranny of uncivilized Arab invaders or stood up against the atrocities of Muslim kings of Delhi were labeled by Gandhi as misguided people; and ignored by Congress-Communist historians. And those revolutionaries who took up weapons against the British oppression were called as terrorists by Gandhi and his successors (including the Trinamool Congress Chief (Mamata Banerjee). This was just a ploy to malign the true and real freedom fighters as contrasted to the fakes like the Congress leaders who have all along been stooges of the Raj and subservient to the white skin that continues to date with an Italian white lady President of Congress (I). The *Bhagwadgita*, written many centuries before the start of the Christian Calendar followed universally, is the oldest treatise on philosophy of life. In Indian courts, any litigant whether an accused or a witness must swear by placing his/her hand on this book before deposing. *But teaching of this greatest book belong to 80% of Indians or Hindus is not permitted in schools as per our Constitution* whereas much newer religions' books like Bible, Quran, etc. can be taught in the schools run by the Minority communities. Is this not most anomalous? Why so? Did Nehru and Gandhi influence the process of writing the Constitution? That was not a big deal. The members of the Constituent Assembly did nothing but put the unwritten Constitution of Britain in black and white.

Moreover, 70% of our Constitution has been taken from the (British) Government of India Act, 1935. Our founding fathers took three years to perform that 'meritorious' job! Was it because pro-Muslim Gandhi and his protégé, an allegedly Muslim b*****d Nehru were staunchly anti-Hindu, and anti-Sikh by corollary? If the Constitution was that perfect, why it has been amended 130 times in its existence for 68 years. Or, in other words, on an average twice in a year of its existence!

Modi is the first PM in first 67 years with a lucid thinking and a clear well-planned realistic road map for country's development, and progress of its citizens irrespective of their caste, creed or religion. His pet slogan is *'Sabka Saath, Sabka Vikas'* (Support from every Person and Progress for every Person). And he fervently believes in it and pursuing it at the ground level. This belief has been corroborated by many including Prem Watsa, the chairman of the Canadian investment firm, who counts as many as 30 achievements of the Indian prime minister. Among them are his efforts to crack down on crony capitalism, financial turnaround of state power distribution companies and his pet projects, including smart cities and Make in India. We think Modi can transform India, particularly if he gets re-elected for two more terms. We, the Hindustanis, think he will. He has an excellent track record, is incorruptible and is business friendly. We expect him to be the Lee Kuan Yew of India, said Watsa in his letter to shareholders."

A True story by Manish Malhotra, an Indian MBA in U.K. amplifies the nature and character of PM Modi. "My close family member is a key member in PMO. Let's call him Mr. A, for simplicity. Mr. A had retired in February 2014 and was happily spending his time with the family. He has spent almost all his career with Congress government. At his daughter's wedding, an array of Congress leaders had come. Kapil Sibal and Ashwini Kumar are his family friends as PM Modi!

In May 2014 after Modi took over, he looked at officers and did a big reshuffle. He still had major gaps to fill. So, he recalled seven officers who had retired recently based on their excellent track record. Mr. A was one of them. He was not too keen as he had post-retirement plans. However, to cut the chase, he was finally convinced to resume work for a year. He is not a fan of BJP and Modi. Then began the mad drill. Life turned upside down. Even on Holi and Diwali days he and the entire team is with Modi. On the day of Deepavali (Hindu festival of Lights akin to Christmas of Christians, he came home at 11 in the night. Last week he agreed to extend his contract by another year. He said in the last 44 years in Government he had never worked so hard and so much. He was recently telling me that he is worried the way Modi is working he may be harming his own health. Apparently, many times he skips regular meals to accommodate some requests and meeting. On his foreign tours, most of the times he does not stay in expensive hotels but takes his nap in the official aircraft allotted. His latest trip to Portugal, the USA and Netherlands was completed in 94 hours including the time spent on flying to all three countries.

Modi is working on an average 18-20 hours a day! When I asked him why he didn't respond to allegations against him, he laughed and said he has reached state of self-actualization. Every meeting runs through for 30 minutes and he always asks the same question to everyone in every meeting: "What more can we do to make India better?" 24x7 he is on over- drive working on it.

Mr. A said, a recent example where they finished a meeting at 12 in the midnight and as they were walking out there were three groups of people waiting for him. Coincidentally, he had meeting on another topic at 8 in the morning the very next day. When they were walking in at 8.00 am, the 3rd group from previous night was walking out! And later, he came to know from his secretary that PM hasn't slept for 36 hours!!!! And this is when it is business as usual and not national emergency. *Mr. A says he does not know whether Modi's health will survive this self-inflicted tough schedule or if he will even win the next general elections.*

However, one thing is clear: In his first 5 years, he will leave behind everlasting legacy!"

On the contrary, Opposition spearheaded by thoroughly corrupt Congress party, its cronies and like-minded regional outfits has not been allowing the Rajya Sabha, where the ruling BJP is in minority, to transact business and hence usher in direly needed reforms that were withheld by the incompetent Manmohan government for ten long years. All the antinational politicians whose existence is at stake must perforce oppose Modi, come what may be. They fail to understand that their actions are damaging the country. On the other side, practically the whole of television and print media led by national newspapers like *The Times of India, The Indian Express, Hindustan Times, The Economic Times,* etc. *except Zee News including its newspaper DNA and to some extent India TV* are blocking the news on all the good work by Modi government. *'Unless there is political, social calm, India's economy won't grow'*, was one of the most revealing articles that appeared on March 18, 2016 12:24 IST in *Rediff.com News*. "*The government must keep bad news out of the newspapers. If you have news about a fight every day, it is not a climate where investment takes place.*' India's GDP growth is likely to rise to 7.8% in fiscal 2016-17 from 7.6% this year, largely driven by higher discretionary demand based on the Pay Commission wage hike, low inflation, high corporate profitability, ongoing implementation of public capex and an accommodative monetary policy stance."

Corruption in the form of multiple high-profile scams all through its ten years of government, including the most sensitive defense deals, of various dimensions has been the hallmark of UPA regime headed by perhaps a thoroughly corrupt, puppet PM Manmohan Singh who has been the proverbial British time 'most obedient servant' of his Italian-born boss. A *WhatsApp* note on a battery of UPA scams making rounds recently, linked metaphorically to the five basic elements according to Hindu religion, has been widely prevalent: *Agni* (*Fire*-Coal; *Vayu* (Air)-2G; *Jal* (Water)-Irrigation; *Prithvi* (Earth)-Adarsh Housing; *Akash* (Sky)-AgustaWestland and Air India scams. The third major one after AgustaWestland and Air India scams is the controversial Aircel- Maxis deal. Scams refuse to stop coming tumbling out of Congress cupboards. There was a bombshell from the Italian court at Milan (equivalent to an Indian HC) when it delivered the 225-page judgement on AgustaWestland Deal with India on VVIP choppers meant for the President, Vice President, Prime Minister, etc. Apparently, the Judgement referred to Congress 'life' president Sonia Gandhi as 'the driving force' behind the deal; PM Manmohan as the 'chief administrator'; Ahmed Patel as the 'political secretary'; Oscar Fernandes as the 'politician'; Tyagi brothers (ACM SP Tyagi and his three cousin brothers) plus nine others as 'part beneficiaries' of bribes; plus, National Security Advisor (MK) Narayanan who was also indicted. Our Indian law is lax and incapable of delivering proper justice in a reasonably quick time unlike the civilized West.

On 27th April 2016, *Rediff.com News* tried to simplify the understanding of AgustaWestland deal via an article, *'Explained: The AgustaWestland VVIP chopper scam'*. "An INR 36 billion deal for helicopters to ferry VVIPs that ran into rough weather... A controversy that now threatens to park itself at the doorsteps of the Congress party... Nitin Gokhale, national security expert and founder *BharatShakti.in*, tells us what the controversy is all about.

What was the need to buy new VVIP helicopters and when did the process begin? 2000: Aware that the Mi-8 VVIP helicopter fleet had only 10 years to go before being phased out, the Indian Air Force suggested to the PMO and to the defense ministry that there was a need to look for suitable and modern replacement. The MI-8 helicopters are a typical Russian product -- sturdy, dependable, but with very little comfort level to offer. Air Chief Marshal AY Tipnis was the then chief of the air staff. A 'Request for the Proposal', RFP, was floated. Six companies responded. One of the key requirements in that RFP was that the competing helicopters must be able to fly at altitudes around 6,000 meters with a full load. After trials, only one helicopter -- the Euro copter's EC 225 -- could fly at that altitude.

In 2003, the IAF sent its evaluation report to the PMO. Brajesh Mishra, then national security adviser and principal secretary to then PM Vajpayee, asked the Special Protection Group that guards India's VVIPs, for its comments. The SPG apparently said the EC-225 was unsuitable because its cabin height was too short (at 1.39 meters) and that neither the VIPs nor the SPG personnel would be able to stand upright inside such a cabin. Mishra then wrote to Air Chief Marshal S Krishnaswamy who had taken over from Air Chief Marshal Tipnis in 2001, expressing concern on *two* points: A single vendor situation had arisen because of the specification that said the helicopters must be able to fly at altitudes around 6,000 meters and that the SPG's inputs were not taken. Having seen that letter briefly, I remember a couple of lines from it. It said, in part: 'It is unfortunate that SPG wasn't taken on board... I suggest you and the defense secretary work out the specifications in consultation with the SPG.' Mishra's point was that the competition must be broadened and the SPG's requirements must be met. So, the IAF, in consultation with the SPG, drew up the entire Air Staff Qualitative Requirement once again. That was in 2003. The new specifications said the helicopters must be able to fly at an altitude of 4,500 meters and that its cabin must be at least 1.80 m in height. Meanwhile, Air Marshal SP Tyagi took over as IAF chief in 2004. It took Air Headquarters and the defense ministry's acquisition wing another three years to issue a fresh 'Request for the Proposal'. That was in 2006. By then Vajpayee's National Democratic Alliance government had been ousted, and the United Progressive Alliance was in power. The new RFP, which went by the specifications finalized in 2003, was issued to six different vendors when Pranab Mukherjee, now India's President, was the defense minister.

Three companies -- the makers of Mi-172, Sikorsky which made the S-92 helicopters and AgustaWestland's AWA101 -- responded to the RFP. Meanwhile, the defense ministry put in place a new concept -- the Defense Procurement Procedure. Under this, all companies that bid for contracts above INR 1 billion will have to sign an integrity pact that binds the companies to give an undertaking that no bribes would be paid or that agents would be used in the contracts. The Russian company that manufacturers the Mi-172 withdrew from the competition at an early stage refusing to sign the integrity contract! That left AgustaWestland and Sikorsky in the race. By now this was late 2007. Fali H Major, himself a helicopter pilot, had meanwhile taken over as the IAF chief. The evaluations and trials of the S-92 and AW101 began and continued over the next couple of years (2008-2009). According to IAF sources, the S-92 was found to be non-compliant on four counts:

1] It could not reach 15,000 feet without maximum power.
2] Its 'hover out of ground effect' was insufficient.
3] Its drift down altitude did not meet the requirement.
4] Its missile airborne warning system was not up to the mark. AgustaWestland, with its three engines, was a bonus, according to IAF test pilots since one engine failure still meant it had two engines to fall back upon.

Sometime in 2009, Air HQ sent its recommendation to the defense ministry and after going through stringent financial and technical requirements mandatory under the DPP, a contract was signed in February 2010. By this time, Air Chief Marshal PV Naik was the air chief. The first of the AW 101 AgustaWestland helicopters arrived in India in late 2012. Two more helicopters followed in quick succession.

When a controversy over the deal emerged in 2013 with the arrest of Agusta's parent organization Finmeccanica CEO Giuseppe Orsi by Italian authorities, the then United Progressive Alliance government cancelled the deal, recovered the advance paid to the chopper manufacturer and instituted a probe against the alleged middlemen and beneficiaries

<u>So, were there middlemen? Who were they and why were they present in getting the deal despite India disallowing them to function here?</u> Allegedly, Guido Ralph Haschke, his partner Carlos Gerosa and London-based consultant Christian Michel were paid kickbacks totaling €47.5

million (cINR4 billion) in the INR36 billion deal for 12 VVIP helicopters with AgustaWestland, the UK-based subsidiary of Italian conglomerate Finmeccanica, in February 2010.

The Central Bureau of Investigation's First Information Report says: 'Guido Haschke and Carlo Gerosa managed to send €5.6 million (over INR 470 million) through the Mohali-based IDS Infotech and Chandigarh-based Aeromatrix Info Solutions Private Limited to India and kept the remaining amount of about €24.30 million (cINR2.05 billion) received from AgustaWestland with them in the account of IDS Tunisia.' Haschke had earlier claimed that €6 million (INR510 million) were paid to IAF officers and €8.4 million (around INR710 million) to bureaucrats, with politicians also getting a cut in the AgustaWestland deal. Prosecutors have claimed that money was paid to close associates of former Indian Air Force Chief SP Tyagi, who is named as a prime accused in the Italian prosecution case. Italian prosecutors have also alleged that another part of the bribe money was paid through UK-based consultant Christian Michel to political entities in India and speculated that senior leaders of the then ruling party, Congress, were among the recipients.

<u>Was Congress president Sonia named in the court hearing in Italy? Why?</u> Prosecutors in an Italian court produced a note purportedly written by Christian Michel revealing that he had advised the people handling the VVIP helicopter deal on the company's behalf to target people close to Congress president Sonia Gandhi, including the prime minister and some of her closest advisers, to win the contract. The note written in March 2008 by middleman Christian Michel to Peter Hullet, India head of the Anglo-Italian company, was produced by the prosecutors in an Italian court where a trial is underway in the bribe scam. In the note, *Michel reportedly termed Sonia as the driving force behind the deal and advised Hullet to 'target' people close to her to clinch the deal.* "Dear Peter, since Sonia Gandhi is the driving force behind VIP will no longer fly in the MI-8. Gandhi and her closest advisers are the people who the British ambassador should target," said the letter of Michel seized by the probe team. This letter was seized from the home of arrested middlemen Guido Haschke in early 2013.

What does the April 16 verdict of the Italian appeals court say about involvement of Indian politicians in the payoffs? Michel's note reportedly mentions among others, Sonia's political secretary Ahmed Patel, Pranab Mukherjee, M Veerappa Moily, then national security adviser M K

Narayanan and Vinay Kumar, a defense ministry official in charge of IAF procurement.

The 225-page judgment of the appeal court in Milan says Haschke identified all the Congress leaders, when their photos were shown to him during the trial by the Italian prosecution. Page Nos. 163 and 164 name Manmohan Singh and details that Orsi used Italian leadership and diplomats to contact the then PM to scuttle the probe by non-cooperation from the Indian Government's side. In Page 163, the judgment produces a handwritten note by Orsi from jail in July 2013 asking his people to contact then Italian PM Monti or Ambassador Teracciano to call Dr Singh. "Call Monti or ambassador. Teracciano in my name to ask him to call the PM Singh," said the note seized from the prison cell of Orsi. The judgment in several areas blames the non-cooperation from Indian authorities including the Defense Ministry and other probe agencies in 2013, when the Congress-led UPA was in power.

What does the judgment say about former air chief Tyagi's role? The judgement has a separate 17-page chapter on SP Tyagi explaining the grounds on which it concluded on the corruption of the former IAF chief. Tyagi is alleged to have intervened in favor of AgustaWestland for the VVIP helicopters competition. The Italian court order said that payments to Tyagi and his family -- including three of his cousins, were made in cash and through wire transfers. [*This report is an updated version of an earlier FAQ on the controversial deal posted in February 2014*]. "Beginning his speech by promising to not take names so that there is no disturbance, the defense minister mentioned an anecdote of Birbal related to a "theft" to suggest that the Congress was unnerved, fearing the truth would implicate it. "The country wants to know who instigated, supported and benefited from the corruption. We cannot let this pass," Parrikar said. He added that the fact that there was corruption in matter is brought out in extensive details in recent judgments of Milan court. "A litany of omissions and commissions at various stages of the decision-making process indicate *malefice* and corrupt actions, driven by a goal to favor a particular vendor," the defense minister said. Hitting out at the UPA government, he said the field trials of the chopper were conducted in Italy even though it was necessary for it to be held in Indian conditions. Parrikar said the helicopter offered by AgustaWestland was still in "development stage" and hence the trials were conducted on a different helicopter. Targeting the previous United Progressive Alliance regime over the controversial

AgustaWestland deal, Defense Minister Manohar Parrikar on Wednesday, the 4th May said the ongoing probe will focus on those named in the Italian court judgement even as he suggested the role of an "invisible hand" in preventing a proper investigation earlier. He, along with Parliamentary Affairs Venkaiah Naidu, rejected the opposition demand for Supreme Court-monitored probe, after which Congress members walked out. Parrikar said even though the reports of wrongdoings and unethical conduct by Finmeccanica, the parent company of AgustaWestland had surfaced in 2012, followed by arrest of its CEO, the action of putting on hold all procurement cases with the accused group of companies in pipeline was approved by (UPA defense minister) Antony only on May 12, 2014 towards the fag end of the its government. "It was the present government which finally issued the order on July 3, 2014," he said. [*Rediff.com News* on 4th May 2016]

There are two other defense deals under scanner of the NDA government. On 6th May 2016, *MSN News*, quoting *News18*, quoted *Firstpost* article: '*Now, Rafale and Pilatus Deals by UPA Also Under Scanner*'. "After the AgustaWestland VVIP chopper deal fiasco punished by the Milan Court of Appeals, two other defense deals signed during the UPA 2 regime surfaced. Air India scam by Manmohan's civil aviation minister Praful Patel (the #2 in NCP, led by Sharad Pawar allegedly the most corrupt and unethical opportunist politician in India, and the then coalition partner in UPA) are under the NDA government's scanner with investigations ordered. According to the Canadian court, there were plans to bribe Praful with $40 million! Secretary, ministry of civil aviation has started looking into that. According to government sources, the Defense Ministry has ordered probe into the selection of the Pilatus and Rafale deals. Decision to probe the two deals comes even as the government and the opposition are engaged in a fierce battle over the AgustaWestland VVIP chopper deal. While the government has accused the Congress leadership of corruption, the opposition has accused them of inaction in the alleged scam case. Sources said that names of officers involved in Agusta negotiations have already been given to the Enforcement Directorate. The Defense Ministry has also asked the ED and the CBI to fast-track the AgustaWestland scam probe.

Earlier in May 2015, Union defense minister Manohar Parrikar had said that UPA government's proposed deal for 126 Rafale fighter jets was economically unviable and not required. He had also raised questions on the tendering process initiated by former (UPA) defense minister AK Antony. According to Parrikar, his predecessor had "hammered" the tender in such a way that the Rafale deal would have never seen the light of the day. Surrounded by hostile neighbors, India has fought numerous wars to protect its sovereignty and as deterrent to any future hostility, it has one of most well-armed, trained and disciplined military forces in the world.

Rafale had won the MMRCA deal in 2012 to supply 126 fighters at a then estimated cost of INR420 billion. The MMRCA race had seen six vendors - Russia's MIG-35 (RAC MiG), Swedish JAS-39 (Gripen), Dassault Rafale (France), American F-16 Falcon (Lockheed Martin), Boeing's F/A-18 Super Hornet and Eurofighter Typhoon (made by a consortium of British, German, Spanish and Italian firms) – taking part. Under the terms of purchase, the first 18 MMRCA aircrafts were supposed to come in a 'fly away' condition while the remaining 108 manufactured under Transfer of Technology. The Indian Air Force has already started inducting Swiss made basic trainer aircraft Pilatus. The aircraft is used for basic training of all IAF pilots, in addition to those of the Indian Navy and the Coast Guard."

Roles of dirty media persons: India Opines published Vijaya Dar's blog, *'AgustaWestland – Bribes to Journalists'*: "The payoffs/bribes by AgustaWestland to Journalists (apparently as much as INR450 million) could not have been equal and there must have been a gradation. According to me the *pyramid* would have Vineet Jain, Aroon Purie, Shobhana Bhartiya, N. Ram, Anant Goenka and Aveek Sarkar in the top layer. The *second layer* would consist of Pankaj Pachauri, Shekhar Gupta, Prannoy Roy, Barkha Dutt, Bharat Karnad and Ajay Shukla. The bribes most likely began from this second layer of the pyramid. The *third layer* would have Sonia Singh, Rajdeep Sardesai, Karan Thapar, Rahul Kanwal, and Rana Ayyub. At the *bottom,* you find Ravish Kumar, Abhisar Sharma, Nidhi Razdan, Bhupendra Chaube, Punya Prasun Bajpai and maybe Anjana Om Kashyap." *Is that the reason none of them talks about this scam?"*

On Tuesday, the 25th April 2016, *MSN News* published *Firstpost* article, *'Fireworks expected in Parliament: BJP to name Sonia Gandhi in AgustaWestland scam'*. "After racking up the Ishrat Jahan issue and the Uttarakhand crisis in the Parliament, it appears that both the Houses are set to see acrimony over another alleged scam. The BJP is presently working on a plan to initiate a debate on the AgustaWestland chopper deal in the Parliament, *NDTV* reported on Tuesday. In a move which could spark a political controversy, the BJP may name Congress president Sonia Gandhi with respect to the controversy, *NDTV* said.

Union minister Ravi Shankar Prasad on Tuesday dared the Congress to come clean on the VVIP chopper deal with AgustaWestland after an Italian court observed that it was "proven" that illegal money had made their way to Indian officials. "Now that bribe-givers have been convicted, what should happen to the bribe-takers? Will (UPA defense minister AK) Antony publicly give a statement on this? Will he accept that his party men are involved in the scam?" he said. This comes even as Sonia launched a sharp attack on the government during her poll campaign in West Bengal, saying, "The way the Modi government is functioning, it is endangering our country's basic structure, our secular values, endangering democracy and our age-old tradition and values." Senior Congress leader Antony was Union defense minister when the VVIP helicopter deal with Italy-based firm AgustaWestland was being finalized and sealed in February 2010 during the UPA government. Antony was quoted as saying by *ANI* on Tuesday that the blacklisting of the company was done by the UPA government. "My request is--please complete the inquiry and punish the culprits," he said. (Later, the Union defense minister Manohar Parrikar dared the Congress to furnish names of bribe-takers in their fold).

In a 225-page judgment, a judge at the Milan Court of Appeals found that bribe was paid by the firm to Indian officials to get the $530 million contract for the supply of 12 AW101 choppers. Questioning why the Indian government at the time did not provide documents with respect to the case, the BJP's Meenakshi Lekhi asked, "Was the UPA government trying to protect the Italian mafia?" as per an *NDTV* report. The Indian government, however, cancelled the deal in 2013 when a controversy over the deal emerged with the arrest of Agusta's parent organization Finmeccanica CEO Giuseppe Orsi by Italian authorities." [With inputs from *IANS*]

The deal was worth INR 36.6 billion out of which 10% is said to have been paid to the Indian bribe-takers: politicians, bureaucrats, Air Force officials. The ratio in percentage terms was 52, 28 and 20 respectively, (as per *Zee News*). The court verdict repeatedly named Congress president Sonia and her three *chamchas* namely Manmohan Singh, Oscar Fernandes, Ahmed Patel. Others facing flak in the court verdict are the then NSA, (MK) Narayanan – originally a long-time *chamcha* of Indira Gandhi since 1958; it was for his *chamchagiri* (sycophancy) to the 'first political dynasty' that he was pulled out of retirement to make NSA for one 5-year term and then the Governor of West Bengal by puppet PM Manmohan. Others indicted: Former Air Force Chief, Air Chief Marshal SP Tyagi, his three cousin brothers and nine others. *The state of affairs in India can be judged from the fact that even Italy has given its verdict, our CBI is still investigating*!

On the same day, *MSN News* reported a news item from *The Indian Express* titled, '*CBI seeks Italian court's order on AgustaWestland graft.*' It went on like this: "The CBI has approached External Affairs Ministry seeking help of diplomatic channels to get a copy of an Italian court's order in the AgustaWestland helicopter deal. Sources say the agency completed domestic investigation, but judicial requests sent to eight countries are still pending. They said the agency cannot react based on media reports and any action will be possible after it gets the copy of the order issued by Milan Courts of Appeal--equivalent of high courts in the Indian judiciary. The sources said once the order, in Italian, is received, the agency will get an authentic translation done before taking note of the observations made by the court there. The Milan Court of Appeals, which overturned lower court's order, sentenced Finmeccanica's former chief Giuseppe Orsi to 4.5 years in jail for false accounting and corruption in the deal of 12 VVIP choppers to India while former CEO of Finmeccanica's helicopter subsidiary AgustaWestland, Bruno Spagnolini, got over four-year sentence. On January 1, 2014, India scrapped the contract with AgustaWestland for supplying 12 AW101 VVIP choppers to the Indian Air Force (IAF) over allegations of kickbacks by it for securing the deal. The then UPA government had also barred Finmeccanica and its group companies from participating in any new program of the defense ministry.

A case was registered by CBI against former IAF chief SP Tyagi and 12 others, including his cousins, for alleged cheating, corruption and criminal conspiracy in the INR36.6 billion VVIP helicopter deal, in which INR36.6 million is alleged to have been paid as kickbacks. The former IAF chief had strongly refuted the allegations against him. CBI alleged in its FIR that middleman Guido Haschke, through his Tunisia-based company, Gordian Services Sarl, entered several consultancy contracts with AgustaWestland from 2004-05 onwards and, "almost on a back-to-back basis he also made consultancy contracts with the Tyagi brothers". Under the cover of these contracts, Haschke is alleged to have spent Euro126,000 (cINR10.6 billion) and Euro200,000 (cINR16.8 billion) to the Tyagi brothers. The allegation against the former IAF chief is that he reduced the height of the VVIP helicopters so that AgustaWestland could be included in the bids."

On 6th May 2016, *MSN News* quoted *News18* on a new dimension on middlemen involved in the now notorious AgustaWestland VVIP Chopper Scam through a news item, *'ED Probes Danish Woman Link to AgustaWestland Deal'*. "New Delhi: The Enforcement Directorate is looking at the alleged role of a Danish woman, Christine Bredo Spliid, in the AgustaWestland deal. *CNN-News 18* has documentary proof of relationship between Christian James Michel and Christine Bredo Spliid. Christine and Michel have shareholding in a United Kingdom based company named Beetle Nut Home Ltd. Documents show Michel's Dubai based company Global Services FZE has the shareholding in the company. Two British nationals of Indian origin, Saahil Parkash Mehra and Sonya Mehra, also have shareholding in the company. Records show both have London based address. Spliid traveled to India during the period when AgustaWestland deal was being finalized. Christine Spliid's address is Flat 3, 10 Chapstow Road, London. Records show Spliid was born on 11th July 1984. Indian sleuths were trying to find out if some part of the kickback money reached Beetle Nut Home Ltd. The records show that Beetle Nut Home Ltd was dissolved in January 2016. Christine Bredo Spliid also holds equity in UK-based Croprotein Ltd and French Crystal."

On 7th May 2016, *Rediff.com News* published an article titled: *'Guns, thieves and a ghost'*. "We get tangled up in our own crooked web on purchases, and the murky arms bazaar knows it, says Shekhar Gupta. The AgustaWestland controversy is the latest scandal to emerge from India's defense acquisitions. We Indians are beyond boring old grandma's wisdom, like don't throw the baby out with the bath water. We just throw away the baby and keep the bath water. Take our military acquisitions, for example. Most new acquisitions become scandals. Many are then terminated, leaving our forces with a fraction of the needed inventory, and short of spares and ammunition. Nobody is caught and punished. Some examples from our times:

1. *Bofors* is the most storied of our scandals. The Army is left with just the guns bought in the first order. Indigenous production was stalled. Even existing guns are short of spares and ammunition. The Army made distress import of ammunition during the fighting in Kargil which, note, was 17 years ago. India has acquired no fresh

artillery in the 30 years after Bofors. Most importantly, nobody was ever punished for the bribery, no money recovered. *A classic case of throwing the baby out but keeping the dirty bath water.*
2. *German HDW submarines*, called Type 209, are a scandal of the same vintage. These were to be the Navy's first SSKs (submarine-to-submarine killers). The program was scuttled. Only two vessels were bought and two assembled in India, 10 years late. Technology transfer, expansion never happened.
3. *This isn't a military acquisition*, but I choose the Indian Airlines purchase of its first Airbus A-320s because it became a scandal at the same time as Bofors and Type 209. Just as the rumors of kickbacks emerged, a new A-320 crashed in Bangalore. It was used to damn the aircraft and the entire lot just purchased, was grounded. The A-320 survived fortuitously.

After Saddam Hussein invaded Kuwait, India needed to airlift tens of thousands of its citizens out of Kuwait. Actor Akshay Kumar was not available in real life to carry out the airlift. The spare Air India and IAF strength was inadequate. Then PM VP Singh had to de-mothball the A-320s. And once they resumed flying, there was no going back. Indian Airlines never recovered from the financial loss of grounding that fleet. Again, nothing was proven, nobody was caught or punished. The setback and humiliation of Bofors led to our most vicious political blood feud. The Congress found its opportunity with the Tehelka sting. The NDA cried entrapment, but Bangaru Laxman and George Fernandes lost their jobs (the latter only temporarily). None except Laxman, who had nothing to do with any real defense deal, was punished by law.

Gandhi family saw bitter revenge in *Tehelka* because it damaged not just the BJP but also Mr. Fernandes, the noisiest Rajiv-baiter on Bofors. But, since Vajpayee's credibility and popularity, and dumping of expendable Laxman helped Fernandes recover, the revenge remained incomplete. A fresh bid was launched towards the later years of the NDA with what was called the 'coffin scam' though nothing was eventually proven. Consequently, however, no major acquisitions took place in Vajpayee's six years, despite a limited conflict (Kargil) and a near all-out war, *Operation Paraakram*. Not one significant non-Russian system was introduced as the government was petrified. Even the Israeli Barak missile system for protecting our naval assets from enemy aircraft and missiles was rendered ineffective as its maker was banned, leaving the Navy's finest ships unprotected. Something similar has happened now with the latest submarine Scorpene entering the seas without torpedoes. The company that makes these, WASS, is a subsidiary of Agusta and covered under the AK Antony ban.

When the Congress unexpectedly returned to power in 2004, it was desperate to find something on the NDA's defense 'scandals.' But nothing was found and the first UPA Union defense minister Pranab Mukherjee was much too wise to launch a witch-hunt. He knew the consequences of perpetuating this feud at the cost of the armed forces. His inability to 'discover' any scandals annoyed 10 Janpath. It probably led to his being moved out of defense, making way for loyalist AK Antony. Antony also did not launch a witch-hunt. He saw keeping his own back and hands clean as his most important KRA. His typical response to the first rumors of a scam, even anonymous complaints, was to call in the CBI and ban the supplier.

In the process, he became not just India's longest-serving defense minister but also one who banned so many suppliers that it was no longer possible to find one completely chaste, particularly in this fast-moving environment of mergers and acquisitions (M&As) in the multi-national defense industry. When he banned Germany's Rheinmetall in 2012 for example, it also excluded nearly a hundred other western armament companies that the conglomerate now owned. He banned companies from Europe, Singapore, even Israel. The joke in South Block used to be that soon he would ban the Pakistani army and end the problem altogether.

As the armed forces got frustrated, I described his approach to defense modernization as 'strapped-in-Latex' and once called him Indian politics' answer to cricketer Bapu Nadkarni who was known neither to concede runs nor get many batsmen out and holds the world record for the largest number of consecutive maiden overs (21) that will probably never be broken. *The greatest irony of the AgustaWestland bribery is, it took place despite Antony. He had to admit that bribes had been taken, cancel the deal, invoke penalty clauses and order inquiries.*

It is an indisputable fact that he acted only after Italian authorities had detected wrongdoing and one Indian newspaper and its reporter had broken and pursued the story relentlessly. He continues to do so even today and set the pace for the rest, some of whom then claim retrospective 'newsbreaks.' Since it is an incontrovertible fact that bribes have been paid by

Agusta, the case must be speedily investigated and the guilty punished. The test, however, is can we have the sagacity to distinguish this scam from the larger issue of modernization?

We can talk about *Make in India*. But most 'Indian' systems will also depend on large imports for engines, avionics, sensors, weapons, guidance systems and so on. These include the most visible ongoing developments like Tejas, ALH, stealth frigates, even the MBT Arjun, nearly 30 years behind schedule.

India should opt for one of three possibilities now. The *first* is, to concede that tender-based, vendor purchases are no longer possible in the murky arms bazaar. All future purchases would be purely on government-to-government basis or what the Americans call FMS (Foreign Military Sales). This is how UPA had ordered the IAF and the Navy's new C-130s, C-17s and P-8Is.

A cruel side: this forced Mr. Antony to do what he detested ideologically, to buy from the US, which became our biggest arms supplier under his watch, for the first time in 65 years. The BJP is now buying two squadrons of the French Rafale through the same route and exploring American artillery. This narrows the buyers' options and negotiating space but get the commission agents out. The second is to bring in a fool-proof system of purchases which is an impossibility given how broken our politics is.

The *third* is to accept the limitations inherent in our system on timely acquisitions (the need for a so-called VVIP helicopter was first approved in 1999 and we still don't have it). You then mold your diplomacy and strategic posture accordingly. That, nobody would want.

So, we will likely keep muddling along, battered by scandals yet shortages, not catching any guilty but getting our soldiers frustrated. In short, keep flushing away the baby and frolicking in the soiled bath water. [*Shekhar Gupta*; Source: *Business Standard*]

Congress President Rahul is on a slippery ground as always in the past since he is addicted to speaking on unfounded falsehoods in Hindustan and abroad. He has been vigorously challenging Modi government on Rafale deal both domestically and abroad. Union finance minister Arun Jaitley jumped into the Frey. On 29th August 2018, *livemint* published a news report by Elizabeth Roche, *'Jaitley takes battle to opposition camp on Rafale fighter jet deal'*. "New Delhi: Finance minister Arun Jaitley on Wednesday took the battle to the opposition camp, challenging Congress president Rahul to answer 15 questions before levelling corruption allegations on the purchase of the Rafale fighter aircraft from France. Rahul had earlier said that the deal signed by the Modi-led NDA government smacked of corruption and crony capitalism. In fact, the Congress has finalized plans for a media blitzkrieg and ground-level campaign to corner the Modi government over the deal in the run-up to the 2019 general elections. The party had also raised the issue during the monsoon session of Parliament. In response to the accusations, Jaitley first took to *Facebook*, accusing the previous Congress-led UPA government of compromising with national security by delaying the purchase of the multi-role fighter aircraft by more than a decade. He also accused Rahul and the Congress party of running a false campaign against the NDA government on pricing and procedural irregularities.

Later in the day, in an interview with *ANI* news agency, the senior BJP leader said Rahul had lowered the standard of debate to the "kindergarten" level and asked him to respond to 15 questions, including the frequent flip-flop by him on the pricing of the aircraft, and whether he was aware that the price quoted by the manufacturer included an escalation cost and a rupee-euro foreign exchange variation clause. The two factors, Jaitley reasoned, made the UPA-shortlisted aircraft 20% more expensive than what was negotiated by the NDA in 2015.

Unfazed by Jaitley's aggressive stance, Rahul shot back on *Twitter*, thanking the finance minister for "bringing the nation's attention back to the GREAT #RAFALE ROBBERY!" and demanded a joint parliamentary panel probe. "Problem is, your Supreme Leader is protecting his friend, so this may be inconvenient. Do check & revert in 24 hrs. We're waiting!"

Anil Ambani-led Reliance Defense has a private tie-up with Dassault Aviation, maker of Rafale, to fulfil the offset obligations following the purchase of the aircraft. Incidentally, Ambani has sued the Congress in an Ahmedabad court for damages worth INR500 billion for falsely implicating the role of Modi government on the grant of such an arrangement.

In his blog, Jaitley said it was based on the request for proposal issued by the UPA government in 2007 that two vendors, Dassault and EADS, were found compliant with the government's requirements. Thereafter "it took the UPA five more years to commence the negotiations and in January 2012, the Contract Negotiation Committee (CNC) determined Dassault Aviation to be L1." "For reasons best known to the UPA government in 2012, the deal was directed to be re-examined, which effectively meant that the entire 11-year exercise was abandoned, and the process was to be undertaken afresh, leading to the depleting combat strength of India's fighter squadron. Was this delay and eventual abatement of the purchase by the UPA based on collateral considerations as had been witnessed in earlier transactions, such as the purchase of the 155 mm Bofors gun?" Jaitley asked, in a tacit reference to the allegations that the Rajiv-led government had received kickbacks following the purchase of Swedish artillery guns in 1986. According to Jaitley, in 2015, "India decided to procure 36 Rafale aircraft from the French government on terms better than the ones conveyed by Dassault in the bid of 2007", adding that the "slow and casual approach of the UPA government seriously compromised national security requirements". Jaitley asked whether Gandhi could deny the fact that the Modi government had no contract with any private company to supply the aircraft."

Saumitra Chaudhuri, a former member of the prime minister's Economic Advisory Council and a former Planning Commission Member, recently delivered the '8th SAGE-MSE Endowment Lecture' on *'India and the Ongoing Global Economic Turmoil: Commonalities and Differences, Risks and Prospects.'* He discussed the state of the Indian economy with Shobha Warrior. *"You spoke about impending global economic turmoil. Are we going to see another 2008?* I don't think we are going to see another 2008. It had some very definite underlining reasons to precipitate the crisis. We don't see any such underlining reason right now. However, because of a combination of factors like the slowing down of the US economy, the European Union crisis, the developing world that had good news earlier does not seem to have any now, and then, of course, the oil price slump. I think the oil price crashing is the googly! In 2014, there was a drop in the annual growth of demand (*for crude*), but in the summer of 2015, the price was $60 and now it is $30. In 2015, the demand grew by 1.8 million barrels which was 0.6 more than average. The situation is weird. While there is higher demand, prices have declined further. That's why I call it a googly of some kind. After Narendra Modi came to power, when the Indian economy grew much above expectations, people attributed it to crashing oil prices and nothing to do with the Modi government's policies. *Do you agree?* I don't agree. I will look at it as two separate issues. One, when the oil prices go down, India is a big beneficiary as far as external payment, the current accounts deficit and subsidy are concerned. We should have benefited, but I believe somehow, we didn't harvest the benefit. If you look at last year's and the year before last's growth figures, they are somewhat comparable.

We see a similar trajectory. There was a positive effect after the change in the government and a feeling that things would improve. The feeling was quite evident in 2014 though it is not that pronounced now. The benefit that India could have reaped due to low oil price does not seem to have materialized.

What could be the reason for this? It is basically because investments are not coming. Companies are not keen to invest, as they are already heavily leveraged by profitability problems from what they have already invested. Why should they take more risk in such a situation? Of course, you have specific problems like the capacity utilization of private IPP (*Independent Power Producers*) has come down significantly in the power sector. The corporates are investment shy now. On the consumption side, it is also under pressure because job creation has slowed down. The retail sale data also shows that sales have not picked up at all.

What should the government do to revive investor confidence? It should step up roads and highways activities. You must remember that public sector investment is very sluggish. Money does not get spent. The government must keep bad news out of the newspapers. If you have news about a fight every day, it is not a climate where investment takes place.

Reports say FDI has increased after Modi's marketing blitzkrieg... There may be some merit in that. A good amount of Japanese investment has come to India. It might have happened because of his (*Modi's*) intervention. FDI coming is a good story. The Economic Survey projects 8% growth next year, but it is said that without 10% growth, India will not achieve the kind of growth needed now. *Do you think so?* There is a problem with the numbers. We have a number from a new data series and we also have numbers from the old data series. Now, the kind of energy, growth and positivity we associate with 7 to 7.5% growth in the past is certainly not there today. Maybe you are talking about two different animals! Maybe they applied different methods.

China says India is manipulating data. I don't think anybody is doing so. I think the difference in method has caused some comparability problem. In 2004-2005, we had 6% growth and if you remember, everything was moving at a galloping phase then. That really is not happening.

Is it because the aspirations of people have increased? I really do not know. It is like looking at two different data. Now everybody wants the government to use the same method and provide us the data for the previous years so that we can compare. Then, we can have a better understanding of the problem. Otherwise, many people will continue asking questions: Look at company sales. Look at profitability. Look at the buoyancy in the market. I am not the only one who is asking questions. India Inc. is also asking, 'Where is this 7.5% growth you are talking about?' Many public-sector banks are in the red with such bad loans that the SC had to ask the government to come out with a list of huge debtors. *Where will this lead to?* There were some bad loans given, and there were some situations created in which bad loans were given. I think a beginning must be made to enforce security. I don't want to take names, but if the shares in that person's name are pledged to you, you should ensure that the government gets its money. It will be a lesson for those who are willful defaulters. You just cannot postpone action.

What kind of impact will the public-sector banks, with the volume of bad loans, have on the economy? The faster you address this issue, the faster you will come out of the bad situation. The longer you postpone, longer the problem will remain and mind you, it is not good for the economy. *Economic Survey projects 8% growth, but what we see is not good news at all -- in fact only bad news like the stock market falling, the rupee falling...* That is why I said, the atmosphere must be more positive. I think the government can do a lot by making the atmosphere positive.

Like? Mainly not do negative things! The *second* is the Treasury benches have the responsibility to take the flak. It cannot behave like the Opposition. I will draw a parallel. In the closing years of the UPA (*United Progressive Alliance government*), every day, we used to hear about one corruption charge or the other. *Quid pro quo* will not let you function. Even if unjustified, the government should not react to all the Opposition charges. The onus is on the government to discharge its duties. The Opposition would criticize. Now we see tension being built up by the government! It is strange. That is the last thing the country's economy needs. *Unless there is political and social calm, the economy will not grow.*

People say the GST Bill is the 'Brahmastra' and by passing the bill, most problems the Indian economy faces today will be solved. I don't think so. *First*, what you have is a Constitutional amendment and not a law. This is not the GST Bill. It is not even written. It must be written. Another thing is it will address different sections differently, and this must be sorted out. It will not happen overnight. It is certainly not a *'Brahmastra'*, but yes, it is certainly an incremental improvement. It certainly won't cure what is fundamentally wrong with us which are of two kinds.

What is fundamentally wrong with us? One, on the investment side, there is a shyness about it as corporates are already heavily borrowed. *Secondly*, on the demand side, lower job creation. The agricultural sector is also in some difficulty. These two are linked. If investment picks up, job creation will also increase and that in turn will boost consumption.

When you say investment, are you talking about only investment from the private sector? Of course, I am talking about the private sector. Public sector investment was around 7 to 7.5% of the GDP for many years and it will remain as it is. It is private investment that drives an economy. Unfortunately, the confidence of the private sector is quite low.

The Economic Survey predicts low growth for the agricultural sector. Between 2009-2010 and 2011-2012, the farm sector created more than 10 million jobs. I don't think that is happening today. People are switching from the farm to the non-farm sector. That's good as non-farm jobs will give more pay and more disposable income. When job creation is weak, we are going to have lots of problem. When people do not find the jobs they expect, there is going to be a social dimension to it. The solution does not lie in increasing the political temperature but calming it!

Can India capitalize on China's slowdown? India can capitalize on certain markets, which China was servicing so far, but we have not been able to do it in a big way. China itself is the second largest market after the US. We should try to sell our goods to China, and I have been advising many exporters to do so. It is a difficult market to crack, but quite a few people have succeeded. Most of the manufacturers can increase the capacity by 40% by simply raising capacity utilization.

From the way you have painted the future, is it going to be tough for India in the next couple of years? It will not be smooth sailing. It is easy to do well when everybody else is doing well. High tide lifts all the boats, but what we have is rough waters now. So, it all depends on how you handle your fate. The fact is you cannot do well internationally if you don't do well domestically."

<u>PM Modi's initiatives</u>: *Make in India* (September 2014), *Digital India* and *Skill India* (both July 2015) and *Start-Up India* (January 2016) and *Stand Up India* (April 2016) should get a fillip with NRIs pooling their resources. A good development appeared on *Rediff.com News* on 16th April 2016: *'Indians give up cushy jobs abroad to come back to their homeland'*. Armed with pricey degrees from colleges overseas, young Indians are returning home in search for greener pastures, finds Anjuli Bhargava. They

are 20-something, have spent four to five years overseas, mostly in the US and the UK, studying and are now back home with fancy degrees in hand. Some were earning good money, career paths in the land of opportunities looked set and the future certain.

What then brings these young adults with promising careers ahead of them back to India – to what will certainly be a struggle even if they are from the privileged set? How do they justify the substantial amount spent on their degrees by their parents and do they feel it was worth it? Mumbai-based education consultant Viral Doshi estimates that unlike 15 years ago when only a handful of students who went overseas to study returned, now almost half of them come back after completing their education. He says visa troubles, lack of attractive opportunities and in some cases plain homesickness are among the reasons, as also India is where the action is today.

Neeraj Batra, chairman of *Oncourse*, the largest private consultancy which has sent over 900 children overseas for studies over the past four years, says that a large percentage of students he knows of are coming back and a lot of it should do with the lack of opportunities overseas and the economic slowdown. "I'd say it is primarily because India is the best option in the present scenario when good jobs overseas are hard to come by."

India in fact presents more options for them, including a thriving start-up culture. Batra says this is like a reverse brain drain. India, as he sees it, only stands to gain. Rich Indians also return to take charge of family businesses. While this is not entirely new, Poshak Agrawal, founder of Gurgaon-based Athena Education, says that in many cases "it's their endeavor to 'professionalize' the businesses from family-owned to process-driven establishments." They apply what they have learnt to help the family business thrive. *The entrepreneurial or start-up bug is another big factor.* Agrawal, who left India to study at Princeton University, says that he always wanted to go the entrepreneurial way and India was where his heart lay, although his degree at Princeton was "priceless". Along with his business partner – a classmate from Princeton, Agrawal now heads a consultancy firm that helps Indian students go abroad for higher studies. "I have an investment banker friend from Princeton who now works in New York in high finance. He once said India is probably like New York in the early 1900s: a land of problems which create opportunities.

Priceless experience: Almost everyone agrees that this reverse migration is not to imply that studying abroad is not worth it. It opens their minds, gives them a holistic education (that the Indian system doesn't), a solid network to fall back on and exposes them to ideas their Indian education could never have given. "A degree is just a stamp but an experience at Princeton is priceless," says Shikha Uberoi, who is soon to launch Indi.com in India, a brand challenge platform. Shikha, who has played tennis representing India at a professional level, did her freshman year at Princeton in 2000-01 but took a decade off to play tennis. She finally finished her degree in 2013. She was always determined to head back to Mumbai and create social impact with media. "I wasn't forced into replacing my passions and ideas with a high paying job, so I consider myself very privileged. I get to do what I love, and I love what I do," she says.

Chiraayu Sethi echoes Uberoi's sentiment. After finishing his schooling at Mumbai's Dhirubhai Ambani School, Sethi earned his degree in civil engineering from Carnegie Mellon in 2011 (with a minor in photography). Sethi says that the education he received was phenomenal, molding him into what he is today. Sethi has friends who are studying engineering here in India and he can see the difference. "Here you are limited to learning what you need to be a good engineer", whereas he got a taste of a bit of everything while studying at Carnegie Mellon, be it history or photography. But never once did he consider working or living outside the country. "My plan was to come back and set up my own enterprise," he says. He knows this will be challenging but he also knows it might be the best time for him to do it. Home-grown Indian start-ups are going abroad, and he thinks it's too exciting an opportunity to miss. Moreover, he'd rather set up his venture in his own environment where he's more comfortable, creating employment that accrues to his country.

There is another set of students which is back partly disillusioned with the life the West offers – riddled with money, materialism and mortgages. Shantanu Garg, a Doon School alumnus who dropped out of Delhi's Shriram College for Commerce after a year and headed to Claremont McKenna College in Los Angeles, got into economic consulting after completing his degree. He worked with a boutique firm, Cornerstone Research, for a while but soon realized that while he was earning good money, he wasn't particularly satisfied with his life there. "I wasn't particularly excited by the work I was doing, and I could see myself getting sucked into a life of comfort." Culturally, too, Los Angeles lacked the political environment he'd grown accustomed to love in India. Garg extricated himself and came right back home. He's now toying between taking the civil services examination and sitting for law entrance. Either way, he couldn't see himself leading a life of "quiet desperation"- quoting Henry David Thoreau.

A search for something more brought back Akshay Saxena who worked with a large consultancy firm in the US after graduating from Harvard University. He realized he wanted to give back to his institute (IIT, Mumbai) and country. After returning in 2009-10, Saxena went on to set up Avanti Fellows, a not-for-profit initiative that helps children from less privileged backgrounds make it into engineering colleges like IIT, a course many want to follow. His and other similar success stories make the risk worth taking." [Source: *Business Standard*]

Unfortunately, it is well known we have the most corrupt politicians, police and bureaucrats. Or, in fact anybody dealing with public is corrupt unless proved otherwise. The public perception is Sharad Pawar is the most opportunist highly corrupt politician in the country. He left Congress (I) on the issue of party president Sonia being of Italian origin. He floated his own political party, Nationalist Congress Party. But he joined the cabinet when Sonia-*chamcha* Manmohan was nominated the PM. His party with nine MPs in the Lok Sabha was allotted two berths: he himself as agriculture minister and Praful Patel as civil aviation minister. It is a matter of common knowledge that both made tons of ill-gotten wealth during the ten years UPA ruled. On *Quora.com* a question was asked: '*How corrupt is Sharad Pawar*'? Shreyash Nadage, *not a Pseudo-secular but a pragmatist*: "Let me admit, this is a wonderful question to answer and I am going to relish it. *First*, let's put a glance at three major and prominent players from the house of the Pawar Dynasty namely Sharadchandra Pawar, Ajit Pawar and Smt. Supriya Sule who is former's daughter. Following are the details of assets the above-mentioned players have revealed as part of affidavit before the election commission of India in year 2014.

1. Sharadchandra Pawar: INR320,626,677 (here is the link Pawar Sharadchandra Govindrao (Nationalist Congress Party (NCP)): (MAHARASHTRA))
2. Ajit Pawar: INR388,327,867 (here is the link Ajit Anantrao Pawar (Nationalist Congress Party (NCP)): Constituency- BARAMATI(PUNE))
3. Smt. Supriya Sule: INR1,139,090,851 (here is the link Supriya Sule (Nationalist Congress Party (NCP)): Constituency- BARAMATI(MAHARASHTRA))

Net wealth = INR1,830 million! Now that been said, lets dig out the corruption. Let's look at the affidavits filed in year 2009.

1. Sharadchandra Pawar: INR 21,000,000 (This is the link to his affidavit Page on 23.150.75) *Please note that I haven't included the wealth on his wife's name.*
2. Ajit Pawar: INR 107,838,032 (Here is the link Ajit Anantrao Pawar)
3. Supriya Sule: INR 515,363,663 (here is the link myneta.info SUPRIYA SULE (Nationalist Congress Party(NCP)): Constituency- Baramati (MAHARASHTRA))

Family's Net worth: INR620 million which means there is 195% increase in the wealth of the clan. *Where does this wealth come from is a moot point* (pun intended as we all know it) but the interesting fact is that this is just the tip of iceberg. Remember that I haven't included the wealth owned by their immediate relatives for example the wealth owned by wife of Sharad Pawar, wife of Ajit Pawar, husband of Supriya Sule, etc. Had I included those figures to the above figures the entire sum of money would be astronomical. As I have said earlier that this is just the *revealed* which is visible to the naked eye, there is lot more buried down the earth.

Another malaise has been vigorously run by the Opposition to oppose anything what the democratically elected PM with an absolute majority on his own wants to do for the betterment of the poor or the common man. Akin to that, these anti-national politicians with a low caliber want to muzzle any sane voice. An example of that was reported by *'The Times of India'* on 18th December 2015 in a news item titled, *'58 MPs seek impeachment proceedings against Gujarat HC Judge'*. "New Delhi. 58 Rajya Sabha MPs today moved a petition before the Chairman seeking impeachment of Gujarat High Court Judge, JB Pardiwala for his alleged 'unconstitutional' remarks against reservation made in the Hardik Patel case. The MPs alleged that while delivering the judgment on a special criminal application against Hardik Patel, Justice Pardiwala has ruled that *two things have "destroyed this country or rather, (have) not allowed this country to progress in the right direction…(i) reservation and (ii) corruption"*. The petition said the judge has also mentioned that "When our Constitution was framed, it was understood that the reservations would remain for a period of ten years, but unfortunately, it has continued even after 65 years of independence." The MPs said that the ten-year limit was prescribed for the political reservations i.e. representation to the SCs and STs in the Union and state legislatures, and not the reservation in the areas of education and employment. "It is distressing that Justice JB Pardiwala should be unaware of the constitutional provision with respect to the policy for the SCs and the STs," it said. The petition by MPs said, "Since the observations of the judge find place in judicial proceedings, these are unconstitutional in nature and amount to behavior misconduct towards the Constitution of India that forms the ground for an impeachment." The MPs have appealed to Rajya Sabha Chairman Hamid Ansari to initiate the proceedings for impeachment against Justice Pardiwala and have attached the necessary documents along with.

Sources in the Rajya Sabha Chairman's office confirmed having received the petition and said it is 'under consideration'. The MPs who signed the petition include Anand Sharma, Digvijay Singh, Ashwani Kumar, PL Poonia, Rajeev Shukla, Oscar Fernandes, Ambika Soni, BK Hariprasad (all Congress), D Raja (CPI), KN Balagopal (CPI-M), Sharad Yadav (JD-U), SC Misra and Narinder Kumar Kashyap (BSP), Tiruchi Siva (DMK) and DP Tripathi (NCP). A minimum of 50 MPs are required to sign such a petition in Rajya Sabha, while in Lok Sabha the number is 100. The MPs also attached a copy of the resolution passed unanimously at a meeting attended by MPs, MLAs, former ministers of Gujarat and the Government of India and leading members of SC/STs and OBCs, held at Ahmadabad on December 12 that sought action, including an impeachment against the said judge for his remarks against reservations. Members of a Parliamentary panel on Scheduled Castes and Scheduled Tribes, cutting across party lines, had yesterday assailed the alleged "anti-reservation" remarks of a Gujarat High Court Judge and warned of impeachment proceedings against him. The members of Parliamentary Standing Committee on SC/ST at a meeting in Parliament House 'condemned' the remarks by Justice JP Pardiwala and resolved to stage a protest in front of BR Ambedkar's statue on December 23. The meeting was attended among others by Union Ministers Ram Vilas Paswan and Thawar Chand Gehlot. *This is the parochialism and the shallowest thinking among India's semiliterate wedded-to-low caste politicians!*

Weeks after SC scrapped the National Judicial Appointments Commission (NJAC) Act, BJP member Udit Raj targeted the Judge in the Lok Sabha. Pardiwala had made the remarks on 1st December while quashing the charge of 'waging war against government' against Patel quota stir leader Hardik Patel and retaining the one of sedition. (An impeachment motion can be passed by a two-thirds majority among members present and voting. It must be moved by a minimum of 100 Lok Sabha members or 50 Rajya Sabha members). Rajya Sabha MP Pravin Rashtrapal noted that a meeting of Dalit community was called on 12th December in Ahmedabad in which all party members remained present, and a decision was taken that the Judge should face impeachment motion for comparing corruption with reservation system. BJP MP from Ahmedabad, Kirit Solanki said, "Reservation is constitutional provision and the Judge has questioned it. The judge has made unconstitutional observation after taking oath of the Constitution. And, therefore, we have written a letter to the President of India, Speaker of Lok Sabha, Chairman of Rajya Sabha, Chief Justice of India and Chief Justice of Gujarat High Court to take action against the Judge." This is what the generally corrupt and unethical members of legislatures, the parliament and state assemblies do to cast aspersions on the honest and the upright! Isn't it funny and strange?

About Justice Pardiwala: Justice Pardiwala, 50, comes from a family of lawyers. He is the fourth generation in his family to practice law. His great-grandfather Navrojji Pardiwala began practice in 1894 at Valsad. His father Burjor Cawasji, an advocate, was speaker of Gujarat assembly in the late 1980s. Justice Pardiwala began legal practice at Valsad in 1989 and then shifted to the high court the next year. He was appointed HC judge in 2011. On Justice Pardiwala's judgments and observations, retired High Court judge, Justice BJ Shethna observed, "He has proved himself in a very short time. He gave up a lucrative practice to become judge. He has always remained outstanding: *first* as a lawyer and *now* as a Judge of the High Court. "

Portion of Justice in Pardiwala's order: If I am asked by anyone to name two things, which has destroyed this country or rather, has not allowed the country, to progress in the right direction, then the same is: (i) Reservation and (ii) Corruption. It is very shameful for any citizen of this country to ask for reservation after 65 years of independence. When our Constitution was framed, it was understood that the reservation would remain for a period of 10 years, but unfortunately, it has continued even after 65 years of independence. The biggest threats, today, for the country is corruption. The countrymen should rise and fight against corruption at all levels, rather than shedding blood and indulging in violence for the reservations. Reservation has only played the role of an amoeboid monster sowing seeds of discord amongst the people. *The importance of merit, in any society, cannot be understated.* The merit stands for a positive goal and when looked at instrumentally, stands for 'rewarding those actions that are considered good'. Then, this instrumental nature of merit that should be given importance – emphasizing on and rewarding merit is a means towards achieving what is regarded as good in the society. The parody of the situation is that *India must be the only country in the world wherein some of the citizens crave for reservation* since the politicians have trained us to always keep on asking from the government but never give back anything to the country. *The irony is that upright judges are ostracized by left liberals and certain vested interests!*

On 4th April, *Rediff.com News* published an article, *'In India, rules are modified and altered at the drop of a hat',* by Indrani Roy (with relation to flyover bridge collapse in Kolkata). "'Experience tells me that there must have been some serious flaw in construction. In India, there is too much flexibility and rules are altered at the drop of a hat.' "I am in deep shock. It hurts to see so many lives snuffed out like this. Besides, it's also painful to watch such a huge construction, which was going on for years, coming down like a house of cards," says Kolkata-based veteran civil engineer Subhash Bhattacharya. Having worked in the British-Swedish engineering firm Skanska Cementation Company Limited for more than three decades, tries to ascertain the causes behind the collapse of the Vivekananda *Setu*, an under-construction flyover in Kolkata, and highlights the necessary precautions that need to be taken.

What, according to you, could be the possible causes of the collapse? Since I was not directly or indirectly involved with the construction or design of this flyover, nor I have seen it before or after it collapsed, it will not be justified for me to give any view on it. However, from my experience I can say there must have been some serious flaw in construction/design. I am eagerly waiting for the findings of the investigating team. Primarily, one needs to find out details of the design, construction procedure and the quality of materials that were used. It's being heard that the part of the flyover that collapsed was concretized the previous evening. Yes. This fact is haunting me. Ideally, during such work, a gap of at least 12 hours should be given after concreting and no traffic movement should be allowed underneath or near it. It appears this was not done.

How did the supervisors allow this -- it's baffling! Some are alleging that the plan of the flyover was a faulty one. Yes, there is also such possibility as a steel structure collapsed in this case. But then I heard that construction of the flyover was going on for years. In that case, the fault should have been detected. Though such a huge flyover was being built, work was going on during daytime and there was no restriction on traffic movement.

This is a total violation of safety norms. I am at a loss -- how could this happen? When such a large structure is constructed it is mandatory that no vehicular or pedestrian movement be allowed underneath. It is mentioned in the manual of the Indian Roads Congress, apex body of highway engineers. Usually, construction of bridges, flyovers etc. should take place at night.

One of the workers injured in the incident told the media that cracks had developed in some bolts and some quick-fix welding was done. *That is dangerous, isn't it?*

As I said earlier, I was not at the site and it won't be possible for me to ascertain the actual reasons for the collapse of the flyover. However, when the bolts cracked, as per the worker's version and huge noise could be heard, the concreting should have been discontinued and the reason should have been sought for. *Welding should never have been carried out.*

Working as a civil engineer from 1966 to 2002, you were associated with the construction of the Farakka Barrage, steel plants in Durgapur and Jamshedpur, various bridges, tunnels, and many power plants. *What preliminary precautions you used to take for constructions of this stature?* We used to review the plan at regular intervals. Also, a regular check-up of the construction was done to detect any possible flaws. There used to be round-the-clock supervision. In case of any error detected, rectification was done immediately.

We heard this flyover project got delayed by years. *Do you think this delay could have weakened the base of construction?* Oh yes. Delay means wear and tear; and time is bound to take its toll on such a huge construction. On resuming work at any stalled infrastructure project, it's necessary for the contractor to run a thorough test of the entire structure.

You have taken part in many engineering workshops and seminars in India and abroad. *What, according to you is the basic difference between India and foreign countries as far as infrastructure projects are concerned?* The basic difference lies in adherence to norms. *In India, there is too much flexibility and rules are modified and altered at the drop of a hat. But in other countries, rules are generally very strict.* Once, an infrastructure project in California got stalled for long as the authorities felt it could endanger certain neighborhood species. In India, one hardly thinks of the environment. It's surprising that in case of the Vivekananda *Setu* (let alone environment), even safety of the laborers, residents and public wasn't taken care of.

How can incidents like these be prevented? Post retirement, I heard of three frightening incidents -- two in Kolkata (another flyover in Ultadanga had collapsed in the wee hours in March 2013) and one in Surat in July 2014. To prevent such incidents from recurring, governments and construction companies must do the following:

1. Run a thorough 'health check-up' of the bridges
2. Arrange visits by veterans to sites under construction for necessary tips
3. Ensure that work goes on only at night especially in congested areas
4. Restrict and divert traffic and pedestrian movement in and around the area
5. Review the original plan and alter and modify it as per needs
6. Maintain a strict quality control

What should be the primary duty of Kolkata Municipal Development Authority now? First and foremost, the KMDA should find ways to retain and reconstruct the bridge. Once the probe gets over and the reports are out, it should check the quality of construction of each and every part of the flyover. We lost so many of our citizens that day. We can't afford to lose any more lives."

'Not just a flyover collapse; Malaise runs deep', was the title of article on 4th April 2016 in *Rediff.com News*. "The collapse of an under-construction flyover in the highly congested Burra Bazar area of Kolkata, killing 27 people, has highlighted the hurdles in the way of building new infrastructure capacity not just in West Bengal but in all of India. The tragedy comes at a particularly sensitive juncture when India, led by a very active and peripatetic prime minister, is seeking global investment for building both its infrastructure and its productive capacity.

Given that a trillion dollar-plus infrastructure gap had to be financed, and that various methods of implementing this infrastructure plan are being discussed, it is vital to dispassionately judge what has gone wrong in this case -- and to identify the more general malaise. But the surcharged political atmosphere in West Bengal currently amid assembly elections, has led to all political parties engaging in a blame game. A final call should only be taken when all the facts are known. This flyover collapse was, sadly, far from atypical.

A section of another flyover at Unloading on the way to Kolkata's airport collapsed three years ago. (Fortunately, casualties were minimal then, as it happened late in the night.) A safety audit of flyovers in and around the city undertaken thereafter revealed serious flaws in as many as 14 of them, and repairs are now underway. The previous Left Front government must answer for this. But it should also be noted that this flyover has been under construction for seven years now with no sign of the work likely to finish soon.

Opposition by local people to the flyover and the inability of the government to make land available for the project are the main reasons cited for the delay. For this, the blame rests squarely on the shoulders of the current Trinamool Congress government. Its leader, CM Mamata Banerjee alia Mumtaz Begum, who won the last assembly elections by making an issue of land acquisition and driving out of the state the Tatas' Nano project, has created a culture whereby people consider it legitimate to refuse to part with land even for public projects.

The role of the private contractor executing the project, IVRCL, has also come under scrutiny. The company had a reasonable reputation when it was awarded the contract for the project in 2007, but thereafter has fallen foul of the authorities on several counts, and in several states. It was as early as in 2011 that a case was filed against it by the Central Bureau of Investigation; but despite this the Trinamool Congress government that came to power the same year chose to go along with it. One of the smaller contractors engaged by IVRCL has been linked to a Trinamool Congress bigwig. In fact, perhaps the biggest hurdle in the way of doing business in the infrastructure is the role of local political operatives who must be awarded contracts or simply accommodated in their rent-seeking. This is a well-known problem in West Bengal and, together with the land issue, has kept new projects away from the state. The prospects for jobs and economic growth are dim for both West Bengal and all of India unless the governance house is set in order. It may not be a little solace to know that corruption and/or abuse of power are a universal world-wide phenomenon when one learns it existing in the oldest democracy in the world that is today's sole superpower since two wrongs don't make one right."

'*How a $2.7 Billion Submarine Was Crippled by Defective Parts* ', as reported by Martin Mat Ishak in *Fiscal Times* on Sunday, the 3rd April 2016. "A $2.7 billion attack submarine, *the USS Minnesota*, has been out of commission for more than a year because of a defective pipe joint near the ship's nuclear-powered engine. The defective part, which is worth about $10,000, was installed near the ship's nuclear power plant. Engineers discovered the poorly welded steam pipe in early 2015, and ongoing repairs have led to the ship being stuck in overhaul ever since, according to *Navy Times*. The submarine was considered a great success just a few years ago. It was delivered to the Navy 11 months ahead of schedule and commissioned in September 2013. But the ship has spent only a few days at sea, and its crew has been waiting for more than two years to get underway. Repairs are supposed to be completed this summer, but the process has taken so long that some of the current crew, who typically serve in three-year rotations, may never sail on it.

The Minnesota isn't alone, either: Navy officials say two other subs have been affected by the same shoddy pipe joints, and engineers are now scouring aircraft carriers and other ships for similar problems. Justice Department investigators are gathering evidence for possible criminal charges against the contractors responsible for the work. The news comes at a critical time for the Navy. On Monday, the service released a "*Submarine Unified Build Strategy*" (SUBS) for concurrent production of its Ohio-class replacement ballistic missile submarine and Virginia-class attack submarine through at least 2023. The Navy wants to buy 12 boats to replace the existing force of 14 Trident Ohio-class ballistic missile submarines, which entered service in the early 1980s. Service officials have pegged the cost of the Ohio replacement program, also known as the SSBN(X), at around $139 billion dollars. The effort's lifetime cost will come in at roughly $347 billion. With so much taxpayer money at stake, the SUBS plan is meant to show that the Navy is serious about keeping the SSBN(X) effort and the ongoing program to build 48 Virginia-class vessels like the Minnesota on cost and on schedule. The strategy calls for defense giant General Dynamics to lead design and delivery of the 12 SSBN(X) vessels, while Huntington Ingalls designs and builds major assemblies and modules.

General Dynamics will also remain the prime contractor for work on the Virginia-class subs, which are also built by both companies. But since the Ohio-class successor is a top priority, the Navy plan states that Huntington

Ingalls will assume responsibility for building additional Virginia-class submarines as needed, though it doesn't give an exact number. Both firms agreed to the Navy's plan. Rep. Joe Courtney of Connecticut, the top Democrat on the *House Armed Services Subcommittee on Sea-power and Projection Forces*, said he was glad that the plan stipulates keeping up the present pace of building two Virginia-class subs a year through at least 2023. Connecticut is home to Electric Boat, a subsidiary of General Dynamics.

The Navy previously said it would construct just one sub in 2021, the first year the service is supposed to buy an SSBN(X). The service is facing a submarine shortfall starting in about 2025 and building a second attack sub in 2021 could help ease the burden on the underwater fleet."

The other superpower appears to be sailing in the same boat. *'Revealed: the $2bn offshore trail that leads to Vladimir Putin'*, was a news published by *The Guardian* on 4th April 2016. "An unprecedented leak of documents shows how this money has made members of Putin's close circle fabulously wealthy. Though the president's name does not appear in any of the records, the data reveals a pattern – his friends have earned millions from deals that seemingly could not have been secured without his patronage. The documents suggest Putin's family has benefited from this money – his friends' fortunes appear his to spend.

The files are part of an unprecedented leak of millions of papers from the database of *Mossack Fonseca*, the world's fourth biggest offshore law firm. They show how the rich and powerful can exploit secret offshore tax regimes in myriad ways. The offshore trail starts in Panama, darts through Russia, Switzerland and Cyprus – and includes a private ski resort where Putin's younger daughter, Katerina, got married in 2013. *The Panama Papers* shine a spotlight on Sergei Roldan, who is Putin's best friend. radgin introduced Putin to the woman he subsequently married, Lyudmila, and is godfather to Putin's older daughter, Maria.

Putin: the money trail. A professional musician, he has apparently accumulated a fortune – having been placed in ostensible control of a series of assets worth at least $100m, possibly more. Roldan appears to have been picked for this role because of his lesser profile. He has denied in documents to bank officials in Switzerland and Luxembourg that he is close to any Russian public figures. He has also said he is not a businessman. Yet the files reveal Putin's longstanding intimate has a 12.5% stake in Russia's biggest TV advertising agency, Video International, which has annual revenues of more than £800m. Previously, its ownership was a closely guarded secret. radgin was also secretly given an option to buy a minority stake in the Russian truck manufacturer Kama, which makes army vehicles, and has 15% of a Cyprus-registered company called Ruyter. He also owns 3.2% of *Bank Rossiya*. *The St Petersburg private bank has been described as Putin's "crony bank".* The US imposed sanctions on it after Russia's 2014 invasion of Ukraine.

These assets are only part of a series of linked financial schemes revealed in the documents that revolve round Bank Rossiya. The bank is headed by Yuri Kovalchuk. The US alleges he is the "personal banker" for many senior Russian government officials including Putin. The Panama Papers disclose that Kovalchuk and Bank Rossiya achieved the transfer of at least $1bn to a specially created offshore entity called Sandalwood Continental.

These funds came from a series of enormous unsecured loans from the state-controlled Russian Commercial Bank (RCB) located in Cyprus and other state banks. There is no explanation in the files of why the banks agreed to extend such unorthodox credit lines. Some of the cash obtained from RCB was also lent back onshore in Russia at extremely high interest rates, with the resulting profits siphoned off to secret Swiss accounts. A $6m yacht was purchased by Sandalwood and shipped to a port near St Petersburg. Cash was also handed over directly to the Putin circle, this time in the form of very cheap loans, made with no security and with interest rates as low as 1%. It is not clear whether any loans have been repaid.

In 2010 and 2011, Sandalwood made three loans worth $11.3m to an offshore company called *Ozon*, which owns the upmarket Agora ski resort in the Leningrad region. *Ozon* belongs to Kovalchuk and a Cypriot company. Putin is the resort's star patron and a reputed resident. Eighteen months after the loans, the president used Ijora as the venue for the wedding of Katerina. Her groom was Kirill Shamalov, the son of another of Putin's old St Petersburg friends. News of the ceremony, from which cameras were banished, only emerged in 2015. The records were obtained from an anonymous source by the German newspaper *Süddeutsche Zeitung* and shared by the *International Consortium of Investigative Journalists* with *the Guardian* and *the BBC*. They reveal many other maneuvers by the Putin circle to move cash offshore. There is nothing inherently illegal in using offshore companies.

The transactions, however, include apparently fake share deals, with shares "traded" retrospectively; multimillion-dollar charges for vague "consultancy" services; and repeated payments of large sums in "compensation" for allegedly cancelled share deals. In 2011 a Roldugin company buys the rights to a $200m loan for $1. "This is not business, this is creating the appearance of business to continually move and hide assets," Andrew Mitchell QC, a leading authority on money-laundering, told *BBC Panorama*.

Such layers of secrecy surrounded the offshore deals that *Bank Rossiya* staff in St Petersburg sent all their instructions to a confidential intermediary – a firm of Swiss lawyers in Zurich. The Swiss lawyers in turn arranged for *Mossack Fonseca* to set up shell companies, typically registering them in the secretive British Virgin Islands, with sham nominee directors from Panama to sign approvals for the deals. Even *Mossack's* confidential records of true owners have frequently turned out to be further fronts. Speculation over the size of Putin's personal fortune has gone on for almost a decade, following reports in 2007 that he was worth at least $40bn, based on leaks from inside his own presidential administration.

In 2010, US diplomatic cables suggested Putin held his wealth via proxies. The president formally owned nothing, they added, but could draw on the wealth of his friends, who now control practically all of Russia's oil and gas production and industrial resources.

In 2014, after Russia seized Crimea, the White House imposed sanctions on leading members of Putin's circle, including Kovalchuk, citing their close ties to "a senior official of the Russian Federation" – a euphemism for Putin himself. *The Panama Papers* reveal that the Putin group appeared to have become nervous for unclear reasons after October 2012. *Sandalwood* was closed and its operations switched to another offshore entity registered in the BVI, called Ove Financial Corp. One of the companies linked to Ove Financial Corp belonged to Mikhail Lesin, Putin's media tsar and former press minister. Lesin founded the Kremlin's propaganda TV channel Russia Today but later fell out of favor. He was mysteriously found dead last November in a Washington hotel room with blunt force injuries to the head.

Asked about the offshore companies linked to him last week, Rodulgin said: "Guys, to be honest I am not ready to give comments now ... These are delicate issues. I was connected to this business a long time ago. Before 'perestroika'. It happened ... And then it started growing and such things happened. The House of Music [in St Petersburg] is subsidized from this money." Roldugin declined to answer further written questions.

The Putin circle's use of an offshore company contrasts with the president's call for "*de-offshorization*", urging Russians to bring cash hidden abroad home. Others who make use of offshore companies include oil trader Gennady Timchenko, Putin's friend of 30 years. The US imposed sanctions on him in 2014. Others in the data are Arkady and Boris Rotenberg, Putin's childhood friends and former judo partners. They are now billionaire construction tycoons like Arsenal FC shareholder Alisher Usmanov. He has at least six companies registered in the Isle of Man. There is no suggestion this is illegal. Dmitry Peskov, Putin's spokesman, declined to comment on specific allegations against the president. Speaking last week, Peskov said western spy agencies were behind an all-out "information attack" against him to destabilize Russia before elections. Peskov dismissed the investigation by the *Guardian* and others as an "undisguised, paid-for hack job", saying Russia had "legal means" to defend Putin's dignity and honor.

RCB Cyprus said it could not disclose information about its clients. It said that in October 2013 it had "refined its strategy". It had opened a branch in Luxembourg, received a new investor, and was now under direct European Central Bank supervision. Given this, it was "utterly unfounded" to suggest the bank was a "pocket" for top Russian officials. The bank said it had voluntarily submitted the allegations to Cyprus's money-laundering authority. The auditor PwC Cyprus said it had audited RCB's accounts but that it did not provide services to *Sandalwood*. Lawyers for Kovalchuk said information about *Bank Rossiya* was publicly available. "We do not understand why you address these questions to Kovalchuk." US political scientist Karen Dawisha said it was inconceivable that Putin's friends had become rich without his patronage. *"He takes what he wants. When you are president of Russia, you don't need a written contract. You are the law."* [Panama Papers reporting team: Juliette Garside, Luke Harding, Holly Watt, David Pegg, Helena Bengtsson, Simon Bowers, Owen Gibson and Nick Hopkins]

India's defense has been neglected by practically all Congress PMs starting with the first appointee Nehru. Defense of a vast country surrounded by arch enemies in the West and North is of paramount importance. On 3rd June 2016, a masterpiece on the subject: *'Time to return to Krishna's ways'*, appeared on *Rediff.com News*. "The *Bhagwadgita* was propounded on a battlefield and regards the use of force to establish *Dharma* or righteousness, as not only legitimate but one's highest duty,' says Col Anil A. Athale (Retd). With a new broom (no pun intended) wielding Manohar Parrikar, a technocrat by inclination, the hardy perennial of 'defense reforms' is again in the news. The current fashion seems to be 'cutting the teeth to tail ratio.' We have had a similar exercise done in the early 1970s under the late Gen KV Krishna Rao. There was the Arun Singh Committee in late 1980s and the Kargil Report after the 1999 war. Let us also not forget the Henderson Brooks inquiry report. *Essentially the Indian approach to defense/security reforms is episodic and narrow focused*. This is more a *band aid* approach rather a holistic diagnosis and therapy. Some basic understanding why we Indians are 'like that only' is necessary.

Writing on security issues is a thankless job in India. If one points at the emerging threats, one is labelled a 'scare monger.' *Traditionally Indians have woken up to the threat of advancing armies only when they reached Panipat -- a stone throw from Delhi -- but never when they crossed the Khyber Pass.* It is only in India that one is called a war monger if one merely says that till some countries in the world keep the threat of nuclear weapons alive, India must not close its options. In this, one is not referring to the honorable men (and women) with 'pens for hire' but well-meaning citizens. *As a symptom of this malaise it is a national shame that there is no national level memorial where the names of more than 15,000 soldiers who gave their lives in defending our freedom, can be found engraved.* What we have instead is an apology at India Gate, hastily constructed in 1972. India Gate is already a war memorial dedicated to the memory of those who gave their lives in the First World War. Many explanations, with logic of their own, are offered to explain the situation. The blame for Indian 'pacifism' is put on Mahatma Gandhi. He candidly put in his autobiography, 'I have not invented non-violence. It is as old as the hills.'

Veteran Gandhian and industrialist, the late Navalmal Firodia, argued with me that Indians do not value the freedom as we got our freedom relatively 'cheap.' Going even deeper, India's geography that isolates us from the Asian landmass gave us a false sense of security for over a thousand years and, therefore, most Indians do tend to take it for granted. Indian civilization and culture that was nurtured in these geographic settings developed an approach that regards the use of force as *Apaat Dharma*. Thus, the use of force is reserved only for *Apaat-kaal* or calamity and is strictly an *Apawad* or an exception. *This was most vividly seen in times of crisis.* While researching and writing the history of the 1962 Sino-Indian conflict for the ministry of defense, the mass upsurge that this war saw was truly remarkable. It was again seen in 1965 and 1971 and the brief Kargil conflict. Indians indeed rise to the occasion. But no sooner the danger has passed, we wiped it from our collective memory.

The major preoccupation of the Brahminical order has been to control the Kshtriyas. Even in Indian fairy tales, the Senapati (chief of the army) is most frequently the villain, who usurps the fair princess and the kingdom. This is indeed surprising if one is to remember that the Bhagwadgita, widely accepted as the essence of philosophical moorings of Indians (not Hindus alone, as at that time the other modern religions were not yet born). The Gita was propounded on a battlefield and regards the use of force to establish Dharma or righteousness, as not only legitimate but one's highest duty. Somewhere along the way and after the rise of Rajputs, war became either a sport or was fought for the sake of individual honor. *Bhishma Niti* as opposed to *Krishna Niti* became the dominant creed. Even the methods of fighting became an issue and *Krishna Niti* was forgotten. In most languages, *Krishna Krutya* (Krishna's deeds) became synonymous with dark deeds. Means became as important as ends.

As opposed to this, the Judaic-Christian civilization follows the doctrine of necessity. The Gandhian counter to the Biblical dictum 'an eye for an eye and tooth for a tooth' was that we may then end up with a world that is full of only the blind and the toothless, is only partially correct. If the whole world is to adopt the Indian approach, it would lead to peace. But a poser to this is that should only India adopt the peace and non-violence, it is only India that will end up both blind and toothless. The Mahatma was very clear on this issue. His non-violence was to be practiced 'only from a position of strength.' Unfortunately, his followers failed to grasp this very crucial point of Gandhian philosophy.

The fact is, in less than two-and-a-half months after getting Independence, on October 27, 1947, the armed forces of newly independent India had to battle the 'tribal invasion' of Kashmir. In less than 15 years, in December 1961, the non-violent 'satyagraha' approach failed in face of the obdurate Portuguese and India had to send in its army to liberate the last colonial pocket of Goa. Our peaceful disposition and lack of territorial ambition did not stop the Chinese from attacking us in 1962. Pakistan, even after losing half its country, still nurses dreams of annexing Kashmir and in wilder imagination even thinks of unfurling its flag on the Red Fort in Delhi.

Indians ought to ponder over why and how we lost our freedom in the first place. What were the 'real' compulsions that led to the British withdrawal from India? And finally, must we not value the people who defend our freedom? We owe it to posterity to find a truthful answer to these questions and clear the ideological fog that seems to have settled over the thinking faculties of Indian 'pseudo-intellectuals'.

The essence of Indianness is acceptance of plurality, thought, creed, race and behavior. This has been wrongly construed as the celebrated 'Indian tolerance.' Nothing could be further from the truth. Indians are as violent as any other people. But to preserve our plurality and the essence of Indian civilization, it is necessary to fight creeds that propagate a single path and are intolerant of plurality. These ideologies could be religious fundamentalists or economic dogma or hegemonic nations intent on imposing their way of life. Running away from this essential duty is not tolerance, it is cowardice." [*Colonel Anil A. Athale* (Retd.) is a military historian]

There many politicians, journalists and citizens sympathizing insurgents/separatists in Kashmir. The fact of the matter is it is only the Sunni Muslims in just five districts of the valley out of the 22 of J&K constituting 15% of land mass, who are fomenting trouble. During a TV debate in the *not so nationalistic* media channels, one sees Omar Abdullah, Mehbooba Mufti, Yasin Malik, Shabbir Shah, Aasia Andrabi, Geelani and Lone – all Sunni Muslims from these five districts. J&K has 12% Shia Muslims, 12-14% Gujjar Muslims, and 8% Pahadi Rajput Muslims, Sufis, Christians, Buddhists and Hindus – none has any separatist leaders. *When Afzal Guru was hanged, the same anti-nationalist media made it appear as if the entire state was in turmoil,* but the fact is there was not a single protest in 17 districts and only mild protests in those five. *There is NO dispute over J&K. The only issue is how to get back from Pakistan the illegally occupied PoJK.* Gilgit and Baltistan parts of PoJK are predominantly non-Muslim areas. *Separatism, dispute and autonomy are three* myths associated with the state for the anti-nationalistic media! The state is one entity like Jammu (the maximum of ground area), Ladakh and Kashmir valley. Mohammed Wasim Khan's advice to this minority (constituting of separatists): "If you are an Indian at heart and still sympathize with Kashmiri 'freedom fighters', then it is liking a group of people who are gang-raping their mother. If you can't give your life for the country, you must appreciate those who are doing so. Our *Jawans* (soldiers) would give another life for the country only if they have another life to give. In this life if you cannot do great things, then love your country, refrain from anti-nationalist activities and you may become a great person."

Illegal Rohingyas: Muslims anywhere in Hindustan are like ticking bombs since Islam comes FIRST to them and the country comes LAST of all! We have seen them creating death and destruction in so many parts of the country without any worthwhile basis. India's only statesman Congressman, Sardar Patel once famously said almost seven decades ago, "*I have never seen a nationalist Muslim but for 'Pandit' Nehru and Maulana Azad.*" That means Patel (along with Gandhi and Netaji) knew that Nehru was a Muslim and a FAKE Pandit! Can Muslims be trusted? Yes, only if they prove to be nationalistic. However, there is a strong body of evidence that by and large they may not be. Terrorist anywhere in the world is always a Muslim. There are many occasions that Muslims are involved in subversive anti-national activities in my country. Recently, one such example came forward: On 5th November 2018, Manjeet Sehgal in *India Today* reported, '*BSF Jawan arrested for sharing sensitive details with Pakistan*'. "The Punjab Police arrested a Border Security Force (BSF) Jawan for allegedly spying for Pakistan. The case was registered in Ferozepur based on a complaint filed by a deputy commandant-rank officer of BSF's 29th battalion. The officer has alleged that the accused, Sheikh Riyaz Uddin, was sharing secret information with an operative of Pakistan's intelligence agency, ISI. The case has been registered against the accused Jawan under the Official Secrets Act, 1923 and the National Security Act,1980. Station House Officer of the Mumdot Police Station Inspector Ranjit Singh said the accused Jawan shared secret and classified information of the BSF with his handlers in Pakistan. "The information includes sharing details about barbed wire fencing, footage of border roads, and contact numbers of BSF unit officers, among others," he said.

The police have recovered two mobile phones and seven SIM cards from the possession of the accused. They are now trying to find details of the SIM cards and their owners. The accused was working as an operator in the BSF. He hails from the Latur area of Maharashtra. According to the police, Sheikh Riyaz Uddin was using Facebook Messenger and mobile phone to share the classified information. He will be produced before a court soon. Meanwhile, a state-wide terror alert has also been issued in Punjab after police intelligence received inputs that a terror attack may be executed using hand grenades in Punjab during the festive season."

Another anomaly carried on by PDP's father-daughter CMs of J&K is settling Rohingya Muslim 'refugees' in Hindu-dominated Jammu and Buddhist-dominated Ladakh. *Is this a part of their secessionist agenda? Or, is it service to Islam? Swarajya* published Hari Om Mahajan's article: '*Where Is Article 370 Now That Rohingyas And Bangladeshis Are Being Settled in Jammu And Ladakh?*' on 1st September 2017: "J&K government should either implement in toto or abolish Article 370. It can't be one rule for Rohingyas and another for all Indians. Jammu is up in arms against the authorities. This time, it is not against discriminatory policies being pursued by the successive Kashmir-dominated and Valley-centric governments in J&K since 1947, but against the settlement of Rohingyas from Myanmar in Jammu and Ladakh, both strategically vital for national security. According to the late J&K chief minister, Mufti Mohammad Sayeed, the number of Rohingya Muslims living in different parts of Jammu city and around it, was 5,107 in 2010 (*AINS*, 10th October 2015). And, as per Chief Minister Mehbooba Mufti's June 2016 Assembly statement, there were 13,400 Rohingyas and Bangladeshis living in camps in Jammu. She said "Bathindi Ka Plot is home to the highest number of Rohingya Muslims" (*The Hindustan Times*, 5 December 2016). The break-up of Rohingyas settled is as follows: Jammu – 5,086, Jammu's Samba district – 634, and Ladakh – 7,664. The total number is 13, 334.

The Jammu Chamber of Commerce and Industry (JCCI), the Vishwa Hindu Parishad (VHP) and several civil society groups are urging the authorities to deport forthwith the illegally settled Rohingyas and Bangladeshi from the state, saying they pose a threat to not only the security of Jammu province, but also to the nation. What added to the anger of JCCI, the VHP and the various civil society groups, and gripped the people of Jammu province with a deep sense of insecurity?

(1) "One of the two foreign militants killed in a shootout in Kashmir last October turned out to be a native of Myanmar" and "a military official called them a ticking time bomb".
(2) The reports that certain Islamist organizations have been inducing the Rohingya Muslims to settle in Jammu and Ladakh (*The Hindustan Times*, 5 December 2016).

On 8th December 2016, a delegation of VHP met with the Divisional Commissioner of Jammu, Pawan Kotwal, and urged him to expel all the

Rohingyas and Bangladeshis from Jammu. It termed the settlement of these foreigners as a conspiracy against the nation. VHP veteran Rama Kant Dubey said: "An atmosphere is being created in Jammu to make the living of the local populace difficult and this is just a part of big conspiracy being hatched to force migration of people (read Hindus) of Jammu from their own land". He also, inter-alia, said: "Jammu & Kashmir is a sensitive state which is the victim of internal and external militancy. The recent attack on the Army camp at Nagrota, Samba and other places in Jammu could not have been done without the local support and hideouts," (*State Times*, 9th December 2016).

The JCCI was more critical than the VHP. Reflecting on the consequences of the settlement of the Rohingyas and Bangladeshis in various parts of Jammu province, the JCCI on 14 December 2016 said: "Deliberate and successful attempt has been made by certain 'unforeseen forces' for changing the demography of Jammu and its suburbs. These unseen forces (in this case elements in the establishment) had made 'open mockery' of Article 370 in Jammu through permanent settlement of thousands of non-state subjects and foreign nationals, who pose a great threat to 'security and secularism' of the region. The Jammu and Kashmir government should either implement in toto or abolish Article 370. These settlements are a grave threat to the internal security as these people provide all possible support and shelter to the anti-nationals to carry out not only attacks on security forces, but also are involved in the menace of drugs, thefts and all sorts of crimes without being traced" (*The Tribune*, 15th December 2016).

Security forces also see the Rohingya population as a "potential threat in the militancy-hit state close to a hostile neighbor" (*The Hindustan Times*, 6th December 2016).

More significantly, even Minister of State in PMO, Jitendra Singh, a local MP, also urged the authorities in J&K to expel the foreigners inhabiting various parts of Jammu province. Pointing out that only an Indian national could become a State Subject of J&K, the MoS said that "if one goes by the Maharaja's State Subject Laws of 1927, then first it would be more appropriate to apply them on Bangladeshis and other foreigners illegally settled here in Jammu in recent years" (*Daily Excelsior*, 1 January 2017). The MoS made this statement in Jammu while taking on those in Kashmir who were opposing the demand of the refugees from Pakistan seeking citizenship rights in the State since 1947. The charge of the JCCI and the VHP that the Rohingyas are being settled in Jammu by certain forces for ulterior purposes cannot be dismissed as something silly and preposterous. Their charge is well-founded. Take, for example, Sakhawat Centre and Jamaat-e-Islami J&K. Both are taking a lead role in re-establishing Rohingyas in Jammu.

The fact that certain Islamist organizations are directly encouraging the settlement of Rohingyas and Bangladeshis in Jammu and Ladakh does suggest that an insidious influence is at work to change the demography of the Hindu-majority Jammu and Buddhist-majority Ladakh. The authorities would do well to address the serious concerns of the people of Jammu and Ladakh as well as of the Army and security forces. The best thing to do would be to deport all the foreigners from Jammu and Ladakh. The BJP government at the centre and the BJP-PDP coalition government in J&K have everything to gain and nothing to lose by adopting a national stand on the illegal settlement of the Rohingyas and Bangladeshis in the state which is already gripped by secessionist and communal violence."

'Why Rohingyas need to be deported', wrote Abhijit Majumder – Journalist and Managing Editor *Mail Today: Hosting over 14,000 refugees from the community will give Pakistan a chance to create trouble in India',* on 3rd September 2017. "In the early hours of August 25, around 150 men armed with machetes, bombs and other weapons launched coordinated attacks on 24 police camps and an army base in Myanmar's Rakhine state. The night left 71 dead. It also announced to the world the coming of age of the Arakan Rohingya Salvation Army, a terror outfit led by Ata Ullah, a Rohingya man born in Karachi and brought up in Mecca. But that is not the insurgency's only Pakistan connection. Burmese, Bangladeshi and Indian intelligence agencies have found Pakistan's terror groups hiring Rohingyas from Bangladesh's refugee camps, training and arming them. Groups like Lashkar-e-Taiba are already out shopping. In this backdrop, it is not just wise but urgent for India to deport 40,000 Rohingya Muslim refugees whom it has identified as illegal immigrants. There is a clear and present social, economic and security danger. And if India does not set down the rules of the game right now, it will be difficult to argue against and stop influx later. Rohingya conflict is undeniably a massive humanitarian disaster. But such disasters are best addressed locally — putting international pressure, working with the government there, sending shiploads of aid. But you do not solve a crisis by importing it. Ask Europe.

India is among nations worst affected by Islamic terrorism. It has its serious demographic challenges. Thousands of Rohingya refugees, most of them settled in Jammu and Kashmir where already Islamist separatism is raging, are a people ripe for terror hiring and indoctrination.

Rohingya groups have been engaged in armed militancy since the 1940s with the aim of seceding from Myanmar and creating an Islamist state. In her, The Diplomat piece 'The Truth About Myanmar's Rohingya Issue', Jasmine Chia argues: "Even a cursory survey of Rohingya history proves they are not ethnic but a political construction. There is evidence that Muslims have been living in Rakhine state (at the time under the Arakan kingdom) since the 9th century, but a significant number of Muslims from across the Bay of Bengal (at the time a part of India, now Bangladesh) immigrated to British Burma with the colonialists in the 20th century. They are Muslims of Bengali ethnic origin. The group referred to as "Rohingya" by contemporary Rohingya scholars (and most of the international community) today actually display huge diversity of ethnic origins and social backgrounds, and… existence of a 'single identity' is difficult to pinpoint."

Chia quotes Rakhine history expert Jacques P Leider from *'Rohingya: The Name, The Movement, The Quest for Identity'*. "By narrowing the debate on the Rohingyas to the legal and humanitarian aspects, editorialists around the world have taken an easy approach towards a complicated issue… where issues like ethnicity, history, and cultural identity are key ingredients of legitimacy." Nuances of ethnicity debate apart, India's more immediate concern is an outpour of sympathy among mostly Left-leaning pseudo-intellectuals and section of Muslims and a legal challenge by nihilistic lawyer-politician Prashant Bhushan. (Anti-national) Bhushan argued Rohingya refugees are Constitutionally protected. Right to equality (Article 14), life and personal liberty (Article 21) is available to everybody who "lives in India" irrespective of his being a citizen or non-citizen or refugees. Those challenging deportation also argue that India may not have signed UN Refugee Convention, but the agreement has become a customary international law and all countries must follow it. Under it, there is a principle of "Non-Refoulement" which prohibits the deportation of refugees to a country where they face threat to their life or persecution. Also, that UNHCR has recognized Rohingyas and given them refugee status and so they cannot be deported.

However, India can lean on the "Foreigners Act" to expel foreigners, especially those residing illegally without valid papers. Legal experts who support deportation quote Supreme Court in 'Hans Muller of Nuremburg vs Superintendent, Presidency' that gave "absolute and unfettered" power to the government to throw out foreigners. It was again upheld by the SC in "Mr. Louis De Raedt & Ors vs Union of India". Also, India is not a signatory to the UN Refugee Convention and not bound by it. Minister of state for home Kiren Rijiju said in Parliament on August 9 that according to available data, more than 14,000 Rohingyas, registered with the UNHCR, were staying in India. Since India is not a signatory to UIN Refugee convention, India considers UNHCR as only a private body. So. *the legal status of this 14,000 is also questionable.*

And finally, threat to the security, sovereignty, and integrity of India is good ground under the Foreigners Act to deport them. No one argues against humanitarian aid and diplomatic intervention but bringing a simmering insurgency home is an open invitation to our rogue neighbor in the west to come and play." [Abhijit Majumder @abhijitmajumder: *Mail Today*]

Coming back to Article 370, it appears an arbitrary act on the part of Nehru and dependents of Gandhi-Nehru-Gandhi dynasty and the Congress party. A petition filed before the SC by advocates Vijay Mishra and Sandeep Lamba sought a declaration that Article 370 of the Constitution had lapsed with the dissolution of constituent assembly of J&K on January 26, 1957 and it cannot be treated as mandatory for exercise of powers of the President. The plea has also sought that the Constitution of Jammu and Kashmir be declared as "arbitrary, unconstitutional and void", claiming that it was against the supremacy of the Indian Constitution and contrary to the dictum of "One Nation, One Constitution, One National Anthem and One National Flag". It has sought declaring as arbitrary some provisions of the Jammu and Kashmir Constitution, which deals with permanent residency and flag of the valley among other issues, for being violative of the Preamble and the Indian Constitution. The petition has said that continuance of two parallel constitutions, one for the Centre and other for the state of Jammu and Kashmir, "reeks of a weird dichotomy" as most of the provisions of the Indian Constitution has already been extended to the state. It has alleged that due to vote bank politics, successive governments did nothing to repeal Article 370 and Constitution of Jammu and Kashmir was adopted much after the Indian Constitution came into force. It also added that the instrument of accession of October 26, 1947 does not talk about separate Constitution or constituent assembly for the state.

On 4th September 2017, *MediaCrooks'* Ravinar posted an article: *'The Rohingya Threat'*. "The old English idiom "Bring home the bacon" meant earn money, economically maintain the family and provide for meals. Bacon forms a good part of Western breakfast and other meals in the normal course of life. Bacon is made from pork which comes from farm pigs and is consumed worldwide. The Muslim community must be made to realize that it's intolerance to customs, practices and food habits and sensitivities of the majority community in the country they live in cannot pass anymore. Limitless Muslim migration to Sweden, Holland, Germany and others has wreaked havoc in these countries with intolerance, rapes, murders, ghettos and no-go zones and terrorism. Many of them in the last decade came as REFUGEES.

Back home, *CommiePigs* specifically hold "Beef festivals" to offend Hindus who consider cows sacred. They do so with impunity. They even slaughter cows in public. The Partition in 1947 was incomplete due to lack of vision by some selfish politicians. When the subcontinent was divided along religious lines, they allowed Muslims remain in India. It should have come with a caveat: *"Muslims will be entitled to live in India so long as they respect the sentiments of the majority and their values. Failing this, the offenders will lose all citizenship rights."* Recently we had riots in Noida over a fake case of a maid being kept captive. The riots were by illegal Bangladeshis working in that area and had built illegal shanties nearby. It's hard to believe that these illegals, from the Muslim community can go to such extent of violence. After the incident, the colonies in the locality getting verifications done in states like UP or Delhi, is something to ponder? *This is what brings us to the question about Rohingya Muslims.* Clandestinely and secretly, the previous Congress governments allowed them in and settled them in various parts of India. These Rohingya refugees from Myanmar have settled in Hyderabad, UP and a large number in Jammu. How these people got to Jammu is a mystery. Article 370 even prevents Indian non-residents of J&K state to have houses in J&K. But the vicious plan of the Congress and Commies becomes clear when one realizes that altering the demography of Jammu bit by bit can completely Islamize the whole state of J&K which can then secede from India with greater force. This is like enabling Pakistan and terrorists in their own design. So, naturally, when the GOI is now acting on a decision to deport these illegal Rohingyas back to Myanmar, their protector in chief proclaims thusly: So, who are these Rohingyas? They are a minority within the State of Myanmar and number around a million from the Rakhine region. After a long history going back to the Indian subcontinent, they were considered an ethnic group in then Burma and now Myanmar. Over period they were deprived of normal citizen and political rights. Consequently, they have been fighting for secession from Myanmar and have a military wing with multiple denominations – one is called The Rohingya National Army and another very violent wing is called the Arakan Rohingya Salvation Army (ARSA). ARSA is designated a terrorist group in Myanmar; it is made up of Muslims. In the most recent attack around August 25, the ARSA killed 96, injured many and displaced over 400 people. Majority of these people were Hindus. So, whether it is India, Pakistan, Bangladesh or Myanmar the ones suffering most at the hands of Islamic terrorists are Hindus. Let's rest that trivial, inevitable truth.

Sickulars in India are now trying to make out the illegally settled Rohingyas as "victims" of Myanmar government when Rohingyas run terrorist outfits in their own country. This is not India's problem and should never be. India faces insurgents in multiple states. With all our might, we can drive these Maoist pigs to Burma, Bhutan or Bangladesh or even Pakistan. Do we? The Rohingyas in India may not be militants or terrorists, but they do not belong here and especially not in sensitive areas like Jammu that is a target for terrorists and enemies to groom them. Whether Rohingyas or 'Ching Funglis from Pappu's Jupiter' – once their identity is "Muslim", the brotherhood will try and groom them to kill Hindus and destroy India. As simple as that. And what the Rohingya killers have done to Hindu kids can be seen in the image on the left.

There is a reason Congressis and their jokers like Shashi Tharoor whine for the Rohingyas. Having settled them illegally in Jammu and other places, their anti-national plans plus a loss of vote-bank would be threatened. They see Rohingyas as a weapon to use to combat the currently unmatchable Modi. Rohingyas have no place in India and do not deserve our compassion. Their treatment of Hindus in Myanmar and possible threat to Hindus in Jammu shouldn't leave anyone in doubt: In August 2016, two Rohingyas were arrested in Bihar from a train and their questioning revealed their plans to join anti-India groups in J&K. They were on the train to J&K. Two were arrested but it is impossible to tell how many slipped through the hole and joined the terror-groups in J&K.

This is a country where KPs driven out of Kashmir are still refugees in their own country and we cannot have any more refugees from abroad with evil intentions.

To digress a bit, what do these refugees from Bangladesh or Myanmar bring to India? We talked about the Noida riots by Bangladeshis. Selfish, idiotic Indians even employ illegals just to save some money. They don't have any idea the damage they cause to India. Most of the illegals merge into slums and rivers of garbage like this sample from Mumbai: Most of these slums that affect a city, like during the recent floods in Mumbai, are ones that were all Indians at one time. But lately, many of these slums harbor anti-nationals and illegals. The Rohingyas and Bangladeshis easily mingle and melt into these slums. Why? Because nobody checks on them. Nobody investigates what goes on in these slums. In many cases, the illegals can multiply and build such slums by parties like AAP in Delhi. They are regularized with Aadhar cards and Voter IDs. *Anti-nationals work to the agenda of India's enemies.* This cannot go on.

Predictably, the anti-national charlatan Prashant Bhushan filed a PIL in SC to stop deportation of the Rohingyas. This was heard and *it is shocking that SC even admits such petitions and hopefully the PIL will be thrown out.* SC itself has strongly ordered eviction of illegal Bangladeshis from Assam in the past: The current BJP govt at the Centre MUST NOT dither and must ensure all the illegals are deported. The older lot from Bangladesh in Assam or Bengal and other places might take longer. But GOI MUST ensure that new lots are not only deported but send a clear warning that those protecting illegals will be prosecuted and action must be initiated quickly. Especially, the first lot of Rohingyas in Jammu must be packed off immediately and then the rest."

For over half a century, the successive Congress governments in Assam had blessed immigration of Bangladeshi Muslims by giving them ration cards thus making them voters to swell its vote-bank. Anti-nation Congress is least bothered in upsetting the demography of the state. Same must have been going for the Rohingya Muslims ever since they have become *persona non-grata* in Burma (Myanmar). Apart from Jammu and Ladakh, they are settled in UP, Rajasthan, Delhi NCR and Hyderabad. On Bakr Eid this year, Rohingyas wanted to sacrifice a buffalo in Faridabad Haryana, close to Indian capital. Locals had hell of a hard time preventing that. Police had to intervene in the ensuing scuffle.

MALADIES AFFLICTING HINDUSTAN AND REMEDIES

Chris Hedges once said about America, his country: "*We now live in a nation where doctors destroy health; lawyers destroy justice; universities destroy knowledge; the press destroys information; religion destroys morals; and banks destroy the economy.*" This statement is more than true for Hindustan, my own country erroneously renamed India post-independence. Hindustan or Hind is still the name preferred by Muslim countries, our famous poets, our present or past politicians and historians! The revered Persian and Urdu poet Sir Mohammed Iqbal wrote in 1906, '*Hindi hain hum, Hindustan hai watan hamara*'. Or, in literal translation in English, '*We are Hindi, and our motherland is Hindustan*'. Iqbal went on to pen, "*Mit gaye Yunan-o Rome-o Misar iss jahan se, per abhi bhi baqi hai nishaan hamara, kuchh to baat hai ki mitati nahin hasti hamari'*. Or, stated in English, "*Greek, Roman and Egyptian civilizations ended but ours still exists today, there must be some substance in ours that it cannot be forgotten or defaced.*" Unfortunately, the anti-national party that has been in forefront for all the wrong reasons for 101 years now helped by her self-centered, highly selfish worthless least patriotic non-Hindu or half-Hindu 'leaders' or precisely owners faking as Hindus tried hard to deface, dishonor, disown or even destroy our ancient Hindu civilization for their ulterior motives from their white masters whom they were indebted for handing them power in a platter!

Hindustan became India because of an allegedly 'ba*****d' Muslim (allegedly born to a leading Muslim lawyer Mubarak Ali and his concubine – a Muslim prostitute Thussu Rehmatbai in latter's *kotha* at #77 Mir Ganj, the red-light area in Allahabad now Prayagraj. That is the real name of revered religious Hindu city that now stands corrected centuries-after the Mughal king Akbar (grandson of invader Babar) had changed the old name Prayag to Allahabad, thanks to the right-thinking Uttar Pradesh CM Yogi Adityanath. This fact on bastardy of Nehru can be verified even today from the convoluted by lanes of the famous city. This undeserving immature megalomaniac usurped the position of the 1st post-independence Prime Minister from his most-deserving 14-year senior statesman leader duly elected in 1946 for the job by the then 12 Provincial Congress Committees out of a total of 15 with none voting for Nehru. Remember the 565 princely states then had no voting rights. This unique disservice to the motherland was done by none other than the most 'crooked' substandard politician of the times today mistakenly/falsely addressed as 'Mahatma'. At best, he was a FAKE. This half-Hindu admitted to the fact that he was a FAKE Mahatma in his 10th June 1946 evening prayer meeting (at his sponsor GD Birla's Birla House located on the renamed *Tees January Marg* New Delhi). Incidentally, Gandhi was killed just before starting a prayer meeting in the same house on the fateful evening of 30th January 1948. *INC government led by his 'adopted son' did not try to find out which of the four bullets fired upon him caused his death* that occurred 30 minutes after being shot at. There remain many unanswered questions since he was not removed to the nearby Willingdon Hospital, no autopsy was performed on him, Godse fired three bullets, from where the 4th bullet came, FIR mentioned two bullets, the court case file talked about three' and so on It was a ploy by Muslim Nehru to discredit Godse and his Chitawapan Brahmins! INC organized the killing of hundreds of Chitwapan Brahmins in Pune and elsewhere in the then Bombay province. What was their fault? The same pattern was followed on 31st October 1984 for five continuous days in Delhi and elsewhere in the country where Congress(I) goons killed mostly by immolation thousands of innocent Sikhs in the aftermath of her two bodyguards shooting Indira from close range. The targeted killings were supervised by the PM in chair! This is *true* color of shameless Congressis! That proved convincingly that basically it is the fault of the gullible unconcerned slave-minded populace of India who could not decide the right party and individual who could run the country dispassionately without personal agenda. In both the instances, the criminal goons belonging to the ruling party responsible for mass-murder of one community were let Scot-free without holding them responsible or facing an independent court trial for such a heinous act!

<u>Why did Gandhi supersede Patel's election as PM?</u> *Firstly*, the credentials of Gandhi as the dictator of INC are questionable and trashed by his more famous adversary and better-known 20-year senior Congressman Jinnah. He ceased to be Four-Anna member of INC after 1934. In what capacity he was the dictator of this nefarious party? Was he a demi-god? Essentially, it was because real or true democracy never existed within the party and consequently in the country. It was always an autocracy by the Gandhi-Nehru-Gandhi dynasty. Hindustan must be a unique country in the world where one single political dynasty has continued at the helm of affairs of a so-called democratic set up for over a century now! *Was it because both he and his 'adopted son' were both allegedly 'Muslims' and sons of prostitutes? Was it because Sardar Patel was a staunch Hindu and his two Muslims contemporaries did not like a Hindu as the PM of a country with 85% Hindus? Who was more intelligent and forthright than either of the Gandhi/Nehru duo? Or, did the duo have NO Faith in Patel? Why did Patel accept Gandhi's autocratic overruling and step down from prime minister-ship??* Respect for an elderly is there in our culture but CERTAINLY NOT at the cost of the future of the motherland. It was well known that Nehru was an immature, short-tempered, pro-British man of loose morality involved with Edwina Mountbatten and quite a few other women of the times. So, was Gandhi who was also fond of young women and used to sleep naked and take bath with so many women including Dr Sushila Nayyar, the sister of Gandhi's PA Pyarelal. Gandhi did not spare his brother's granddaughter and grandson's wife! Wasn't that SHAMEFUL? 'Two of a feather flock together' is well known. Was that another reason in favor of Nehru's nomination as the would be the PM after British exit? My country comes first and anybody or anything else afterwards, if we consider Patel as a true patriot! It appears that Patel is 'wrongly' addressed as India's 'Iron Man'. However, he proved he was made of paraffin wax since he could be cut and molded into any form or shape! These and many more related accusations will always remain on the two Muslim stalwarts' faulty behavior and actions!

<u>There are **numerous** maladies/threats afflicting our psyche as also our motherland Hindustan</u>**:**

1] <u>***FIRST and foremost chronic, recalcitrant and ongoing threat is the Congress party itself:***</u>
INC and its present Avatar Congress(I) have been the bane of the country for over a century. The democratic set up hitherto prevalent was to elect the party president year after year. Naturally, governments run post-independence by this anti-national party have inflicted the most, many a time irreparable, damage to my people and my motherland! This nefarious party sabotaged both the history and geography of the subcontinent. The

criterion for membership to this useless party has all along been, *'One has to be a graduate of the school for scoundrels, where sycophancy and* Swami-bhakti (personality worship of the nominated dynast president of the party from Gandhi-Nehru-Gandhi dynasty) are the main attainments needed. 'Unfortunately, its pigmy 'leaders' ruled over Hindustan for 80% of its independent existence. There were only five years (1991 to 1996) when a non-dynast PV Narasimha Rao was at the helm of affairs of the party and the government. Like his predecessors Indira and Rajiv, he kept the post of party President while as the PM of the country. *One notable difference was he was the only Hindu (Brahmin) to adorn the chair.* All other 'dictators' of the party before and after him were non-Hindus from FAKE Mahatma to FAKE Gandhis. Its PMs have been from FAKE Pandit (Nehru) to FAKE Economist (Manmohan). The three generation of dynasts from Nehru to Indira to Rajiv were Muslims though the last named converted to Christianity at the Orbassamo church near Turin before marrying an Italian Catholic Christian Sania Antonia Maino. This, in brief, tragically the hierarchy of Gandhi-Nehru-Gandhi dynasty projecting them as Fake Hindus was a ploy to fool the ignorant unconcerned stupid Hindustanis who were ever ready and always willing to be fooled. Paradoxically, the three PMs were cremated according to Hindu rites whereas they needed to be buried as per their religion, Islam. Thus, it was the biggest fraud on the gullible Hindustanis of a slave mentality! In this way, this party has been distorting history right for the past 101 years!

The party always comprised of sycophants, known as CHAMCHAS in the colloquial Hindustani. A proof of sycophancy or CHAMCHAGIRI exists even today. On 19th November 2018, *Yahoo News India* published, *'Bharat Mata nahi, Sonia Gandhi ki jai, senior Congress leader'*. "A senior Congress leader from Rajasthan, during a public gathering, apparently stopped his aide from shouting *'Bharat Mata ki jai'* and instead ordered him to raise the slogan, *'Sonia Gandhi ki jai'* In the video of the incident, which has gone viral on social media, the former leader of the opposition, Dr Bulaki Das Kalla, was clearly seen muzzling his aide and asking him to change his slogan. Kalla stopped his party leader from raising "*Bharat Mata Ki Jai*" in Muslims locality. Said we will lose Muslim votes as a result. He told him to shout *'Sonia Gandhi, Rahul Gandhi & Ahmed Patel Jindabad'* instead of *'Bharat Mata ki Jai'*. No sooner that the aide begins to chant 'Bharat Mata Ki Jai', Kalla was seen intervening and whispering something into the supporter's ears. Immediately after, the aide promptly changes his slogan. Kalla is a five-time MLA from Bikaner. However, he lost the last two Assembly elections from the same constituency and his name was conspicuously absent from the first list of candidates released by the Congress. But after a huge uproar by his supporters, the party decided to bend its rule of not giving tickets to those who have lost two consecutive elections and granted him one. That should be reason enough for him to swear his undying allegiance to the Nehru-Gandhi clan. But was it proper of Kalla to ask his aide to switch from 'Bharat Mata' to 'Sonia Gandhi'? [Tajinder Pal Singh Bagga@TajinderBagga]

During the last years of Nehru, undeservedly made taller than life leader, a question regularly posed to him, 'Who after Nehru?' remained purposefully unanswered. A cunning Nehru didn't want to admit that he has all along been grooming his sparsely educated non-matriculate 'daughter' for the job. Indira Gandhi nee Priyadarshini as she preferred to be called used to say, *"Tell a lie hundreds of times. It becomes truth."* Congress party has been consistently following this nefarious practice and fool the gullible masses. The practice of repeatedly telling the same lie is continuing with FAKE Gandhi, Raul Vinci, the current Congress(I) president. *His blatant lies of Rafale deal have made him a Notorious* liar. The CEO of Dassault had no option but to come out openly to refute the false notions perpetuated by this immature naïve dynast.

On 13th November 2018, *Rediff.com News* published, *'I don't lie; Dassault CEO responds to Rahul on Rafale deal'*. "On the pricing issue, CEO Dassault Aviation, Eric Trappier said that the present aircraft are cheaper by 9%. In an exclusive interview to *ANI*, Eric rubbished allegations made by Congress president Rahul that the former lied about the details of the Dassault-Reliance joint venture for offset contracts in the Rafale Jet deal. "I don't lie. The truth I declared before and the statements I made are true. I don't have a reputation of lying. In my position as CEO, you don't lie," said Trappier when asked to respond to Rahul Gandhi's charge that Dassault was covering up for possible cronyism in awarding the offset deal to Anil Ambani-led Reliance Group.

Speaking to *ANI* in the Dassault hangar housed in Istres-Le Tube Air base located north of the French city of Marseille, Dassault's CEO Eric Trappier said that they had prior experience dealing with the Congress party and the comments made by the Congress president made him sad. "We have a long experience with the Congress party. Our first deal was with India in 1953 with Nehru and later with other prime ministers. We have been working with India. We are not working for any party. We are supplying strategic products like fighters to the Indian Air Force and the Indian government. That is what is most important," said Trappier.

When pressed further for the reason behind Dassault's choice of Reliance as an offset partner which had no experience in manufacturing fighter jets, Trappier clarified that the money being invested was not going to Reliance directly but in a joint venture that included Dassault. "We are not putting the money in Reliance. The money is going into the JV. I put my know-how free of charge on how to produce people. I have engineers and workers from Dassault who are taking the lead as far as the industrial part of this deal is concerned. At the same time, I have an Indian company like Reliance who is putting money into this JV as they want to develop their country. So, the company is going to know how to produce aircraft," added Trappier. Trappier further clarified about the investments being made by Dassault, adding that Reliance would match the amount since the shareholding pattern is 49 per cent Dassault and 51 per cent Reliance as per prescribed government norms. "We are supposed to put in this company together about Rs 800 crore as 50:50. For the time being, to start work in the hangar and to pay workers and employees, we have already put in INR400 million. But it will be increased to INR8 billion, which implies INR4 billion by Dassault in the coming five years," said Trappier. He added Dassault has seven years to perform offset. "During the first three years, we are not obliged to say with who we are working. We have already settled work and agreement with 30 companies, which represents 40% of total offset obligation as per contract. Reliance share is 10% while rest 30% is a direct agreement between these companies and Dassault," Trappier said.

On the pricing issue, the CEO said that the present aircraft are cheaper by 9%. "The price of 36 helicopters was the same when you compare with 18 flyaway; 36 is the double of 18. So as far as I was concerned, it should have been double the price. But because it was government to government, there was some negotiation; I had to decrease the price by 9%. The price of Rafale in a flyaway condition is less expensive in '36 contract' than '126 contract'," he said. When asked about initial agreement with Hindustan Aeronautics Limited and the subsequent breakdown of talks with the Indian PSU for production of Rafale jets, Eric said that if the initial deal of 126 jets went through they would not have hesitated to work with HAL and Mukesh Ambani-led Reliance. "It's because the 126 didn't go smooth that Indian government had to reconfigure to urgently acquire 36 from France. And then I took the decision to continue with Reliance, and HAL even said in the last few days that they were not interested to be part of the offset. So, it has been done by my decision and the decision of Reliance to invest in a new private company," added Trappier. He added that Dassault was earlier in discussions with several other companies for offset tie-ups. "Obviously, we could have gone to Tata or other family groups. At that time, the decision to go ahead was not given to Dassault. We were in 2011, Tata was also discussing with other flying companies. We finally decided to go ahead with Reliance as they have experience in big engineering facilities," Trappier said. Talking about the aircraft, the Dassault CEO explained that the present planes will have all necessary equipment but not weapons and missiles. "The weapons will be sent in a different contract. But the aircraft with everything other than weapons will be dispatched by Dassault," he said." [With inputs from *PTI, Smita Prakash*. Source: *ANI*]

Indira passed the baton to her older pilot son Rajiv since the younger – a conversant politician knowing the country's needs died in an air crash. After Rajiv's assassination for his *Karma*, a non-dynast PV Narasimha Rao became the PM while continuing as president of Congress(I). After Rao's departure, the party could not find a Hindustani to head it and they nominated Italy-born Sania Antonia Maino erroneously known as Sonia Gandhi, Now, it is time to pose similar question to 'erstwhile Life-President' of Congress(l), 'Who after Sonia?' Or, 'What would be the future of Congress if Sonia dies suddenly?' Of course, she nominated to the throne her sparsely educated immature son Raul Vinci erroneously called Rahul Gandhi. Of course, Raul is better educated than 4th Grade dropout mother from an Italian medium Elementary School. Vinit Dawane, MBA student, 'Practitioner of Spirituality', and Technologist answered like this: "If Sonia dies suddenly then the future of Congress-I in India would have following effects:

1] Congress leaders will use her death to gain the sympathy and possibly sweep the next General Elections. They will keep all the issues like development, employment, terrorism aside and only focus on schemes like 'Food Security Bill', 'Right to Information Act', etc. and try to show the voters that 'How visionary her leadership was.'

2] Her death would be a chance to either Rahul Gandhi or Priyanka Vadra to become the next PM of the country. Other sycophants like Digvijay Singh (Who can't win a Lok Sabha seat) will also use this opportunity to win the general elections and would possibly be awarded a Ministry also.
3] She will be awarded *Bharat Ratna*, like her senior dynasts – husband, his mother, and maternal grandfather – posthumously for her 'sacrifice' for the country.
4] Some International airports, Big Fat and Hit Government Schemes will be named after her.
5] If India can eradicate poverty in future, then she would be projected as the 'Visionary' who helped to bring the Revolutionary schemes like MNREGA, Food Security Bill, etc. for the masses. (People will even forget that someone known as Manmohan was the PM at the time when these schemes were implemented)."

The author of this book does not agree to Vinit Dawane's contentions simply because Indira who was assassinated for her *Karma* of being a staunch anti-Hindu and anti-Sikh, created a wave of sympathy among our gullible, not-so realistic, unconcerned voters with slave mentality and the already due general elections were advanced by only a month or two. Of course, Sonia is also expected to die because of her serious disease possibly Ca Cervix under treatment at Memorial Sloan Kettering Hospital, New York at enormous public money expenditure! The glaring differences today are the widespread use and reach of media, both print and television; Sonia is going to die a natural death from the cancer. Considering the numerous bunglings of Congress PMs from Nehru to Manmohan and the level of political awareness of young Indians who today constitute brute majority among the electorate, one strongly believes that Congress (I) is finished for all times to come. The Mahatma gave a call for disbanding Congress which another Gandhi Rahul had to----- accomplish seven decades later. After all, someone had to dig the last nail in the coffin of the oldest prejudiced, communal but failed party. Who can be better than 5th generation dynast Rahul Gandhi or Raul Vinci – the way the Indians may like to 'remember' this nut, who says there is no consensus between the ruling BJP and the opposition Congress: Either party's supporters want Rahul to continue leading the fading lackluster 'grand old party'.

This (author's) view is strengthened by the most recent expose by *Times Now, Zee News, Republic TV,* and others, on the strong collusion of Congress's notoriously crooked managers like Chidambaram, Digvijay, Khursheed, Manmohan, Pranab, Shinde, Sibal, et al., having always been under the diktat, thumb or 'watchful' eye of an imported, white and sparsely-educated lady unfamiliar with India's civilization, culture or history. These and so many other loyal CHAMCHAS always worked under her directions. Sonia must have been the gang leader in the mischievous agenda of defaming and falsely/unethically implicating Narendra Modi, the then most popular BJP leader and the then high-performing Gujarat CM who beat Congress-I hollow in three successive assembly elections after the highly 'publicized' 2002 Gujarat Riots for wrong reasons. He was, after all a future potential candidate for prime minister-ship of India, Sonia knew!

The masterminding of the fabrication, falsification and submission of distorted whole gamut of facts to the Gujarat High Court in the case of a well-documented L-e-T terrorist Ishrat Jehan – the notorious Mumbra teen, noted collaborator and suicide bomber of L-e-T is going to wholly discredit Congress-I. This will certainly disintegrate this party further. It is already reduced in stature to nothing more than a regional outfit. This will finish the undeserving 'First Political Family' that happens to be the 'Gandhi-Nehru-Gandhi Dynasty' for all times to come. It has been ironical that ever since the cremation of its greatest leader, Lokmanya Bal Gangadhar Tilak on the sands of Bombay's Chowpatty beach on 1st August 1920, Congress was always led by an anti-Hindu dictator although the Hindus made up over 80% of the subcontinent. Just to enumerate, the first one to take charge by sheer cunningness was the pro-Muslim double-faced Gandhi who 'professed' to be Hindu till his death on 30th January 1948. 'Muslim' Nehru took over from where his benefactor had left. Then the baton was passed on to his daughter who was 'Muslim' by self-confession and to her pilot son (of which religion nobody knows) after she was assassinated. For a few years following Rajiv's assassination, the president of Congress (I) was non-dynasts i.e. Narasimha Rao and Sitaram Kesri before the pendulum swung back in favor of Rajiv's white widow when Kesri was unceremoniously ousted. The rest is the history of the past three decades. Historically speaking, the Congress presidents have been from an illiterate K Kamaraj to sparsely educated dynasts Indira and Sonia; the only exception was better educated Narasimha Rao who like the dynasts chose to be Congress-I president and India's PM simultaneously. Even yesteryears Bollywood heartthrob Rishi Kapoor slammed Congress. "New Delhi, May 19: After his scathing attack on the 'Gandhi family,' veteran actor Rishi Kapoor took to his Twitter handle to thank people, who have supported him and his thought behind those particular tweets. "Thank you all for your unprecedented unconditional support, love and solidarity for what I said, *Mera Bharat Mahaan*!" "Thank you, thank world over! Your reaction coming is unprecedented. I meant it from my heart, and you know it. And I know you know it!" In his series of tweets, the 'Kapoor and Sons' actor snapped directly at the political system of India, especially the grand old 'Gandhi family'. The 63-year-old actor took to his *Twitter* handle to ask question over naming of the roadways, airports and railway stations on the names of "Gandhi family" members through a series of tweets. "Change Gandhi family assets named by Congress. Bandra/Worli Sea Link to Lata Mangeshkar or JRD Tata Sea link. *Baap ka maal samjh rakha tha*? (Did you consider it your father's property?) If roads in Delhi can be changed why not Congress assets/property ke naam? Was in Chandigarh, *wahan bhi* (there also) Rajeev Gandhi assets? *Socho* (Think)? Why?" The actor, with these allegations, added the fact that the names should be after people from every genre, who have contributed to the society. "We must name important assets of the country who have contributed to society. *Har cheez Gandhi ke naam* (Everything in Gandhi's name)? I don't agree. *Sochna logo* (Think, people)!" he tweeted. Kapoor then asked for suggestion from people on whether the names can be after film personalities like Dilip Kumar, Dev Anand, Ashok Kumar, Amitabh Bachchan and others. "Film City should be named after Dilip Kumar, Dev Anand, Ashok Kumar or Amitabh Bachchan? Rajiv Gandhi *udyog Kya hota hai* (What is Rajiv Gandhi industry? *Socho dosto* (Friends, think)! Imagine Mohamad Rafi, Mukesh, Manna Dey, Kishore Kumar venues on their name like in our country. Just a suggestion: *Why Indira or Rajiv Gandhi International airport? Why not after JRD Tata, Bhagat Singh, Dr. Ambedkar* or, on my name say Rishi Kapoor. As superficial! What one says? Raj Kapoor made India proud in life and even after his death. Certainly, more than What has been perceived by politics." [*ANI*]

Congress, being a party of substandard leaders and sycophants with no inherent wisdom or talent, reacted in a nasty manner to Rishi Kapoor's pragmatic criticism. On 26th May 2016, *Business of Cinema* reported: "Recently, Bollywood veteran actor Rishi Kapoor had tweeted questioning on why all the properties are named after Gandhis. Rishi Kapoor had strongly lashed out at Gandhi family members especially Indira and Rajiv. Days after his tweets, Congress workers have made a comeback by hanging a placard over a Sulabh toilet with his name. In the series of tweets, *Kapoor had expressed his displeasure over the name of Delhi as Indira Gandhi International airport!* Well, it seems Congress supporters made a point to respond to Rishi Kapoor. On Monday, Congress workers gathered at the Shivaji Park area in Allahabad and hung a placard over a public toilet with Rishi Kapoor's name written on it. Well, Kapoor has reacted to it saying that he is thrilled and that at least he will be of some use to someone as these people (Congress) are of no use to anyone. Kapoor always shows his honesty by *tweeting* his views. But it seems this time he can be in trouble for raising his point of view."

Much good had happened for India both inside and outside the country even during the first two years of PM Modi's regime. Full term of five years ushered in a trend for the reversal of bad times unfortunately accumulated for India due to the misrule, nepotism, favoritism and thorough corruption started by the undeserving first PM Nehru and his even more undeserving Congress successors till the last *puppet* PM Manmohan. *All of them unnecessarily occupied the Delhi 'throne' without doing good during the first 67 years of her independent existence.* Given that, our masses will be well advised to re-elect Modi for one, if not two more terms. When that happens, it will catapult India into the Top League of Nations in the world! Time should not be too far away when India becomes the top global economy given the disciplined approach and entrepreneurship by the Indian business community. I may not be boasting when I say: "We Indians are more intelligent, hard-working and honest as compared to the whites in their own country given the commanding heights the Indian Americans, constituting just 1% of the population, have scaled in that highly competitive and successful nation.

As a matter of fact, the not-so-patriotic FAKE Mahatma ruled over the minds of the most stupid, gullible compatriots, least interested in country's affairs or her real history – the irresponsible Hindustanis, *I reproduce just one of the many most damaging anti-national acts by Congress(I)*:

One of the most sinister acts of this anti-national party: A highly talented Hindu Brahmin, Lt Col Prasad Shrikant Purohit, a senior member of the Army Intelligence Unit had done tremendous service to the nation by unearthing certain discomforting facts: the anti-national activities of SIMI working in tandem with Pakistan's ISI under protection from 'anti-national' Congress (I) leaders and its government headed by dummy accidental PM Manmohan; some bizarre anti-national acts by that party's 'life' president Sonia Gandhi aka Sania Adige Maino running the party as a private limited company; her cancelled scheduled meeting with Hafiz Saeed – chief of banned L-e-T now called J-u-D, always under protection of Pak ISI – the international terrorist on whose head the US government has kept a bounty of ten million dollars but roams freely in Pakistan often visiting the border with India; and many more sensational pieces of information like Dawood Ibrahim's 2005 visit to his native Bombay now known as Mumbai (obviously under protection of the ruling Congress governments at the Centre and in Maharashtra); terrorist roaming in Kashmir valley in red beacon cars; successfully busting fake currency racket by certain Indian politicians; anti-national activities by certain persons or groups; and so on. *Purohit was clandestinely arrested prior to 26/11 since he had documentary evidence of this coming ghastly terror attack on India's financial capital.* Thus, there was a well thought of concerted plan by the then UPA government. Earlier the *MAHACHAMCHA Manmohan allowed the breach of Constitution by creating extra-Constitutional position of 'super prime minister' for his boss and allowing her to run the National Advisory Council. Arrest of a highly patriotic officer of our brave army, the only secular organization in Hindustan, raises many disturbing questions*: It was a deliberate attempt to label the Hindus as terrorists. It is an open secret that PM Manmohan was aware of the 11/26 ghastly terror attack plot well in advance. Like a true crooked antinational anti-Hindu, he did not make any attempt to thwart it. Instead another equally big CHAMCHA Digvijay Singh got written a book to show it was Hindu terror that caused the most-deadly terror attack on Indian soil ever. The book was to be released after the terror attack! Unfortunately for Congress president Sania Maino, Manmohan and their party a Braveheart Head Constable Tukaram of Mumbai Police caught the last of the ten Pakistani terrorists alive! The rest is history.

There are many questions that this anti-national Sikh, his Italian boss and their anti-national party cannot answer. *At whose behest Purohit was unlawfully kept in prison for nine long years without a charge-sheet by faceless Manmohan? Can the most useless and worthless PM give a cogent reply? Why was Col Purohit handed over to civilian Maharashtra ATS run by a crook and a most-obedient Congress-servant Hemant Karkare and tortured daily?*

And even threatened with damage to his wife, sister and aged mother? Why Manmohan and his cabal consisting of Sushilkumar Shinde, P Chidambaram, Pranab Mukherjee, Sharad Pawar, Salman Khurshid, etc. did not act on any/all the very sensitive information provided in Purohit's letter to Manmohan?

And there were many more such anti-national acts! *Why the Congress (I) even after repeated electoral debacles is still hellbent in protecting anti-nationals, Muslims and their activities?* From before Gujarat Assembly elections and possibly under instructions from Cambridge Analytica, President Raul Vinci started behaving like a Hindu by visiting Temples, wearing the *Sacred Thread (Janeu)* over his shirt. As per the Vedic tradition it must be around the body but under any garment a Hindu Brahmin wears. The public can easily make out between a FAKE Hindu from the real. Raul Vinci is a Catholic by birth.

The true patriot Purohit never budged from his correct and justified stand. One can only wonder and imagine and profoundly appreciate the strength of his will power that he did not wilt under non-stop persecution and torture for nine long years. *Will PM Modi punish the wrong doers in the whole plot from Sonia-Manmohan combine to Maharashtra ATS' corrupt and subservient officers to Purohit's army colleagues?* Thoroughly unbiased investigations must immediately begin: with first attack outside J&K on revered Hindu spaces at Akshardham in Gandhinagar; and the creation of the bogey of 'Hindu terror' by the above named anti-national individuals thereby maligning the fair name of one billion peace-loving Hindus living globally. Statuary action must be taken against Col RK Shrivastav and his superiors who were ordering and falsely imposing his (Shrivastav's) actions, going right up to the then COAS Gen Deepak Kapur who broke all rules and regulations for certain pecuniary benefits; and surviving members of ATS Maharashtra – Addl DG Parambir Singh, Inspector Arun Khanvilkar, and Assistant CP Mohan Kulkarni. Hemant Karkare's misconduct must be placed on record and the 'Ashok Chakra' given by biased Manmohan for his 'service' to him and his outfit must be withdrawn! Kudos to Purohit who still went back to his Intelligence unit and continues to serve the country to the best of his ability and capability.

Finally, and inevitably, Lt Col Purohit was released under orders of the SC Bench on 21st August 2017. The well-known news anchor Shweta Singh tweeted two days later: *"After remaining in jail without a charge-sheet for nine years, only a Hindustani army man can say 'Jai Hind'. Superstars and persons retired after a decade of occupying high Constitutional* *positions [Hamid Ansari, a Vice President for ten years] can only see India is 'insecure' (for Muslims)."* There was a big slap on the *Sickulars*, an eponym for so-called 'seculars' and pseudo-intellectuals, via a tweet by Spaminder Bharti@atomeybharti: *"Ishrat Jehan is innocent unless proven guilty in court. Purohit is guilty unless proven innocent in court."*

On 21st August 2017, *Scoop Whoop News* flashed an article compiled by Ritu Singh: <u>*All You Need to Know About Colonel Purohit Who's Granted Bail After 9 Years in Malegaon Case*</u>. "Nine years ago, the arrest of Lt Col Prasad Shrikant Purohit rattled the nation as it was the *first time* that a serving Army man had been booked for a terror act. The Supreme Court today granted conditional bail to Purohit, the main accused in the 2008 Malegaon blasts case, after nearly nine years in jail. A bench of Justices RK Agrawal and AM Sapre said they are setting aside the Bombay High Court order by which the bail was denied. The apex court said it has imposed certain conditions on Purohit while granting bail. On 17th August, Purohit had told the apex court that he has been caught in the "political crossfire" and languishing in jail for nine years. Purohit had moved the apex court challenging the Bombay High Court's order dismissing his bail plea.

<u>*What is the Malegaon case*</u>? Seven people were killed and nearly 80 others injured when a bomb strapped to a motorcycle exploded in Malegaon on 29th September 2008. Malegaon is a communally sensitive textile town in Nasik in north Maharashtra [Source: *PTI*]. The 4,000-page charge sheet had alleged that Malegaon was selected as the blast target because of a sizeable Muslim population there. It had named Sadhvi Pragya Thakur, Purohit and Swami Dayanand Pandey as the key conspirators. However, Thakur was last year given clean chit by the NIA.

<u>*Who is Prasad Shrikant Purohit*</u>? Hailing from a Maharashtrian Brahmin middle class family, Purohit was born to a bank officer in Pune. After completing his education from there, he was commissioned into Maratha Light Infantry in 1994 after he cleared out of the Officer's Training Academy at Chennai. He served in the counter-terrorism operations unit in J&K between 2002-2005 and was later shifted to Military Intelligence due to health reasons, says a report by the *Indian Express*. As per his neighbors, Prasad Purohit was a soft-spoken man, and superiors in the Army remembered him as a bright, hard-working recruit, says an *NDTV* report.

<u>*Involvement of Abhinav Bharat Trust?*</u> Purohit was *alleged* to be associated with a retired Major Ramesh Upadhyay who had set up *Abhinav Bharat*, an extreme right-wing group, alleged to be behind the 2008 blasts. The

trust though was formed to promote Hindu values but was allegedly a front to carry out attacks against Muslims. Not just Purohit, Thakur, Pandey, Swami Aseemanand, and others were falsely implicated in the Malegaon blast were also members of the Abhinav trust. The charge sheet had alleged that it was Pandey who had instructed Purohit to arrange explosive RDX, following which he stole 60 kg of RDX, some of which was used in the blast. He was also charged with funding and training the group. According to the NIA, Purohit held meetings in Faridabad on January 25 and 26, 2008, where the formation of a *Hindu Rashtra* was discussed. Purohit allegedly read over the constitution of *Abhinav Bharat*, discussed about the formation of a "Central Hindu government in exile in Israel and Thailand. *This was essentially anti-Hindu agenda of then ruling Congress (I).*

What Purohit said in his defense? Purohit accepted that he had attended meetings of Abhinav Bharat but said he had acted as an army officer and passed on the information to his senior officers about group's activities. Purohit argued that even assuming the charges that he had supplied the bomb were true, even then he should have been out of jail as the offence attracted a maximum imprisonment for seven years." [Famous journo Tufail Ahmad @tufailelif: 'Lt.-Col. Purohit told the SC that he was acting as Army mole and was not involved in terrorist activity']

On 28th August 2017, *'Big News: Colonel Purohit Reveals This Big Connection of Dawood Ibrahim and Sonia Gandhi'*, by Ankit Sharma was reported on *IndiaPolitics*. "Slowly and steadily we are able to understand why Lt Col Purohit was interned by the UPA Government that was (super)led by Sonia. Soon after he came out of the jail, he started revealing information that we never imagined in our wildest of the dreams. Yes, Purohit said that Dawood was in Mumbai in the year 2005. Now this raises question on the Ruling Government because how the most wanted criminal could so easily sneak into our nation? The report dated 27th July 2011 during UPA regime lists the findings of a DGMI probe that began soon after Purohit's name came up in the blast case. It not only detailed his involvement with Hindutva radicals and his alleged role in the Malegaon blast but also accused him of dealing in arms illegally and selling ordnance weapons.

India's *The Most wanted terrorist*, Dawood Ibrahim was in Mumbai. Yes, Lt colonel Purohit has all the detail of Hindustan's enemy #1 Dawood's visit to Bombay. Dawood – the ring master of anti-national anti-Hindu film industry run by bastard or legitimate Muslims and pro-Muslims as well as impotent 'purchased' or 'sold' unpatriotic Hindu producers, directors, distributors and actors. Dawood became the master of terrorist activities in the country and its funding through his illegal drug trade. Officers had successfully gained access even to the people with whom Dawood had links and movements in the country. Perhaps this officer (Purohit) knew something more that could destroy that (antinational) Congress(I). Dawood's visit had grabbed the attention of few newspapers and it was published on June 5th or 6th 2005. Dawood was acting like a pivot between ISI and the Naxals. Instead of supporting Lt Col Purohit's Report, it was suppressed, and Col. Purohit tortured. *Does the torture of high-ranking patriotic army officer by bought over civilian police Chamchas of the Congress is allowed in any civilized country of the world?*

"I am serving the Flag...I am serving the president...," said Purohit. One must appreciate his will power. *Even after undergoing series of non-stop tortures, he did not give up. He still wants to serve the nation, hats off to his real patriotism.* At another end we find people like Kanhaiya Kumar who insult and abuse our army! *Indian Army Court (Probe) gave clean chit to Purohit but those who are part to Hindu terrorism conspiracy are unprepared to accept this fact and logic."*

Unlike members of his clan, Mani has named political personalities, IAS and IPS officers. He has either indicted them for their wrongdoings or appreciated others for their good work, such as former IB officer Rajendra Kumar, whom he has mentioned multiple times and credited him for destroying several sleeper cells of Pak ISI that were flourishing in the country. The book has been divided into 14 chapters. In one chapter, titled "Seeding of Hindu terror", he has shared several anecdotes to prove how the Congress led UPA government had forced the MHA officials to manufacture a false narrative on "Hindu terror". Mani mentions how he was summoned by the then Home Minister Shivraj Patil to his chamber and was asked to share information on terrorist attacks. At the time, two more individuals, whom Mani identified as senior Congress leader Digvijay Singh and former Maharashtra IPS officer Hemant Karkare, were sitting there seeking information from him, while Patil sat in his chair totally unconcerned about what was happening. According to Mani, both Singh and Karkare were unhappy with his information that "a particular religious group was in most of the terror attacks". This was in June 2006 and according to him it was during this time that the "first seed of the canard" that there existed Hindu terror was sown. This promulgation of the theory of Hindu terror, according to the book, led to many knots among the various agencies that work under the MHA as agency people were asked to change the narrative from terror to Hindu terror. According to him, "At a time when we had the best team in the 18th division, the attitude of the government in power and intent to cover every terror attack was making this country a cannon folder for those with evil designs against India".

Mani says the most challenging time for him came during the time of the Mumbai attack as almost all the top officials of IS division were in Pakistan. According to Mani, this was all part of a design which has been explained in great details in the book. And with a less than adept Home Minister at the helm, which Mani has tried to prove by giving examples, the terrorists got crucial hours to "secure" themselves. In this chapter he has named IAS officers, politicians and Bollywood personalities for playing a questionable role during and after the attack.

The behind the scenes developments in the MHA, when the tragic attack was taking place, and when the post attack investigation started, which could only be known to someone who was in the inside, has been vividly mentioned in the book. It also talks about how credible inputs about an impending terror attack on Mumbai were not heeded to by the MHA due to intervention from "top political office". Consequently, it was the agencies and officials who got the blame for not being able to stop the attack. PM Manmohan had wind to the impending Mumbai terror attack but for the reasons best known to this impotent person he did precious little to thwart it! Maybe it was Congress(I) plan to implicate Hindu Terror since a book was already written and kept ready to be released by another important *Chamcha* Digvijay Singh, Congress(I) general secretary.

A full chapter has been devoted to the happenings in MHA when P. Chidambaram became the Home Minister. Mani shares how the initial two DGs of NIA were picked without following any due process and how the NIA acted as the personal favorite of the Home Minister and "big brother" to other agencies. According to him, the NIA introduced a non-existent "Hindu terrorism" concept. "In every case assigned to NIA they overlooked the first set of evidences and replaced it with the evidences supporting the Hindu terror narrative". It is worthwhile to mention here that senior officials with the NIA, with whom this correspondent used to interact during the UPA times, have admitted off the record that they had no evidence of any organized Hindu terror. The most interesting part of the book is titled "*The whispering rooms*", in which, Mani included several incidents that may sound unbelievable at firs but will eventually sink in.

Like how the CBI sat on requests by the Indian representative to UN when he sought evidence against Dawood Ibrahim which only the CBI had since the "political quarters, when P. Chidambaram was the Home Minister, were against providing any hardcore evidence against Dawood to the UN". He also writes about how an iconic property in Lutyens Delhi [7, Lok Kalyan Marg – the residence of our Prime Minister—Mani has chosen not to mention] was "sold" to an NRI.

Perhaps a more interesting part of the chapter, which will leave the reader wishing that some more pages were devoted to it, is when Mani narrates incidents regarding how our intelligence agencies stopped several terror attacks. Many of these incidents have not come out in the public domain before. He has also written about how there are a set protocols, safeguards that the MHA carries out before any "surgical strike". According to him, Mani received no such orders to implement these safeguards during 2006-2010, the time when UPA government says that it carried out surgical strikes. So, did the UPA government carry out the 26/11 terror attack? That is something the book leaves on the reader to decide.

Hindu Terror: Insider account of MHA is a recommended read for both laymen and experts who want to get a first-hand account of, among other things, how common political interference is in matters of national security. On 30th July 2018, Pushpinder Guleria said: '***Shame to Congress party and its leaders. Modi ji should win with total majority in 2019. Vande Matram***', among Replies to '*Book by MHA officer reveals how UPA manufactured Hindu terror narrative*'."

Winding up of Congress(I) is very much the need of the day. Dynast president Raul Vinci aka Rahul Gandhi is working overtime to hasten the end of Congress-I. He is thereby fulfilling Patel's forecast [recorded by the Cycle Rickshaw pedaler who was ferrying Patel] communicated to Nehru in 1946 while the former was seated on a manual Cycle Rickshaw, *"When the so many dynasties who ruled India for even centuries are not remembered today by the masses, our People are going to forget Congress in 60-70 years."*

On 8th November 2018, *Rediff.com News* published, '*Rahul is working untiringly for Modi*', "'Rahul is only making a pathetic public spectacle of his lack of judgment and good sense by hallucinating that somehow, the Congress, or whatever political combine is cobbled together, will displace the BJP at the coming Lok Sabha election by constantly harping on the Rafale deal,' argues retired civil servant BS Raghavan. It has hit the jackpot with the Congress President, Rahul, no less, working assiduously and untiringly for Narendra D Modi's triumphant second term with an increased majority in the 2019 Lok Sabha election. In 2014, Sonia Gandhi and Mamata Banerjee also worked hard for Modi, but not as much as Rahul. Sonia, by calling Modi the *'merchant of death'* and Mamata, by characterizing him as *'a donkey'* ensured that the BJP was installed with a majority on its own for the first time ever in three decades, putting an end to the chaotic coalition era. Cho Ramaswamy, the editor of *Tughlaq*, before a huge gathering on the occasion of his annual communion with the weekly's readers, to which he had invited Modi, held the audience in splits by playing on Sonia's title, elaborating how Sonia was dead right and how Modi was truly the 'merchant of death' to loot, plunder, corruption, venality, incompetence, indiscipline and a host of other ills and evils afflicting the Indian polity."

This time, a few others had joined Rahul who has repeatedly called Modi a *'chor'* (thief) and are lending him a helping hand. Shashi Tharoor has called Modi a *'scorpion on a Shivling'*, claiming he got it from an unknown RSS source. AP Finance Minister and TDP leader Yanamada Ramakrishnudu upped the ante by describing Modi as 'an anaconda swallowing institutions'. Mamata, Mayawati, Nara Chandrababu Naidu and those of their ilk are yet to get into the act. If all of them pull together in the same vein, Modi's majority may even soar to greater heights. Rahul is pitching for a record-breaking performance by hitting Modi the hardest of all, by holding the wrong end of the stick. He has got hooked to the Rafale deal and is flogging it day in and day out in a way that borders on some mania. For one thing, no other political party or leader, has joined him, except perhaps Sharad Pawar and that too once, and in a fleeting fashion. *Which means that all those other parties and their leaders, knowing their opinions, have arrived at the conclusion that there isn't much political or electoral juice to be squeezed out of it.*

Ironically Rahul has been unable to substantiate with solid evidence any of his charges against Modi and the government on aspects of the deal, such as the exorbitant price; the forced choice of Reliance Defense as one of Dassault Aviation's many offset partners, Anil Ambani thereby benefiting, thanks to Modi, to the extent of INR300 billion; and Reliance Defense being paid an initial kickback of INR2.84 billion as a first tranche with more to come. Eric Trappier, the CEO of Dassault Aviation, has categorically denied all allegations of corruption, crony capitalism and inflated profits on the deal which predates Modi as well as then French president Francois Hollande. According to him, Dassault had been in discussions with the 'Ambani family' since 2012.

'We stick to the laws of France and laws of India and the law of the contract,' Trappier said. 'We are totally against corruption. If there is any investigation in France or India, we are not only open to the investigation, [but] it is our duty [to respond]. We will prove there is no corruption.' He also rejected the contention that the Indian side had nudged him to give the offsets to Anil Ambani's Reliance Group. 'It has been a long time since we are discussing with Reliance,' said the CEO, referring to an agreement Dassault inked with the Mukesh Ambani group to discharge offsets as part of an earlier deal for 126 jets that was being negotiated with the previous UPA regime. Trappier claimed that India had got a better deal for the 36 jets in 2016 compared to what it would have paid for the 18 that the previous government was pursuing as part of the 126-jet deal. 'Compared to the same price, India brought down the cost by 9%', Trappier said, adding that Reliance Defense will get only INR8.5 billion worth of offsets, not INR300 billion. As regards Rahul's charge of Dassault Aviation paying the 'first tranche of kickbacks' of INR2.84 billion to Anil Ambani, in a hard-hitting rejoinder, Reliance Defense has described it as a 'shameful and deplorable' falsehood. Based on such study as I have made of the deal from material in the public domain and drawing on my own experience of negotiating such international agreements, I see nothing suspicious. It is a government-to-government deal, and France has strict laws as per UN requirement, against any surreptitious kickbacks and handouts. It is a hard State and sternly enforces its laws. Both Dassault's MD Eric Trappier and Reliance Defense Chairman Anil Ambani have strongly and convincingly refuted Rahul's outlandish statements. In any case, there is no evidence whatsoever to support the allegation that Modi brought about the deal to line Ambani's pocket. Thus, other than some clapping by his own cheerleaders at meetings addressed by him, the issue has left the people cold. The media too, which gave it a run initially, has moved on.

Rahul is only making a pathetic public spectacle of his lack of judgment and good sense by hallucinating that somehow, the Congress, or whatever political combine is cobbled together, will displace the BJP at the 2019 Lok Sabha elections by constantly harping on the Rafale deal. It may well be that a large section of the Indian electorate is unlettered and unversed in finer points of governance. But it has shown repeatedly that it has a will of its own, unshaken by all the disputations of the intellectuals among them.

Also, it applies its own independent criteria and forms its own independent judgment of persons, parties and public policies. Kamaraj in Tamil Nadu in 1967, Vajpayee in 2004, Indira in 1977, and Sonia in 2014 learnt it the hard way. In my judgment, as a dispassionate critical observer of the national scene, in 2019 too, the people summoned their native collective wisdom honed for millennia to bear on Modi's performance in office. To them what matters most is the consolation of knowing that the leader has genuine concern for their plight and an awareness of their needs and aspirations, and is earnest in his effort to help them better their lot and has the desire and ability to move forward and fast, making up for all the past neglect. They are going to judge him on criteria such as the ability to go to the root of a problem and knowing where the shoe pinches, his earnestness, determined effort to deliver, courage in decision-making to that end, commitment to public welfare and the nation's good, kindling a sense of self-pride and bolstering national pride and raising India's stock in their own eyes and in those of other nations, and the capacity to run the government as a disciplined team. They note that whoever has seen Modi in action -- heads of States and governments, hard-nosed honchos of business and industry, political, economic, financial and public affairs analysts heading think-tanks, the commentariat of the media and India-watchers in general of other countries -- have paid high tributes to the way Modi is devoting himself to his mission. They are not going to take the measure of him on the yardsticks of what agitates the elitist, English-educated, intellectuals most of whom are completely out of sync with the mood of the man in the street, the farmer, the village artisan and schoolmaster and the average home maker, sprawling themselves on topics such as demonetization, GST, NPA, relations with the RBI, swallowing of institutions and the like.

If anything, debates on these topics will seem sterile and puerile to the average voter, before specific and tangible goals set by Modi for himself, his government and the nation such as the *Swachch Bharat Abhiyan*, *Ayushman Bharat*, *Jan Dham Yojana*, *Beit Bacha, Beit Pahoa*, *Make in India*, *Start-up India*, *Digital India* and *Smart Cities*. (S)he has the inborn intelligence to understand that they cannot yield results for the asking in a country of such size, complexity and diversity, but that they should be given time to show results. In my opinion, and this is also patent from the opinion polls held so far, the generality of the people think that Modi makes the grade in all these respects and continuity of his leadership is imperative for maintaining the tempo of executing these schemes and taking them to fruition. Flowing out of these basic postulates, I am convinced that the outcome of the 2019 election -- the return of Modi and BJP with a significantly increased majority -- is a foregone conclusion." [BS Raghavan, retired IAS, was secretary of the National Integration Council during the prime ministerships of Jawaharlal Nehru, Lal Bahadur Shastri and Indira Gandhi.]

2] *__Kashmir imbroglio:__*
It is very fundamental to understand the root cause of contention between Hindustan and its daughter country Pakistan. The main culprit is undeserving, unelected, immature, inexperienced, womanizer and playboy Nehru, wrongly labeled the *first* prime minister by hired historians. *Netaji* Subhas Chandra Bose was the *First* prime minister when he formed the first government of the India subcontinent 'in exile' in Rangoon on 21st October 1943. Bose retained defense, foreign affairs and home portfolios, Chatterjee was finance minister, and soon 12 countries including Japan, Germany, Italy, Afghanistan, Philippines, Thailand and Manchuria recognized the government and set up their embassies. The salutation was *'Jai Hind'*. The Indian flag (tricolor) was first hoisted in Andaman & Nicobar on 31st October. A big battle was fought in Nagaland during which 26,000 men and officers of INA vs 53,000 of British Royal Indian army lost their lives!

Nehru was nominated as the *second* PM in 1946 by his 'Bapu'. Gandhi admitted in his first autobiography in Gujarati [the only language he knew well] published in 1925 that *he learned wheeling and dealing from his father Karamchand, the Dewan of Rajkot state, who used to cut deals by cheating others.* The reasons, for Gandhi defrauding the most mature well-deserving elder statesman Sardar Patel and, in a way, senior politician MA Jinnah of their rightful election or position respectively as Hindustan's first post-independence prime minister, are dealt with elsewhere in this book. Suffice it to say, the two 'Muslims' – Gandhi and his 'adopted son' Nehru were British agents who never wanted an intelligent INC leader Jinnah to be prime minister of undivided India and senior INC leader – a Hindu Patel to be at the helm of affairs after Partitioning the subcontinent. *They both were scared to hell and very clear in their dirty minds that a right-thinking truly patriotic statesman would sideline the two 'showmen only' with no real substance and hardly any quality/strength and thereby accomplish their lifetime burning aspirations to rule the country and set up a dynasty as if the country was their fiefdom*! Moreover, Gandhi was under pressure from

Britain to install a pliable and easily maneuverable prime minister who could be molded like rubber. Immature stupid Nehru truly fitted the bill. A reference is made by a few that Nehru threatened Gandhi that he would split INC If not made the PM. And, thereby delay the 'transfer of power' from the experienced wily Whites to the inexperienced naïve Browns.

What was the need for Partition? Was it to seize the complete power for the duo by excluding the mature and senior Congressman Jinnah who had joined the INC 20 years before Gandhi? Just to gain ten-and-half months from the stipulated day at too colossal a price: Ten million Hindus and Muslims uprooted from their homes and hearths by the most conservative estimates; one million killed, at least 75,000 young Hindu women and girls abducted and raped; countless Hindustanis killed in the religious frenzy – trains overflowing with Hindu and Muslim migrants were slaughtered on both sides of the 'artificial' borders disclosed only on 18th August 1947 i.e. four days after the two States came into existence! *Did it ever happen in world history that a country is carved out without declaring its boundaries?*

The freedom of Hindustan was inevitable. The uncalled for undesirable unnecessary Partition of the subcontinent must have been avoided at all costs. In a compromise formula, Jinnah could have been easily the first Governor General or Head of the State and Nehru the first PM of the dominion. The brief given to Mountbatten by his second cousin, King George VI as well as the British PM, Major Clement Attlee was to leave Hindustan as it was on 30th June 1948. Partition was too high a price to bring forward that date by ten-and-half months! *The chain of events in handing over or 'gifting' one-third of J&K to Pakistanis a classical story of one high magnitude blunder after the other continuously contemplated by an emotional megalomaniac fool called Nehru. The sequence of developments leading to the man-made colossal Kashmir fiasco amply proves the gulf existing between a truly patriotic, unselfish wedded to his country, proper and richly deserving Chief Executive in the form of George Washington, the First President of the USA on one hand and the least patriotic, selfish, self-centered, substandard, undeserving first prime minister of Hindustan!* Countries like buildings are strong only if their foundations are strong. That explains how far America moved in her first 71 years of existence as an independent nation. Our corrupt inept rudderless leaders could achieve little for their country. But for their own self, they amassed large swathes of unaccounted wealth that can easily last their next seven generations. Gandhi-Nehru manipulated the creation of unwanted two Pakistans on either side and consequently losing one-fifth area of her land thus creating a smaller India.

Nehru's *first* big blunder was to appoint the husband of his beloved Edwina who happened to be the last British representative or Viceroy as the first Governor General of partitioned Hindustan. So, the Constitutional Head (Viceroy) of slave Hindustan and that (Governor General) of free Hindustan was the same! Was it an irony? Most of the newly independent countries in British Commonwealth chose a person of their country as the Constitutional Head rather than a Brit. Hindustan although being the largest among the liberated British colonies chose the undesirable or unwanted. *Does it mean Nehru possessed little IQ and commonsense! This blatantly wrong decision bared the so many flaws in Nehru's character and personality:*

1. Only a skin-deep patriotism having hardly any love for his country or motherland.
2. A slave mentality having faith only in his erstwhile white masters. This flaw has prevailed all throughout from the days of formation of this anti-national party named INC on 28 December 1885 to the present day 134 years later!
3. His mediocre IQ-must have been the same as that of his mentor- the FAKE Mahatma. Plainly speaking, both were duffers. Hence, picked up an education (study law in London) after matriculation where they did not have to exert to study but attend Banquets on Saturday, and Wednesday – as per Gandhi's admission in his 1925 autobiography he wrote in Gujarati. Both never practiced as barristers even for one day!
4. A loose moral character much like that of Gandhi. By choosing Mountbatten, Nehru was *buying* a few more years to live close to his lady love Edwina and continue the affair and romantic life to his liking!

There was a tacit understanding between INC and IUML that Mountbatten would be the governor general for both the countries. On 12th August 1947, Jinnah, the life President of IUML, backtracked and appointed self as the governor general of the country he created with express contribution by Gandhi-Nehru. It is said that Mountbatten advised Nehru to rescind his decision to make room for an Indian as the *first* governor general. Nehru did not want to lose the company of his lover, Edwina so soon! He persevered with his foolish *antinational* decision 9without cabinet approval) to appoint an enemy who ruled the *slave* Hindustan, a Brit as the first governor general! Nevertheless, this major blunder led to a spate of much anticipate foolish blunders by the habitual blunder-master – the opportunistic emotional fool Nehru was known to be!

<u>Second</u> blunder was his audacity to handle Kashmir although his senior Patel as Home and Minister for states had done commendable job of forcing the 562 princely states, big and small, to accede to the Indian Union. Nehru appointed his *Chamcha*, Ramaswamy Iyengar as special minister for Kashmir. *Why did the hell autocratic clueless stupid Nehru keep Patel out of this most important state*? Had Patel been legitimately in charge Kashmir, there would NOT have been any Kashmir problem that India is facing for 72 years. [Thanks to present farsighted PM Modi, the Special Status of J&K was abolished on 5th August 2019]! A weak and clueless Iyengar was at a loss to understand his job let alone accomplishing it. *Chamchagiri (sycophancy) – a cult created by cunning cheat Gandhi, has been the bane of Congress party since 1917 and continues in full flow even after 101 years*! **When merit is sacrificed, the results are meritless**.

On 22nd October 1947 (within two months of its creation), Pakistan invaded Kashmir by sending its army in the garb of *Qabailies* (tribals). Mountbatten knew it before-hand as both British army C-in-Cs (of the two countries) were reporting to and in touch with Mountbatten who in turn was in touch with British Prime Minister, Attlee. But the Brit did not let Nehru know of it. He must have thought if Nehru was ever ready to be fooled, why not make an ass of him! *Maharaja* Hari Singh was at a total loss as the Muslims in his army joined hands with invaders. He was foolish enough to think of independent existence much like Nizam of Hyderabad and Nawab of Junagarh.

<u>Third</u> blunder of Nehru was even more poignant and damaging. He appointed Mountbatten as the Chairman of the Defense Council. How can a man in senses with a reasonable IQ appoint an enemy on the strategically important key defense position? Nehru's two seniors (Sardar) Patel and (Rajaji) Chakravarty Rajagopalachari were much more competent than Mountbatten far more suitable persons. Mountbatten's appointment was without approval by the Union Cabinet! So, *Nehru was taking the most stupid decisions keeping all the other senior leaders in the dark!*

<u>Fourth</u> blunder of Nehru was to wait endlessly for Hari Singh to call for Hindustan's help. It may be worth mentioning that Kashmir was bequeathed to Hari Singh's ancestor Gulab Singh. He was the erstwhile '*traitor*' general of great Maharaja Ranjit Singh, the Lion of Punjab who

ruled over the huge state of Punjab of the Punjab including the then Kashmir equivalent to present J&K and Gilgit-Baltistan. The other extreme was the most patriotic and famous General Hari Singh Nalwa who remains the only Hindustani to rule over Afghanistan which the most powerful British army could not subjugate even after many battles! After extra-hectic activities on the fateful 27th October involving many Delhi-Srinagar-Delhi air dashes by Menon, the former PA to the Viceroy but now Patel's, King Hari Singh signed the accession document in Srinagar. Officers and men of our Army were airlifted to Srinagar in numerous sorties using all types of aircrafts available. Jinnah had left the capital city of Karachi in the south, the largest in West Pakistan. He was camping at nearby town of Sialkot to closely monitor the Indo-Pakistan war from close quarters. Incidentally, that was the only city connected by rail to Jammu. This way, Nehru wasted five precious days leading to the loss of almost half of Kashmir state territory to Pakistanis.

Fifth blunder was decision of Plebiscite in Kashmir for deciding its accession to India. This was on the advice of fifth columnist Mountbatten who never wanted the merger of Kashmir into India. It was part of the British agenda to create a bone of contention between the newly liberated countries. As expected, the sane statesman Patel was opposed to such an action on our part. Nehru never listened to his senior's judgement and spurned his logical advice. Nehru compounded the blunder by announcing it on the All India Radio on 2nd November 1948. Countries are pushed into oblivion if its founding leaders like stupid Nehru lack the sense of proportion. British PM Attlee congratulated Nehru for this statement as that tantamount to pursuing the British agenda of creating a permanent rift between the two neighbors so that Britain as also America, the emerging world power could fish in troubled waters and continue exerting their influence in South Asia. From then on, America more than Britain started increasingly pro-Pakistan stance. For America, there was another grudge too, President Harry Truman offered an olive branch to Nehru during his first official visit in 1949. Truman wanted Nehru to join the capitalist camp abandoning pro-USSR stance. The Communist Nehru declined. Hence, from 1950 onward, America whole-heartedly started supporting Pakistan politically, financially, militarily and diplomatically! This India-bashing continued for 68 years. It was left to the first apolitical President Trump to reverse this time-honored American policy and show Pakistan its place.

Prior to this, Nehru's _Sixth_ blunder was to approach the UNO solely on the advice of Mountbatten, thereby propagating the British agenda of destroying Hindustan. *It is unimaginable that a slave mentality person like Nehru could be so totally dumb*! Though being insiders, both Sardar Patel and Lt Gen Cariappa, in charge of army's Kashmir operations, were bitterly opposed to the same having been able to see through the British game yet Nehru had closed his eyes like the pigeon closes his eyes to approaching cat! The pigeon believes that cat will not come if its eyes are closed. I learned it from horse's mouth: Cariappa's PA – a colonel in the Indian army – happened to be the father-in-law of my friend and class fellow at (Glancy) Medical College, Dr Yashbir Mehta. During the celebrations of the golden Jubilee of our 'Class of 1963' at Amritsar during March 2013, Yashbir's wife and daughter of the Colonel told us, "My father used to say that our Army needed just five more days to vacate the whole of Kashmir from occupation by the invaders. Cariappa asked silly Nehru "to delay approaching UNSC by 7 days at the most so that we can reclaim the whole of Kashmir state." Nehru was under the spell of Edwina and hence a pawn in the hands of Mountbatten. Or, in real terms, he was continuing to a slave to the white skin. Incidentally, as a physician with decades' experience in clinical research, I can vouch that slavery is transmitted by a dominant gene. Hence slave Indians are producing slaves for generations every time after they became followers of Gandhi, the Fake Mahatma or even Fake Hindu, for a century since 1917. That means they have already added five generations of persons with slave mentality and most of them are members/followers of Congress party that is bent upon destroying Hindustan. Incidentally, the draft of Nehru's proposal to the UN was shown to his '3rd father' Gandhi during the last days of December 1947. There were three suggestions put forward by Nehru as dictated by his supremo Mountbatten. These were:

1. Kashmir merging with India,
2. Kashmir merging with Pakistan, and
3. Kashmir remains an Independent country.

Britain and her agent Mountbatten were for the last option so that both the new neighbors are ever fighting with each other. Gandhi, the only person Nehru respected and abided by, struck down the third proposal (of remaining as an independent country) much to the relief of Patel, the only sane and truly patriotic Hindustani among the whole lot of actors or players in Kashmir imbroglio!

Why Nehru was playing into the hands of his white masters by acting in an anti-national manner? Obviously, he was immature childish politician who most undeservingly snatched the highest post in newly 'independent' Hindustan courtesy Gandhi who, in fact, had bargained his re-entry into INC in 1928 by promising/offering its ailing president Motilal that he (Gandhi) would ensure that latter's son Jawaharlal becomes independent India's first PM! The anti-national man stood by it and maneuvered to achieve this most dangerous and detrimental to the country act!

3] *National Character or Lack of it?*

Do Hindustanis possess the national character befitting the citizen of the country with once greatest civilization? The answer is a vehement No since the effects of mental slavery inflicted by nearly a millennium-old slavery especially the last 200 years of that under the British are evidently omnipresent. Medically speaking, Slavery appears to be transmitted by a dominant gene. Hence, a slave can produce only another slave. There are subtle differences between we Hindustanis and those from advanced/developed countries. Wes are basically dishonest and essentially lawbreakers. We hardly behave as patriotic people except during war or cricket match against Pakistan. We are insensitive to others' needs especially those of females and senior citizens. Atrocities against girls and women in the form of female feticide, molestation and rapes of girls as young as six months have been reported. Bride-burning for non-receipt or lack/deficient dowry (as per the brides' husband's or his parents' expectations) happens often and looks as if it were a pastime for the greedy. Much-talked about equality between the two sexes appears to be a pipedream. The list goes on and on. We try to follow corrupt practices in practically every walk of life. Rather than follow the law of the land, we look for short-cuts to obviate or bypass the rules. For example, we prefer to bribe the traffic constable rather than follow the traffic rules. Thanks to politicians right from the days of the FAKE Mahatma, ware constantly being divided by religion, caste, sub-caste, religion and any other parameter the wily crooked politicians use to garner votes. We don't believe in hard work and fair competition but reservation. Any SC/ST can get to a medical college with even 40% or less marks whereas a candidate from non-reserved category may not be successful with even 90% marks. We want reservations for any and every necessity of life!

4] *<u>Misguided directionless Youth.</u>*

Stemming from lack of training to build the national character from an early age and Nehru, being a mental slave of the British, blindly following Raj-introduced Macauley system of education by doing away our millennia-old Gurukul system of education relegating the most perfect Sanskrit to oblivion. Muslim Nehru had hatred for Hindus and Hinduism. His sinister ban on the teaching of Hinduism as a subject spoke of his gross immaturity but proved his credentials of being born to Muslim parents. His hatred against the religion of 85% of India's post-independence population was evident in his every action. Paradoxically, he also put an embargo on the study of Bhagwadgita, the foremost treatise in the world on philosophy of life. At the same time study of Quran and Bible in schools was encouraged. I am constrained to say that the present PM Modi who comes from humble background also could not notice this anomaly. Or, maybe his hands appear to be full and he may revert to the most important topic of early education later.

Japan is a classic example where patriotism is taught throughout the elementary school curriculum so that the child becomes an ideal citizen before embarking upon formal education. Teaching in our schools and colleges is too much inadequate and lopsided so much so that a PhD is prepared to work as a peon for lack of opportunities. No doubt the institutions for higher learning like the IITs and IIMs have high standards. But the irony is bulk of those qualifying from these august institutes prefer to leave the motherland for greener pastures in developed world. Hence, public expenditure on these institutes is a waste of our resources that could better be put for better use. There is more hype than reality in my country. My compatriots are double-faced, show contradiction in them and trying to maintain a face on what we are not. There is extremely wide gap between speech and action. Laws exist on any and every issue but those are not followed at all or, at best, tardily acted upon. 'Right to Education' is given primacy on paper only. The government has failed to provide proper schools conducive to our multimillennial-old Hindu culture and civilization. *Edifice is bound to crumble if its foundations are weak. That is the fundamental ailment in basic education. Our planning is lop-sided. We plan for today and implement it tomorrow – that has been the fallacy and fault of our prime ministers from FAKE Pandit to FAKE economist.* The result is for everyone to see and discover. Even the history of our country particularly of the freedom struggle has been changed and distorted to fulfill political agenda of the Congress party that was anti-India right from its inception on 28th December 1885! Apparently, PM Modi is right and justified in making *Congress-mukt* Bharat!

However, this will certainly obviate future damage but what about the colossal damage already inflicted by this nefarious party over the past 101 years? Our primary education system needs drastic improvement and refurbishing. The soonest it is accomplished the better it will be. We have already lost the first 71 years since independence. Any further delay will only confound the issue. The day to day conduct in society of our children requires a sea change! Partha P Chakrabartty's article, *'Indian govt's porn ban is empty, illusory measure; tackling sexual assault needs real intent and action'*, published by *MSN News* on 30th November 2018 is worth reading

"The porn ban covers less than 2% of porn websites online. Since it is clearly not about banning porn, what is the porn ban about? To understand what the most recent porn, we must start with a number: 827 websites were blocked under the most recent order by the Uttarakhand HC.

How did the High Court come up with this number? Its story begins with the tragic 2012 Delhi gangrape case. In the wake of the tragedy, an Indore-based advocate, Kamlesh Vaswani thought pornography was the chief cause for crimes against women and embarked on a crusade against porn websites. It was he who came up with a list of 857 websites when he filed a public interest litigation in the SC in 2013 to get these sites banned. SC put the then UPA government on notice, which expressed its helplessness in the matter of acting against pornography websites whose servers were outside India. The case ran till July 2015, when then CJI HL Dattu ruled that the SC cannot tell adults what to do in the privacy of their room. That would be where the list would have died its natural death, but like Mihir Virani on *Kyunki Saas Bhi Kabhi Bahu Thi*, it found a way to be reborn. Vaswani passed the list on to Pinky Anand, a top lawyer in the BJP government, who then passed it on to the ministry of telecom for "appropriate action". Was this action the careful crafting of laws that regulate cyberspace? Or perhaps a committee to find out the ill effects of pornography and how best to fight them? No. The government did what was easiest for it to do: send a circular to internet service providers asking them to ban the list of websites.

After realizing their order had no defensible legal basis and facing both critique by intellectuals and ridicule and jokes from the masses, the ministry backtracked in 2015. It was not a pretty retreat, with the government first trying to put the blame on the SC, and then telling

ISPs to "voluntarily" block websites. One of them, Reliance Jio, took the government up on its offer.

Which brings us to the present day. Again, it is a court order that has prompted this ban. Once again, it is a horrifying gang rape in a Dehradun school that has prompted the order. According to reports, four students assaulted a girl after they watched porn clips. The court has hoped that this order to internet service providers will "avoid an adverse influence on the impressionable minds of children." But did the court find out how best to go about achieving this goal? Or encourage the government to find out? No, it turned to Vaswani's list instead. The government found 30 websites to be not pornographic, and so we arrived at the number 827.

Now that we know of how the ban came about, we can infer everything that this ban is not about. *Firstly*, this is not about internet censorship. It is a very tightly defined ban and does not spread to other parts of the internet. Equally, it is a ban that the Supreme Court has found constitutionally indefensible, meaning it will be struck down were it to be challenged. That the government has chosen to implement a ban rather than pass legislation shows that legislation would likely be unpopular. If we want to discuss internet censorship, there is the much more pressing use by the government of internet blackouts and arbitrary bans, particularly in J&K. It'd do us well to pay attention to that instead.

Nor is this ban about punishing 'safe' pornographic sites and therefore diverting traffic to unsafe sites as Pornhub.com's brilliant public relations team has argued. They are right that they have more controls than smaller players, but anyone can upload a revenge porn video on the website, and have it spread widely, well before it can be flagged and taken down. Also, a lot of the content is unregulated, meaning that a lot of videos repeat toxic narratives, objectify women, and misrepresent sex and consent. It is hard to see Pornhub.com as a solution to the nastier consequences of pornography. Luckily, we have the enterprising Cindy Gallop and her lovely website, makelovenotporn.tv, to show us how it is to be done.

Next, the ban is not about preventing sexual assault. Even a cursory analysis of the effect of porn on sexual assault shows that increase in access to pornography reduces cases of sexual assault. There are many causes of sexual assault: rape culture led by our esteemed leaders, toxic masculinity, and the absence of any conversation around sex, leave alone a comprehensive program of sex education. But these issues will take sensitivity, intelligence, creativity and effort to solve, and will also require questioning religious traditions and social customs, something this government is particularly loath to do. If anything, the tragic court cases have been used as an excuse to implement the porn ban. That this has precious little to do with sexual assault is made even clearer by how utterly ineffective this ban is. Remember how Reliance Jio voluntarily blocked websites on the list? Pornhub.com circumvented it by switching to Pornhub.net. If porn was truly causing sexual assault, and was a dragon that needed slaying, would our measure be so utterly ineffectual?

This brings us to the final point that this ban is not even about banning internet pornography. If it was, it would start by finding out how many pornographic websites exist. The number in 2010, according to Ogi Ogas, the author of A Billion Wicked Thoughts, was 42,337 of the million most popular websites in the world. That makes our porn ban cover less than 2% of popular pornographic sites" a fig leaf that wouldn't even hide the genitals" and this is all the way back in 2010. Other estimates count the total number of porn websites in the millions.

So, *if it is not about any of these things, what is it about*?

First, like with our *Statue of Unity*, it is about perception rather than action. Solving the real problems here" sexual assault, and our silence around sex that is filled up by the toxic narratives of pornography" is complex and challenging. Much easier to make a show of doing something about pornography, which will appease the anti-porn constituency in your electorate, while doing so little that the pro-porn electorate will not be too outraged.

Second, it is about the limits of national governments in the internet age. If anything, this porn ban is likely to educate our youngsters in the use of proxies and routers, making them even more proficient at circumventing other bans the government may implement. Governments are helpless to regulate a land where anarchic coders are constantly coming up with ways to defeat control and surveillance.

Third, it is about another opportunity lost for a meaningful conversation about the prevention of sexual assault, and even the harmful effects of porn. Pornography is not innocent. There are entire communities of people online with lives significantly disrupted by porn addiction. Revenge porn has devastating consequences for those featured in it. And the most horrifying pornography problem in India is not online websites" it is rape videos being sold offline.

Unfortunately, the government cannot hope to regulate internet pornography. States have too little influence over the internet, and they cannot meaningfully influence the supply of pornography. Given a force that you cannot stop, the only appropriate response is to arm the citizenry with ways to deal with this onslaught. This should have been used as an occasion to have India take the lead on comprehensive and progressive sex education for all its adolescents, including a discussion on the ethical and proper use of pornography. Mixed in with it could be a sexual assault prevention training program like Kenya's that conducted workshops with both girls and boys in schools. The program has demonstrated its efficacy in studies. If anyone from the government is taking note: please stop investing time and effort in empty, illusory measures. The harms here are real. They need real intent and action from you.

5] *Reservations and Dirty Vote-Bank politics.*

Dr BR Ambedkar wanted 22% reservations for Schedules Castes and Scheduled Tribes for the initial ten years from 26th January 1950. However, these got extended every ten years. In 1990, PM Vishwanath Pratap Singh implemented the 'Mandal Commission Report' thereby enhancing the quantum of reservations to 49%. It is noteworthy to know that this report was gathering dust for over a decade under his two predecessors, Rajiv and Indira. There were wide-spread agitations across the country. Several self-immolations by high caste university students did not deter Singh for he was of the firm opinion that low caste voters would be lured and vote for his party in future although his was a minority government. Singh did not last more than a year as the PM and had to resign because of his sheer incompetence. But he sowed the seeds of a deep-seated division between the high caste (unreserved) and the low caste (Reserved) populations. The tragedy with this country has been undeserving prime ministers from 2nd PM Nehru to the last Congress(I) PM Manmohan. Tragically each one of the 14 of them did more damage than good to the country. Consequently, Indian masses has been at the receiving end for the first 67 years of the so called 'independence'! Some states wanted the reservations to go beyond 70%. Thanks to the Supreme Court that put a cap at a maximum of 50% for all types of reservations. Extreme degrees of populist measures unheard of in any civilized country are being employed in my country by different PMs and CMs. Objective is vote-catching with least consideration towards the country or equal benefits to all classes of citizens. Although secular on paper, politicians have divided the country on religion, caste and sub-caste or even regional! basis.

6] *Fake Secularism or 'Pseudo-secularism':*

Just before independence in 1946, Two important sinister developments with far-reaching consequences took place. Congress party (then INC and now Congress-Indira) shed its secularism by robbing the right of the duly elected PM Patel with 80% vote. 'Half-Muslim' and FAKE Mahatma nominated 'Muslim' Nehru and a FAKE Pandit instead. This anti-patriotic action of the dictator not only signaled the end of democracy within the party and hence the government but also proved the forerunner of many serious problems the country is facing till date. It also marked the setting up of a dynasty within the purported democratic country. Since then the Hindus have been at the receiving end. Immature Nehru committed numerous blunders. He considered India his property and promoted his sparsely educated 'daughter' thus completing the job of his mentor in establishing Gandhi-Nehru-Gandhi dynasty. Now, 72 years after independence, time is just ripe for the Hindus to unite and throw the wrongdoers out of the window. There are very rare moments when the Hindus in India stood unitedly when their religion was in trouble. But the unity of Hindus after the Sabarimala judgement displayed like never and they showed the world how the unity of Hindus cannot just save themselves from their suppressors but also send fear in the minds of anti-Hindus! In sending a big blow to the communist government that wants to send women from the restricted age group, thereafter the Kerala government was hell-bent in sending women activists, who were from other faiths, the Hindus took an oath of donating not even a penny to the temple. Instead of money, the box for donation was filled with 'Hundis' or chits that read 'Swamiye Shardana Ayappa'. This way, Hindus succeeded in inflicting heavy damage to the coffers of Sabarimala Temple's income.

7] *Presence of anti-national Muslims sheltered and financed by Congress party.*

There is a long list of Muslim traitors. One such noteworthy recent example has been Hamid Ansari who was given an unprecedented second term as Vice President for bailing out the NDA government on the issue of Lokpal Bill when Anna Hazare's movement for introducing a Lokpal was at its crescendo, and the country especially its youth was up in arms against the NDA government arguably the most inefficient and thoroughly corrupt since independence being headed by a worthless pseudo-economist accidental PM, a truly worthless *Chamcha* Manmohan who was -merely a pawn in the hands of the scheming Congress(I) president with strong anti-India bias and anti-Hindu import likened to Italian mafia by many an analyst!. Realizing his 'importance', Ansari was kept as Vice President pf the country for unprecedented second term by the highly corrupt UPA government under an accidental PM, a meek mindless puppet and the most revered *Chamcha* of the Italian owner of the ruling Congress(I). It may not be out of place to name the t*hree most important traits of this good-for-nothing PM Manmohan who have always been: Swami bhakti (worshipping one's master) indulging in Chaplusi (seeking undeserved favors) and Chamchagiri (always playing a second fiddle). Manmohan proved to be the biggest slur on the fair name of brave, intelligent, self-respecting highly patriotic Sikhs since he possessed qualities directly opposite! Manmohan had 'qualities' diagonally opposite.* Ansari's ancestors were-associated *with Khilafat Movement* and the INC for a very long time. He was made Vice President by the same anti-national party-led government. He even got an unprecedented second 5-year-term for the first time in 60 years in lieu of saving the UPA government during a debate on Lokpal! His favor for MAHACHAMCHA and a stooge of Italy-born Sania Maino, who nominated undeserving Manmohan as the PM of the most corrupt government, was to abruptly stop the ongoing Rajya Sabha debate at midnight on 31st December 2011 when it was clearly going against the UPA. Thus, he saved the highly corrupt and inept UPA government from falling by abruptly terminating the Rajya Sabha session on the all-important Lokpal Bill. Thus, he gave lease of life to the beleaguered Manmohan government! *Two*: Ansari's statement on his last day in office that 'Muslims feel insecure in India' has a basis: *A PIL filed in 2015 and the subsequent report by the CAG has found gross irregularities and huge misuse of money in the working of Rajya Sabha TV (RSTV) controlled by Ansari.* The budget of *RSTV* is bigger than any government channel. It does not accept any advertisements as a source for revenue. Like the Congress whom he supported, defended and saved all the time while in office, he proved to be an anti-national crook of the first order like some others from his community. His irregularities inviting/anticipating reprisals from all around even from PM Modi, is the real cause of his 'insecurity'!

Islamic Another stooge of Congress(I) has been the controversial Islamic preacher Dr Zakir Naik. Party general secretary Digvijay Singh – an important Chamcha of Sania Maino – used to be frequently seen in the fora addressed by Zakir. Once the Congress(I)was booted out of the Central government Naik has been on the run. Being a Muslim country, Malaysia gave him asylum. On 12th November 2018, *One India's* Vicky Nanjappa's article, 'A poison called Zakir Naik and his role in radicalizing Kerala detailed by an ISIS recruit', appeared on *Yahoo News*. "New Delhi, Nov 12: The heat is back on Dr. Zakir Naik, the controversial Islamic preacher, who is hiding in Malaysia. His name has emerged right on the top of the investigations being conducted by the National Investigation Agency, which is probing the case of the missing persons from Kerala, who have joined the Islamic State in Afghanistan. Nashidul Hamzafar, the 26-year old management student from Kerala's Wayanad was in September arrested by the NIA after he became one of the first ISIS recruits to be deported from Afghanistan. During his interrogation, *he details the role played by Islamic preachers such as Naik and what sort of an influence they had on him, which ultimately prompted him to join the ISIS*. Hamzafar says that he was not attracted to the ISIS ideology for long. I found them to be too brutal and the outfit only scared me, he says. My ambition was to pursue my education and find a good job in Dubai. A lot changed when one of his friends, Shihas sent him an audio clip regarding the Islamic State. My perception towards the outfit changed. Then I began listening to audios of Zakir Naik, Noman Alikhan among others. Their speeches inspired me and my approach towards life changed. I began telling my family members to become stringent followers of Islam. I told them not to watch television or even lend money for interest. These were anti-Islam, I would tell them, Hamzafar told the NIA.

Going by his statements, it becomes clear that the likes of Zakir Naik through his Islamic Research Foundation and the Kerala based Peace Educational Foundation have played a huge role in the radicalization of youth in Kerala and elsewhere in the country. He said that in May 2017, he had left for Bahrain for a job. He however maintained contact with Shihas and others who had joined the ISIS in Afghanistan. Shihas who was working in the media department for the ISIS advised me to reach Iran after I expressed interest in Hijra. I came back to Kerala and then left for Oman in October 2017. From there I reached Tehran. From there I left for Isfahan, where I was picked up by a man and left off at a safe house.

<u>*A poison called Naik*</u>: A Mumbai court had framed charges against Arshi Qureshi by a group of like-minded youths from Kasaragod district of Kerala. It was also stated that some members of the Zakir Naik run

NGO, Islamic Research Foundation too were involved in the radicalization process. It was further alleged that those 'motivated' the youth to join the ISIS. Investigations revealed that Qureshi was also involved in unlawful activities and spreading hatred against India.

NIA recently said that members of the *Popular Front of India* had conspired to kill Sasi Kumar, a spokesperson of the Hindu Munani. The murder of the leader from Coimbatore was carried out to create terror among the people, the NIA has also said in its supplementary charge sheet. During investigation, NIA conducted searches at the houses of 4 accused persons on March 18 and recovered PFI donation receipts, PFI literature, PFI Unity March CDs, mobile phones, Compact Disks and pen drives, DVD of Zakir Naik of Islamic Research Foundation and other incriminating documents relating to PFI."

Muslims, by and large, may be nationalistic. Lack of proper formal education and even on the fundamental tenets of Islam makes them an easy prey for predators like fundamentalists like the Mullahs and eccentrics like the likes of Zakir Naik. *One should not be constrained to say that monotheism is a fundamental flaw in the major global religions of Christianity and Islam*!

8] *Congress party produced more anti-nationals than any other political outfit.*

As the oldest party, it ONLY worked for the high office rather for the country or its well-being. Having been in power for over half a century, the damage caused by its 'leaders' has been colossal. Aside from -Muslims Nehru and Gandhi, scores of others continued to contribute their unholy part. *Let me tell my readers about some of their herd of anti-nationals in the not-too-distant past --who helped the terrorists.*

i] *Mufti Mohammed Syed*, a Congressman since 1965, was the Union home minister in VP Singh's cabinet in 1990. He released 13 terrorists in exchange of his medical intern daughter Rubiya Syed who was allegedly abducted by terrorists. However, she was returned totally unharmed. Was it a drama created by this anti-national Kashmiri Muslim who founded PDP in 1999?

ii] *Saifuddin Soz* was once a minister in Congress government in J&K. In August 1991, his daughter was 'kidnapped'. The result: seven hard-core terrorists released from prison.

iii] *Ghulam Nabi Azad* is the blue-eyed boy of Sonia, the Italian origin Catholic owner of the party, and a former J&K chief minister for one full term of six years and now leader of the Opposition in Rajya Sabha. On 22nd September 1991, he released 21 terrorists from the prison in lieu of freedom of his wife's brother from 'abduction' by so called terrorists.

iv] *Abdullahs*: This dynasty close to the 'first political family' has ruled over J&K for most part since independence. Sheikh Abdullah, the founder, was close to Nehru being Muslims. Sheikh Abdullah is alleged to be the 'b*****d' son of one Motilal Nehru and his Muslim maid. Hence, he was very close to Nehru as both shared time during their childhood years in the household of Motilal. Nehru had too much faith in him and preferred him over and above Hari Singh, the king of erstwhile princely state of Kashmir even though the latter had signed the instrument of accession like his any other contemporary king. Sheikh was scandalously installed as the first Kashmir PM much against Patel's advice, ousting the King who as a Hindu was totally disliked by Nehru. Post of J&K state PM was downgraded as CM to fall in line with the political scenario. Sheikh started the secession movement in the state through his party, National Conference, that, on surface, sounded like Indian National Congress. 'Indian' is missing in the name of the Kashmiri party since its job is secession. Both parties are in fact anti-national in their deeds and actions. Nehru claimed to be the owner of INC after pro-Muslim Gandhi's 1948 assassination. In 1953, Sheikh had to be removed for sedition charges because of his attempted secession and was put in jail by the Sadr-e-Riyast, Dr Karan Singh son of erstwhile king Hari Singh. Farooq, the 2nd generation dynast and his son Omar, the 3rd generation, continue the nefarious agenda of the founder under explicit support from Congress.

v] *John Dyal* – the odd Christian seditionist among anti-national Muslims – is heavily funded by his master and the Vatican to criticize the Hindu PM at every forum and act in a questionable manner: We have been talking of Muslim seditionists this far. John happens to be the main anti-Hindu in *Today's Hindustan*. It is well-known that John Dyal was closely associated with Sonia in the unconstitutional National Advisory Council which was acting in place of docile but highly corrupt Manmohan wearing the garb of honesty, the dummy PM for ten years under 'super PM' Sonia. John is the champion in the art of mispresenting the Hindus and their Organizations on the foreign soil furthering his master's agenda. He has repeatedly denounced India polity and system on platforms abroad. Such anti-national acts have been willfully ignored or covered up by the not-so-nationalistic mainstream media and the powers that be i.e. the then 'super prime minister' Sonia whose agenda he was supporting and furthering.

vi] Sania Adige Maino, followed by son Raul Vinci and daughter Bianca aka Priyanka Vadra. This trio appears higher at 6th, 7th and 8th in Francois Gautier's book on all-time *'50 anti-Hindus'*. Incidentally, the 1st position is occupied by Thomas Babington Macauley who changed our education system from Gurukul system in Sanskrit to the present Public-School Christian model in English. Thus, it damaged our culture irretrievably. At #2 is INC; and at 3rd Nehru who along with Gandhi, are the duo who did the MAXIMUM, difficult-to-retrieve, permanent culpable damage to the country! Bollywood lyricist Javed Akhtar and his second wife are at #10 & #11.

The fact remains that Congress, right from her inception, has been a well-wisher of the Raj and fully subservient and slave to the white skin. This anti-national party has always nurtured, protected, sponsored and supported pseudo-intellectuals whose main job is denigration of Hindus and our most ancient civilization and culture. This has been continuously and consistently tarnishing the fair name of Hindustan abroad. It does not matter to this party so long as Hindus are demonized. Present Congress (I) president and all his *Chamchas* continues to berate and demonize our present PM Modi who, in the only general election he contested, cut this party to size with number of its MPs coming down to paltry 44 from 205 earlier. From Gandhi-Nehru onwards, Congress liked this coterie spreading the venom here and abroad since it always remained an anti-national party. *Time has come to expose, disband and destroy this insidious anti-national network of a nefarious clique run by persons of doubtful credentials and integrity!* This could be one of the recipes for *'Achhe Din'* (Good Times). *It is a question of NOW or NEVER!*

On 14th October 2017, the anti-India British newspaper, *Sunday Guardian* published MD Nalapat's article, *'India's fake secularists and phony liberals'*: "The fact that a *Dalit youth appointed as Head Priest of the Manappuram Shiva Temple in Kerala has been entirely ignored by the phony liberals. A dictionary would show that secularism mandates equal treatment for people of all faiths.* Ancient India welcomed people of faiths entirely different from what was then practiced within the subcontinent. Conversely, it would be difficult to argue that all faiths were treated the same during the six centuries when the Mughals ruled much of India, or during the three centuries when it was the turn of the British to be the masters. While there was probably discrimination against Dalits and some "backward castes" during what may be called the Vedic (i.e. pre-Mughal) period, it was the Hindus who were at the receiving end of discrimination during Mughal rule. The mistreatment continued into the British period. The new colonial masters ensured that much of the Hindu temples and their lands and properties that were left after the Mughal period were taken over by the state, while prime plots of land in the cities were gifted for the construction of churches. Hence, while there existed historical grounds for post-1947 affirmative action in support of the Dalits, as also some "backward castes", the continuation by Jawaharlal Nehru and his successors of Mughal and British-era policies that discriminated against the Hindu community was uncalled for. Nehru seems to have been taken aback during 1935-46 by the growing support of Muslims in the subcontinent to the concept of Pakistan. He apparently concluded that the best way of preventing the re-igniting of separatist sentiments among the Muslims who remained in India after Partition was to give them additional privileges. The post-1947 provisions relating to minorities in the laws and practices of the country have instead had the predictable effect of increasing rather than reducing feelings of separation between "minority" and "majority".

Unexpectedly for a BJP PM, Vajpayee retained in full the practices initiated by Nehru, rather than ensure a transition to genuine secularism through doing away with differential treatment by the Central, state and local governments to people of different faiths. Modi appears to have decided to put off to his second term such a rectification of colonial practice through phasing out the Nehruvian distortions of the secular ideal. The PM has instead been focusing his efforts on creating a cashless economy and a zero-tax evasion society during his first term. It speaks for the self-confidence of Modi that such feats are being attempted through the same colonial model of administration and law that the country has been choking under throughout its seven decades of "Independence". Thus far, PM has not accepted the counsel of those who have called for a complete break from the past in matters of both personnel as well as policy and has decided instead on a policy of a more gradual incremental change.

Moving in lockstep with fake or pseudo-secularists are India's phony liberals. They can be equated to the Democrats in the US. They look to cues from the *CNN* and the *BBC* while fashioning responses to events. Which is probably why they have almost entirely ignored such events as a Dalit youth being appointed as the Head Priest of the Manappuram Shiva Temple in Kerala. The concept of caste as a consequence of birth belongs in the same lunatic asylum as Adolf Hitler's racial theories, and yet to the "liberals", the temple appointment is not even a hundredth as important as demanding that the Rohingyas get resettled from Myanmar to India. The 22-year-old Yadukrishna represents the spirit of his faith before its calcification began through the adoption of "caste by birth". The "liberal" media seems to be almost ignoring the new Manappuram Shiva Temple Head Priest and his guru, Aniruddhan Tantri, who is quoted as having correctly pointed out that the Vedic concept is that "one becomes a Brahmin by his or her deeds and not by birth". If India had more genuine and less fake liberals, by now there would have been hundreds of Yadukrishnas conducting rituals in traditional style at Hindu temples across the land.

Another sign of the distance our country needs to traverse before it can earn the tag of being "liberal" is the shoddy example of the Indian Navy. Another of the numerous institutions in India still loyal to the hypocrisies and misperceptions of the Victorian era (at a time when the UK has moved far beyond such tommyrot), the Navy has dismissed simply for having undergone a sex change operation at her own cost, and that too while on leave. Both the Army and Air Force have shown the absurd prejudice against the induction of women in combat wings to be wrong, and so should the Navy. PM Modi has often spoken about the need to ensure justice for women, and Defense Minister Nirmala Sitharaman should, therefore, step in to ensure justice for *Sabhi* (All).

India is ranked even below North Korea in health and nutrition. The primary reason for this is a hypocritical and self-obsessed ruling class. "Liberals" in India such as Palaniappan Chidambaram oversaw the passing of laws that would have raised eyebrows even in North Korea or Saudi Arabia. 21st century India has become the easiest country in the world to get arrested in. Genuine secularism and liberalism are needed to cleanse the nation of the havoc caused by toxic policies. India has millions of truly liberal heroes and heroines such as Sabi. We have millions of genuinely secular citizens such as Yadukrishna. They need to be celebrated and empowered so that India evolves into the genuinely secular and liberal state, it needs to be, to thrive and even to survive."

Comments on the foregoing write-up evoked interesting responses. Some examples are:

A] <u>Srichar B</u>: The fake liberals are mostly from the so-called convent educated urban elite. They are beholden to Nehruvian socialist ideology even today while the world has moved forward. They would want to champion the causes of Muslims and Christians and seen as flag holders of the Secular thought, without recognizing the areas where Hindus have moved forward in accepting that it is necessary to accept and live with what history has bequeathed. With so overt and irrational support by these fake liberals and secularists, we are now seeing a push back by the Hindus. Having seen support, many Muslims still do not want to integrate and put country before religion and want to have sharia in places within the country and indulge in converting Hindus to their faith. Christians on the other hand believe it is their obligation to convert the Hindus to their faith in large numbers luring them with money and rice bags. Many Hindus have converted to Islam and Christianity and never needed the sanction of their religion to do us. That's Hinduism, where individuals have choice to practice any faith.

B] Sanjiwan Kumar: Pure spirituality reveals that the Supreme Father is one, we may call it God, Allah, Ram, Waheguru or Akalpurukh. Names are many, but the God is one. This oneness leads to oneness of all Prophets like lord Ram, Lord Jesus, Lord Krishna, Prophet Muhammad or Guru Nanak. This oneness further leads to oneness of all religions. And this oneness leads to oneness of whole mankind as a huge family. Or, we can say universal brotherhood. This is the essence of all religions, and this is pure secularism.

C] Mohan: The appeasement of minorities and handouts of crumbs is for what Congress, TMC and Communists have been well established. *No wonder even after 70 years of independence, we continue to remain a third-rate country and are lagging in all human, social and civic indices.* Slave mentality and reservation system must go if India wants to stand shoulder to shoulder to the democracies in the developed world.

9] Judiciary.

Legislature, Executive and Judiciary are the Three pillars of Democracy. Media may be added as the Fourth. Unfortunately, the Apex Court likes to show its undeserved supremacy at every step in its tussle against the Administration. *The foremost flaw is the British Raj-started Collegium system for appointment of Judges in the SC and High Courts* since the British rulers wanted to have like-minded judges. N0 surprise then the anti-national communal Congress party has been happy with it since it wanted a committed anti-Hindu judiciary in instituting Congress's corrupt ecosystem by appointing Judges who would to servient always. This was witnessed on 12th January 2018 when during the working hours of the SC, four senior-most judges namely Justices Chelmeshwar, Ranjan Gogoi, Kurien Joseph and Madan Lokur addressed a press conference. The four Congress Chamchas and the Left were feeling the heat since the CJI Deepak Misra was taking rational decisions against the interests of their masters. It is on record that Communist D Raja came to meet Chelmeshwar just after conclusion of the unprecedented press meet. After his retirement, Joseph was seen by everybody is spilling the beans. He made it obviously clear that the four Judges were remote-controlled touts of the anti-national party cited above.

Let me analyze the events controlled by the three 'Muslim' PMs and their Catholic descendant who is tirelessly working to earn his undeserved place. 'Muslim' Nehru enacted many bizarre acts some are open like *Hindu Code Bill,* in place of Common Civil Code, and linguistic division of states. More importantly he performed (mostly behind the scene) acts detrimental to the interests of the democracy and hence the country by taking undue advantage of his undeserving nomination coupled with the fact that illiteracy and ignorance were rife – a literacy rate of mere 9%. *Most sinister in the fact that the majority of populace possess slave mentality – the ailment that is very slowly and tardily getting respite.* It is well documented that 'Muslim' Nehru was strongly anti-Hindu and anti-Sikh. 'Muslim' Indira nee Maimuna Begum was the *first* PM to openly advocate and work for judges committed to her. So much so, she superseded three senior-most SC Judges as she believed they would not toe her line. Rajiv ('Khan') overturned the classical SC decision to grant alimony to a divorced Muslim woman, a Triple Talaq victim, in her 60's. The present Catholic owner mother-and-son duo Sania Maino and Raul Vinci are openly pro-Christian and pro-Muslim but strongly anti-Hindu and anti-Sikh. It is glaringly clear in the Congress-I or even TRS manifesto for assembly elections in Telangana. Salient features are:

1] ONLY-for Muslim hospitals will be created where no Hindus, Sikhs, Buddhists and Jains will be entertained even if their disease requires emergency treatment.
2] Free electricity for only mosques and churches but NOT Hindu temples or Sikh gurudwaras.
3] Urdu as second language.
4] Muslim youth to get preference and special consideration for jobs over the Hindu and Sikh.
5] Only Muslim students will get massive INR2 million loan for higher education. This template in the official manifesto will create Telangana 'Muslim First' state. This will be a prelude to Muslim First India where Hindus and Sikhs will become second rate citizens. The question is who is Raul Vinci to change the system in a secular country like Hindustan?

Big flaw in appointment of Judges: A grasp of 300 families control the Apex Court in appointment of a Judge. The primary job of the SC is to interpret the Constitution. Instead it is passing orders on matters that are not strictly connected to it. Another lacuna in its working *SC is anti-Hindu and anti-Sikh bur pro-Muslim and pro-Christian*. This means it is against four-fifths of Hindustanis as well as opposed to the country's interest. SC is anti-government as well. This does not augur well for it and the country. SC Judges being ignorant on Hindu culture and civilization MUST be given academic classroom teaching so that they may understand the nuances of Hindu religion. That may help wisdom to dawn upon them. Supreme Court's outreach must be curbed if we as a country want to move forward and stand in the line of foremost nations of the world! Another flaw is that

Judges have double faces like bulk of their countrymen. On the retirement of SC Judge Kurien Joseph on 29th November 2018, CJI Ranjan Gogoi, among other things, said, *"The compassion from court is not a charity of a judge, but a bounden duty of a constitutional court. When you approach the question of compassionate appointment, the first thing is the judges should have compassion. Unless the judges have compassion there is no point in interpreting the law on compassion appointments."* Although Gogoi knows it he does not use this compassion; In just two minutes of hearing postponed the hearing on the Ram Mandir case for three months! Was he obeying Congress(I) mandate?

One classical example is <u>*34 years taken to pronounce sentence on two culprits during the Congress-sponsored and supervised by the then PM Rajiv Sikh-genocide*</u>. On 21st November 2018, *MSN News* reported: *'First Death Sentence In 1984 Anti-Sikh Riots Case, One Life Term'*. *"NEW DELHI*: One of the two attackers convicted of killing two Sikh men during the 1984 riots has been sentenced to death by a Delhi court. The other convict will spend life in prison. Naresh Sherawat, 68, and 55-year-old Yashpal Singh were convicted of killing the two men in south Delhi's Mahipalpur during the riots. They have also been fined INR 3.5 million each. *Yashpal Singh's sentence makes it the first death punishment in the 1984 anti-Sikh riots.* On November 1, 1984, Hardev Singh and Avtar Singh were at their grocery shops in Mahipalpur when a mob armed with iron rods, hockey sticks, stones, kerosene oil attacked them and set their shops on fire. They fled toward the latter's residence, but the mob followed them and set it on fire. Hardev Singh and Avatar Singh were charred to death. The Supreme Court-appointed Special Investigation Team, formed in 2015, probed the 60 cases it had reopened out of the total 293 and succeeded in getting conviction in the first case last week. It has filed "untraced report" in 52 cases and of the eight cases being investigated, charge-sheets have been filed in five while the rest, in which senior Congress leader Sajjan Kumar is an accused, are pending investigation. The verdict has given "Sikhs a ray of hope", said Union minister Harsimrat Kaur Badal. The records say that over 2,800 Sikhs were killed across India after former PM Indira's assassination by her two Sikh bodyguards. Official figures are much lower than the actual numbers, historically speaking. The violence in many cities and towns across the country, but mostly in and around capital Delhi, saw people dragged out of their homes and burnt alive. [*Times of India*; edited by *Nidhi Sethi*]

The other classic illustration of the lopsided working of our Judiciary is its abject inability to hang the four convicts of the dastard Rape and Murder of a young 23-year paramedic even after four dates fixed for their hanging. The Four committed the most heinous crime on 19 December 2013 against which the whole country stood together as one with countrywide protests and candle marches. *Judiciary failed to hang the criminals till the date of writing this book on 6 March 2020!*

The irrational and unpatriotic working of the Indian judiciary cannot be better exposed than its handling of the high-profile *National Herald* Cheating case wherein seven accused include the owners [ex-President and President of Congress(I)]. The perusal of this case tells the world that Indian judiciary is either grossly incompetent or can be bribed to purchase justice! On 16th November 2018, *Yahoo News* was kind enough to trace the long painful judicial history of this case at different levels of our Judiciary right up to the Supreme Court, thanks to the painful compilation by *Firstpost*. '*National Herald case: Delhi HC adjourns hearing till 22 November; judicial deferments make it enter fifth year.*' is the apt all-embracing title of this news item on Friday, the 16th November 2018. "The Delhi High Court on Thursday adjourned the hearing of the plea of Associated Journals Ltd (AJL), publisher of the National Herald newspaper, against the Centre's order asking it to vacate its premises and said that the status quo be maintained till 22 November, which is now the next date of hearing. The Delhi High Court on Thursday adjourned the hearing of the plea of Associated Journals Ltd (AJL), publisher of the National Herald newspaper against the Centre's order asking it to vacate its premises and said that the status quo be maintained till 22 November which is now the next date of hearing. The publisher had approached the high court on Monday challenging the 30 October order of the urban development ministry, ending its 56-year-old lease and asking it to vacate the premises in the press enclave at ITO in Delhi. Appearing for the publisher, Abhishek Manu Singhvi argued in court that the prosecution has ulterior political motives, *ANI* reported.

The court, which had earlier fixed the date of hearing in December, agreed to hear the matter on 15 November after Advocate Sunil Fernandes, appearing for the AJL, said there was urgency in the matter as they have been asked to hand over the possession to the Centre by that date and they had received the order of the Land and Development Office (L&DO) on 30 October after which the courts had closed for a vacation. Meanwhile, the SC would (on 4 December) hear the final arguments on Sonia and Rahul Gandhi's petitions challenging a Delhi HC order refusing to give them relief in a case of reopening of their tax assessments for 2011-12. Earlier, Delhi's Patiala House Court on 17 March deferred the hearing till 21 April. Without exception, all these dates are getting postponed. Now we are in 2020 without progress!

Earlier, a Delhi court which had issued summons against Sonia, Rahul and others, on 7 August had deferred till 28 August the hearing in the case filed by BJP leader Subramanian Swamy pertaining to the acquisition of the *National Herald*. Metropolitan Magistrate Gomati Manocha postponed the matter after the counsel appearing for the accused informed the court that Delhi High Court had stayed the criminal proceedings pending before the trial court till 13 August, *PTI* reported. Meanwhile, on 26 May 2018, Swamy's application to the trial court seeking a directive for the defendants to verify material filed by Swamy in the National Herald case was denied. On 11 March 2016, the trial court after hearing Swamy's plea had allowed the examination of the balance sheets of the Congress party, AJL and Young Indian from 2010 to 2013, which was later overturned by the Delhi HC.

Apart from that, on 30 April 2017, the Punjab and Haryana HC deferred the hearing on the petition of AJL, seeking a copy of the enforcement case investigation report (ECIR) registered by the ED till 19 July 2017. The hearing was deferred after the high court was told that a related matter was pending before the Supreme Court as well. Also, a district court in Delhi on 26 December 2016 had dismissed a plea by Swamy seeking documents in the National Herald case. However, on 12 February 2016, the Supreme Court granted an exemption to all the five accused in the case from personal appearances while refusing to quash proceedings against them. Later, on 12 July 2016, the Delhi High Court set aside the trial court judgment allowing examination of balance sheets and other documents of Congress party and other two companies, the AJL and *Young Indian*. The next hearing in the court was then scheduled to be on 20 August 2017.

In 2015, the Delhi HC on 7 December had dismissed the appeals of Sonia, Rahul and five others which included Motilal Vora, Oscar Fernandes, Suman Dubey and Satyam Pitroda and ordered them to appear in person before the trial court on 9 December. But they did not appear in the court and, on their lawyers' request, the trial court ordered them to appear before him in person on 19 December. He disallowed their request for exemption from personal appearance. On 19 December 2015, the Patiala House court granted bail to all but one and ordered them to appear in the court on the date of next hearing 20 February 2016.

In the same year, when the third judge of the Delhi HC " Justice PS Teji" started hearing of the controversial case on 9 October, he did not heed to the demand of senior lawyer Kapil Sibal representing the Congress president Sonia Gandhi for postponing the case to November for arguments and fixed the date of 15 October 2015 for next arguments. "I have synopsis (written arguments) of all parties. No need of much time to argue," Teji had said rejecting the demand for posting the case. Meanwhile, on 27 January 2015, the Supreme Court of India directed Swamy to make a case for speedy trial in the Delhi HC.

Earlier in December 2015, first Justice VP Vaish heard the appeal of Sonia and Rahul and ordered for a temporary stay in the summons of the trial court. In January after ordering for a daily hearing, Justice Vaish recused from the case. Justice Vaish had ordered for daily hearing after Swamy approached SC in December 2014 citing delay from the side of Delhi High Court. In his petition to SC, Swamy said that the apex court on several occasions gave directions that higher courts should take a decision within six weeks on the appeals against the verdicts of the lower courts. Justice Sunil Gaur, the second judge also shifted from the case though he collected synopsis from all parties in September, promising speedy decision in the sensitive case. Both Justice Vaish and Justice Gaur left the case after hearing the matter for more than six months.

It all started when on 1 August 2014, Swamy was served notice to file a reply in the Delhi HC. On 28 August 2014, the metropolitan court fixed 9 December 2014 for the next hearing. On 12 January 2015, the judge of the Delhi HC recused himself from hearing the case and directed that the petitions be directed before an appropriate bench. The Congress top leadership approached the high court after Metropolitan Magistrate Gomati Manocha summoned them on the petition filed by Swamy on 26 June 2014. The Congress top brass was summoned to appear on 7 August, after the trial court found prima facie case in the acquiring the assets of National Herald's publishing company by floating a new private company. [With inputs from Agencies]

Our Supreme Court NEEDS to take a NEUTRAL stance in hearing cases of different communities. However, it chose to be pro-Muslim much like the party that ruled India for over half a century. Is SC scared of Muslims and Christians? SC regularly interferes with blatant disrespect to Hindus and their customs. *Why did it pass orders on Jalaikattu, or ban explosives on Deepavali, or lifted ban on entry into Sabarimala temple of females 10 to*

50 years of age; and umpteen of other instances directly interfering on affairs connected with Hindus! Why did it refuse to hear plea on mass murder and eviction of 500,000 Kashmiri Pandits from the valley? Whereas, it said that it would decide whether the alien Rohingyas Muslims can be treated as refugees and that it would decide whether they should be deported to Myanmar. It is worth remembering that Triple Talaq has already been banned long ago in at least 22 Muslim countries. The SC at best gave a split 3:2 judgment on its ban i.e. the three – Hindu, Christian and Parsee judges banning Triple Talaq and the two -the Sikh CJI Khehar and Muslim judge – dissenting thereby disagreeing to abolish Triple Talaq! Even in the MOST important recent case of Triple Talaq, an inhuman practice that is destroying the lives of tens of thousands of Muslim women, there was a three-to-two majority judgment, the Sikh CJI and Muslim judge dissenting by stating it is a matter of their religion. This was against the Hindu, Christian and Parsee judges who opted for a ban. So, personal whims and fancies crop up even in interpreting the Constitution of India and pronounce a judgment! This raises many valid questions: Is our SC worth its salt as the ultimate seat of justice? And, can it be called sane or even truthful in performing its most important but delicate function possessing far-reaching consequences? Isn't it frankly pro-Muslim and anti-establishment? The functioning of such an institution URGENTLY NEEDS to be STREAMLINED, RECTIFIED, and VASTLY IMPROVED. Otherwise, it needs to be DISBANDED soon if it cannot deliver a PROPER judgment as per the Statute! We Indians need conscientious, dispassionate and honest judges who abide by the Constitution rather than act on their whims and fancies or other extraneous non-legal factors. *There must be a mechanism to review the judgements delivered by various courts starting from Sessions Courts to High Courts to Supreme Court. Or, at least its most important judgments impacting large populations of citizens must be reviewed,* Afterall, since any judgment is the analytical conclusion by a Judge who is a vulnerable human being aligned with a political party of his/her choice and can be easily approached or influenced in various manners especially a hefty bribe as we have witnessed in a number of cases pertaining to celebrities and/or politicians given the present circumstances and the scenario that has prevailed over the last seven decades since independence!

Indian government issued an ordinance to abolish 'Triple Talaq'. As per the practice followed in my country, any ordinance must be ratified by both houses of Parliament. The BJP government was wary of discussing it there since it does not have majority in the Rajya Sabha. So, the matter came before the Supreme Court. The SC created lot of fuss on the issue of 'Triple Talaq'. The SC fears Muslims and this evil practice pertained to the Muslim community. It is well-known that giving divorce to one's wife by saying 'Talaq Talaq Talaq' is a highly criminal act and demeaning to the women. Still, *the SC failed to give a unanimous verdict to abolish this horrendous practice by Indian Muslim men.* This is although 22 Muslim countries including our daughter countries like Pakistan and Bangladesh abolished long back. It was a split 3:2 judgement – the Sikh CJI and the Muslim Judge against abolishing whereas the Hindu, Christian and Parsi Judges were for its abolition. *Can you expect any good from such a bunch of nuts adorning the high seats of justice?*

The SC has hardly any respect for Hindus' and Sikhs' sentiments and practices and rituals. SC Judges need exhaustive training and 'education' on Hindu and Sikh religions and their customs before they can start thinking rationally and give rational judgements! It gives quick judgements be it Jalaikattu, exploding of crackers during the most Important Hindu and Sikh festival of Deepavali, entry into the famous Sabarimala shrine of females 10 to 50 years of age, just to give a few examples. However, the SC is hell scared to abolish the nasty and gruesome practice of sacrificing millions of lambs and he-goats on Bakr-Eid! On 16th November 2018, *Rediff.com News* brought out, *'Won't come back till I enter Sabarimala'*. "'If we do not enter the temple, then history won't be made, and all wrong rituals will get continue to be followed.' 'If they resort to violence against women and abuse them, how can they be Ayyappa Swamy's bhakts?'

On September 28, 2018, the SC delivered a historic verdict (although contrary to the Ayappa principles/practice) permitting women in the age group of 10 to 50 to enter the Sabarimala temple in Kerala. Earlier, only girls below the age of 10 and women above the age of 50 [who were not menstruating] could worship at the Ayyappa shrine in south Kerala. Soon after the judgment, large-scale protests erupted in the Sabarimala area as some women devotees belonging to the traditionally 'barred' age group tried to make their way to the temple. Despite police protection, these women could not enter the shrine.

Trupti Desai, who successfully entered the Shani Shingnapur temple in Maharashtra and the Haji Ali dargah in the country's financial capital, has left for Sabarimala. "I am ready to sacrifice my life for this cause," Desai, below, who heads the Bhumata Brigade, told *Rediff.com's* Syed Firdaus Ashraf on Friday. *Alas! She could not do all that she was professing*!

What kind of security measures are you expecting from the Kerala government? We have mailed a letter to the Kerala chief minister (Pinarayi Vijayan) and the DGP (director general of police) about our visit to the Sabarimala temple. So far, I have not got any response from them, but I have heard that they are not ready to give us any kind of VIP security. I want to tell them that we do not want any VIP security, but when we have been threatened with our lives, we have asked for normal (police) protection. But, if despite the Supreme Court order, we do not get security and we are attacked on the way to Sabarimala, who will be responsible for it? Will the Kerala CM or the DGP be the responsible for any attack?

Why do you want to enter the temple in the face of so much opposition? Post-SC decision, the Sabarimala temple was open only for six days. After that, the temple was open only for two days. Now the Sabarimala temple would be open till January, so there is more time to visit the temple this time. Already 500 women did online booking to enter the temple. All these women are in the age group of 10 to 50. I have decided that I will not come back from Kerala to Maharashtra till I enter Sabarimala. I don't have a return ticket booked from Kerala to Maharashtra.

Don't you feel that you should wait for some more time since the review petitions on the Sabarimala issue in the apex court is coming up for hearing in January? Don't you think your attempt to enter the temple will create a law and order problem in Kerala? We are not creating a law and order problem. It is the protesters who are creating a law and order problem. The SC order came on September 28 and those who do not believe this order, they have filed review petitions. I have a simple answer to those people who oppose the entry of women in Sabarimala, that since the review petition is coming up for hearing in January 2019, they must allow women to enter the Sabarimala temple till then. Whatever decision the Supreme Court takes in January we will abide by it. But, legally, at this moment, women can enter the Sabarimala temple, and nobody can stop us or indulge in violence.

How many women from your team will attempt to enter Sabarimala? There are seven women including me right now from Maharashtra who want to enter the Sabarimala temple. We are not at all scared to enter the temple because this is our right. I am ready to sacrifice my life for this cause because the people who oppose our entry have a different kind of mindset. We are fighting against that mentality. Be it Shani Shingnapur, Haji Ali or the Mahalakshmi temple, we were attacked there too. Here, in Sabarimala, we feel that if we do not enter the temple then history won't be made, and all wrong rituals will get continue to be followed. To the protesters of Sabarimala, I say that if they want to protest, they can do so by *Ahimsa*, but not resort to violence.

If they resort to violence against women and abuse them, how can they be Ayyappa Swamy's bhakts? Devotees say Ayyappa does not want women in the age group of 10 to 50 to enter the temple. Ayyappa Swamy never said such things. No God has discriminated against man and woman. Nowhere it is written in the Puranas that women in the age group of 10 to 50 must not enter the temple or for that matter menstruating women are not allowed inside (any temple). This is done by men who do not want women to come up. They want to give women secondary status in life. They are stopping women from entering the Sabarimala temple by *dadagiri* (up Manship) and *goondagiri (hooliganism)*. Nowhere has Ayyapa Swamy discriminated against his devotees, and he will never do that. You proved your point at Shani Shingnapur, then at Haji Ali too. Some people say you are doing all this for publicity. Earlier too, I had stated that I will go to the Sabarimala temple. I waited for more than a month after the SC judgment and you have seen that different women tried to enter the temple. It wasn't me who tried to enter the temple first. I am putting my life in danger. Then how can anyone say that I am doing a publicity stunt? We are fighting for our rights and such allegations are only a conspiracy to defame women. Devotees say they will guard the temple for 60 days till the review petition comes up for hearing. The SC has given rights to women to enter the Sabarimala temple. It is the police who should act against the people who do not allow us to enter Sabarimala. Protesters have a right to protest, but they can only protest in Gandhian ways, but they are not doing that. They attack women and resort to violence which is not right.

When you went to Shani Shingnapur and then later to Haji Ali, such large-scale violence did not exist. What is difference between those places and the Sabarimala temple? In Maharashtra, when the (Bombay) high court gave an order -- be it for Shani Shingnapur or the Haji Ali dargah -- the trustees of those places welcomed the order. Though some people did protest and locals (women) said they are not going inside Shani Shingnapur or Haji Ali, but women (outsiders) who want to go inside, they will let them go. So, we went inside Shani Shingnapur and Haji Ali. In Sabarimala, local women do not want us to enter and they want all of us also to wait (till the age of 50) because they believe that this is their tradition. I feel that those who do not want women to enter the Sabarimala temple are the contractors of Dharma. Nowhere has Lord Ayyappa has discriminated between men and women.

Do you think you will succeed in Sabarimala just as you succeeded in Shani Shingnapur and Haji Ali? I am sure about our success. Already 500 women in the age group of 10 to 50 have done online booking at the Devasthanam board for a darshan.

Have they got the permission? They have not got permission, but they have done the booking. Now when they reach the Sabarimala temple, it is the job of the government to give these women protection. [*Syed Firdaus Ashraf/Rediff.com* in Mumbai]

Likewise, on the issue of Ram Mandir at Ayodhya, the SC dilly-dallied for 69 long years ever since the matter came up before it in 1950. <u>This proves a few points</u>:

1] The SC is not efficient in its working.
2] It is anti-Hindu and scared of taking any decision against Muslims.

This is because most judges come from only 300 families ever since independence or even during pre-independence era as well. The intriguing story of the ascent of present CJI Ranjan Gogoi, son of Keshav Chandra Gogoi, former Congress CM of Assam, is an open secret: On his father's recommendation and support, Ranjan started as an advocate in Assam High Court in 1978. In 2010, he was made a Judge of Punjab & Haryana High Court. Within five months, he was promoted as Chief Justice of the same HC. Ranjan passed an order removing Jats from OBC. That became the basis of a fierce violent agitation which literally burnt many towns in Haryana. In 14 months, he was promoted as Judge of the Supreme Court.

Some months ago, after CJI Misra had ordered day to day hearing on Ram Mandir case, senior Congress(I) leader advocate Kapil Sibal approached Ranjan's court to postpone the hearing to July 2019 I.e. after the next general elections. On the advice/instructions of Congress(I), Ranjan was one of the four senior Judges who held a press conference in January during the working hours of the SC casting aspersions on the then CJI Deepak Misra. This was a ploy to exert pressure on the CJI so that he goes slow on the Ram Mandir case. This strategy of Congress(I) worked. CJI put the case on a low priority. On 2nd October 2018 when Deepak Misra retired, Ranjan Gogoi became the CJI in just eight years! On 29th October 2018, when the hearing on Ram Mandir started after a long gap, CJI Ranjan immediately in 2 minutes' hearing postponed the hearing of the case to January 2019, ostensibly to please his Congress(I) bosses! Although the low priority case on Sabarimala temple was heard on priority and judgment against the sentiments of the devotees was passed immediately by Ranjan. Somebody wrote on *WhatsApp* and quite rightly so, "*My Lord, it is neither fair nor proper to hurt the sentiments of one billion Hindus in order to please Sania Antonia Maino, the Italian lady and her imbecile Italian son, Raul Vinci.*"

So, the question naturally arises whether an Institution like the Apex Court has any sanctity and why not it be scrapped? It is well-known that Lord Rama was born in Ayodhya. Moreover, the Archeological Survey of India convincingly proved that the existing Ram Mandir was destroyed by 1st Mughal king Babar's general known by name Babri to build a mosque. Hindu genocide went on at full swing during the 800 years of reign by Muslim invaders who became kings in Delhi. *Draconian Hindu genocide wherein at least 200 million Hindus were killed, countless Hindu girls and young women abducted, raped, auctioned and converted into Islam* has been conveniently removed from history by the Left liberal paid conscienceless historian Chamchas of the anti-national, anti-Hindu and anti-Sikh INC and its present Avatar Congress(I). Notable shameless among these are Irfan Habib, Mushirul Hasan, Romelia Thapar, Ramchandra, Guha, Vijay Rashad, et al. Hindustan has 80% population as Hindus. I am afraid we Hindus have no faith in the credibility of this rotten outdated institution known as the Supreme Court or the Apex Court that is hell scared of Muslims!

The sentiments of the Hindus vis-à-vis Ram Mandir are best exemplified in an article, '*Ram temple was there, is there and will be there*', that speared in Rediff.com News on 15th November 2018. "'I'm sure the central government must be thinking over how to pave the way for construction of the temple.' After RSS Sarsanghchalak Mohan Bhagwat sought an ordinance facilitating the construction of a Ram temple in Ayodhya, the movement has gathered fresh steam. Voices demanding an ordinance have increased after the Supreme Court postponed the matter of the land dispute to next year, a decision it reinforced on Monday,

November 12. Manish Shukla, the BJP's spokesperson in UP, recently invoked the party's Palampur resolution of 1989 to assert that his party is committed to building the temple. "A temple should be constructed at the birthplace (of Lord Ram). It is not a normal temple. It is like Amritsar's Golden Temple, it is equally important as Mecca or the Vatican," Shukla tells Rediff.com's Utkarsh Mishra.

What do you have to say about the Supreme Court postponing the hearing on the Ayodhya issue to next year? It's a verdict of the honorable Supreme Court and as a member of a party that respects the law and the Constitution, I respect the verdict. However, like crores of people, I was also disappointed that an initiative that could have led to the construction of the Ram temple was delayed. As a devotee of Lord Ram, as someone who has faith in the temple movement, I was certainly disappointed.

You recently invoked the resolution your party adopted during the Palampur convention in 1989. The resolution says that the issue will be resolved 'through mutual dialogue between the two communities or, if this was not possible, through an enabling legislation'.

Which way do you prefer? There are only two ways which can lead to the construction of temple, either the Supreme Court gives a verdict, or a law is brought to this effect. It is a practice that if a matter is sub judice, an ordinance over it isn't promulgated. But it is a technical issue for the government to consider. And I am sure the central government must have been thinking over the technicalities, of how to pave the way for construction of the temple. Ever since the Palampur convention, we firmly believe that a temple was there, is there and will be there.

RSS chief Mohan Bhagwat and Vishwa Hindu Parishad leaders demand an ordinance on the issue. What do you have to say about it? We welcome what Bhagwati said. He expressed the sentiments of crores of Indians. We are with him on this issue.

What about the demand that a mosque should also be constructed along with a temple near the disputed site? Look, the issue is still sub judice. But a temple should be constructed at the birthplace (of Lord Ram). It is not a normal temple. It is like Amritsar's Golden Temple; it is equally important as Mecca or the Vatican. So, it is not just any temple. And therefore, at the site, only a temple should be constructed.

There are leaders who continue to give inflammatory statements on the issue. Why does the government not tell them that they should not do it as the matter is sub judice? Everybody has a right to express their opinion in a democracy. The government acts only when someone's speech can cause a law and order problem.

If your party wins a majority in 2019, what would it do to facilitate the construction of the temple? See, the matter is still with the court. I can assure you that we will win 73 seats in UP. [Utkarsh Mishra]

On 1st November 2018, *Rediff.com News* published, '*BJP MP likely to introduce private member's bill to build Ram temple*': "BJP Rajya Sabha MP and RSS ideologue Rakesh Sinha suggested this morning that he would soon introduce a private member's bill in Parliament seeking the construction of a Ram temple on a 'disputed' site in Ayodhya. The Ayodhya Ram *Janmabhoom*i case is currently in the Supreme Court. The court recently said that it would decide in January when to begin hearing the case. Sinha today tweeted, "*To those who keep asking the BJP and the RSS about when Ram temple will be constructed, I have a straight question: Will you support my private member bill?*" Sinha also questioned why the Supreme Court was delaying hearing the matter and said that the issue of a Ram temple in Ayodhya is a "top priority for Hindu society. Will Rahul Gandhi, Sitaram Yechury, Lalu Prasad Yadav and Mayawati support the bill," Sinha also asked. "They frequently ask the date to @RSSorg @BJP4India, now onus on them to answer." He also asked how many days the SC took to give the verdict on Article 377, the Jallikattu issue, and the Sabarimala temple ban. "But Ayodhya is not in priority for decades and decades. It is a top priority of Hindu society," he asked. [*ANI*]

On 2nd November 2018, *India Today* published, '*Will launch 1992-like agitation for Ram mandir if needed: RSS*'. "The 1992 agitation being referred to by the RSS was a country-wide rath yatra undertaken to demand the construction of a Ram temple in Ayodhya. The RSS today said that it would take up an agitation as in 1992 "if needed" in order ensure the construction of a Ram temple in Ayodhya. The 1992 agitation being referred to by the RSS was a country-wide rath yatra undertaken under the leadership of senior BJP leader Lal Krishna Advani. This rath yatra provided a base for the larger movement to build a Ram temple in Ayodhya. The movement ultimately sparked major communal tension and nation-wide riots after Ayodhya's Babri Masjid, which is believed to have stood on the location where a Ram temple was present, was demolished by Hindu 'kar sevaks', who were part of the rath yatra. The RSS spokesperson Bhaiyyaji Joshi today said that the organization was ready to carry out a similar campaign like the rath yatra of 1992 to press for its demand to build

Ram Mandir in Ayodhya. Joshi also expressed disappointment over the SC delaying hearing the Ayodhya title suit. A decision on the suit is expected to resolve the legal question of who owns the land where Babri Masjid once stood and where a Ram temple was once believed to have been present.

The SC is hearing appeals filed against an Allahabad HC judgment that had divided the land in three parts. This week, the SC said it would decide in January next year when to hear the appeals. "We were expecting good news before this Diwali. But the Supreme Court refused to give a verdict," Bhaiyyaji Joshi said today before questioning why the matter was not a priority for the Supreme Court. "The court said its priorities are different. Because of this, Hindus feel insulted. It is surprising that the feelings of crores of Hindus are not a priority for the court," Joshi said. Joshi also spoke on the increasing clamor that the Narendra Modi government bring in a law to construct a Ram temple in Ayodhya. "Those who want to demand an ordinance to facilitate construction of ram temple should go ahead. Whether it can be brought in or not is something that the government must decide," Joshi said.

10] *Irresponsible Biased Anti-national Media and Corrupt 'sold out' Journalists.*

Media can be unfaithful to the news anywhere including the West but more so in my country. This is illustrated by this reporting from America: 'Well at Least I Tried…'. "A Harley Davidson biker is riding by the zoo in Washington, D.C., when he sees a little girl leaning into the lion's cage. Suddenly, the lion grabs her by the collar of her jacket and tries to pull her inside to slaughter her, under the eyes of her screaming parents. The biker jumps off his Harley, runs to the cage and hits the lion square on the nose with a powerful punch. Whimpering from the pain the lion jumps back, letting go of the girl, and the biker brings the girl to her terrified parents who thank him endlessly. A reporter has watched the whole event. The reporter, addressing the Harley rider, says: 'Sir, this was the most gallant and brave thing I've seen a man do in my whole life.' The Harley rider replies: 'Why, it was nothing, really. The lion was behind bars. I just saw this little kid in danger and acted as I felt right.' The reporter says: 'Well, I'll make sure this won't go unnoticed. I'm a journalist, you know, and tomorrow's paper will have this story on the front page. So, what do you do for a living?' The biker replies: "I'm a U.S. Marine." The journalist leaves. The following morning the biker buys the paper to see if it indeed brings news of his actions and reads on the front page: "U.S. MARINE ASSAULTS AFRICAN IMMIGRANT AND STEALS HIS LUNCH".

Andrew Brietbart, noted American conservative commentator and editor who died in 2012, had once this to say about media manipulation: "Feeding the media is like training a dog. You can't throw an entire steak at a dog to train it to sit. You have to give it little bits of steak again and again until it learns the tricks." In Hindustan, this training appears to have been accomplished long since, unfortunately for the country, single unethical, hungry-for-power and not so nationalistic as a party, Congress ruled for an unnecessarily inordinately long period of time i.e. 56 of the 71 years since independence. With traitors and separatists and anti-national elements, aided, abetted or purchased by anti-India 'financiers' within and outside the country, in full steam everywhere and their fiery 'hate India' speeches publicized by anti-nationalistic media also working on an agenda set by anti-India barons or organizations abroad, this poses a piquant situation for the nationalist BJP's Union government as to my country.

Western media, led by the *BBC* and *The Guardian* in Britain; *The New York Times, Washington Post, Wall Street Journal, the Economist* and *Financial Times* in the USA; *Der Spiegel* in Germany; and *Le Monde* in France, have been out there for many years to defame and denounce India at the slightest pretext or even without it. Likewise, America-controlled social media platforms like *Facebook, Twitter, etc.* are inimical to Hindustan's interests. They would ever like the Western hegemony to be maintained. And, consequently, not let my country ever to emerge stronger and beat their capitalist countries and MNCs in their own game. They can't believe and tolerate that India may have already become the 3rd largest economy. My country should be the largest global economy in the times to come as this will end their perceived superiority. *BBC's* depiction of Nirbhaya gang-rape on 19th December 2012 and projection of the most brutal teen age offender including his jail interview was aired against the request of Government of India. *BBC* still shows us Snake Charmer's land under the alibi of raising public awareness on the plight of snake charmers in India although that trade was banned long ago in 1991. How is the *BBC* concerned with the internal affairs of India? And why not? In 1962, foolish PM Nehru with a pro-West slave mentality arranged a Snake-Charmer's show at his official residence to bemuse the visiting US First Lady, Jacqueline Kennedy. *How is it that the Indian PM had no better idea to entertain our VIP visiting guest from his arch enemy, America?*

Factually speaking, he failed to comply with President JF Kennedy's request to provide a blueprint for Indo-American co-operation because of his Communist antecedents! It is worth remembering that those were the times America was providing food grains to India under PL480 program. *Was Nehru patriotic enough? Apparently, he was NOT.* Non-existent nationalism/patriotism cannot be inculcated overnight. A comment currently making rounds on *WhatsApp* amplifies this in this way: 'The level of nationalism on Republic Day or Independence Day is about 10% and on the day of Indo-Pak cricket match it goes up to maybe 80%'. It is NOT possible to have these important events on a day to day basis. However, such anti-national elements and sentiments spewing venom must be neutralized IMMEDIATELY to prevent any further collateral damage to the country since Indians by and large are hardly nationalistic. We are fence-sitters who care a hoot for their motherland and are insensitive to other countrymen's needs and aspirations especially the females and the elderly!

I would like to quote *The New York Times:* An editorial in the *NYT* condemned Modi Government action on the JNU issue. Will the editor have a similar view if Americans protest in support of Osama bin Laden? Balaji Viswanathan has been studying US history for a decade. and is a Most Viewed Writer in JNU. He commented: "One should not take the *NYT* too seriously for India-related news. They are the ones who drew the infamous racist cartoons when India launched its mission to Mars, MOM. The *NYT* apologized for the cartoon - That is one among their dozens of news items that form a pattern of prejudice against India. Read *NYT* for their books list and art-related reporting, but their reporters are terrible for subjects outside liberal arts - say foreign policy, defense or economics. DO NOT use *NYT* if the subject is India. Among the US publications, *Washington Post* is anti-India so much so during its owner and Amazon's Proprietor Jeff Bezos was clearly told by PM Modi that *Bezos must mend its Washington Post before India can think of doing business with Amazon. TIME and CNN on the liberal side, Wall Street Journal* and *CNBC* on the conservative side have slightly better reporting on India – even if sometimes they too suffer from the old stereotypes possibly because it is there in the psyche of the Americans that they can police the world! Across the pond, *Guardian* and *Economist* who also went to nadir in their India reporting in the past decade seem to be recovering. The recent articles in those publications are coming out of the extreme prejudice they were heaping on India. While they are going in the right direction, BBC seems to have gotten significantly worse in the past four years and I have put them in my personal blacklist." [it is not a big list – just *The New York Times* and *BBC* are there for now].

Maybe the situation is changing for the better on the social media if this *MSN News* is to be believed. On Thursday, the 22nd November 2018, it published: 'Step up': Twitter's apology over photo angers Indian activists'. "A group of Indian journalists and activists has accused *Twitter* and CEO Jack Dorsey of 'misrepresentation and half-truths' [*Anushree Fadnavis/ Reuters* Provided by *Al Jazeera*] New Delhi, India - Women journalists and activists in India have hit back after *Twitter* apologized for a photo of its top official holding a photo that criticized patriarchy propped by India's caste system. *Twitter* accounts sympathetic to India's far-right branded Twitter CEO Jack Dorsey's holding the sign as "hate-mongering". The placard that read "smash Brahminical patriarchy" referred to the highest Hindu caste and its alleged sanction for patriarchal oppression of women. The controversial photograph was taken during Dorsey's recent India trip, when Twitter hosted a closed-door discussion with a group of women journalists and activists. The poster was handed to Dorsey by Sanghapali Aruna, a Dalit activist. Dalits fall at the bottom of India's complex, and often brutal, caste hierarchy.

On Monday, Vijaya Gadde, a top *Twitter* official, apologized on behalf of the company following a massive backlash from mostly upper caste Indians, who were incensed by what they read as "hate speech" against Brahmins. On Wednesday, a group of journalists and activists, who were at the meeting with Dorsey, accused Twitter of "misrepresentation and half-truths". A statement issued by a group of women journalists and activists said the apology came as a "disappointment to all of us dealing with abuse, harassment and legal threats". "This is also in sharp contrast to Twitter's strong stand in favor of women and marginalized communities in other countries," it said. "We call on Twitter to step up and not capitulate to bigotry, disinformation and bullying and to address in serious terms the problem of trolls threatening the life and liberty of scores of women and marginalized communities online," the statement added.

Divided over a placard; Frequent instances of so-called "honor killings" where young inter-caste couples are killed most often by irate upper caste families reflect just how tightly caste holds India in its grip. A recent *Reuters* poll said India is the world's most dangerous country for women while Dalits have suffered thousands of years of exclusion and extreme poverty. "Traditionally, Brahmins have had power and privilege over others and had control over knowledge, resources and women's sexuality. That power hierarchy is still intact," Aruna, founder of rights group *Project Mukti*, who gave the placard to Dorsey, told *Al Jazeera*: "Lower caste women, and those from minority communities, are vulnerable to injustice and oppression from upper caste men in positions of authority." On the other hand, Indians sympathetic to Hindu nationalists, like journalist Chitra Subramaniam, said the *Twitter* CEO's photo with the placard was "an incitement to violence". A government official said the placard was "a fit case for registration of a criminal case for attempt to destabilize the nation". TV Mohandas Pai, former finance chief at software company Infosys, accused Dorsey of "hate-mongering" against the Brahmins. Religion and caste often clash violently with women's' rights in India. In recent weeks, conservative Hindu groups have prevented women from entering an ancient Hindu temple in southern India, defying a Supreme Court order that lifted a centuries-old ban on women devotees.

Social media and far-right groups: *Twitter's* apology sparked outrage over the perceived inability of social media giants to stand-up to far-right bullying in India. "Jack wasn't advocating any campaign. The poster wasn't trying to create animosity between groups. *Twitter* had no reason to apologize, except they feared a backlash from the right-wing and the government," Tejas Harad, editor at the *Economic and Political Weekly*, told *Al Jazeera* from Mumbai. Dorsey had also met Hindu nationalist leader and Indian Prime Minister Narendra Modi during his India trip. "The poster upset many because upper castes in India don't like to publicly acknowledge the caste system. It embarrasses them," said Harad. Meanwhile, *Twitter* said it is committed to remaining "apolitical". "We are proud of the fact that *Twitter* is a platform where marginalized voices can be seen and heard, but we also have a public commitment to being apolitical. We realize that the photo may not accurately represent that commitment and we apologize for any offence caused," a Twitter spokesperson told *Al Jazeera*.

Hate online: But *Twitter's* apology, and its distancing itself from the anti-caste placard, has left many disappointed. "These platforms back movements against oppressive structures if it benefits them. Take the case of feminism. *Twitter* had introduced special emojis for the #me-too hashtag. Is the feminist movement not political?" asked Harad. Analysts point out that social media channels have given its users a platform to be heard and a role in catalyzing democratic voices in many parts of the world.

"Twitter's apology itself is a political stand," said Aruna."Our communities need to be protected from any kind of hate speech and bullying that can translate into physical violence including lynching. We don't want India to be the next Rakhine state."

Earlier this year in the US, Twitter faced flak for "verifying" and handing out "blue ticks" to several hate groups and white supremacists. Twitter, like other social media platforms, is struggling to curb online hate in countries like India, home to its fastest growing userbase. As per networking giant CISCO, India's internet market will exceed 800 million by 2021. Meanwhile, online hate against critics of the government or right-wing groups has reached unprecedented levels in the past few years. *"Twitter* accounts which repeatedly spew hate, post death threats - no action is taken against them. So many anti-Dalit messages go unpunished. Criticize upper caste oppressive systems, and you are swiftly apologizing for it. This is worrying," said Harad."

Likewise, the *Facebook* CEO Mark Zuckerberg was hauled and grilled by both the US and the UK administrations for 'selling' personal data of millions of *Facebook* users to the notorious British company Cambridge Analytica, now in deep trouble even in its own Britain! This firm is accused of helping Donald Trump win the 2016 American Presidential Election. The author refuses to buy this 'achievement' on the part of *Cambridge Analytica*! He won because of blue collar Americans and Trump's slogan, *'Make America Great'*. Owner-cum-dictator of inherited ownership of Congress(I), Sania Antonia Maino is alleged to have entered a $10 billion contract with the same Cambridge Analytica in 2017. The company is supposed to help her good-for-nothing son Raul Vinci climb the 'hereditary throne' of PM of Hindustan. However, the company failed to turn tables against the BJP in Gujarat assembly elections in December 2017 although the party has been in power there for the past 22 years. Even anti-incumbency didn't work. This is although the narrative and rhetoric has sharpened though based on falsehood and half-truths. Hindustanis especially those under-35 who constitute 65% of the population are wiser than their ancestors and CANNOT be fooled by the empty slogans of the anti-national Congress(I)!

Media and journalists pose a danger of same or bigger magnitude as compared to the faulty judiciary we have been tolerating ever since independence or even before that. During its over five decades-long misrule, the anti-national and most corrupt Congress party has been installing 'pimps' in administration by way of cultivating IAS cadres, media persons, 'independent' institutions like judiciary including the Supreme Court, Election Commission, CBI, ED, IB, et al. Maximum damage happened during the latest decade-long (2004-2914) misrule by the most inept, highly corrupt Mahachamcha and principal stooge of the dictator of Congress(I) – the Italian Sania Maino, the 'eunuch' Manmohan Singh – the pseudo-economist. He had no aptitude as a PM but generated multibillion-dollar scams perpetually one after the other. One is surprised why *the Guinness Book of Records* had not so far included his name as 'King of Scams'. He 'purchased' several journalists, 'activists' as also pro-Gandhi historian Ramchandra Guha. In India every (wo)man has a price! This list is exhaustive but notable beneficiaries (to be used later on as 'pimps' in future) are: Ramchandra Guha-Padma Bhushan in 2009; owner of *Hindustan Times* Shobhana Bhatia-membership of Rajya Sabha and Padma Shri in 2005; Teesta Setalvad used against the then Gujarat CM Narendra D Modi-*Padma Shri* in 2007; notorious Critic of Narendra Modi Vinod Dua-Padma Shri in 2008; Thrice-married to Muslims Barkha Dutt-Padma Shri in 2008; Rajdeep Sardesai-Padma Shri in 2008; and the most 'notorious' Chief Editor of *Hindustan Times* Shekhar Gupta-Padma Bhushan in 2009, just to name few notable persons most frequently 'used' by Sania Maino and her coterie. This is just tip of the iceberg. So, how can anybody expect TRUTH from media? Moreover, then PM Manmohan used to take almost of them for foreign jaunts at public expenditure year after year. So, how can any sane Hindustani expect any of them being truthful and do good for the country? Their main job has all along been to continuously criticize NDA government led by the most able ever PM Modi; not publish the spate of positive developments within the country and on its image in foreign lands; and in the process they keep on maligning the fair name of Hindustan within Hindustan as well as abroad!

Now it has been playtime for the sold media in the ecosystem created and perfected by the Congress party for over six decades. Vinod Dua is the ultimate Congress stooge known for long to genuflect and prostrate before the dynasts. Fortunately for the country though unfortunately for him or the dynasts, Dua got sucked by #*Me Too movement*. Accused of sexual misconduct. And surprisingly met sudden death – another proof of the Karma theory as enunciated by Lord Krishna in Bhagwadgita. Congress-pliant ecosystem within the Judiciary and institutions like ED, CBI, etc. are working overtime to disrepute the popularly mandated present NDA government through intrigues and possibly on the diktat of dynasts. And thereby they are derailing the development of the country that has been pushed with great elan, gusto and will power.

There has been a deliberate attempt to create a confusion in the minds of citizens that their verdict in 2014 was a mistake and perhaps a wrong decision. For this, the best of jugglers or spin masters are trying to do their best in exhibiting their prowess. To add to their viliferous campaign, Sania Maino allegedly hired last year for a 5-year contact *Cambridge Analytica* – a notorious company charge-sheeted in own Britain and alleged to have helped Donald Trump to have won his presidential election – from a whopping $10 billion. The situation is much like Dhritrashtra in the famed Mahabharata. Sania wants to hoist her good-for-nothing son Raul Vinci on the dynastic chair of prime minister of India!

Remember the notorious Press Conference during working hours of the Supreme Court of four Judges of which the present CJI, the son of erstwhile Congress CM of Assam was a part. We were told that the entire system within SC has gone wrong because of the then CJI Deepak Misra. Now in office, has he taken any tangible steps to address the issue for which he mocked and rebuked his boss Deepak Misra? The obvious answer is a BIG 'NO'. Is it because the priorities of the 'Supreme Kotha' have surprisingly changed now and nobody dares question him?

I can recall the forewarning one of the brightest legal luminaries Harish Salve who had successfully contested the case against Pakistan in the International Court of Justice at the Hague; that too for a 'handsome' fee of Rupee One! In recent times, he had predicted in 2014 itself that no stone will be left unturned by Congress-I to disparage the BJP government and bring it down by its cleverly crafted ecosystem. How mighty close he has been in his prognosis perhaps better than the soothsayers. Being the son of an eminent Maharashtrian Congressman, it is possible that his many years withing the Congress-I edifice mad him aware of Congress treachery!

11] Undoubtedly, <u>*we face the most explosive daunting situation* today</u> because of an unfortunate curious combination of three: *external* threats and *internal* factors of the 'Break India', Award Waapsi and Pseudo-intellectual Gangs interspersed with *nature's* fury now and then. The last one exists since we have been unnecessarily and unreasonably tinkering with environment and habitat thereby destroying the ecology for too long a period now. 'Our brave, highly disciplined, patriotic and extra-efficient armed forces are competent enough to guard our frontiers and get over *external* threats from any offender', is the unanimous perception of all my nationalistic compatriots. The only notable snag had been the freeze on buying new defense equipment by the useless supposedly 'honest' ex-defense minister AK (Saint) Antony under the puppet and useless decade-under long decadent PM Manmohan of erstwhile UPA government – both these men being first rate *chamchas* of Sonia, the Italy-born white 'life' president of the Congress-I or -Indira. Believe me, this (sycophancy) has been the only way to flourish in this non-sensical party for the worthless leaders serving it for a century now!

There are hired authors, pseudo-intellectuals and lackeys outside the party. They have been doing all sorts of non-sensical acts under the patronage of Congress party flushed with funds mostly in black money. These undeserving hired hoodlums raise their voice periodically when dictated by their benefactors and start 'returning' their awards just before any vital state election of the general elections. More of this drama was seen in months in the run-up to General Elections during April-May 2019! These *Chamchas* do so just to please their masters in the Congress-I since they are paid for it and they all had undeserving awards just bestowed upon by UPA government when in power. One is so-called historian Ramchandra Guha. A controversy erupted recently in October-November 2018, when he decided to reject an offer for a teaching job in Ahmedabad University. *BBC* reported on it like this: "A leader of the student wing of the local BJP said that they had met an Ahmedabad University official and told him they didn't want Guha to teach in the city. *We said we want intellectuals in our educational institutes but not anti-nationals*", he said, adding that they had quoted *"anti-national content" from his books to the official."* The complaint said, *"Guha's writings have encouraged divisive tendencies, alienation in the name of independence of the individual, freeing terrorists in the name of independence of the individual, and separating J&K from the Indian union. And Guha is a Communist."*

In actual reality, the GOP as it prefers to be called has been run as a private limited company by a dictator from FAKE Mahatma to FAKE Gandhis for a century now ever since 1917. The undemocratic practice was maneuvered by the wily rook, MK Gandhi who founded the Gandhi-Nehru-Gandhi dynasty, also known as the 'First political family'. Now, we find a third generation *Fake Gandhi* after Indira (Maimuna Begum) and her daughter-in-law Sonia (Sania Antonia Maino). The current 'owner' is Rahul Gandhi nee Raul Vinci, an Italian citizen. This is tragic since a nationalist Hindustani Congress(wo)man is NOT allowed to run the thoroughly corrupt, inept, stale and rudderless unwieldy party at the verge of extinction or natural death. How right and prophetic the statesman Patel was in 1946 when he told Nehru, "Don't make INC as your personal property as it is not going to last forever. In 60-70 years, Hindustanis will forget this party."

My views have been corroborated by Aakar Patel who headed the anti-India *Amnesty International* here. On 15th December 2015, *Rediff.com News* published, '*Why the Congress is a private limited company*'. 'It seems clear that what the Gandhis have done is, if not criminal, at least improper. The fact is that having never had to work for a living, having never had to look for a job like the rest of us, having always lived in government housing their entire lives, it is only natural that they should see no difference between personal property and everything else,' says Aakar Patel. There is one essential difference between BJP and Congress(I): BJP is like a public limited company in which shares are held by many people. Congress is a private limited company in which shares are held by one family. One can say that BJP is a tightly held company, because it is associated with the RSS, which is also a family of sorts. But there is no insistence on pedigree.

The smart outsider stands a good chance of taking over the company on merit, as the prime minister has shown. In the Congress, no matter how talented the individual, he or she must be resigned to the fact that the top two jobs will never be open to anybody other than the family members. Secondly, no matter how lacking in talent or competence, since they hold all the shares, the family's performance and actions are never questioned by their employees. Because of this distinction, the party's members behave in a peculiar fashion. Evidence of this emerged in the last few days, when it was revealed that the Gandhis were facing trial in a property matter. First it was said that they would fight it out in court, which was sensible. But later the party said that this issue was political (it very clearly is not) and they would blame the government for it. To anyone who looks at the matter, it seems clear that what the Gandhis have done is, if not criminal, at least improper. They are arguing that they did not benefit financially from the transaction and even if it violated some law nobody made any money. We are not surprised that they have taken such a casual attitude. The fact is that having never had to work for a living, having never had to look for a job like the rest of us, having always lived (free) in government housing their entire lives, it is only natural that they should see no difference between personal property and everything else. *The Indian Express* reported that before this change in strategy from court battle to political battle was decided on, Sonia was advised by Ghulam Nabi Azad, Ahmed Patel, Bhupinder Singh Hooda, Kapil Sibal and Abhishek Manu Singhvi. Others named in the report were Motilall Vora, Oscar Fernandes and Sam Pitroda.

What is common to all these people? It is, of course, that none of them is in the Lok Sabha. None of them needs to be elected or face the population (electorate). Their advice would likely not have been about the political but the personal. Their whispers would have been all concerned with protecting the family and little of it would have been to do with protecting the party and the damage to it. Nobody in the Congress, of course, has said that the party should distance itself from the matter by letting the family fight it in court and not raising it politically. *Anyone who would even consider this, let alone suggest it, would be fired immediately from the party. This is another difference it has from the BJP.*

It is inconceivable that Modi would have faced such charges and would not have to deal with internal dissent. Even his inability to win Bihar, despite trying very hard, brought up resentment against him. A charge of financial impropriety would have been difficult to survive. *One could say many things about intolerance in the BJP, but it is true that it is far less tolerant about corruption than the Congress(I).* Since it was decided to make it political, the court case has become another in the long list of things that the Congress(I) has used to disrupt Parliament. The party has been using this disruption as a tool of becoming relevant again. This is fine. And all parties use it as a tactic, and it is effective. *But is flitting from one thing to another sensible?* One day it is the alleged corruption of chief ministers and the foreign minister, the *next* day it is the casual and careless (but definitely not deliberate) remarks of Union minister VK Singh, the *third* day it is intolerance, the *fourth* day it is this personal court matter, the fifth day it is again corruption. It boggles the mind that somebody thought up this strategy and somebody else approved it. *It is the misfortune of Indians that at a time when a serious debate was needed on some of the doings of the government, the Opposition is serving up this sort of rubbish.* [Aakar Patel is Executive Director, Amnesty International India. The views expressed here are his own].

12] _Anti-national Muslims_: Patel said in 1948, "I have never seen a nationalist Muslim but for Pt. Jawaharlal Nehru and Maulana Abul Kalam Azad." Obviously, *the great Indian statesman knew that the FAKE Pandit was in fact a Muslim. Stemming from the traitor anti-national Muslims, the internal threats are numerous.* An important one needs mention: It is the small fraction of anti-national Muslims – who have been and are being nurtured and nourished by this anti-national Congress(I) its Cronies and its like-minded regional political parties all along – for the sake of vote-bank politics – for whom religion has precedence over everything else including the country. The danger of many Pakistans: mini or big emerging lurks and looms large. The notable biggies are Kashmir valley, Kerala, West Bengal and Western UP. To compound its deleterious effect, the largest majority i.e. the Hindus (80% of Indian population) are scrupulously kept divided by the same anti-national parties. Congress-I is singled out since it and its parent INC ruled the country for 55 of the 71 years of Indian democracy's existence

A *terrorist wielding a pen causes far more damage than the one with a gun.* The former (like Dr. Zakir Naik) misguides a horde of gullible Muslims whereas the latter (like Burhan Wani) can -kill many innocents and destroy a limited number of properties. Therefore, some 'intellectuals', preachers and clerics assume importance being too detrimental to the society anywhere in the -world. We have several of them inciting those with an orthodox bent of mind, coaxing, cajoling, pressurizing to perform acts of terror against the humanity in general but all the people other than Sunni Muslims. One Congress-supported anti-nationalist above-mentioned Naik of Mumbai has been in the news but for wrong reasons. The Maharashtra CM has requested the Police Commissioner to investigate and go through the tapes of his 'preaching', lectures and talks. Incidentally, he is alleged to have been invited many a time by the then ruling Congress to give lectures to IAS and IFS officers. Does it imply that Congress promotes terrorists? On 7th July 2016, *Rediff.com News* published an article: *'Decoding Zakir Naik: A TV preacher or a threat'*? "*Absconding* Islamic preacher Zakir Naik has been in the news for some time especially after it was disclosed that one of the five Bangladeshi terrorists who killed 22 people at a restaurant in Dhaka was his known followers.

Here is what we know about him:

- Naik, a medical doctor by education, not only influenced the Dhaka attackers alone. Even the chief of Islamic State's Hyderabad module told the National Investigation Agency that he was deeply influenced by his teachings.
- Unlike other preachers who like to dress in traditional clothes, Naik usually wears a three-piece suit (with pants fitting above the ankles) and a tie, but teams it up with a skull cap, and speaks English fluently. Arabic is his other preferred language.
- Naik is banned in the United Kingdom and Canada for hate speech. He is also among 16 banned Islamic scholars in Malaysia.
- Naik once advised Sania Mirza that she should dress up modestly, even when she is playing tennis. He has also said that wife beating is not necessarily a bad thing, has rationalized stoning, and has said that using a condom is like killing a human being.
- His TV channel 'Peace TV' is banned in India but is run in many languages -- Bangla, Urdu and Chinese among others -- and has a 200 million-strong viewership in Bangladesh. It is not known how he funds the TV network. He has around 14 million followers on *Facebook*.

Controversial statements:

- On 9/11: It is a blatant, open secret that this attack on the Twin Towers was done by George ---Bush himself... Even a fool will know that the 9/11 attacks were an inside job.
- On Osama-bin Laden: If he is fighting enemies of Islam, I am for him. I don't know him personally. If he is terrorizing America, the biggest terrorist, I am with him. Every Muslim should be a terrorist. The thing is that if he is terrorizing a terrorist, he is following Islam.
- On girls' education: Girls shouldn't be sent to schools where they lose their virginity by the time they pass out. Schools should be shut down.
- On homosexuals: They should be killed.
- On Islam: It is superior to all other faiths. Non-Muslims should not be allowed to have places of religious worship in an Islamic country."

On Saturday, the 9th July 2016, *Rediff.com News* followed its earlier reporting: "Acknowledging that Islamic preacher Zakir Naik's speeches were provocative, Baghpat MP Satyapal Singh and now a Union minister formerly Mumbai police commissioner said, "In 2008, we sent a report to government questioning Zakir Naik 's source of funding and speeches. His organization should be banned by FCRA. We filed a report on the event in which 12 people converted to Islam at the venue, they have transformed at least 12 girls and boys into Muslim from Hindu and Jain. At that time, we have sent a report. They get funding from outside." Singh also said that Naik misinterpreted and misquoted religious books. "We have mentioned in the report that such things can be dangerous and sought immediate action from the government. But nothing was done at the right time," he added. In October 2008, a two-day program by Naik's Islamic Research Foundation at the Azam Campus ground in Pune Camp became controversial after "religious conversions" at the venue. Twelve persons, mainly youths, 'converted' to Islam voluntarily in Naik's presence at the full-packed open program, the premises of an educational organization run by the Maharashtra Cosmopolitan Education Society. [Source: *ANI*]

On 4th November 2017, *The Quint* published: '*Zakir Naik Embraced by Malaysian Govt Because Islam Sells*'. "When Zakir Naik emerged from a prominent Malaysian mosque last month, fans swarmed about him, seeking selfies with the Indian Muslim televangelist whose hardline views-- have sparked a criminal investigation back in his home country. Accompanied by a bodyguard, Naik was making a rare public appearance at the Putra Mosque in Malaysia's administrative capital, where the prime minister and his cabinet members often worship. Naik, who has been banned in the UK, has been given permanent residency in Malaysia, and embraced by top government officials. Critics see Naik's presence in Malaysia as another sign of top-level support for hardline Islam in a country with substantial minorities of Christians, Hindus and Buddhists, and which has long projected a moderate Islamic image. [*Reuters*]

<u>We have intelligent truly nationalistic (patriotic) citizens too.</u> One comes across several of those. Ms. Meeta Somani's 10th September 2017 *Facebook* post, '*What if an Indian had written this... Would anyone have believed*', makes interesting and meaningful reading; "*Article by Maria Wirth:* Though I have lived in India for a long time, there are still issues here that I find hard to understand. For example, why do so many educated Indians become agitated when India is referred to as a Hindu country? Majority of

Indians are Hindus. India is special because of its ancient Hindu tradition. Westerners are drawn to India because of Hinduism. *Why then is there this resistance by many Indians to acknowledge the Hindu roots of their country? Why do some people even give the impression that the Hindustan which valued those roots would be dangerous? <u>Don't they know better</u>?*

This attitude is strange for *two* reasons. <u>*First*</u>, those educated Indians seem to have a problem only with "Hindu" India, but not with "Muslim" or "Christian" countries. Germany, for example, is a secular country, and only 59% of the population are registered with the two big Christian churches (Protestant and Catholic). Nevertheless, the country is bracketed under "Christian countries" and no one objects. Angela Merkel, the Chancellor, stressed recently the Christian roots of Germany and urged the population "to go back to Christian values." In 2012, she postponed her trip to the G-8 summit to make a public address on Katholikentag, *'Catholics Day'*. Two major political parties carry Christian in their name, including Angela Merkel's Christian Democratic Union. Germans are not agitated that Germany is called a Christian country, though actually I would understand, if they were. After all, the history of the Church is appalling. The so-called success story of Christianity depended greatly on tyranny. "Convert or die" were the options given—not only some five hundred years ago to the indigenous population in America, but also in Germany, 1,200 years ago, when the emperor Karl the Great ordered the death sentence for refusal of baptism in his newly conquered realms. This provoked his advisor Alkuin to comment: "One can force them to baptism, but how to force them to believe?" Times, when one's life was in danger for dissenting with the dogmas of Christianity, are thankfully over. Today many in the West do dissent and are leaving the Church in a steady stream. They are disgusted with the less-than-holy behavior of Church officials and they also can't believe in the dogmas, for example that "Jesus is the only way" and that God sends all those who don't accept this to hell.

The <u>*second*</u> reason why I can't understand the resistance to associate India with Hinduism is that Hinduism is in a different category from the Abrahamic religions. Its history, compared to Christianity and Islam, was undoubtedly the least violent as it spread in ancient times by convincing arguments and not by force. It is not a belief system that demands blind acceptance of dogmas and the suspension of one's intelligence. On the contrary, Hinduism encourages using one's intelligence to the hilt. It is an enquiry into truth based on a refined character and intellect. It comprises a huge body of ancient literature, not only regarding dharma and philosophy, but also regarding music, architecture, dance, science, astronomy, economics, politics, etc. If Germany or any other Western country had this kind of literary treasure, it would be so proud and highlight its greatness on every occasion. When I discovered the Upanishads, for example, I was stunned. Here was expressed in clear terms what I intuitively had felt to be true but could not have expressed clearly. Brahman is not partial; it is the invisible, indivisible essence in everything. Everyone gets again and again a chance to discover the ultimate truth and is free to choose his way back to it. Helpful hints are given but not imposed.

In my early days in India, I thought every Indian knew and valued his tradition. Slowly I realized I was wrong. The British colonial masters had been successful in not only weaning away many of the elite from their ancient tradition but even making them despise it. It helped that the British-educated class could no longer read the original Sanskrit texts and believed what the British told them. This lack of knowledge and the brainwashing by the British education may be the reason why many so-called "modern" Indians are against anything Hindu. They don't realize the difference between Western religions that should be believed (or at least professed) blindly, and which discourage, if not forbid, their adherents to think on their own, and the multi-layered Hindu Dharma which gives freedom and encourages using one's intelligence.

Many of the Indian educated class do not realize that those who dream of imposing Christianity or Islam on this vast country will applaud them for denigrating Hindu Dharma, because this creates a vacuum where Western ideas can easier gain a foothold. At the same time, many Westerners, including staunch Christians, know the value of Hindu culture and surreptitiously appropriate insights from the vast Indian knowledge system, drop the original Hindu source and present it either as their own or make it look as if these insights had already been known in the West. As the West appropriates valuable and exclusive Hindu assets, what it leaves behind is deemed inferior. Unwittingly, these Indians are helping what Rajiv Malhotra of Infinity Foundation calls the digestion of Dharma civilization into Western universalism. That which is being digested, a deer for example, in this case Hindu Dharma, disappears whereas the digester (a tiger) becomes stronger.

If only missionaries denigrated Hindu Dharma, it would not be so bad, as they clearly have an agenda which discerning Indians would detect. But sadly, Indians with Hindu names assist them because they wrongly believe Hinduism is inferior to Western religions. They belittle everything Hindu instead of getting thorough knowledge. As a rule, they know little about their tradition except what the British have told them, i.e., that the major features are the caste system and idol worship. *They don't realize that India would gain, not lose, if it solidly backed its profound and all-inclusive Hindu tradition.* The Dalai Lama said some time ago that, as a youth in Lhasa, he had been deeply impressed by the richness of Indian thought. "India has great potential to help the world," he added. *When will the Westernized Indian elite realize it?"* [Maria Wirth, a freelance writer who has lived in India for the past 33 years]

<u>Ms. Maria Wirth's open letter to Dr. Zakir Naik and his ilk makes an interesting reading</u>:

"Hindus generally don't criticize other religions although Christianity and Islam not only criticize but demean Hinduism badly. Naik is only one example. Do Hindus know what is preached in the innumerable churches and mosques across India? I know for sure that Hindu gods are called devils by Christian missionaries. Yet, Hindus neither defend their gods nor challenge the Abrahamic dogmas despite having a solid philosophical basis for their beliefs, which is lacking in Christianity and Islam. Naik had ridiculed Ganapati and thrown a challenge to prove that Ganapati is God. I assume he means by God the Supreme Being that Muslims call Allah.

Now what do we know about Allah? Foremost, Allah is great and merciful, and the faithful as well as the unfaithful are loudly reminded of it five times a day. He also knows what all human beings are doing but is separate from them. It is claimed that Allah has communicated his final words to Prophet Mohamed. Those words are in the Quran. Allah declared that Islam alone is true. So, all human beings must follow Islam because other paths are wrong. And they must hurry up, because every human being has only one life. Those, who do not accept Islam during their lifetime, will be thrown into eternal hellfire where "boiling water will be poured over their heads that not only melts their skin but also the inner parts of their bellies…" (Q22.19-22) Clearly, here is where Allah's mercy ends. He does not brook any dissent. And the Azan, which started compassionately, ends with: "Oh Allah, guide us to the Right Way. The Way of those whom You have favored, not of those who have earned Your wrath…" (Al-Fatiha) This means, Allah is merciful only to his followers or Muslims and he is wrathful to those who are not Muslims.

Dr. Zakir Naik, I am confident that I got the concept of 'God' in Islam right because Christianity has a similar concept. And I dare to claim that it is not true. Can you prove (and this challenge goes also to Christian clerics also) that Allah/God is indeed so unfair and divisive? Can you prove there will be this huge cauldron of fire where billions of people will burn for ever after Judgment Day? Do these claims of "eternal hellfire for unbelievers" not rather have the purpose to keep the flock in check? To divide and rule?

There are about 2 billion Christians, who are told they must remain Christians, otherwise they can't go to heaven. And then there are about 1.5 billion Muslims who are told that they must remain Muslims, otherwise they can't go to paradise. Both religions had plenty of time to sort out which one is true, but they did not do it. Why? Because they cannot prove it. They can only make claims and counterclaims and fight among themselves, between Muslims and Christians and with heathens or infidels. They do this for the last 2000 years.

Under these circumstances, can anyone claim that Islam or Christianity is beneficial for humanity? Is it not time to have a thorough check of what REALLY is the truth? About the absolute Truth, Dr. Zakir Naik, your ancestors, the Indian Rishis, made valuable contributions and you can be proud of them. In ancient times, long, long before Christianity or Islam appeared on the scene, the Rishis had a very mature understanding of *Brahman* which would be 'Truth' or 'Supreme Being' or 'God' in English. *Brahman* is not personal, not a superhuman entity somewhere in heaven, not male or female, not jealous of other gods, not revengeful if ignored, but it is *Sat-Chit-Ananda*, the conscious, one essence in all names and forms – like the one ocean is the essence of all the waves. The Rishis realized that this universe is a wrong perception of *Brahman*. They called it *Maya*, not true, only apparently true. For anything to qualify as absolute Truth, it should be always – past, present and future – and it must be self-evident.

The *Rishis* concluded that nothing fulfils these criteria except pure thought free consciousness. This consciousness is here and now, always, everywhere. Yet we miss it because we focus only on things or thoughts, emotions, etc. – like, when we focus a torchlight in a room only on the furniture and miss the empty space. Infinite space, which throbs with life and love is good metaphor for *Sat-Chit-Ananda* – highest truth that underlies names and forms (*nama-rupa*). Science has meanwhile discovered the *Sat*-aspect of the truth. Oneness is there. To discover that this Oneness is also aware (*Chit*) and blissful (*Ananda*) scientists would need to turn to their own consciousness to research further instead of looking outside. Let us see whether the scientists will support also the claim of the Rishis that this whole manifestation is alive and full of bliss.

In one point, however, you are right, Dr. Zakir Naik: There is only one Truth, one God, which the wise call by different names. But the nature of it you got wrong. It does not send non-Muslims or non-Christians eternally into hellfire. The Supreme Being is indeed merciful and great. But you wanted to know whether Ganapati is a deity. May I explain a bit of your ancestors' tradition which struck me as most profound when I came to know of it?"

Sanatana Dharma is not only about intellectually knowing *Sat-Chit-Ananda*, but about realizing it. Since *Brahman* is all pervading, it must be also in us (*Ayam Atma Brahman*). So, we can tap and feel it. For this, however, we need to follow certain rules. We need to purify ourselves, lead a moral life, speak the truth, etc. To eat plenty of meat and have plenty of sex is not conducive for this purification. Yet one factor is very conducive: *Bhakti* – love for God.

Here Hindu Dharma brings in Ishwar. The concept of *Ishwar* is close to the Abrahamic notion of a personal God but more benevolent. There is, of course, no eternal hell for unbelievers. Everyone gets chance after chance in life after life till he realizes that he is not a separate wave, but one with the ocean. *Ishwar* is God with attributes and has innumerable aspects, as this universe has innumerable aspects or human nature has innumerable aspects. These aspects are personified in different deities and the devotees can choose the one who is dearest to him. It helps to develop love for the invisible Truth – for example through *Ganapati*.

Those *Devas* are mistakenly much maligned by Christianity and Islam. They are not separate entities but kind of access points to the one *Brahman*, which is otherwise unimaginable. It is possible to feel familiar with them, to love them, to talk with them. And the scriptures leave no doubt that *devas* are ultimately *Brahman*.

And here, Dr. Naik, you may get an answer to your question whether Ganapati is ultimately the Supreme Being. The *Ganapati Atharvashirsa Upanishad*, which is part of the Atharva Veda, states: "*Tvameva kevalam karta si, tvameva kevalam dharta si, tvameva kevalam harta si. Tvameva sarvam khalvidam brahmasi, tvam saksadatma si nityam.*" It means: You alone are the creator, you alone are the sustainer, you alone are the annihilator. All this is Brahman and you are that Brahman. You are indeed the Atman eternally. This declaration, however, is not unique for Ganapati. It is said for other deities, too. Yet the fact that this is written in a sacred text, is not proof enough. There are plenty of sacred texts in this world and if everything in them is blindly accepted as true, we end up with all kind of proclaimed truths which are not true. We need to verify what is declared as truth on the touchstone of reason, intuition and experience. If it contradicts all these, it is not worth believing it and certainly not dying for it.

The proof that all deities are *Brahman* is because only *Brahman* really exists. *Brahman* is like the ocean. The waves are not separate from it. The name with which one worships the Divine, does not matter. What matters is how much devotion one feels. The greater the devotion, the more miracles can happen. Ganapati is loved by millions of Hindus worldwide. He is the door through which they try to access *Sat-Chit-Ananda*.

Sanatana Dharma is very ancient. And yet the Rishis had such deep insights, for example that the world is a wrong perception of what is true, like seeing a snake at dusk when in fact there is only a rope. Westerners who ridiculed Hindus because they believe that the world is an illusion keep now quiet as science supports the Hindu view. Meanwhile NASA scientists have detected the building blocks of DNA in meteorites. The Max Planck Institute in Germany published the first picture of the whole universe. It had an oval shape. Could it be possible that those who ridicule Hindus for worshipping a Shiva lingam might soon rethink their attitude, as well, lest they embarrass themselves? Great men have come and gone in India's ancient civilization. Some have been made into gods. There is nothing wrong with it. The Divine is in all. It should make you reflect, Dr. Naik that science keeps validating the insights of the Rishis, for example the mindboggling age of the universe, or the ultimate Oneness of all.

Attempts to vilify Indian tradition by you and others are successful because the British weaned Indians away from their tradition and most people know little about it. Yet if you are sincere, you will realize that the wisdom of your ancestors scores high over the worldview and the mind set of Abrahamic religions. The attitude of "We alone are right, and you go to hell if you don't accept our religion" is doing great harm to humanity. It may be helpful for world dominion, but do you want to live in a world where everyone should wear a straitjacket?

If I were you, Dr. Naik, I would be worried especially about one thing: what if you wake up after death and there is NO paradise waiting for you? What if all those Jihadis, who were inspired by you, cursed you after realizing there was no paradise for them? What if you are taking birth again in another form and reap the fruits of your actions of this life where you consciously or unconsciously distorted the truth? Rebirth is not only mentioned in the Indian texts. There is also plenty of evidence for it – over 3000 cases are documented in the archive of Virginia University.

Dr. Naik, I don't know how deeply you believe what you preach. I know from personal experience how effective brainwashing in childhood can be. But I also know that it is possible to get out of it, and it seems the older one is, the easier.

For me, it was a great relief to come out of the Christian religious straight jacket and I would encourage you to also genuinely enquire into the truth. Your concept of God is not Truth. You quote a book as support. Truth does not fit into a book. Truth is THAT WHAT TRULY IS. Your ancestors, the Indian Rishis, spoke from experience, not from book knowledge."

Naik absconded possibly with Congress party's help being their blue-eyed boy. Congress (I) general secretary Digvijay Singh, advisor to Rahul and closely associated with 'first political dynasty', used to share the dais with Zakir Naik many a time during UPA regime. Naik initially took citizenship of Saudi Arabia that is a haven for Salafist and Wahhabis. Then he moved to another Muslim country Malaysia where he lives in piece of mind under the protection of the government. When the government of India requested for his extradition,

13] *Islamic terrorism:* Islamic terror is a global phenomenon. Terror is expected wherever Muslims reside. *We in India have been bracing against Pak-sponsored terrorism for many decades now.* The whole world refused to believe this fact labeling it as our internal problem. The perception changed when the prime sponsor of terrorism, America got the taste of its own medicine through infamous 9/11 carried out by US prop Osama bin Laden – a Pak-based, Pak-supported criminal-minded terrorist who lived for many years after carrying out the dastardly terrorist attack for the first time – near the biggest army garrison under its total security. Then Britain and other Western powers faced terror attacks like the 7/7 in Britain. And more recently, France suffered terror attacks in Paris. It was only then it dawned upon the Western Powers that terrorism is a menace and global phenomenon. Paradoxically, the only 'superpower' America never learned any lessons and continues to financially and militarily support Pakistan in a big way! It is a well-known fact that any terrorist anywhere in the world is always a Muslim. Then why the American President Obama and even the Indian PM Modi always say: "Terror has no religion." One can understand for Obama as his father was a Kenyan Muslim. Does Modi have the compulsion of vote-bank politics? Or, like the not-so-nationalist Congress leadership, it is his policy of Muslim appeasement? So that he has also to appease Muslims much like the Congress and all other 'secular' or precisely speaking 'sickular' parties. When one goes through the list of India's '50 most wanted criminals', one finds they are exclusively Muslims. Whenever anyone is arrested or killed for acts of terror, everyone is found to be a Muslim. The terrorist organizations across the globe namely ISIS, al-Qaeda, Taliban, Boko Haram, Hamas, et al. are all generally Sunni Muslims. Does that imply that *Islam is the religion of Terror*? If it is so, why not to admit that fact?

This is not for any specific religion, but it's true...nothing against Islam, but...? You decide...

The Shoe Bomber was a Muslim; The Beltway Snipers: Muslims; The Fort Hood Shooter: Muslim; The Underwear Bomber: Muslim; The U-S.S. Cole Bombers: Muslims; The Madrid Train Bombers: Muslims; The Bali Night Club Bombers: Muslims; The London Tube Bombers: Muslims; The Moscow Theater Attackers: Muslims; The Boston Marathon Bombers: Muslims; The Libyan U.S. Embassy Attack: Muslims; The Buenos Aires Suicide Bombers: Muslims; The Israeli Olympic Team Attackers: Muslims; The Kenyan U.S, Embassy Bombers: Muslims; The Saudi, Khobar Towers Bombers: Muslims; The Beirut Marine Barracks Bombers: Muslims; The Beslan Russian School Attackers: Muslims; The First World Trade Center Bombers: Muslims; The Bombay (Mumbai), India Attackers on all occasions: Muslims; The Achille Laura Cruise Ship Hijackers: Muslims; The Nairobi, Kenya Shopping Mall Killers: Muslims; The September 11th 2001 Airline Hijackers: Muslims; The Sydney, Australia Lindt Cafe Kidnapper: Muslim; The Peshawar, Pakistani School Children Killers: Muslims; and so on.

Think of it: Hindus living with Jews = No Problem; Baha'is living with Jews = No Problem; Jews living with Atheists = No Problem; Sikhs living with Hindus = No Problem; Hindus living with Baha'is = No Problem; Christians living with Jews = No Problem; Jews living with Buddhists = No Problem; Shinto living with Atheists = No Problem; Buddhists living with Sikhs = No Problem; Baha'is living with Christians = No Problem;

Buddhists living with Shinto = No Problem; Buddhists living with Hindus = No Problem; Hindus living with Christians = No Problem; Atheists living with Buddhists = No Problem; Confucians living with Hindus = No Problem; Atheists living with Confucians = No Problem;

Now: Muslims living with Jews = Problem; Muslims living with Sikhs = Problem; Muslims living with Hindus = Problem; Muslims living with Baha'is = Problem; Muslims living with Shinto = Problem; Muslims living with Atheists = Problem; Muslims living with Buddhists = Problem; Muslims living with Christians = Problem; MUSLIMS LIVING WITH MUSLIMS = BIG PROBLEM!

SO, THIS LEADS TO: They're not happy in Gaza; not happy in Egypt; not happy elsewhere.

Q: *In which country are they happy?*

For answer, read the following: They're not happy in Libya; They're not happy in Iran; They're not happy in Iraq; They're not happy in Yemen; They're not happy in Pakistan; They're not happy in Syria; They're not happy in Lebanon; They're not happy in Nigeria; They're not happy in Kenya; They're not happy in Sudan; They're not happy in Morocco; They're not happy in Afghanistan.

So, where are they happy? They're happy in Australia; They're happy in Belgium; They're happy in Denmark; They're happy in France; They're happy in Germany; They're happy in Holland; They're happy in Italy; They're happy in Norway & India; They're happy in Spain; They're happy in Sweden; They're very happy in UK; They're happy in the USA & Canada. It's because of 'Loads of Welfare Benefits' in all these places. *They're happy in almost every country that is not Islamic!* And who do they blame? Not Islam... Not their leadership... Not themselves... THEY BLAME THE COUNTRIES THEY ARE HAPPY IN! And they want to change the countries they're happy in, to be like the countries they came from... where they were unhappy! *Do you believe all this?*

Finally, they will get hammered! Islamic Jihad: AN ISLAMIC TERROR ORGANIZATION; ISIS: AN ISLAMIC TERROR ORGANIZATION; Al-Qaeda: AN ISLAMIC TERROR ORGANIZATION; Taliban: AN ISLAMIC TERROR ORGANIZATION; Hamas: AN ISLAMIC TERROR ORGANIZATION; Hezbollah: AN ISLAMIC TERROR ORGANIZATION; Boko Haram: AN ISLAMIC TERROR ORGANIZATION; Al-Nusra: AN ISLAMIC

TERROR ORGANIZATION; Abu Sayyaf: AN ISLAMIC TERROR ORGANIZATION; Al-Badr: AN ISLAMIC TERROR ORGANIZATION; Muslim Brotherhood: AN ISLAMIC TERROR ORGANIZATION; Lashkar-e-Taiba: AN ISLAMIC TERROR ORGANIZATION; Palestine Liberation Front: AN ISLAMIC TERROR ORGANIZATION; Ansaru: AN ISLAMIC TERROR ORGANIZATION; Jemaah Islamiyah: AN ISLAMIC TERROR ORGANIZATION; Abdullah Azzam Brigades: AN ISLAMIC TERROR ORGANIZATION; Al-Shabab Somalia: AN ISLAMIC TERROR ORGANIZATION ....

AND A LOT MORE! *Please think of it seriously*! *Undoubtedly, Islam is the religion of terror*!

ISIS and the period of anarchy: American President Bush's unwarranted intervention in Iraq destroyed the most liberal Arab country. Coupled with hasty withdrawal by his half-black successor prepared a ripe field for the emergence and rise of ISIS. Ironically the deadly terrorist organization is funded by an arch US-ally Saudi Arabia. Hence ISIS is not an orphan. Its father is America and the mother Saudi Arabia. ISIS is knocking the door of India having moved eastward to Afghanistan and Pakistan to our west and Bangladesh to our east. ISIS flags can be seen outside and atop mosques in Srinagar after every Friday Namaz! Incidentally and unfortunately, senseless Muslims from many countries including Xinchiang region of China as also some from India, country with the second largest Muslim population in the world, are flocking to it.

On 7th July 2016, *Rediff.com News* published: '*Everything about ISIS had indicated that this would be a violent Ramzan*'. "A violent, divisive Ramzan (Ramadan) sends out exactly the message ISIS wants to send to religious Muslims outside its fold: It plays on their faith and fears, says writer Tabish Khair. He wrote this essay 2-3 days before *Eid-ul-Fitr*. Eid marks the end of Ramadan, the holy month of fasting for practicing Muslims, a month that should be lived simply and peacefully, with an effort to avoid negative thought and action. Anger, violence, and hostility are to be renounced. Some traditions even claim that, if possible, enemies are to be reconciled in this month. But I need hardly remind the reader that, this year, the month of Ramzan has been ripped apart by Islamist violence incidentally claiming its victims mostly in Muslim countries.

Over the past week alone, there have been bombings in Saudi Arabia, and far more deadly attacks in Iraq, Turkey and Bangladesh. I could list all of them, but I prefer not to repeat stories of villainy and violence in the month of Ramzan. If I must tell stories from this week, I would prefer to talk about the 20-year-old Bangladeshi (Muslim) man, Faraaz Hossain, who chose to not abandon his Indian and American friends when he was given that option by the terrorists during the atrocity at the Holey Artisan Bakery in Dhaka on July 1. He was killed along with them.

That date, July 1, is part of the answer to the question that most people are asking today: *Why this spate of violence by Islamists during the peaceful month of Ramzan?* There are two complementary answers to it. Both the answers have to do with ISIS and its ilk, but, alas, they also have to do with trends among many peacefully religious Muslims. July 1 was a Friday. The executioners of ISIS who struck at the Holey Artisan Bakery were probably motivated by the common fundamentalist conviction that a Muslim should not be in a bakery on a Friday during the fasting of Ramzan. This grisly logic is nevertheless rooted in a tendency among other (peaceful) religious Muslims: There has been growing intolerance of differences within the communities of Islam. It has become increasingly difficult in many Muslim Mohallas to be a Muslim and practice the faith differently. It is possible for most Hindus, Buddhists, Christians and even Jews to practice little or nothing of their faiths and yet to be accepted within large sections of their communities. This is seldom the case among Muslims, if they live with other religious Muslims. I have Jewish and Christian friends who are confirmed atheists, but can move openly, freely and with mutual respect among religious Jews and religious Christians. This is almost impossible to imagine in most Muslim societies today.

ISIS, in that sense, is a natural outgrowth of peaceful fundamentalist movements like Wahhabism, which have been relentlessly narrowing down the definition of what it is to be a Muslim. That ISIS and its ilk have killed far more Muslims than non-Muslims is a direct consequence of this. Fundamentalism finally consumes its own children, because it increasingly disowns most of them. The other answer is the millenarianism of ISIS and its roots elsewhere.

As Graeme Wood pointed out in *The Atlantic* last year, there is a difference between 'jihadists' -- who can be motivated by many political factors, including nationalist protest in the Middle East -- and the 'jihadists' of ISIS. Wood noted that much of what ISIS does 'looks nonsensical except in light of a sincere, carefully considered commitment to returning civilization to a seventh-century legal environment and ultimately to bringing about the apocalypse.' He went on to argue that at least the ideologues of ISIS are, consciously or unconsciously, motivated by a desire for apocalypse. This is not as far-fetched as it sounds.

Almost everyone who has grown up among religious Muslims at least in the subcontinent knows the mythical prophesy of apocalypse, which follows a period of totally anarchy among Muslims, and then the restoration of Muslim glory for a few decades. This is a central myth in Sunni sources.

Consciously or unconsciously, ISIS sees itself as embroiled in the period of anarchy which must be crossed before Muslim glory is restored and then apocalypse comes. *This period of anarchy is significant*: as it is supposed by some Sunni ideologues that it would be distinguished by violence of Muslims against other Muslims, by a total divisiveness of the kingdom of Islam. Hence, violence during the holy and peaceful month of Ramzan fits this picture.

Looking back, and knowing what we know of ISIS, I wonder why religious Muslims did not expect this from ISIS. Everything about ISIS had indicated that this would be a violent month. A violent, divisive Ramzan sends out exactly the message ISIS wants to send to religious Muslims outside its folds: It plays on their faith and fears. Once again, it is not enough for religious Muslims to just disown ISIS. ISIS has not come from outer space; it has grown up among religious Muslims.

The many political troubles in Muslim lands, some are due to external interference and others by manipulation, continue to provide ISIS and its ilk with their desperate foot-soldiers, the ideology driving such militant organizations is based on tendencies also present among many peacefully religious Muslims. These include intolerance of internal difference and a negative, proto-apocalyptic view of the future. *Sadly*, unless religious Muslims face up to these tendencies and do something about them, ISIS -- or something like it -- will always be able to get the odd (vainglorious, frustrated or confused) Muslim to kill many other Muslim (and non-Muslim) men and women during the Ramzans to come. Eid, I grew up believing, was the festival when you embraced even your enemy. If so, perhaps this Eid, very religious Muslims can try to embrace differences 'within the fold,' including those of gender. Differences 'outside the fold' will prove easier to accept as a natural consequence. And even apocalypse might start to seem less pressing." [*Tabish Khair*, an associate professor in the department of English, University of Aarhus in Denmark, is the author of The *New Xenophobia*. His latest novel, Jihadi Jane, has just been published by Penguin in India.]

Our air force destroyed Pakistan's in the 1971 Indo-Pak war so much so, its long-time ally, financier and supporter American had to requisition fighter planes from Jordan and its most powerful nuclear-powered aircraft carrier and 7th fleet *Enterprise* set sails from South China Sea. After traversing Straits of Malacca, it developed cold feet. Obviously, it was under the fear that if the Indian Navy helped by its USSR counterpart may hit and damage the *Enterprise* thereby sinking American prestige forever!

Situation may have changed now on the balance of strength of Indian and Pakistan air forces because of America's continued unstoppable arming of Pakistan with sophisticated modern heavy arms. Then Obama has the cheek to say that America and India are natural allies and friends. On 31st March 2016, *Rediff.com News* published an eye-opener of an article, '*Can the IAF fight the next war effectively?*' "In the light of India's increasingly 'darkening' threat environment and the convergence of strategic interests between China and Pakistan, the IAF's declining combat capabilities are a cause for concern, says Brigadier Gurmeet Kanwal (Retired).

In a rare public admission, Air Marshal BS Dhanoa, Vice Chief of Air Staff, said while briefing the media recently on the eve of Exercise Iron Fist, a fire power demonstration of the Indian Air Force that 'numbers are not adequate to execute a full air campaign in a two-front scenario.' Independent corroboration of the vice chief's assessment has been provided by the well-known analyst Dr. Ashley J Tellis, Senior Research Associate, Carnegie Endowment for International Peace, Washington, DC. In an impressive monograph, *Troubles They Come in Battalions: The Manifold Travails of the Indian Air Force* (Carnegie Endowment for International Peace, March 2016), Dr. Tellis analyzes the IAF's force structure and suggests measures to improve its combat efficiency to meet future threats and challenges.

Dr. Tellis highlighted India's increasingly 'darkening' threat, environment, in view of the convergence of strategic interests between China and Pakistan and their rapidly modernizing air forces. While noting approvingly that 'the IAF remains exemplary among air forces in the developing world,' he writes that it is gradually losing the combat edge that it has enjoyed since the 1971 War with Pakistan because of the superior fighter aircraft in its inventory and larger numbers. Dr. Tellis accepts the aspirations of Indian analysts for a combat strength of 60 squadrons for the IAF to be able to effectively dominate the skies in a two-front threat environment. However, he points out that the number of the IAF's frontline squadrons has been steadily declining. 'Today, against the authorized total of 39.5 squadrons,' he writes, 'the IAF can barely muster 32 squadrons of fighters... China and Pakistan field about 750 advanced air defense/ multi-role fighters against the IAF's 450-odd equivalents.' The large-scale depletion in the IAF's combat capability can be attributed to 'serious constraints on India's defense budget, the impediments imposed by the acquisition process, the meagre achievements of the country's domestic development organizations, the weaknesses of the higher defense management system, and India's inability to reconcile the need for self-sufficiency in defense production with the necessity of maintaining technological superiority over rivals.'

Dr. Tellis systematically analyzed the present holdings and future requirements of fighter aircraft in the lightweight (MiG-21/Tejas LCA), medium-weight (Rafale MMRCA) and heavyweight (SU-30MKI/PAK-FA Indo-Russian fifth generation fighter) segments and concludes that the IAF faces serious challenges in all of them. 'The Tejas Mark 1 is handicapped by significant technological deficiencies; the prospects for expanding the MMRCA component to compensate for the Tejas' shortcomings are unclear; and the IAF's reluctance to proceed fully with the PAK-FA program could undermine its fifth-generation fighter ambitions.'

Dr. Tellis discussed the options available to India in each segment in detail. According to him, India should be cautious about acquiring more than six squadrons of the Tejas LCA; it should opt for the 'cheapest' Western MMRCA available and enlarge its requirement in this segment; and, it should continue to invest in its collaboration with Russia for the fifth-generation fighter aircraft PAK-FA. He dwells in length on the advantages and shortcomings of the major Western contenders in the middle-weight segment, including the two European aircraft, the Rafale and the Gripen NG, and the two American aircraft, the F-16IN and the F/A-18E/F Super Hornet. He writes that both Boeing and Lockheed Martin would be amenable to manufacturing their fighters in India with transfer of technology. However, India has faced difficulties with American technology in the past, partly due to its reluctance to sign some of the foundational agreements like CISMOA, BECA and LSA. As a case in point, the C-130J transport aircraft for the Special Forces came without some high-tech equipment.

Dr. Tellis highlights the difficulties envisaged in integrating just 36 Rafales in an aircraft fleet that is already 'widely diversified', that too at a price of approximately $9 billion -- almost one-fourth of India's current defense budget. However, he does not comment on the view of some non-aviator Indian analysts that the MMRCA (Medium Multi Role Combat Aircraft) is too expensive, especially if acquired in small numbers, and that the IAF should acquire larger numbers of the Russian-designed SU-30MKI and encourage the indigenously manufactured Tejas LCA, in line with the government's policy thrust to *'Make in India'*. While this view has some merit even though the serviceability rate of the SU-30MKI leaves much to be desired, the LCA is still three to five years away from being declared fully worthy of undertaking combat operations. If deal to acquire 36 Rafale fighters does finally go through, it may be prudent to manufacture these in India with transfer of technology -- provided the terms offered by the company are suitable.

Dr. Tellis emphasizes importance of providing accurate and timely 'close air support' to army in the required quantities. This facet of air force operations will be critically important in a future conflict due to the limitations imposed on the maneuver in mountains by the difficulties presented by the terrain and not to risk crossing Pakistan's so-called nuclear redlines in the plains. Hence, it is necessary for the Indian armed forces to augment their firepower capabilities by an order of magnitude. He carefully analyzes the requirement of acquiring dedicated close air support aircraft to support ground operations and concludes that the American A-10 Thunderbolt would be a good option for India. When the MiG-27 enters the phase of obsolescence in five years' time, it would be good for India to begin inducting an aircraft that is designed to strike targets on the ground like the A-10 or the Russian SU-39. The process for acquiring such an aircraft must begin now. Simultaneously, the holdings of precision-guided munitions must be significantly enhanced to achieve stocking levels of up to 30%. Also, the time has come to introduce unmanned combat air vehicles (UCAVs) or combat drones into service in large enough numbers to influence operations on the ground. He brings to bear his considerable knowledge and experience as an analyst with Project Air Force at the RAND Corporation and later at CEIP to analyze a complex subject and explain it in easy-to-understand terms. His latest offering should be compulsory reading for policy makers and members of India's strategic community."

[Brigadier Gurmeet Kanwal (Retired) is Distinguished Fellow, Institute for Defense Studies and Analyses and former Director, Centre for Land Warfare Studies, New Delhi].

Fortunately for the IAF and the country, PM Modi ordered 36 fully loaded Rafale (Rafael) fighter aircrafts from France in 2016 through a government-to-government deal obviating the middle- men that were the practice by the erstwhile corrupt UPA government under its titular head Manmohan. In October 2018, during President Vladimir Putin's two-day visit to New Delhi, India and Russia signed for four Units pf S-400 defense system – world's most advanced and unimpregnable air defenses system that holds no challenge from even the US!

Relations with America are on the mend and at a much better level, thanks to PM Modi's foreign policy and personal equation and relationship with President Donald Trump. On 15th November 2018, a news item, *'India best trade negotiator, Modi a friend', says Trump at White House Diwali celebrations.* "President Donald Trump participates in a Diwali ceremonial lighting of the Diya in the Roosevelt Room of the White House, Tuesday, Nov. 13, 2018, in Washington. On Tuesday, he described India as "very good negotiators" as he celebrated Diwali in the White House along with top Indian Americans and said he is "grateful" for his friendship with Prime Minister Narendra Modi. "The United States has deep ties to the nation of India, and I am grateful for my friendship with Prime Minister Modi," Trump said before lighting the ceremonial Diya in the historic Roosevelt Room of the White House. It is the second consecutive year that Trump has celebrated the largest festival of India and Indian Americans in the White House. "We're trying very hard to make better trade deals with India. But, they're very good traders. They're very good negotiators. You would say right. The best. So, we're working. And it's moving along," Trump said referring to the India-US trade deal negotiations that have started between the two largest democracies of the world. Along with nearly two dozen top Indian American officials of his Administration, President Trump had invited the Indian Ambassador to the US, Navtej Singh Sarna, his wife Dr Avina Sarna, and his special assistant Pratik Mathur to be present during the White House Diwali celebrations, a rare. "India is the world's largest democracy and the relationship between our two countries connect as a bulwark for freedom, prosperity, and peace," Trump said. "Modi is my friend and now her (Ivanka) friend and has great respect for India and the Indian people that I can say," said the US

President as he introduced his daughter to the audience, who was present in the room. "Absolutely," replied Ivanka, who had visited India last year. She was the first top official of the Trump Administration to travel to India.

Sarna in his brief remarks thanks the President for this great honor for India and this great Indian community putting. "They feel very welcome here and so integrated with the American society," he said. "I think, we are looking at one of the best times we ever had in India-US relationship," Sarna said, which was agreed by Trump. "I think, that's true. Very close, closer than ever before," said the US President. In his remarks, Trump welcomed senior Indian American officials gathered at the White House for Diwali celebration. "As we light the Diya in the White House, we are joined by in a fellowship with all of those who light lamps in their own home, cities and places of worship. America is a land of faith and we are truly fortunate to have these wonderful traditions woven into the tapestry of our national life. And that is true," he said.

Trump said that he is thrilled to celebrate Diwali at the White House. "I'm honored to host this beautiful ceremony at the White House. Very, very special people. We're gathered today to celebrate a very special holiday observed by Buddhist, Sikhs and Jains throughout the United States and around the world. Hundreds of millions of people have gathered with family and friends to light the Diya and to mark the beginning of a New year: very special new year," he said. "Our nation is blessed to be home to millions of hardworking citizens of Indian and South East Asian heritage to enrich our country in countless ways. Together we are one proud American family. Do we agree with that? I think so. I think we do. Right? Better, believe it," he said. Trump said Americans of Indian and South East Asian heritage have done an incredible job and identified several of them by name including the chairman of the FCC, Ajit Pai; Manisha Singh, Acting Under Secretary of the Department of State; Seema Verma, Administrator of the Centers of Medicare and Medicaid Services; Uttam Dhillon, Acting Administrator of the Drug Enforcement Administration; Neil Chatterjee, Chairman of the Federal Energy Regulatory Commission and Raj Shah, the Deputy White House Press Secretary.

The first White House Diwali celebrations was held in 2003 under the then US President George W Bush, who never attended Diwali celebrations in person. A senior administration official represented him. It was mostly held in the India Treaty Room of Executive Office Building, which is part of the White House complex. Since 2003, Diwali celebrations at the

White House has become an annual tradition. In 2009, President Barack Obama lighted the ceremonial lamp in the East room of the White House. The event was attended by about 200 guests. In 2013, First Lady Michelle Obama celebrated Diwali in the East Room. Immediately before the celebrations, she participated in a Bollywood dance with local students in the State Dining Room. In 2016, Obama celebrated Diwali in the Oval Office with a group of Indian Americans officials from his administration. In 2016, Vice President Biden hosted a Diwali reception at his official residence Number One Observatory Circle. In 2017 President Trump celebrated his first Diwali in the Oval Office with Ambassador Nikki Haley, senior officials from his administration and a small group of Indian Americans. Over the years, it is being celebrated by the Indian Americans in Pentagon and the State Department. For the past several years, Diwali is also being celebrated at the US Capitol by Rep and Senators, being hosted by India Caucus.

14] *__Nature's most sinister danger signal is 'Climate Change'__* because of our incessant tinkering with the environment for centuries without adopting safeguards. This phenomenon can only be tackled with the co-operation of every country of the world. Unfortunately, there is no real consensus on the line of action as there is a diarchy between the developed nations and the developing countries. Likewise, pollution remains a colossal problem and a threat to development and progress. Latest international research studies have shown that *over 5.5 million people die prematurely every year due to air pollution alone.* Half of these are in India and China, validating what earlier country-specific studies repeatedly hinted at. What is worse, the death count is projected to swell in coming decades even if pollution is contained at the present level.

Another likely danger of great import could be the increase in the frequency of earthquakes in south Asia, very well elaborated on FIRSTPOST in Anshu Lal's 14th April 2016 article, *'Natural time-bomb: Alarming frequency of earthquakes in South Asia should worry us'*. The region witnessed:

> 13 April: Earthquake of magnitude 6.9 strikes Myanmar, tremors felt in east India,
>
> 10 April: Six killed in Pakistan after 6.6-magnitude earthquake hits Kabul, tremors felt in India,

8 April: Mild tremor of magnitude 4.2 hits Nepal,

22 February: Moderate earthquake of magnitude 5.5 hits Nepal,

20 January: 6.1-magnitude earthquake strikes China,

4 January: 6.7-magnitude earthquake hits Manipur in India, 11 people killed.

When headlines like these become a bit too common, you know that they point to something bigger. It has been three and a half months since 2016 began. And since that time, we have seen six major earthquakes in South Asia. That means on an average, there were two earthquakes in South Asia every month. It is safe to say that the number of earthquakes in or affecting South Asia have risen to an alarming frequency, even before the beginning of this year. And apart from the fact that the effect of these earthquakes is devastating, the regularity of these tremors has created fears that South Asia could witness a situation like the one after the 2015 Nepal earthquake, which resulted in the death of over 8,000 people. But something even more worrying than the fact that the frequency of earthquakes has increased is the fact that researchers and scientists have predicted that an earthquake even more destructive than the 2015 Nepal earthquake may hit South Asia in the Himalayan region. After the Manipur earthquake in January, the disaster management experts in the Ministry of Home Affairs (MHA) had warned that an earthquake of magnitude 8.2 or even greater could hit the already ruptured Himalayan region. The 2015 Nepal earthquake was of magnitude 7.9 on Richter scale.

According to this report in *The Times of India*, a series of earthquakes since the 2011 Sikkim earthquake re-ruptured the Himalayan region which had already developed cracks due to previous earthquakes. "The current conditions might trigger at least four earthquakes greater than 8.0 in magnitude. And if they delay, the strain accumulated during the centuries provokes more catastrophic mega earthquakes," the report quoted Roger Balham, seismologist of University of Colorado, as saying. The report had also said that over half of the Indian landmass was prone to earthquakes. Experts at the National Institute of Disaster Management (NIDM) had further said in the report that stress in the mountains of the north-east had increased since the Nepal earthquake and the collision between the

Himalayan plate in the north and the Indo-Burmese plate in the east had put the entire region at risk.

Another report in *The Wall Street Journal* said that scientists were concerned about the area west of the Nepal earthquake, where the plates were still locked. It is possible that the 2015 earthquake "failed to rupture the locked portions of the Himalayan thrust beneath and west of the Kathmandu basin because of some persistent barrier of mechanical and structural origin," the report quoted a paper published in Nature Geoscience as saying. The report added that the stress in the locked western Himalayan region could be released by an "after slip", which could cause a large earthquake. Scientists have been predicting a massive earthquake ever since the 2015 earthquake struck Nepal.

According to this April 2015 *IANS* report, experts had said even then that a temblor of equal intensity is "overdue" in northern India. "An earthquake of the same magnitude is overdue. That may happen either today or 50 years from now... in the region of the Kashmir, Himachal, Punjab and Uttarakhand Himalayas. Seismic gaps have been identified in these regions," BK Rastogi, the director general of the Ahmedabad-based Institute of Seismological Research, had said. This is because the movement of tectonic plates generates stress over time, and rocks at the surface break in response. When the stress accumulates, every 100 km stretch of the 2,000-km-long Himalayas can be hit by a high-magnitude earthquake. "The accumulation of stress is going on everywhere. But where it will reach the elastic limit, we don't know nor also when. But what we do know is that it is happening everywhere (sic)," Rastogi had added. [With agency inputs]

15] The *internal* factors weakening my country such as aping the Western education system unsuitable for our milieu and abandoning teaching our school children on our oldest Hindu civilization, culture and rich heritage such as Ramayana, Mahabharata, Bhagwadgita, Kautilya Shastra; our discoveries dating back to the times when the presently advanced West was totally uncivilized, backward, illiterate and rudimentary, ours was shining brightly. We produced great inventors & discoverers, established philosophers, writers and poets including the greatest, Kalidasa; ancient age-old celebrated real heroes from the not too distant past such as Maharana Pratap, Chhatrapati Shivaji, Guru Gobind Singh and their likes; and in the recent past great revolutionaries to name a few, Swami

Vivekananda, Aurobindo Ghosh, Netaji Subhas Chandra Bose, Ras Behari Bose, Chandrashekhar Azad, Bhagat Singh, Ashfaqullah Khan, Ram Prasad 'Bismil' and their ilk. Our children and students are not taught our rich history. Not even the true story of freedom struggle. It was only one person to whom the honor of obtaining independence should be credited. And he is Subhas Bose who fought the British on the war front. Lord Clement Attlee who introduced 'India Independence Bill' in British parliament on 16 June 1946 testifies that during his visit to Calcutta in 1952. When asked about INC and its Gandhi, he said, "We had finished them long ago." When Sir Winston Churchill was interviewed by a journalist who asked the question that Gandhi would go to 'Fast unto death' and there would be public unrest, he replied, "Who is bothered about the half-naked Fakir. His life matters a shit to us." *All this and many other most relevant facts have been erased or blocked from history.*

16] *Reluctance to follow our multi-millennia-old culture and civilization* *i.e. almost total degradation of moral and other values; administration's inability to enforce the law of the land; deeply fractious society that is hardly nationalistic except in times of war, major calamity or cricket/hockey match against Pakistan; lack of proper education and the system to impart it; presence of unsuspecting pseudo-seculars, pseudo-intellectuals, separationists, traitors and anti-nationalists in sizeable numbers; illegal immigrants, Kashmiri separatists and Pak-sponsored terrorists duly sanctioned/ supported/protected by pseudo-secular anti-national political parties; corruption to the core with politicization and dishonesty in every walk of life; black money parked in safe tax havens abroad; religion-/caste-based reservations in education and government jobs; unduly long and relatively lax and lop-sided unequal judicial process* (based on a faulty assumption that the guilt has to be proved by the government investigating agencies rather than the offender) pose a more ominous challenge. *Vote-bank politics destroyed the fabric of unity.* We are emotional reactionaries lacking in analytic acumen. We believe in hearsay/statement by others without thinking or exercising own critical judgement. We are easily swayed over by false propaganda. Late PM Indira used to say: *"A lie repeatedly uttered maybe 100 times or more becomes the truth."* Worth issue is practically everyone is for sale provided you pay the price.

It is worth quoting a foreigner (a New Zealand citizen) to elaborate this point: This may be a hard-hitting (below the belt) observation by a white. This view on rampant corruption here is worth noting. "Indians are Hobbesian i.e. 'Culture of Self-interest'. Corruption in India is a cultural aspect. Indians seem to think nothing about corruption, it is everywhere. Indians tolerate corrupt individuals rather than correct them. No race can be congenitally corrupt. But, can a race be corrupted by its culture? To know why Indians are corrupt, look at their patterns and practices.

First: Religion is transactional in India. Indians give Gold, Cash, and anticipate an out-of-turn reward. Such a plea acknowledges that favors are needed for the undeserving. In the world outside the temple walls, such a transaction is named 'bribe'. A wealthy Indian gives not cash but gold crowns and such baubles. His gifts can feed the poor. His 'pay-off' is for God. He thinks it will be wasted if it goes to a needy man. In June 2009, *The Hindu* published a report of Karnataka minister G Janardhan Reddy gifting a crown of gold and diamonds worth INR 450 million at the famed Tirupati Temple. India's temples collect so much that they don't know what to do with it. Billions are gathering dust in temple vaults. Indians believe that if God accepts money for his favors, then nothing is wrong in doing the same thing. Therefore, Indians are corruptible. Indian culture accommodates such transactions morally. There is no real stigma. An utterly corrupt Jayalalithaa can make a comeback, just unthinkable in the West!

Second: Indian *moral ambiguity towards corruption is visible in its Past*. Indian history tells us of the capture of cities and kingdoms after guards were paid off to open the gates, and commanders paid off to surrender. Personal rivalries led to the traitors inviting foreign mercenaries to attack their perceived rivals. Classical examples: Raja Jaichand bribed by Khawaja Chishti of Ajmer *Dargah* for inviting Mohammed Ghori of Afghanistan to attack his close relative and the last Hindu king of Delhi, Prithvi Raj Chauhan for the 18th time after Ghori's earlier 17 successive defeats inflicted by Chauhan; Mir Jaffer by Robert Clive in the 1757 Battle of Plassey; Mir Qasim by the British in order to defeat the powerful Tipu Sultan, the Muslim king of Mysore; or Gulab Singh, who was later bequeathed the J&K province of the most powerful Sikh King Maharaja Ranjit Singh, in the two Anglo-Sikh Wars of 1846 and 1849. *This sort of traitor-ship is unique to India*. Our corrupt nature has meant limited warfare fought compared to ancient Greece and modern Europe. The Turks' battles with Nadir Shah were vicious and fought to finish. In India, fighting was not needed, bribing was enough to see off the armies. Any invader willing to pay cash could brush aside India's kings, no matter how many tens of thousands of soldiers were in the infantry. Little resistance was offered by the 50,000-strong army of Nawab Siraj-ud-Daula when Clive bribed Mir Jaffer and all Bengal (present day Bangladesh, West Bengal, Orissa, Bihar and Jharkhand) folded to an army of 2,000 whites and 8,000 Indian sepoys. There was always a financial exchange to taking Indian forts. Golconda was captured in 1687 after the secret hind gate was left open for inexplicable reasons. Less powerful Mughals vanquished the most powerful Marathas in *Third Battle of Panipat*; and, the Rajputs with nothing but bribes and buying over other minor Rajput kings for example Raja Man Singh by Akbar to break the back of great warrior Maharana Pratap. It is a different story that Pratap's younger brother Shakti Singh who was also on the side of Akbar rescued Pratap giving him his own horse after Pratap's Chetak was fatally wounded; and Pratap could regain practically the whole of Chttaur before he died. The Raja of Srinagar gave up Dara Shikoh's son Sulaiman to tyrant Aurangzeb after receiving a bribe. There are many cases where Indians participated on a large scale in reason due to bribery. The question is' *'Why Indians have a transactional culture while other 'civilized' nations don't?'*

<u>Third</u>: Indians do not believe in the theory that they can rise if each of them behaves morally, because that is not the message of their faith. Their caste system separates them. They don't believe that all men are equal. This resulted in their division and migration to other religions. Many Hindus started their own faith like Jains, Buddhists, Sikhs and many converted to Islam and Christianity. The result is that Indians don't trust one another. *There are no Indians in India, there are Hindus, Muslims, Christians, Sikhs and what not! Indians choose to forget that only 800 years ago they all belonged to only one faith i.e. Hinduism. This division evolved an unhealthy culture. The inequality has resulted in a corrupt society. In India, everyone is thus against everyone else, except God. And even He must be bribed."*

17] <u>Politics is the last refuge of scoundrels.</u>

As said by a downright honest prime minister of Britain some centuries ago has become a reality and norm in my country. We have the most corrupt, inept, rudderless not so patriotic rather anti-national politicians. Any undesirable/opportunistic person who wants to break the law of the land with impunity breaks away from his/her normal moorings, joins a political party, or even floats one and becomes its autocratic dictator. There examples galore. I cite just two: First, a person denied chance to lead the party he was working for since birth floats another i.e. Raj Thackeray leaving SS to float his own MNS. Second, an IIT Kharagpur graduate (via a backdoor entry into the Institute) and ex-IRS officer, starts running an NGO (along with a friend who is now his deputy) while well in service and becomes an activist winning Magsaysay Award, joins the bandwagon of an honest Gandhian and real well-wisher and reformer, gains popularity and public praise becomes an opportunistic and forms a political party – Aam Admi Party – totally against the advice of the same mentor. He starts cheating the masses through his brand of politics. [see @anilkohli54]

The New York Times' report on this: Fireworks have become increasingly popular at religious festivals in India, set off by children and adults in streets and in parking lots, as well as on temple grounds. Religious groups and temples, flush with donations, compete to create the loudest, brightest displays. Accidents are common, though the scale of devastation on Sunday was unusual. Hours after the explosions on Sunday, the police in Kerala opened an official criminal investigation of two top temple officials, PS Jayalal, the temple president, and J Krishnankutty Pillai, the temple secretary, could not be reached immediately for comment. S Chandrakumar, a police inspector in the temple town, said the police had begun investigations of 17 people, including the temple leadership, on allegations ranging from culpable homicide to violating the orders of a local authority. On Sunday, the Kerala government ordered a judicial inquiry into the temple deaths, which must be completed within six months. The medical officer of Kollam, Dr. CR Jaysankar, said many of the deaths occurred when pieces of concrete, knocked loose by the explosions, fell on members of the crowd. Some of the dead were burned so badly that they were unrecognizable, according to a statement from Thiruvananthapuram Medical College, which received some of the first victims. The explosions began around 3 a.m., and rescue operations were still underway as of 9:30 a.m., with some people still trapped. The force of the explosions caused buildings and electrical lines to collapse as far as 50 feet away. Neethu Reghukumar, a *CNN-IBN* television reporter at the scene, said by telephone that the fireworks were being set off in a small area next to the temple, less than 300 feet away from houses, when high-intensity fireworks being stored in a concrete building inside the temple premises caught fire after one of the devices landed there. A huge explosion brought down the building, and an adjacent building also collapsed, Ms. Reghukumar said. Many houses in the vicinity were damaged, their windows, doors and walls cracked, she said. The explosions also tore apart bodies, witnesses said in television interviews. One woman interviewed on *CNN-IBN* described finding human remains inside her house and on the roof. PM Modi commented on the episode on *Twitter*, saying, "Fire at temple in Kollam is heart-rending & shocking beyond words." Television stations showed PM Modi arriving in Kerala on Sunday afternoon and heading to visit the vicinity of the temple and victims in hospitals. Puttingal temple is 40 miles from the state capital, Thiruvananthapuram. Residents believe that a goddess appeared on an ant hill that is now the site of the Hindu temple.

On 11th April 2016, *Rediff.com News* reported an article, '*Eyewitness: People disappeared without a trace after the explosion*'. "'*I lost several of my friends, a lot of people I know are severely injured and in hospital. It will take time for all of us to recover. You can't blame any single political party for using their influence to get the fireworks okayed. It is an election year, and everybody wants to please the people.*' Lallu S, a journalist working for *Asianet News*, was born and brought in Paravur where the temple tragedy occurred on the morning of April 10. Like previous years, he was on leave to be a part of the temple festival and was witness to the gruesome tragedy. In this interview, 35-year-old Lallu talks about spending his childhood at Paravur and attending the Puttingal temple festival every year. He spoke to *Shobha Warrier* of *Rediff.com*: "My house is just one-and-a-half km from the temple. We have been staying there from my grandfather's days. This temple has been part of not only my growing up years, but even my grandfather's. Every year, my grandfather used to tell us stories of how it was in his childhood. This is one of the oldest temples and is very famous not only locally, but in neighboring areas too. Its origin can be dated back at least 300 years. It is said that originally the temple was built by the Nair community of the area, but there was a several decades-long disputes about the ownership which went up even to the Supreme Court. I think it was less than two decades ago that the Supreme Court verdict gave the ownership to the four major Nair *karayogams* (community organizations) in the village. Till the verdict came, the temple was under the control of a receiver. Now, a committee constituted by members from each *karayogam* takes care of the temple. After the Supreme Court verdict, the temple was renovated on a very grand scale.

The firework is an age-old tradition practiced in the temple. It is not something that began in recent times. It is believed that Goddess Devi is very fond of fireworks and even the *vedi* (dynamite, a very popular offering in all Devi temples in Kerala). The seven-day festival attracts tens of thousands of people daily from nearby districts of Alleppey and Trivandrum, even Tamil Nadu. The culmination of the festival is the competitive fireworks which is unique to this temple. When I say the Puttingal temple is one of the two temples in Kerala that has a *Kampa pura* (proper storehouse for explosives for the fireworks), you can imagine how important fireworks are to the temple festival. Those who raised their voices against the fireworks are the people who came to live near the temple very recently. People like Pankajakshi Amma (the woman who complained against the fireworks) built the house just a few years ago. When I was a child, there used to be so much vacant space around the temple we used to play cricket there. There were only 50 houses in the whole area, but today, there are many new houses built around the temple. As this was the most sought-after prime land in the village, people with money started buying land close to the temple, and then they started complaining about the fireworks. Now the entire temple ground is surrounded by houses. They are the people who were against the fireworks because they feared it would damage their houses.

Those who have grown up there never objected to the fireworks because it was part of our lives. Every year, our friends and relatives from other parts come to our home to be a part of the festival. So, when those who came to settle here much later object to something that was part of our lives, those who have been staying here for decades used to get a bit offended. All of us who grew up in the village make it a point to take leave and come to Paravur to attend the festival. We may miss Onam, but none from the village miss the temple festival. The uniqueness of the festival is it is not just Hindus, but the entire village, Christians and Muslims included, actively participate in it. There was a ban on fireworks in Kerala after a tragedy, which lasted for 10 years. It was only during that period that we didn't have any fireworks. Even then, people from other places used to come here anticipating at least small fireworks. I still remember as children we used to wait eagerly till morning for the fireworks to happen. Even in those days, with the police around, there used to be at least a small firework display here. This year when it was first announced that there would not be any fireworks as permission was denied by the collector, there was disappointment among the local people. I was in Paravur on three-day leave. On the last day of the festival, by 7 in the evening, all the festivities would end, and the finale is the fireworks for which everyone looks forward to. If it is music performances by well-known singers as culmination in other temples, it is fireworks for this temple.

My friends and I used to sit in an area near the temple, just opposite the store house. We had occupied a place there when one of my friends dragged us to his house. He insisted on all of us sitting on his home terrace, just 150 meters away from the temple. It was past midnight that the competitive fireworks started. Till 3 am, it went on well. That was when the explosion happened. The place where we had sat and all those who were sitting there disappeared completely without any trace after the explosion. When we first saw the first explosion, we thought some of the explosives which had not burst initially must have burst. Only later, did we realize what exactly happened. Then we ran to the ground and what we saw was unexplainable. Parts of bodies were strewn all over and people were wailing in pain. Those who were not hurt gathered the injured and put them in buses and took them to hospital. Every single person who was there, irrespective of caste and religion, was involved in the rescue. I lost several of my friends, a lot of people I know are severely injured and in hospital. It will take time for all of us to recover.

You can't blame any single political party for using their influence to get the fireworks okayed. It is an election year, and everybody wants to please the people. When people of the area want fireworks, the local politicians also will try to make them satisfied. The candidates from all the three major political parties worked to get permission and you cannot blame them for that. See, till last year, everything was going on smoothly and nobody expected something of this sort to happen. If this had not happened, it would have continued next year too. You cannot blame the temple authorities too as the pressure from people to have the temple festival in a certain way is too much. At present, people of this village are in such a huge shock that they are not able to say whether they want fireworks again. But I believe banning something is not the answer." [*Shobha Warrior/Rediff.com*]

18] <u>Atmospheric and Mental Pollution are taking a heavy toll of ours and country's health.</u>

It is especially so that of our children and coming generations as pollution leads to many pathologies within our body and social systems. An interesting blog by Sundar A.S., '*Is 'Pollution' Becoming India's Passion?*' appeared on *India Opines*. "Let me make it clear that my intention is not to criticize what is happening in India. My attempt is more of an introspective nature aimed at correcting ourselves. I feel that there are lot of issues in India which are just denied and allowed to be as it is. This is indirectly denying an opportunity for correction. Please read my blog 'Say Sorry and see the change', on how admission of guilt can lead to correction.

Gasping for breath.... I think I am the best person to write on this problem as I have been a victim of this air pollution for the last decade or so. In fact, I have changed my residences and places of stay because this persisting pollution problem. I had a robust respiratory system gifted by God, till people living around my residence chose to challenge it. In fact, I was staying in a down south town in Tamil Nadu well known for its educated people. The place is scenic and was a part of God's own country until 1954.The town is so literate that you will find a post-graduate in every house even during as early as the 1970s. The town is so beautiful endowed with nature' s bounty but every morning I wake up, not to the chirpy sounds of sparrows but to the disturbing smoke set by my loving neighbors.

GARBAGE Is 'Pollution', Becoming India's Passion? They gather all the dried leaves falling from the trees in the compounded houses and set fire like a towering inferno! The fire rises ten feet or so setting environment into a smoky cloud you can hardly see through! Don't think that this fire is set only in one house near my residence. In fact, simultaneously around five neighboring houses set fire almost at the same time! Struggling for breathing I venture out fast to save myself early in the morning! Alas! As I come out, I find the municipal people who clean all the garbage put them all in a place in the road and set fire with glee! So, I run away to a school ground. Thankfully, school people do not wake up that early to set up their fire ritual. Often my breathing had reached critical conditions that I had to rush to a hospital! On my way to the hospital I find smoky fumes from fires set in houses and roads everywhere say around 100-meter apart! The place I am mentioning is known for respiratory problems and none of the doctorates there realize that it is the pollution that they so much love, that is responsible for the respiratory problems. When I told the doctor attending me, he was smiling and responding: "Well, that's part of the culture here!" He would be happy as he gets more respiratory disease patients! This, in fact, led me to wonder whether pollution and garbage is an essential part of Indian culture!

Testing your driving skills? The coconuts strewn all around will eventually add on to 'Pollution'. As I go for my daily walk, I find broken pieces of coconut strewn all over the street every Friday. This is part of the religious ritual of breaking a coconut in front of the shops by dashing it against the road. As the coconut breaks into pieces of various sizes with sharp edges they get strewn all over the road. The two wheelers crossing the road do a zig zag drive avoiding the sharp edges of the coconut pieces and the entire coconut gets wasted as even beggars do not pick up pieces strewn over dirty roads. Even animals do not or cannot eat them. However, let us understand that the intention behind this ritual is good. The coconut pieces are meant for the poor to pick and eat when it is broken. They could have broken it neatly and arranged it in a plate for anyone to eat. It is simply not in our culture to do so.

Here are the other polluting practices of India:

- All religious rituals involve flowers and are strewn all over during the function. It is never cleaned up later.
- Death/Funeral Procession –Flowers thrown all through the roads and water bodies.
- Marriage/Puberty Functions
- Feeding fish/crows –Rice thrown just like it all over
- Garbage disposal—Throwing in the streets
- Crackers during festivals

Why not clean the mess we created ourselves? Even our most pious river Ganga is heavily polluted. Ganga pollution Is Becoming India's Passion!

In countries like Canada, you are responsible for the cleanliness of the frontage of your house. Here in my country, we clean our house and throw the garbage in front of our neighbor's. If every one of us keep 100 sq. ft. of road in front of our house clean, the entire stretch is bound to be neat. Let us join hands to create an awareness in this regard and make India an orderly and pollution-free place to live for all. Let us forget trivial issues like beef, etc. and focus on making our place a better place to breathe and walk. After all it's our country! If we do not keep it neat, who will?"

19] **Our fundamental problem in this once great country has highest degree of politicization.** Our dirty and not so nationalistic politicians want to control every aspect of our lives. They are adept in making illegal money and exerting undesirable political pulls and pushes into practically any issue. It is not surprising that fireworks were used in the temple compound totally against the High Court orders. As dust is settling down, *Rediff.com News* confirmed that in an article titled, *'Political interference ensured fireworks at Paravur temple'* on 13th April 2016: "Kummanam Rajasekharan, who heads the BJP's Kerala unit, visited Paravur along with PM Modi and BJP President Amit Shah hours after the Puttingal temple tragedy. Rajasekharan spoke exclusively to Shobha Warrier/*Rediff.com* about the horrific fire and its aftermath. *When I interviewed you earlier, you told me that Kerala's temples should not be under the control of the Devaswom Board and the state government.* The Paravur temple was administered by a trust.

Do you still think Kerala's temples should not be under the control of the Devaswom Board? Are you saying accidents did not happen in the temples controlled by the Devaswom Board? Accidents happen only because the administrators are not ready to strictly enforce rules. At Paravur also, rules were disobeyed. That was why such a huge tragedy happened. The casual attitude towards breaking rules by the temple administrators is the reason behind the tragedy. It is not because the temple was under the trust that the tragedy happened; it was because of their attitude to rules. Some people feel that temples under the Devaswom Board would have been forced to follow rules and regulations while the others may flout them.

Do you feel so? Rules and regulations are for all to follow and obey; they are not for the temples under the control of the Devaswom Board alone. If the argument has any strength, how did tragedies happen in those temples?

So, you stick to what you said about the administration of temples even today? Who administers the temples, and how accidents happen have no connection at all? What happened at Paravur was a disregard for laws. They didn't follow safety norms and disobeyed the order by the district administration that denied permission.

The question is how did the temple get permission to go ahead with the fireworks? Eyewitnesses say that till 8 pm, it was announced that the collector had denied permission and that they were trying to change it at the higher level through influential people. They say that it was due to political influence that they got permission finally... Exactly. That's the truth. It was only due to political interference that the fireworks happened. The problem lies in the interference of politics in such places. Because of political pressure and interference, administrators find it difficult to enforce rules strictly. *Temples are infested with politics and political activities and that's why rules are not obeyed, and safety not given priority.* This should stop. We must question this attitude.

Local people say that because elections are around the corner, political leaders were pressurized to please the local community that wanted the fireworks to continue... Yes, what we see is the vested interest of political parties. Just to get a few votes, political parties played with fire, they gambled with the safety of the people.

Did the BJP try to influence the higher ups? Do you think the BJP has the power to influence the government of Kerala? It was the Congress leaders who did this. At the temple venue itself, did they not thank the leaders, naming each one of them for making the fireworks happen at the last minute? Some of them were hailing the efforts of these leaders in getting permission.

Thrissur Pooram, the biggest temple festival in Kerala, will happen soon. Reports say they are going ahead with fireworks and parading elephants. Should this be allowed? We have rules and regulations in this country and the temple must strictly follow them. If the administrators see to it that all safety rules are followed correctly, nobody should be worried. (However, after the interview was conducted, the Kerala high court banned hi-decibel firework displays in the state.) We also have rules to be followed if you have elephants under the custody of the temple.

After the Paravur tragedy, many people feel that fireworks and parading elephants at temples should be totally banned. We also have boat races during Onam. If a boat were to capsize and God forbid, many people were to lose lives, would we ban boat races completely? If somebody falls while plucking coconuts, will we ban it? If people are ready to obey the rules and if the administrators are ready to enforce the rules, we can go ahead with all these events.

You mean, banning fireworks is not the way to react to the tragedy? Yes. What happened there was that rules were flouted. So, we should see to it that those who flouted the rules are identified and punished. [Shobha Warrior of *Rediff.com*]

'*As a visitor from abroad, what shocked you the most about India?*', was a question posed in *Quora Digest to* a foreigner, Sommer Shields-*Part flower child and rescuer of ants & part businesswoman.* Upvoted by Sudhanva Rajasekar, an Indian, answered like this: "'I was asked this question today by a colleague after we filmed a live studio show: My response was: 'How long do you have? Let us have a coffee so I can tell you the whole story.' Okay, there are a few big things here and then some other small things: The *first* thing was so shocking that I spent the first few days after learning this, planning how I was going to bring this to the attention of the world...

A] _SHARING: SHARING YOUR WATER_: Westerners reading this, you are going to be shocked!! Indian people share their water... with EVERYONE. Let me give you a little hypothetical situation: You're in India, walking around in Summer time, it's hot, very hot, you have no water, yet a family near you has a bottle, they will SHARE that with you... DO YOU COMPREHEND WORLD. Indian people share their water!! What then?! Other cultures do not do this, it unheard of in fact!

Another situation I experienced: I returned to Los Angeles after 4 months in India. Went for brunch at a Hollywood Cafe, in fact I was having brunch at BEACHWOOD CAFE in North Hollywood. They were charging people for water in a terrible drought. This is the worst kind of opportunism... charging people for a free resource!? I traveled through the whole of India and EVERY single place I EVER went offered a jug of water to drink.... THIRD WORLD COUNTRY.... MMMMM I think not! Indian people are more culturally mature, and this concept of SHARING WATER should be emulated by the world.

B] _RESPECT_. Teenagers and even young adults are so rude in many places. Teenagers and young people in India are respectful of others and their parents. I can't even begin to explain the differences. The young people in India will take over the world - I'm not being overly biased. I am being honest. Let me explain: Western teens are pre-occupied with themselves and many have little respect. Indian teens are extremely respectful, studious and read...they read and study a lot.... (just look at the secrets of successful people like the late Steve Jobs and others like Richards Branson - both whom I've met at different occasions... They read... they read a lot plus they had/have respect for others!

C] _Togetherness and sense of community_. People in India, have a strong sense of community values, everyone is treated like a family member. Maybe some people will find this overwhelming, but Indian people are caring and will care for you! You will be invited to eat on the floor with a family. You will be treated as if you were part of the family. The whole community is strong and works as one entity. How amazing is that! We in the West have lost this trait. There are numerous studies to back up the health/psychological, not to mention life-lengthening. effects on people that have a strong sense of community.

D] _Patriotism_: One of the most memorable examples of this was when I was on a road trip through India and stopped off in the middle of the Thar Desert. I stopped as I saw a make-shift set-up where people were selling wares and I came to discover this was a camel auction. The little children with smiley, sun-kissed faces and dusty clothes were so patriotic, but they have been living with bare essentials. They told me how much they loved India! I also experienced patriotism throughout the whole of India, I visited a school of teens who were so excited to chat with me and tell me about how much they loved their country. Even adults were so positive about the future of their country and culture. This positivity and patriotism are not as common in other countries… people complain about everything…

E] *Last, but not least*: Let me introduce you to this concept of what my Indian friend and I now named: 'highway pooping' LOL!! Okay, seriously to the Western people seeing people poop outside is unique, I guess I covered a lot of ground. So, of course, there were places where people go and make their business outside. My 74-year old father put it to me like this: "People in Paris were doing this in the 70's'. it just goes on to show that every country and probably every culture has gone through plumbing growth… Still I like our saying of 'highway pooping'…. basically, when you drive past people doing their Biz… You say, 'Highway pooping!' it's a little road-trip humor… and I guess immature and just us being silly!!"

SMILE AND BE KIND… It makes you feel better and more attractive to others!!! I hope you enjoyed this post. If you visit India take note of how respectful the young are and how strong the values of the people are, and thus cherish your stay there in India!"

20] **_Black Money_**: Different estimates have been given to the quantum of black money in circulation within the country as parallel economy or sent abroad by Hindustanis year after year all these years. The present government is committed to bringing it back since it was one of the election pranks. Consequently, the formation of a panel to unearth black money was the first act of the NDA government on its very first day in office. There has been some success in this direction, but it must be a long way to go. On 14th January 2015, *'The political roots of black money'* by Subir Roy on *Rediff.com News* made an interesting reading. *"Going off cash does not offer a major solution to the problem of black money.* Cashless transactions are one of the very important solutions to tame black money and should be promoted, PM Modi noted. There is a problem of emphasis here. It is good for people to use as little cash as possible as non-cash (through book transfers in banks) transactions leave a trail that law enforcers like income tax authorities or those tracking money laundering find extremely useful.

But going off cash does not offer a major solution to the problem of black money. *Moral responsibility is the prime backbone to curb black money.*

To understand what works best in fighting black money it is critical to understand what black money is and is not. It is income that is not declared for Income Tax purposes. This can be simply tax evasion by a businessman or a professional engaged in legitimate activity. It can also be much more serious criminal offences like handling money that fuels trafficking in drugs or humans. An enormous amount of black money flows in and out of the banking system and remains black. A government official can take his family out for a lavish meal at a five-star hotel or buy the choicest Scotch whisky from liquor shops with cash taken as bribe. Once these sales enter the books of the hotel chain or the legitimate foreign liquor importer who pay taxes, black money becomes 'white'. Then if the hotel chain's or the liquor importer's liaison person pays a bribe to any official (there are ingenious ways of cloaking it as a legitimate cashless transaction), the amount paid, which will not be declared by the official as income to the tax authorities, becomes black money again. Before going any further let us get a red herring out of the way. During its election campaign, the BJP had promised to bring back black money stashed away by Indians abroad.

How this is anymore black than black money that stays within the country is unclear? It seems there is greater interest in grandstanding on black money than doing something serious about it. Had the latter been the case the primary reason why black money thrives would have been addressed. *Black money thrives because it plays a critical role in Indian elections and no political party of any consequence appears interested in putting an end to this.* Had it been so the way elections are fought would have changed beyond recognition by now. It is widely believed that it costs at least INR50 million and often much more to contest a parliamentary seat today, whereas the Election Commission-approved ceiling for such expenditure by a candidate is a mere INR 7 million. What is fascinating is that many candidates, going by their declared expenses (on paper), do not even spend up to the permitted ceiling!

The Economist, in a report in May last year, picked up a frequently cited quote of Atal Bihari Vajpayee, saying that 'every legislator starts his career with the lie of the false election return he files'. Closer to today, the late Gopinath Munde, then deputy leader of the BJP in the Lok Sabha, in 2013 publicly admitted that he had spent INR80 million for his 2009 parliamentary election, and then, on being issued a show cause notice by the Election Commission, denied the statement by saying it was 'rhetoric'.

Thus, how much gets spent in fighting elections is hardly a well-kept state secret. It is easy to see what such electioneering lets loose. A person who has spent INR50 million in getting elected will want to recoup that principal, plus inflation plus a reasonable return to create a corpus with which to fight for his re-election. Thus, in five years he will want to making close to INR100 million in black money or more. If legislators who rule the country face this kind of compulsion to generate black money for their own political future, how can they be expected to put in place a system that will bring an end to the generation of black money? It is, therefore, unsurprising that there is a big hole in the rules on permissible election expenses. While there is a cap on what a candidate can spend for his election, nothing like that exists for political parties. What is more, donations up to INR 20,000 are not treated as donations and can be reported without any details. So, all that a party needs to do to account for, say, INR 10 million, is to claim that it received it in the form of 500 donations of INR 20,000 each! Other rules, in this regard, are either of minuscule size and consequence (companies can now officially make political contributions) or routinely flouted (filing returns on expenses within 90 days of an election). *There is no attempt to change the rules where they matter.* The entire political class, across parties, is complicit in this. [Source: *Business Standard*]

A follow up of the election promise of BJP shows there has been some success in recovering black money parked abroad. On 28th June 2016, *Jagruk Bharat* reported under, *'MODI EFFECT: Foreign Countries Allow India to Recover INR 130,000,000,000 Black Money'*. "The government's crackdown on those individuals who stashed undeclared income in overseas bank accounts has started yielding results with the Income Tax authorities having unearthed more than INR130 billion from just two sets of information received in 2011 and 2013. In at least 400 cases of Indians with deposits in HSBC, Geneva, the details of which were received from the French government in 2011, the Income Tax (I-T) authorities have unearthed undisclosed income of INR81.86 billion, the highest disclosure ever from offshore bank accounts, and raised a tax demand of about INR 53.77billion against such account-holders till March 31, 2016, according to an I-T assessment report. In the HSBC case, the government had received information about 628 bank accounts. Of these, at least 213 were found "not actionable" as they either had no money in them or they belonged to nonresident Indians. Also, in some cases, the entities remained untraceable. "Out of the actionable cases, assessments have been completed in 398 cases, including those settled by the I-T Settlement Commission as well as cases where assessment proceedings have been dropped," according to the I-T report. A HSBC spokesperson declined to comment. Based on another set of information disclosed in 2013 on the website of the International Consortium of Investigative Journalists (ICIJ), a Washington-based organization, I-T officials have detected undisclosed income of INR50 billion in foreign bank accounts allegedly linked to 700 Indians.

So far, the I-T department has filed 55 prosecution complaints before criminal courts in the ICIJ cases on charges of willful attempt to evade tax. The basis has been false statements made by these entities during the verification process. In the HSBC Geneva case, tax authorities have launched prosecution proceedings in 75 cases, a majority for willful attempt to evade tax. The criminal courts have taken cognizance in most of these prosecution complaint cases, paving the way for the Enforcement Directorate to initiate actions under the stringent Prevention of Money Laundering Act (PMLA). The recently enacted Black Money Undisclosed Foreign Income and Assets Act has made the "willful attempt to evade tax "as a predicate offence under the PMLA, giving the ED powers to attach and confiscate properties of an accused equivalent to the amount stashed abroad. The I-T report said many Indians whose names appeared in the ICIJ cases had filed declarations under the black money declaration window scheme, which the government had launched for a limited period during 2015. However, those individuals against whom the department had already launched probe were not eligible for any relief."

'What Is Mossack Fonseca, the Law Firm in the Panama Papers?', was the title of the news item published by David Graham on *The Atlantic*, reported by *MSN News* on 4th April 2016. "We're proud of the work we do. Jürgen Mossack was already a citizen of the world when he first hung his shingle in Panama City in 1977. Born in Germany and raised and educated in Panama, the twenty-something had gone to London to work as a lawyer in 1975, returned two years later and began practicing. Since then, the firm he founded has become a global behemoth—hundreds of employees spread around the world, with special expertise in creating tax shelters for wealthy global elites. The firm is also, according to documents in the 'Panama Papers', deeply involved with all manner of unsavory and possibly illegal practices across continents.

The enormous document leak, reported by *Süddeutsche Zeitung*, the International Consortium of Investigative Journalists, and others worldwide, offers a new view of Mossack Fonseca, the firm that Jürgen Mossack established. The leak consists of a stunning 2.6 terabytes of data, dating back to 1977. The documents purport to show Mossack Fonseca's dealings with world leaders, company officers' internal discussions about court cases, and communication about sheltering money obtained through crimes. The Panama Papers put a much greater focus than ever before on a firm whose stock in trade is maintaining opacity for its clients—a strategy it has pursued for itself. Even within the world of attorneys who create shell corporations, Mossack Fonseca has been described, by *The Economist* in 2012, as "tight-lipped." But a silhouette of the firm's history can be drawn from reports and court cases over the years.

Mossack reportedly comes from a colorful family. His father, Erhard, moved the family to Latin America after World War II. The ICIJ reports: Erhard Mossack served in the Waffen-SS during the war and U.S. intelligence files show he offered to spy for the U.S. government, possibly simply to shield himself. He later offered to spy for the CIA, from Panama, on Communists in Cuba. *Süddeutsche Zeitung* reports that Germany's Federal Intelligence Service declined to hand over documents relating to Erhard Mossack due to possible security risks.

Jürgen Mossack's practice only became Mossack Fonseca in 1986, when it merged with the tiny firm run by Ramón Fonseca, a Panamanian novelist, lawyer, and politician. Once Fonseca once reportedly told a journalist, *"Together we have created a monster."* That same year, 1986, according to the Panama Papers, Mossack learned he was involved in a front company for men who had robbed 3.5 tons of gold—£26 million at the time, and more now—from a Brink's-Mat depot near London Heathrow Airport in 1983. "The company has not behaved illegally," Mossack wrote in a memo copied to Fonseca. "But it could be that the company invested money through bank accounts and properties that was illegitimately sourced." Instead, MF served as legal advisers to a new shell company created for Gordon Parry, who was on the lam and later served 10 years in prison for laundering money from the robbery. London's Metropolitan Police had seized shares in the previous shell company, but under Mossack's tutelage, The Guardian reports, Parry was able to outfox police by diluting the seized shares, then reconstituting the company. That trick involved "bearer shares," which seem to have become something of a MF specialty. A 'bearer share' grants control of an instrument or company directly to whoever possesses a physical certificate. The ownership is not recorded or registered anywhere else. Bearer shares are banned in some countries because of the high potential for fraud and money laundering.

One place where MF took advantage of the possibilities posed by bearer shares was the British Virgin Islands. MF first expanded there in 1987; the BVI are now home to 40 percent of the world's offshore companies, according to some counts. According to the Panama Papers, MF's use of the tool grew steadily through the 1990s. But in 2005, the BVI cracked down on bearer shares, so MF simply switched that business to Panama. While MF's use of bearer shares spiked sharply at home around that time, it since appears to have declined significantly.

MF has always been relatively open about its work creating tax havens. On its website, the firm advertises expertise in jurisdictions including "Belize, The Netherlands, Costa Rica, United Kingdom, Malta, Hong Kong, Cyprus, British Virgin Islands, Bahamas, Panama, British Anguilla, Seychelles, Samoa, Nevada, and Wyoming (USA)." (Nevada and Wyoming are notorious among U.S. states for their loose regulatory regimes; in 2011, a professor told Reuters, "Somalia has slightly higher standards than Wyoming and Nevada.")

In 2001, Ramses Owens, a top MF lawyer, spoke on the Isle of Man—itself a tax haven—to drum up business. "I would maintain that Panama is one of the world's best kept secrets in terms of its long established and sophisticated financial regulatory system," he said. "Because Panama has much to offer, I decided to set the record straight and embark on a series of presentations." Owens spoke along with an MF lawyer based on the isle and another based on the Channel Island of Jersey—yet another tax shelter. ("Ramses also likes to break into a little salsa to liven up the proceedings," a reporter with the Isle of Man Courier noted.)

MF has had its share of legal and regulatory troubles abroad, even before the wave of investigations likely to follow on the Panama Papers. In 2012 and 2013, BVI regulators fined the company for violating money-laundering protections on several occasions, including one involving the son of toppled Egyptian dictator Hosni Mubarak. In the mid-1990s, MF helped the tiny South Pacific atoll of Niue establish itself as a magnet for offshore companies. "Importantly, Niue offered registration in Chinese or Cyrillic characters, making it attractive to Chinese and Russian customers," ICIJ notes. But after the State Department suggested Niue was a center for money laundering and several banks quit doing business there, MF's relationship with the government cooled. Even as it encountered problems overseas, MF remained in good stead at home—a fact that wasn't simply a product of its size or legal acumen. The company also had close political ties through Ramón Fonseca. Fonseca is something of a renaissance man: In addition to this work as a lawyer, he has also published several novels, two of which won the Ricardo Miró Prize, a national literary award. When Panamanian President Juan Carlos Varela entered office in 2014, Fonseca was named an adviser. He was also acting president of Varela's political party. Still, authorities were scrutinizing MF around the world. In a 2014 feature for Vice, Ken Silverstein traced the bank's connections to Rami Makhlouf, a wealthy Syrian businessman and a cousin and close associate of President Bashar al-Assad. From 2000 to 2011, MF was the registered agent for Drex, a shell company Makhlouf used in the British Virgin Islands. MF also dealt with alleged "bagmen" for dictators including Zimbabwe's Robert Mugabe and the late Muammar Gaddafi of Libya.

In 2015, Mossack Fonseca's cozy links to several large banks became troublesome. HSBC CEO Stuart Gulliver admitted he had put some of his money in a Panamanian shell company created for him by Mossack Fonseca, a move he said he undertook for privacy. German authorities raided homes and an office of Commerzbank in Frankfurt in spring 2015, and reportedly told journalists they were considering charges against MF employees over tax evasion.

And in the U.S., MF was caught up in another arcane battle. An American hedge fund has been seeking to recoup billions from Argentina after a government default in 2001. (That story, involving escapades like the seizure of an Argentine naval ship in Ghana, is worth reading up on as well.) Tracking down allegedly laundered money, the plaintiff hedge funds ended up in Nevada. The plaintiffs sued MF and its local affiliate, MF Nevada, seeking information. But the Panamanian parent company claimed—somewhat laughably—that MF Nevada was not affiliated with it but simply engaged in business with Mossack Fonseca. MF Nevada's primary employee was Patricia Amunategui, a former cocktail waitress. The Panama Papers show Mossack Fonseca employees speculating worriedly about whether Amunategui can testify without giving up the game. In the end, a judge ruled in favor of the hedge funds and against MF.

Meanwhile, in Brazil, MF is caught up in the corruption scandal that toppled President Dilma Roussef's government. The President was impeached. In the "Operation Car Wash" or "*Lavo Jato*," contractors are alleged to have conspired to drive up the price of contracts from Petrobras, the powerful state oil company while paying kickbacks to politicians and executives. MF is alleged to have helped some of the defendants set up operations to launder money from the scheme. In March, Fonseca resigned his posts as presidential counselor and party chair, vowing to defend his honor. Now, with the huge leak of the Panama Papers, Fonseca and Mossack will have a much greater task ahead in mounting their defense. It seems Fonseca was right that the two lawyers created the monster. Now they will have to find a way to keep it from devouring its creators."

The Indian Express' took up the publishing of Panama Papers from 4th April 2016 displaying one part daily. Apparently, there are 500 Indians with offshore accounts. The Reserve Bank of India which is a part of the Team set up by the FM at the instance of the PM. Both Modi and Jaitley made it clear that those of us who did not use the window period for declaring black money last year and found guilty will not be spared. Conspicuous among them are: Legendary actor Amitabh Bachchan; his daughter-in-law – a former Miss World and Bollywood actor Aishwarya Rai – her father, mother and brother; Harish Salve, senior advocate and son of late Maharashtra Congress leader NKP Salve; Owner of Mehrasons Jewelers, Ashwani Kumar Mehra, wife Mala Rani, sons Deepak Mehra and Navin Mehra and daughters-in-law, Pooja and Shalini; Anurag Kejriwal – the expelled Delhi president of Lok Satta Party; Gautam and Karan Thapar, sons of Brij Mohan Thapar owner of BILT, controlling Crompton Greaves Limited; Satish Govind Samtani, Vishlav Bahadur and Harish Mohnani – all from Bangalore; investment management and IT consultant based in Panchkula, Gautam Seengal; Prabhash Sankhla - retired MP government employee living alone in Indore, his daughter Sheetal Singh and son-in-law Rajeev Singh, both Canadian nationals from Toronto; Vinod Ramchandra Jadhav, chairman of Pune-based Sava Healthcare; $10 million as capital: 10 members of KP Singh's DLF family, three British Virgin Island firms; cricketer Ashok Malhotra, who runs a cricket academy in Kolkata; Panchkula-based Ranjeev Dahuja and Kapil Sain Goel run Berkeley Automobiles, with dealerships of Hyundai and Tata Motors, in Chandigarh; Vivek Jain, a B.Com graduate, running an agriculture equipment store in MP and Nahar Pinkesh.

The Indian Express' published Part-3 of *Panama Papers* on 6th May 2016. The headlines on pages 1, 17 and 19 included: Currency maker offered payoff for its Indian deal-De La Rue authorized 15% commission to agent in India; Mossack Fonseca set up firm linked to Niira Radia; *'Offshore Accounts*-Some reasons may be valid but will probe': Rajan, Governor Reserve Bank of India; 'Have already ordered probe': Justice (MB) Shah (who heads the Special Investigation Team on Black Money); (Amitabh): 'don't know any of the companies'; 'His (Iceland's foreign minister Gunnar Bragi Sveinsson) Boss is Casualty' – all on front page. Amid freeze in Iceland, warmth in Delhi-Iceland foreign minister may cut short India visit (in view of Iceland PM Sigmundur David Gunnlaugsson Bachchan becoming first casualty of the Panama Papers revelations); 'Embarrassing that Padma Awardees figure in Papers; BJP hits back at Congress, Sonia - 'Congress leaders keep asking us every evening where is INR1.5 million?' Let me answer. "This is the story of kidnappers who after abduction come back to see what the police are doing so that they can change their tactic... Congress is the kidnapper who has abducted India's future, money, development and prosperity. And every evening it asks us where is where is our money, development and prosperity... Don't ask us, ask respected Soniaji. If the Almirah is opened, then all the money is inside," said BJP spokesperson Dr. Sambit Patra – all on page 17. *Iceland PM resigns, 1st Panama casualty*: Iceland Government-Gunnlaugsson quits ahead of no-confidence vote, hours before asking President to dissolve parliament; Panama leaks: Sharif forms high-level probe panel – on page 19. Pages 11 to 13 were fully devoted to Panama Papers. The headlines: Rosy Blue also in HSBC List, Diamond dealers are tax haven's best friends, At least 24 offshore companies linked to diamond major Rosy Blue in Mossack Fonseca files; Gambel family also in list; Currency note maker offered to pay for deal-from the front page on page 11. The List-Part Three: Bellary baron, tank tycoon, top industrialist, Responses: Idea is to expand, keep creating and closing companies; it was not my money; it's too long ago to remember now; why should I tell you? Persons' names: Moturi Srinivas Prasad, Satish K Modi, Sanjay Pokhriyal, Prasanna V Ghotage and Vaman Kumar, Bhavanasi Jaya Kumar, Bhaskar Rao, cricketer Ashok Malhotra, Pradeep Kuashikray Buch, Preetam Bothra and Sweta Gupta, Rahul Arunprasad Patel, Bhandari Ashok Ramdyalchand, George Mathew, 'Why drag me in brother's business: (Gautam) Adani' – all on page 12. Mossack Fonseca's bag of tricks, Spies, deals hidden in plain sight, Firm helps CIA operatives and other characters from the world of espionage set up offshore companies to obscure their dealing; Under fire, Cameron says he does not benefit from offshore funds, Labor leader Jeremy Corbyn calls for setting up independent investigation; Credit Suisse, HSBC deny role in tax avoidance net; China blocks news reports on Panama Papers – all on page 13.

The complexity of the process can be gauged from this *BBC News* on 3rd April 2016 given under *BBC Panorama* and titled '*Panama Papers: Mossack Fonseca leak reveals elite's tax havens*' by Richard Bilton. "A huge (11 leak confidential documents have revealed how the rich and powerful use tax havens to hide their wealth. Eleven million documents were leaked from one of the world's most secretive companies, Panamanian law firm Mossack Fonseca. They show how Mossack helped clients launder money, dodge sanctions and evade tax. The company says it has operated beyond reproach for 40 years and has never been charged with criminal wrongdoing. *The documents show links to 72 current or former heads of state in the data, including dictators accused of looting their own countries.* Gerard Ryle, director of the ICIJ, said the documents covered the day-to-day business at Mossack Fonseca over the past 40 years. "I think the leak will prove to be probably the biggest blow the offshore world has ever taken because of the extent of the documents," he said, "Panama Papers - tax havens of the rich and powerful exposed." Eleven million documents held by the Panama-based law firm *Mossack Fonseca* have been passed to German newspaper *Suddeutsche Zeitung*, which then shared them with the International Consortium of Investigative Journalists. *BBC Panorama* is among 107 media organizations - including UK newspaper the Guardian - in 78 countries which have been analyzing the documents. *BBC* doesn't know the identity of the source. They show how the company has helped clients launder money, dodge sanctions and evade tax.

- Fonseca says it has operated beyond reproach for 40 years and never been accused or charged with criminal wrongdoing,
- Tricks of the trade: How assets are hidden? And taxes evaded?
- Panama Papers: Full coverage; follow reaction on Twitter using #Panama Papers; in the *BBC News app*, follow the tag "*Panama Papers*", or
- Watch Panorama at 19:30 on *BBC One* on Monday, 4 April, or catch up later the *BBC iPlayer* (UK viewers only).

The data contains secret offshore companies linked to the families and associates of Egypt's former president Hosni Mubarak, Libya's former leader Muammar Gaddafi and Syria's president Bashar al-Assad. There is a list of 500 popular and powerful Indians including actors Amitabh Bachchan and daughter-in-law Aishwarya Rai with her parents and brother, legal luminary Harish Salve – a close confidant of previous UPA regime, businessmen, and so on.

Russian connection. It also reveals a suspected billion-dollar money laundering ring that was run by a Russian bank and involved close associates of President Putin. The operation was run by *Bank Rossiya*, which is subject to US and EU sanctions following Russia's annexation of Crimea. The documents reveal for the first time how the bank operates.

Media caption. A huge leak of confidential documents has revealed how the rich and powerful use tax havens to hide their wealth. Money has been channeled through offshore companies, two of which were officially owned by one of the Russian president's closest friends. Concert cellist Sergei Roldugin has known Vladimir Putin since they were teenagers and is godfather to the president's daughter Maria. On paper, Roldugin has personally made hundreds of millions of dollars in profits from suspicious deals. But documents from Roldugin's companies state that: *"The company is a corporate screen established principally to protect the identity and confidentiality of the ultimate beneficial owner of the company."*

Mossack Fonseca data also shows how Icelandic PM Sigmundur Gunnlaugsson had undeclared interest in his country's bailed-out banks. He has been accused of hiding millions of dollars of investments in his country's banks behind a secretive offshore company. Leaked documents show that Sigmundur Gunnlaugsson and his wife bought offshore company *Wintris* in 2007. He did not declare an interest in the company when entering parliament in 2009. He sold his 50% of Wintris to his wife for $1 (70p), eight months later. Gunnlaugsson is now facing calls for his resignation. He says he has not broken any rules, and his wife did not benefit financially from his decisions. The offshore company was used to invest millions of dollars of inherited money, according to a document signed by Gunnlaugsson's wife Anna Sigurlaug Pálsdóttir in 2015. *'Beyond reproach'.* In addition, *Mossack Fonseca* supplied a *front man who pretended to own $1.8m, so the real owner could get the cash from the bank without revealing identity.* Mossack Fonseca says it has always complied with international protocols to ensure the companies they incorporate are not used for tax evasion, money-laundering, terrorist finance or other illicit purposes. The company says it conducts thorough due diligence and regrets any misuse of its services. "For 40 years *Mossack Fonseca* has operated beyond reproach in our home country and in other jurisdictions where we have operations. Our firm has never been accused or charged in connection with criminal wrongdoing. "If we detect suspicious activity or misconduct, we are quick to report it to the authorities. Similarly, when authorities approach us with evidence of possible misconduct, we always cooperate fully with them." *Mossack Fonseca* says *offshore companies are available worldwide and are used for a variety of legitimate purposes."*

21] **_It is well known that we Indians though thoroughly dishonest would never admit our guilt._** Our Law holds every accused innocent unless proved otherwise. *Funniest Clause*: 'Law stipulates that one hundred guilty persons may escape but one innocent must not be punished'. That means the onus is on the State to prove the guilt of offenders of the law of the land. The result is legal process goes on and on and invariably nothing comes out. The founding fathers of our Constitution were either naïve to adopt strict legal procedures or, they wanted to protect the corrupt and mighty people. Amitabh Bachchan came out saying he was falsely implicated in 'Panama Papers since he is innocent. This myth was broken in a few days when the *DNA* headline on 8th April read, *'Who paid Amitabh's INR60-crore debt?'* DNA reveals the buried Income-Tax department investigation against the Bollywood actor for tax evasion. "This English newspaper reproduced the actor's letter dated 22nd December 2009 to the (then) Union finance minister, Pranab – a staunch sycophant of first PM Indira and years after her death switched his loyalties to her daughter-in-law Sonia after having been rejected by Indira's son Rajiv and kept out of power for former's full term over five years as Indian PM. Sonia was the 'life' president of Congress (I) since 1998 after duly elected incumbent Sitaram Kesri was unceremoniously shunted out. Pranab Mukherjee happened to be the President who retired on 26th July 2017. *India is the only 'democracy' in the world where pygmies and chamchas can occupy the highest Constitutional office of the country that is: President or Prime Minister.* Letter printed on page 4 of the said newspaper was as follows:

"December 22, 2009.
Respected Pranabda,

Further to our telephonic conversation the other night, I wish to reiterate that, the Notice received by me from the Investigation Department of the Income Tax, Mumbai, wherein a finger of suspicion has been raised towards me, in the matter under reference, is most unfortunate.

I am enclosing herewith a copy of the Notice and our earlier relevant response, which apparently has not been given any trust or merit. The way circumstantial evidences have been created to implicate me are distressing. I have remained always an honorable citizen of the country, loved by the masses and decorated by just not the Government of India, and its Income Tax Department but by numerous foreign nations as well. I believe I have always conducted myself and my affairs within the tenets of the Law of our land and abided by them. However, I have continuously felt that frivolous and mischievously designed media reportage has become a convenient instrument by which cases have been built against me by the Department, including if I may, the one that I write to you about today.

I plead my innocence in the case under reference and make a plea that I be spared from any further harassment. If I have erred or the Department has proof of evidence against me, the Hang me. And if not, then do spare me this humiliation and allow me to exist in peace and the joy of my creativity – a creativity that has for the previous 40 years brought happiness and joy and, if I may modestly state, great pride to our wonderful nation, to millions of people around the globe.

I look upon you to treat this matter with compassion, an attribute you have always been renowned for.

With warm and sincere regards,
signed
Amitabh Bachchan"

The Income-Tax department. despite having glaring evidence of tax evasion against Bachchan, put its investigation on the backburner. DNA revealed the entire Income-Tax investigation of tax evasion, suspicious transactions and payments to offshore tax havens allegedly made on behalf of Bachchan. The payments totaling over six million Great Britain Pound sterling, routed through Mauritius, were made for repaying a loan allegedly taken by Bachchan. The amount used for the purpose was not declared by Bachchan as his income and tax was not paid on it...

The connection between Bachchan and Subrata Roy – the founder and chairman of Sahara India – is well known. ….. In 1998, Bachchan and his wife Jaya toured town and villages across India promoting Sahara's non-banking finance schemes and even allowed their faces to be used on posters promoting those schemes. It is through these schemes that Sahara unlawfully mobilized over INR270 billion from small investors in towns and villages… *The bank accounts of Lahiri Productions – an insignificant loss-making company – showed that INR60 crore (600 million) was paid in two installments by Sahara One Media & Entertainment Ltd. On 24th March 2003, an amount of 460 million was paid. On 9th April 2003, 140 million was transferred."* Incidentally, Subrata Roy is lodged in Tihar Jail Delhi since March 2014 for his inability to pay back hundreds of billions of rupees he had clandestinely raised from the banks and had made many unsuccessful attempts to retune even part of the borrowed money. It is worth remembering that Subrata Roy started his business with a paltry INR5,000 only!

Was Bachchan saved because of Pranab's intervention and gag on Income Tax department? If such a person of doubtful integrity is made the President of India, whose fault is this? Obviously, it is that of the Congress president who wanted to get rid of him from the UPA cabinet. Maybe it was a hope that a trusted lieutenant like Pranab could be of much greater use to the party in future as the President of India! But one thing is abundantly clear that the quality of our Presidents except Dr. Sarvpalle Radhakrishnan (the 2nd), Dr. APJ Abdul Kalam (the 12th) and perhaps Dr. Rajendra Prasad (the 1st) – all holding doctorate in their respective fields – has been rather poor, unfortunately!

22] **One knows full well: 'Justice delayed is justice denied.'** *Our judiciary esp., Supreme Court and High Courts, is the weakest link among the three pillars of democracy. The earliest these anomalies are rectified the better it is for the country and its willfully ignorant, irresponsible and dishonest citizens.* Our country is in dire need of *character-building* to imbibe and practice values enshrined in our civilization and culture. Above all it urgently requires all sorts of reforms including administrative, economic, judicial, police, political and social. Vote-bank politics practiced by all political parties and our compatriots' total failure to elect the right PM in the first 67 years after independence have ruined the country. With an astute, honest and forward-thinking person at the helm of affairs who has his hand over the pulse of people and knows full well the needs of the country, we must expect the process must be accomplished in the next couple of decades. *In less than two years, he catapulted the country to greater heights globally in line with respected nations of the world*!

23] ***Thoroughly corrupt autocrat 'owners'/proprietors/dictators of practically every Opposition party*** of different hues and colors, especially the Gandhi-Nehru-Gandhi dynasty that has been fooling the country for a century and fallaciously always considered the 'Delhi throne' its birthright, can't digest the fact that a poor Dalit *chaiwallah* (tea-seller from a Backward Community/Class) became the PM with absolute majority on his own, something happening first time in three decades. Those antinational elements in Congress are embarrassed that he is performing far better than their own ten-year lackluster regime riddled with mega-scams involving trillions of rupees. Moreover, the last two Congress governments led by Rao and Manmohan were in minority. Congress appears to be in a shamble. Thus, this oldest but most corrupt party appears to be on its last legs being on an irreversible path of decline. For INC, it was initiated in 1917 by a (Bania) *'genuine'* Gandhi-later named *Mahatma* (by Nobel Laureate *Gurudeva* Rabindra Nath Tagore) with a double face and toothless smile. And now, a century later, demise of its offshoot Congress (Indira) will be accomplished by another (Roman Catholic) *fake* Gandhi- the 5th generation scion of the infamous dynasty. The crooked politicians belonging to the Communist party, the Congress and its crony regional parties have joined their dirty hands in nefarious anti-people anti-national act by disrupting the proceedings in the Rajya Sabha (Upper House) to block economic agenda of Modi government and thereby stall the benefits flowing out to our citizenry. This way they are compounding the miseries of the common man especially those of the 600 million poor plus the middle classes. *Time alone will tell how far these unscrupulous antinational politicians succeed. It is dependent upon dawning of wisdom on our countrymen, when that occurs!*

Congress (I) governments were/are known for their sycophancy and abject surrender to the whims and fancies of its autocratic white lady president and her good-for-nothing son who has still to come out of his diapers at 48 years of age; have been notorious for policy paralysis, sky-high corruption, multiple high value mega scams and irregularities in every sphere of governance and bureaucracy. The latest among long list of its misdeeds came into public domain on Saturday, the 20th February 2016, when *Firstpost.com* published: *'Congress-must Lutes (Congress-free Lutyens)? Modi government wants 24, Akbar Road and 3 other bungalows vacated'*: "The Congress party has been asked to vacate four government bungalows in the heart of the Capital including a sprawling building at 24 Akbar Road Congress(I) headquarters following cancellation of their allotment. AICC Treasurer Motilal Vora confirmed the same. The four bungalows in its possession that also included: 26, Akbar Road; 5, Raisina Road and C-II/109, Chanakya Puri. The 24, Akbar Road has been the party headquarters since 1978; 26, Akbar Road is the office of the Congress frontal wing Seva Dal; 5, Raisina Road has Youth Congress and NSUI(I) offices. The Chanakyapuri bungalow C-II/109 is being used as a residence. The Ministry of Urban Development directed the Congress that it pays the penal fee till the bungalows are vacated. In a statement, it said that as per the policy on Allotment of Land to Political Parties for building their own party offices, Congress Party was required to vacate in June 2013 the four bungalows that are in its possession. The Ministry said this is because Congress Party was handed over possession of land at 9-A, Rouse Avenue in June 2010 and as per the policy it was required to vacate the four bungalows within three years i.e. June 2013, which was not done. The Ministry of Urban Development last month has informed the Congress party that the said allocation has been cancelled with effect from June 2013 and it will be charged "damage rate of license fee" from that month for the said bungalows till they are vacated, as per the policy. Subsequently, Congress party made a request seeking further three years' time to vacate these bungalows, it said. Urban Development Minister M Venkaiah Naidu has directed the concerned to examine the request of the Congress. [*PTI*]

An interesting question, '*What are the good & bad deeds of Nehru, Indira, Rajiv, Sonia and Rahul to Indian People and politics of India*?', Milind Joshi wrote, "I differentiate between politics and politicking. *Nehru did the following*: 1] Created right atmosphere to sow the seeds of democracy in this young nation. 2] He codified Hindu Law and helped Hindu community to become socially more relevant to changing times. Whatever position we find Hindu women today would have been unthinkable without these reforms. 3] He successfully made the military sub-servient to the civil government, de-politicized them and this ensured that India did not go Pakistan way. 4] He laid the foundations of industrial base in the country. 5] His idea of public sector gave immense opportunities to people with humble background to aspire, work hard and achieve. 6] He ensured that our relationship with other countries developed in the initial phase. 7] By far the only weakness shown by him was his idealism in geo-political realities. As a result, he ended up giving us problems of Kashmir and later of Tibet. His handling of border matter with China and giving China the permanent seat in Security Councils were blunders.

Lal Bahadur Shastri was an honest Congressman having a conscience too – an extremely rare attribute (phenomenon). He was the first PM who ordered the Army Chief, Gen JN Chaudhry to attack Pakistan on the international border. His predecessor Nehru could never do that. However, at Tashkent Summit, totally against the promise he had made to the President and the people of Hindustan before departing for the Summit in erstwhile USSR, forfeited the initiative by agreeing to return the three important areas won by our army in the 1965 Indi-Pak war: 1] Haji Peer Pass, overlooking and controlling the road to Muzaffarabad, the capital of PoJK, clearly 8Km inside Pak-held Kashmir, 2] Peer Panchal Hills range in Jammu region, and 3]Kargil area strategically overlooking the Srinagar-Leh Highway. Shastri had to pay the price for unpardonable blunder with his life. He sustained the fatal 3rd heart attack. So, his conscience killed him!

Indira was a very smart and decisive politician. She had shrewd understanding of the geo-political realities and this resulted in her exemplary leadership during 1971 war. This was pinnacle of her glory. If she was born in Britain people would have stated that she was fit to be a war time PM only. She initiated the Missile program of India. I am afraid but I should give you more of her misdeeds. 1] She was a thoroughly non-democratic person. Imposition of emergency only to serve her personal ends was the biggest and lasting blot on her reputation. 2] During her time the PMO gained in power – beginning of centralization? 3] Her policies made states and local bodies dependent on center financially. Bereft of financial independence the root of democracy was hit. Federalism suffered its first serious blow. 4] Under the garb of meritocracy, she gave importance to personal loyalties over the loyalty to the Constitution. She played it dirty in promotions in government, military, PSUs and you name it. She played havoc with practically every institution. 5] She gifted Sikh militancy to India. The Frankenstein ultimately consumed her. 6] Making false promises came easy to her, biggest being *"Garibi Hatao"* (Remove Poverty). Integrated Rural Development Program failed to achieve even an iota of what Dairy Federation could through involvement of people. 7] The first nuclear explosion was high on emotive value and low on real benefits. The timing was wrong, and the scientific institutions of India paid dearly.

Rajiv, the reluctant politician, gave an important gift to India. The investment in telephony and thrust on computerization is something which changed the horizons of the market. His positive deeds stop here. *Negatives are:*

1] The post-Indira Gandhi Murder Riots (Sikh genocide) are a blot on the nation. I can, only legally, give him benefit of doubt in his role to control it.
2] Legislation post Shah Bano case is one of the most retrograde steps taken by any government in independent India.
3] Bofors brought PM under corruption clouds. Whatever be the legal decision ultimately, this was the first scam which affected common man's perception of corruption at the highest places.
4] With the decision of 5th Pay Commission, he dealt a death blow to the PSUs versus government jobs. What his grandfather created, he finished off.
5] He created another Frankenstein monster in LTTE and was consumed by it. IPKF was an unmitigated disaster, ill thought and implemented even worse.
6] The importance of Parliament nose-dived to a level hitherto unknown.

To the credit of Sonia, she held Congress (I) together, took it to an unlikely electoral 'victory' in 2004 and later during 2009. Since she did not become the PM, it will be inappropriate to comment on her achievements or failures although she acted as the *de facto undemocratic 'super' prime minister,* and dictated the dummy, meek, week, pseudo-economist, spineless CHAMCHA Manmohan who was accidental unelected/unelectable but the selected PM on paper only. However, I must say that Sonia devalued the post of the PM to the level where a nominated PM ruled the nation for a decade. This was like what the FAKE Mahatma did in 1946 by selecting Nehru with zero vote at the very heavy cost of rejecting the duly elected (by 80% votes) PM Sardar Patel. Who was Gandhi to do so thereby unleashing the greatest disservice to his motherland? This was the type of patriot he was! Or, was this his animosity for the great Sardar? *By 1940, Patel was already disagreeing with the FAKE Mahatma on the fundamental ideas of the future independent Indian State and even on the question of nonviolence in this, the seemingly last leg, of the freedom movement.* Likewise, after Indira's assassination, the top Indira-CHAMCHA President Zail Singh invited her son Rajiv to become the country's PM before he was even elected as the leader of the ruling party! In all executive decision making I give her benefit of doubt because I do not comment on hearsay. *Rahul Gandhi* has achieved nothing thus far and without express executive powers one cannot blame him for the ills of UPA II, thus no comments. *Our tragedy has been anti-national unscrupulous 'leaders' stayed at helm of country's affairs.*

The crude and underhand below-the-belt tactics of autocratic Congress (I) dynast 'life-time' white ex-president has been in the form of 'behind-the-scene' action since the 16th May 2004, when Sonia *appointed* her most obedient servile and docile *chamcha – an unelected and unelectable* Manmohan as PM. He was thoroughly obliged realizing little that being foreign-born Italian citizen, she could never have been accepted as one. FIRSTPOST article, *'UPA could tolerate terrorists but not Modi as PM': Sonia comes under fresh fire over Ishrat affidavit'* on Tuesday the 19th April 2016 20:55 IST attests to the same 'intolerance' of the party high command and her main *chamchas*. "Firing a fresh salvo at Sonia Gandhi over the Ishrat Jahan issue, BJP on Tuesday suggested that the Congress chief had asked the then Home Minister P Chidambaram to file a second affidavit in the case as UPA could "tolerate terrorists but not Narendra Modi as PM". Party spokesperson Sambit Patra asked Chidambaram to let the nation know: "Who is she who wrote the conspiracy? Because we all know that in the Congress party diktats come from a singular address. You know the address. The remote control lies with her," he told a press conference, making a clear reference to the Congress chief. The remote control is only at one place which is 10 Janpath, he said, referring to Sonia's residential address. He alleged Sonia, the then PM Manmohan and the Union home minister Chidambaram 'suppressed' information provided by the NIA and the FBI, the US probe agency, about Ishrat being a terrorist and a threat to Modi's life. *"Why did you suppress it? What was the need?* Because you could not tolerate these two persons (Modi and Amit Shah). *You could not tolerate him as you feared him becoming PM. You tolerated terrorists*. Chidambaram's conspiracy has been blown off. The conspiracy to eliminate important leaders from India, conspiracy to eliminate Narendra Modi, conspiracy to fail Amit Shah. The lid has been blown off and you today have been caught red handed. The UPA government's action hit at the root of democracy. It knew that Ishrat was a suicide bomber deputed by the L-e-T to eliminate Modi. Not only did they keep quiet, they conspired to stand with terrorists, he alleged."

The MHA in the UPA government stood for *"manipulative hush-hush affairs"*, Patra said, alleging that by 'deleting' Headley's reference to Ishrat, it "was trying to protect the perpetrators of 26/11". Quoting some intelligence reports, he said, she was a L-e-T suicide bomber. Asked of the government would take any action, he said law will take its own course and conspirators will be in the dock. Ishrat was killed in an encounter by Gujarat police in 2004. A 'court-monitored' CBI probe had found the encounter fake (since vital pieces of information were suppressed or distorted). And a major row erupted after the UPA government filed in September 2009 a second affidavit which, unlike the first, did not make any reference to her suspected L-e-T links." [*PTI*]

It is a tragedy that there are criminal cases against the bigwigs of the Congress(I) including the longest-serving president, Sonia Gandhi nee Sania Maino; her son Rahul Gandhi nee Raul Vinci – the current dynastic president; CHAMCHAS close to Sania like P Chidambaram, Shashi Tharoor et al. Everyone among them is on bail for the criminal charges under which they are being tried. Raul has the 'credit' of not one but many criminal cases against him. The latest being the one filed by Kartikey, the son of MP Chief minister Shivraj Chouhan, on 30th October 2018 for his speech the previous day sating Kartikey's name appears in 'Panama Papers'. Thus, *Congress(I) can be aptly called the Bail Party*!

24] *'Pseudo-secularism' or 'Sickularism':* *Pseudo-secularism or Sickularism in public perception has been practiced by the communal Congress* ever since 1917. CPM's Chief Sitaram Yechury maintains: "Shouting *Pakistan Zindabad* (Long Live Pakistan) slogans is not anti-national." A message making round on the *WhatsApp* illustrated this in proper perspective. "When apprehended (Kanhaiya Kumar), they say why arrested? When not arrested (Umer Khalid), they say why he has not been arrested so far? When revolting slogans for revolt against the motherland are raised (in university campuses or Kashmir valley), they are innocent since it is freedom of expression When police arrest a traitor (Kanhaiya), they say produce in a court of law. When the Supreme Court awards death sentence (Afzal Guru, Yaqub Memon), they say it is a judicial murder. When a terrorist is killed in police encounter (Ishrat Jehan), they (Nitish Kumar) says she is Bihar's daughter, was an innocent school-going student. When they are told by a foreigner (David Headley) that she (Ishrat) was a terrorist, they say why encounter and why not she was taken to court? They create drama and ruckus at midnight. A battery of dozen or more senior advocates force the CJI to open the Supreme Court at 3am, he (Yaqub Memon) is presented as innocent (after the due course had gone on for six years or more). His funeral procession in Mumbai is joined by tens of thousands, in sharp contrast to that of the most illustrious President of India during the recent times (APJ Abdul Kalam where the attendance is thin despite the presence of the Indian PM; and the procession hurls expletives against the Court and the Government. And incidentally both were Muslims.

What sort of nationalism or secularism is this? Some say, 'we will break India into parts, Inshallah, Inshallah, they say they did not say that. When videos are produced, they say this is 'freedom of expression'. When such people become terrorists, they say why did the Government not act earlier. Was it sleeping? When a traitor (Kanhaiya) is manhandled a bit outside the court, these anti-national politicians and the supporting sold out media raise a hell. When 250,000 Muslims, many illegal Bangladeshis, descend on the roads causing loot and arson burning Hindus' properties and even the police station where the records of illegal immigrants are kept, the same anti-national gang is totally dumb or say it was anger. When a Hindu speaks something against this anomaly, he (Kamlesh Tiwari) is humiliated and jailed indefinitely. When a Muslim (Umer Khalid) speaks against the country, they label it under 'freedom of expression'. When a Muslim (Ikhlaq) is beaten to death by a mob in Dadri UP, the same anti-nationals raise the bogey of intolerance all over the country although law and order is state's prerogative and that state is ruled by the pro-Muslim Samajwadi Party, one of the same nefarious gang. When a Hindu is burnt alive in Pune or Kerala, the same ugly group is totally mum. When a Hindu (Prashant Tiwari) is cut into pieces by Muslim hooligans in Agra in the same state, no arrests are made. Why there are double standards? What sort of 'secularism' is this? *Why all these political belonging to Opposition are extremely anti-Hindu? Any answers for that..............*"

[Late on, the forensic report confirmed the existence of 1kg beef in the refrigerator of Ikhlaq!]

The irony is huge support/sympathy by anti-national parties for terrorists and anti-national paid/puppet Communist student leaders of various universities (being groomed as the future leaders of that party) but not for the army/paramilitary personnel fighting terrorism. Let me ask one question from Congress-I President Sonia: *Is it a sheer coincidence that your Kapil Sibal is the advocate for terrorists and traitors like Afzal Guru, Yaqub*

Menon, Ishret Jehan, Hardik Patel and Kanhaiya Kumar & Party? Prof Madhu Kishwar tweeted, "*If Muslim terrorists get killed, #sickulars become hysterical with grief. But NO outrage over murder of Muslim Kashmiri police/ military officer cracking terror networks.*" Or, "over an *Assassinated NIA DCP also Muslim. But such murders don't seem to upset #sickularists or even Rahul Coz of sympathy 4 assassins?*

Then Bihar and UP were two states with no semblance of law and order. Apparently, those were run by mafia since the ruling parties have far more *goondas* (ruffians) as politicians. Hence the administration is too lax and ineffective. Just an example: "On 11th January 2014, thousands of activists of the 'Azad Bharat Vidhik Vaicharik Kranti Satygrahi' -- splinter group of followers of spiritual guru, Baba Jai Gurudev who passed away in 2012 -- illegally occupied hundreds of acres of government land at Jawahar Park in Mathura on the pretext of holding a protest. The encroachers burnt down nearly 2,400 trees at the park, which comes under the horticulture department of the state government, to facilitate their stay. They continued to stay there illegally for two years, though they had permission to just hold a two-day protest. After a year, based on a petition by a Vijay Pal Singh Tomar, the Allahabad High Court on May 20, 2015 directed the principal secretary (home), district magistrate of Mathura and senior superintendent of police to take "all necessary steps and precautions" to ensure that a public park is "not allowed to be encroached upon in this manner". In April 2016, a 48-hour ultimatum was issued by the district administration asking the encroachers to vacate the land. But the impasse continued till the police force moved in June 2 to remove the encroachers. *Why did the local administration and police take a year to execute the court direction remains a mystery?*"

25] **Corruption in public life.** Corruption has been rife for a very long time. INC and its present Avatar Congress(I) have been corrupt if one must believe in its dictator Gandhi in what he said in 1940, "Corruption is so rampant in INC that I would like its decent burial." Any individual willing to fight against this dragon must do on his/her own peril. Source: in the INC. He or his descendants did precious little except lip service. Since this nefarious party ruled over the country for 75% of her post-independence existence, it was quite natural for corruption to be rooted deeply in the psyche and working of its administration and the public. People feel that if their work, legitimate or otherwise, can be accomplished with a bribe, there is no 'harm' in that. Any person deciding to fight against this unwanted dragon must do it on its own peril. The following case illustrates this deep-seated practice (problem) fully. I narrate a case that illustrates this. On 1st September 2018, *Rediff.com News* »published, '*What happens when you speak truth to power*'. No one was surprised when Rajendra Singh was found shot and killed in broad daylight, not far from the local police station, notes Geetanjali Krishna. "I can't get the photograph of Rajendra Singh out of my mind. He is laughing, proud moustache curled upwards and eyes looking fearlessly at the camera. He looks like a man who isn't afraid of anything, even death. And from all accounts, that's exactly what he was. Here's his story: Sixty-two-year-old Rajendra Singh used to live in East Champaran, Bihar. Till 2010, he ran a petrol pump and lived comfortably with his family. Things in his village were, however, far from ideal and Singh used to raise his voice against any case of corruption he came across. After he was beaten up and left for dead, possibly by people he had threatened to expose, Singh decided to become a full-time activist and whistle-blower. "His first case was when he exposed the embezzlement of rations in the local anganwadi," narrated his son-in-law Rajesh Ranjan when I recently met him in Delhi.

Next, he took up the matter of corruption in MNREGA and in schoolteacher appointments. "Things really heated up when he discovered that contraband confiscated by Sangrampur police, which included timber and three quintals of marijuana, had been misappropriated," said Ranjan.

Singh refused to back down and withdraw his complaint despite, first polite intercessions, and when these didn't work, violent threats. "Instead of acting on his information, the police filed the counter case against him for impeding government functioning," said he. The cases against him continue to pile up and often when he had no money to pay a lawyer, he argued them himself in court. Undeterred, Singh filed over 100 Right to Information applications and continued to discover and expose corruption. Until June 2018, Singh had survived three more assaults after that first murderous attack. He was attacked with a knife, almost run over by a jeep and then, brutally assaulted with an axe.

How many more murderous attacks could he survive, his family wondered? Ranjan said these experiences convinced Singh that he would soon be dead. This only compelled him to dig deeper into yet another case of corruption. The village headman had appointed his brother-in-law and other relatives/friends as teachers in the government school. They had furnished fake degrees to secure the posts. Singh filed an RTI query seeking information on these appointments, after which all these teachers were forced to resign. "By this time, he felt he could be killed any day," said Ranjan. Finally, in 2017, Singh wrote to the DIG of Muzaffarpur, detailing all the threats and attempts on his life. No police protection was given. In fact, *the police did not even act on his letter.* "My father-in-law started living each day as if it were his last," Ranjan narrated. "He stopped giving any family members lifts on his bike, fearing our proximity to him might endanger us," he says, adding Singh began repaying all his debts, big and small. Ranjan recalled how Singh began calling his two daughters more frequently during this time. *Each call felt like a farewell.* No one was surprised when Singh was found shot and killed in broad daylight, not far from the local police station. The Braveheart paid, not only the price for being a whistle-blower and anti-corruption crusader, but also the price of belonging to a country that is yet to implement a law to protect people like him." [*Geetanjali Krishna/Rediff.com*]

26] *Cities/Roads named after Muslim Invaders.*

In no country in the world, roads or towns are named after invaders. It is a strange paradoxical situation here only. Here one finds thousands of roads named after Muslim invaders who not only killed 200 million Hindus if not more, but also desecrated our temples, defiled and abducted our women and even sold them by auction, We proved to be so spineless that we did never ever object to such nonsensical actions. Even 72 years after independence, barring reversion of a few names of some import city, nothing has moved in the right direction. This raises serious questions about our patriotism and even our integrity. It is high time we learn from other countries.

27] *Road Indiscipline: Free Parking, halting/blocking the road and Jaywalking.*

Our roads are free for all. Every type and grade of vehicle can be found on the road. Our citizens are averse to follow discipline. Firstly, pavements or sidewalks do not exist. If these are there, people try to occupy it for any reason. One finds mini shops on pavements. Many times, even the roads are not spared. Politicians are playing havoc and creating anarchy. Vote bank politics and populism are the norm. Of late since May 2014, things have started to be sorted out although the process will remain awfully slow. If one thing is done i.e. free parking and stopping on at least important roads are banned, that will give a new lease of life to the roads. Certainly, it will drastically reduce the accidents. The rate of accidents is enormously high.

28] <u>Film Industry's Anti-nationalism and Bizarre paradoxes.</u> *Last but not the least* Bollywood, Tollywood or Kollywood has done wonders in terms of the number of movies churned out year after year and the tons of money it generates, thanks to the stupid clueless poor Hindustanis who throng to watch mostly useless commercial films! Bollywood has the label of being run by the most wanted gangster and country's enemy #1 Dawood Ibrahim operating from Karachi and Dubai. Like the bulk of our political parties and main-stream media, Bollywood is pro-Muslim and staunchly anti-Hindu and anti-Sikh. It may not be wrong to say that it is anti-Hindustan as well. Most of the times, it shows Pakistan in a much better color as a tolerant country whereas we are intolerant. One of the main reasons for this is they must sell their movies in Pakistan which has a sizeable market for Bollywood movies. Good characters in Bollywood movies bear Muslim names and the bad ones are all Hindus especially Brahmins. Post-independence, this situation has worsened decade after decade thanks to the anti-national Congress party that maneuvered to rule the country for four-fifths of the post-independence era. This was once again possible since our masses, perhaps the most stupid in the world, are totally unconcerned about the country. And this party of crooks and its many offshoots are all in the same bracket. All these are projecting to be pro-Muslim although NOT doing anything for them or non-Muslims as well as their main objective is work for their own families having set up dynastic parties and amass wealth!

On 21st November 2018, *MSN News* brought out a hidden facet of tinsel industry via an article, *'Not everything is starry and glamorous in the world of Stars'*. "Not everything is starry and glamorous in the world of stars. However, only some have the courage to talk about the controversies surrounding their personal lives. Here, we have compiled a list of stars who shocked the world by spilling the beans on their deep dark secrets. *Former Miss Universe Sushmita Sen* said, "Six months ago at an award function, a 15-year old boy misbehaved with me as he thought I wouldn't realize because of the crowd around. But he was wrong. I grabbed his hand from my behind and was shocked to see he was just 15. I held him by his neck and took him for a walk. I told him if I make a hue and cry, his life would be over. He denied having misbehaved at first, but I sternly told him to acknowledge. He realized his mistake, said sorry and promised me that it will never happen again. I didn't take action against him because I understood that the 15-year-old was not taught that such things are an offense and not entertainment," *Deepika Padukone* shocked her fans by talking about the phase when she was battling depression. She had consulted many psychiatrists and had been under medication for a long period of time. She revealed her situation as she did not want anyone else to go through such a low phase. Drawing from her own experiences, Deepika has also opened an NGO that focuses on spreading awareness about mental health and provides help to those suffering from depression and other forms of mental illnesses. *Shama Sikander*, a popular TV actress, revealed suffering from a bipolar disorder. In an interview, she even disclosed that she had attempted suicide while going through a tough, emotional phase. She talked about how she felt hopeless, directionless and extremely gloomy during that phase of life. *Sri Reddy* was in news from past few days. The Telugu actress shocked the nation by stripping in public. She alleged that she has been denied the membership of Movie Artistes Association because of her casting couch allegations. For over a month, she kept alleging that biggies from the Telugu film industry are exploiting female actresses and are asking sexual favors for the roles. The actress also roped in director Sekhar Kammula in the war and alleged that director harassed her sexually. After multiple warnings to the Telugu film industry, she started sharing her pictures with industry biggies on her social media accounts. He also claimed that Suresh Babu's son Abhiram Daggubati sexually exploited her. *Kalki Koechlin* was sexually abused at the age of nine. The actress shared, that she spoke about a 'bygone' incident of her life, so that parents can be more open about "s** and private parts", with their children. Kalki said that she allowed the abuse to happen as she was unaware of what was happening and regretted not having the confidence to talk to her parents about it. *Richa Chadha*, the "*Gangs of Wasseypur*" actor revealed that *Bulimia is a common disorder that plagues Bollywood* and she, too, has been a victim of it. "I was told I should gain weight, then lose weight. I crumbled under the pressure like a wrecking ball had hit me. Bulimia is when you consistently hate what you look like, and compulsively induce vomiting, throw up all the food you eat, accompanied often by binge eating. You become drastically unhealthy, low on nutrition, with lack of sleep. I hated myself, gained weight in a strange way and felt like a failure." Richa, who was invited to give a talk at TEDxDTU, also spoke about how the various "fix-ups" she was told to get, made her insecure about her looks. *Vidya Balan*, while registering her new house in Khar, the "Dirty Picture" star had to play dirty by greasing the palms of officials. The actor even took a pledge of 'bribe bandh' on stage, assuring the audience that she would never opt for the easy way out to get things done quickly. *Chitrangda Singh*: To prepare for her role in director Sudhir Mishra's "Inkaar", she recalled her personal memories of having experienced sexual harassment. "Since I spent most of my growing years in Delhi and Meerut, I have had my share of such experiences; a couple were really bad ones," said Chitrangada. *Hrithik Roshan* disclosed his stammering problems that made his childhood difficult. The actor said that he was scared to wake up in the morning as he had to face people and talk to them every day. As a result, he was also bullied in school. *Aamir Khan* once revealed that he, along with his team of "Satyameva Jayate", had to undergo group therapies post the show. He shared how the crew was disturbed after the show and had to overcome the hard-hitting realities of the subjects explored during the two seasons. *Ranbir Kapoor:* During an interview, he was asked if he had cheated someone in love and he said, "Yes, I have, out of immaturity, out of inexperience, out of taking advantage of certain temptations, out of callousness." He further added, "You realize it now, when you grow up and you value it more. I have realized that now." *Rishi Kapoor*: In his autobiography, titled '*Khullam Khulla: Rishi Kapoor Uncensored*', he admitted buying his debut Filmfare award for Best Actor for his film, "Bobby". The veteran actor had confessed saying, "I was just 21 at that time, fiercely competitive. when a person I met promised that he could get me an award if I paid ₹30,000, I agreed." *Anurag Kashyap*, the filmmaker divulged that he was sexually abused in his childhood for as many as 11 years. In an interview, Anurag said that he was very small at that time and his abuser was 22 years old. Although Anurag was obviously filled with bitterness for the painful childhood, he said that he has forgiven the man. *Govinda,* the man with an impeccable comic timing and killer dance moves, admitted to being in relationships outside marriage. He refuses to divulge any details though saying, " Somethings in life should not be spoken about publicly. It's best kept a secret."

'Zero *to DeepVeerKiShaadi, Rising Sikh Protests Against Bollywood',* appeared on *The Quint* on 21ˢᵗ November 2018. "A few groups amongst the Sikh community in India seem to have a bone to pick with Bollywood. In 2018, three big films have earned the wrath of Sikh representatives over their title or their scenes. Here's a list of the instances when some Sikh groups cautioned against the depiction of the community in films or when certain B-Town celebrity behavior was a breach of decorum.

1] *Protest Against Karenjit Kaur*: The Untold Story of Sunny Leone: She launches the web series Karenjit Kaur based on her life. SGPC objected to the use of "Kaur" in the title of the aforesaid Zee5 web series based on the life on the Bollywood actor and former adult film star - Sunny Leone. The show's title is a reference to her birth name, Karenjit Kaur Vohra. Diljit Singh Bedi, SGPC's additional secretary and spokesperson, reportedly said that the usage would hurt Sikh sentiments as Sunny did not follow the teachings of the Sikh gurus. Indian politician Manjinder Singh Sirsa, a member of the Shiromani Akali Dal party and general secretary of the Delhi Sikh Gurdwara Management Committee (DSGMC) wrote to Subhash Chandra, the chairman of Essel Group, asking for a change in the title and threatened to take a stern stand against the team, to which Chandra had a factual and fitting reply. Many other communities similarly reacted with protest warnings outside their offices.

2] *Protest Against Manmarziyaan*: Abhishek Bachchan plays Robbie in Manmarziyaan. A scene in Anurag Kashyap's Manmarziyaan had reportedly left some members of the Sikh community disgruntled. A Sikh organization filed a petition against the film in the Jammu wing of the Jammu and Kashmir High Court on 18 September, pushing the director to issue a clarification. A scene in the film shows Robbie (Abhishek Bachchan) removing his turban before going away from his house for a smoke. Since Sikhism prohibits smoking or the use of tobacco, the scene caused a controversy and was deleted from the film's screenings in Punjab. Producer Aanand L Rai then took responsibility for ordering voluntary cuts to the film, despite CBFC clearance. In a statement to Mumbai Mirror, Aanand said, "The decision of deleting the scenes was taken by Color Yellow Productions. I thought if they are hurting someone's sentiments, I might as well take them out as that's not what my film is about." The Sikh Sangat of Ambala had also gathered in a meeting at Gurdwara Manji Sahib in Ambala to stand against the screening of the film. They demanded the registration of a FIR against the actor Abhishek Bachchan, Taapsee Pannu and the writer, director and the producer of the film. the Sikhs under the leadership of the SGPC also registered a complaint against the film to the city magistrate.

3] *Protest Against 'Zero'*: Shah Rukh Khan in the controversial poster of Zero. The trailer of Zero sees Shah Rukh wearing the 'Gatka Kirpan' (Article of Sikh Faith) – a dagger extremely sacred to the Sikhs. The Sikh Sangat complained to the Delhi Sikh Gurudwara Management Committee (DSGMC). As per the Sikh Rehat Maryada (code of conduct and conventions for Sikhism, approved by the SGPC) only Amritdhari Sikh individuals can wear the Kirpan. "I have received a number of complaints from the Sikh Sangat for hurting the sentiments of the Sikhs by movie Zero directed by Aanand L Rai. In the film, Shah Rukh Khan has been shown wearing "Gatka Kirpan" (Article of Sikh Faith) and their movie promo has created outrage among Sikh community worldwide," said Manjinder Singh Sirsa, General secretary, DSGMC. He filed a complaint against Shah Rukh Khan and Aanand L Rai in a Delhi police station for the same, demanding that the scene and poster be withdrawn. According to an *ANI* report, a petition has been filed in Bombay High Court by Amritpal Singh Khalsa seeking removal of scenes of Shah Rukh Khan displaying a 'Kirpan'. According to the petition, 'display of the Kirpan in such a way is blasphemous and the scene should be removed immediately from the film. Sirsa responded to the makers saying that Aanand L Rai and Shah Rukh would have to issue a public statement on the matter and clarify their stand.

4] *Protest Against Ranveer Singh and Deepika Padukone's Anant Karaj Ceremony in Italy.* An Italian Sikh organization has alleged that the Anand Karaj ceremony that took place on 15 November, violated the Sikh code of conduct. According to Sukhdev Singh Kang, Indian Sikh Community Italy president, the Akal Takht 'hukumnama' sternly prohibits taking Guru Granth Sahib to a place other than a gurdwara. The celeb wedding took place at Villa del Balbianello, Lake Como in Italy. According to The Tribune, Kang also said that he would be writing to Akal Takht Jathedar for necessary action. Akal Takht acting Jathedar Giani Harpreet Singh has said that the matter would be taken up with the five high priests once a complaint is received.

29] *#Me Too:*

It is well-known that Bollywood and its constituents can do anything for the sake of money. It is an open secret that people (females) get exploited and are propositioned in lieu of work. It is a shameless industry involved in free sex at every stage but has always tried hard to keep that under layers of webs, covers and wraps. *Typical duplicity of majority of Indian mind can be witnessed here in its worst form.* The Casting Coach is omnipresent though in denial mode. Every new actress must be pass through that without exception. It is true for the daughters of big actors or directors too! However, it is only rarely that an actress ever mentions that. Is involved in this shameful behavior but some of them are at more privileged hierarchy namely every man performing an important function in the process of filmmaking. Those are: film producers and directors, casting and art directors, cinematographers, lyricists, music directors in the case of new female singers, senior actors, and so on. The list can be endless.

This campaign gained momentum during September-October 2018 and is becoming stronger by every passing day. When Tanushree Dutta opened-up on sexual harassment at the hands of Nana Patekar on the sets of her 2008 film *Horn Ok Pleassss* during an interview in September 2018. *Little did this forgotten heroine know that she would become the face of one of the most empowering movements in India – The #MeToo movement.* emboldened by her, many females connected with the Bollywood started blurting out the sexual predators one by one. The process is on and likely to gather momentum in the coming times. There is support from the important vocal women ministers particularly Maneka Gandhi and Smriti Irani in the Union cabinet of the NDA government. Starting with Nana Patekar it has engulfed some other equally better-known names such as producer-directors Subhash Ghai and Sajid Nadiadwala, celebrity consultant Suhel Seth, veteran actors Alok Nath and Nana Patekar, music director Anu Malik, directors Subhash Kapoor and Vikas Bahl, producer Atul Kasbekar, lyricist Verimuthu, and a score more. Important fallout of this movement is that the accused are losing plum roles or contracts one after the other.

'Lipstick Under My Burkha' actor Aahana Kumra accused Sajid Khan of indecent behavior. Aahana said in an interview to *The Times of India* that while Sajid never touched her, he did call her to his house and his room and asked her inappropriate questions. "I had a meeting with Sajid about a year ago, knowing the fact that he is a shady guy. I met him. He did the same thing that Saloni (Chopra) has written about him. Same drill — Go to his house, you are escorted to his room that is quite dark. He makes you watch what he's watching," she said. Aahana says that she was assertive in how she responded to him and let him know that her mother was a policewoman. "But he still asked me bizarre questions like, 'Would you have s*x with a dog if I gave you Rs 100 crores'? He didn't touch me," she added. Sajid has been accused of sexual harassment by three actors and a journalist. He has since stepped down from his position as the director of Housefull 4. The film's lead actor Akshay Kumar also tweeted that he would not work with 'any proven offenders and all those who have been subjugated to harassment should be heard and given the justice they deserve'. The film's shoot has also been suspended since. In her interview, Aahana also accused casting director Anirban Blah of making sexual advances towards her. He has also been accused of sexual harassment by four women. "Anirban met me at the lobby of a five-star hotel and said, 'There's a room here. Let's negotiate there.' I walked out of that meeting because I wasn't comfortable. It didn't go down well with me. That's 'normal' conversation he has with women. The day I chatted with him, I was shaken," she said.

Outside film industry, Suhel Seth was a well-respected celebrity. Ever since several women, including model Diandra Soares, filmmaker Natasha Rathore and writer Ira Trivedi, accused Seth of sexual misconduct, Tata Sons stopped dealing with *Counselage*, a brand consultancy firm owned by Seth. Similarly, Nana Patekar is axed out of couple of Hindi movies. Oscar-winning music director AR Rahman who has collaborated with him in number of projects vouched for his misconduct. And even Rahman's sister corroborated on media news on Verimuthu. Actress Mumtaj said, "There was one director who crossed the line. I scolded him so much and hit him with a slipper that he later never tried anything. He later started addressing me as *'vaanga amma ukaraunga amma* (come madam, sit madam)." Top Bollywood actor Akshay Kumar and one of the top TV stars Ronit Raj need special mention. The latter added a new dimension to #Me Too. Recalling an incident that occurred almost a decade ago, Romit shares, "I was called in a coffee shop by a creative director, who posted pictures with some of the biggest names in the industry — actors, producers, and designers. He has been quite influential [that way]. So, I was happy that I would be getting an opportunity to work with him. This person claimed that he was bisexual, but he [in reality] was actually gay." However, Romit quickly clarifies that he has nothing against anyone's sexual orientation or preference. There is a long list of celebrities supporting #Me Too movement: Raveena Tandon, Malaika Arora, Saif Ali Khan, Deepika Padukone, Radhika Apte, Sushmita Sen, Soni Razdan, Twinkle Khanna, Aditi Rao Hydari, Tapsi Pannu, Neha Dhupia, Sonakshi Sinha, Yami Gautam, Prachi Desai, Athiya Shetty and Mrunal Thakur.

Latest on the block is Nawazuddin Siddiqui implicated by Niharika Singh. She wrote on 10th November 2018, "The last few weeks have been interesting for women in India. The Hollywood inspired *#Me-too movement* has made its belated foray into the Indian mainstream media and stories of various forms of harassment and abuse are finally beginning to take center stage. A few men have been asked to step down from their positions of power and some women can heave a sigh of relief as they form solidarities amongst their ilk, process trauma and perhaps begin to get closure of some kind. I decided to write this piece to expand my own understanding of what constitutes abuse, who we choose to punish and whom we are willing to forgive. Like most Indian women, especially those from marginalized backgrounds, my entire life has been dotted with various forms of exploitation. Sexual, physical, emotional, verbal, economic - I've been through it all. Every time I've tried to extricate myself from one abusive situation, I found myself caught in the vortex of another. I've had to discover myriad ways to disengage, break patterns, forgive, heal, and reclaim my strength in order to survive, grow and find peace. My father is from Uttar Pradesh, and my mother from Rajasthan; both belong to 'untouchable' communities. An alliance was formed through a *Times of India* matrimonial ad in the early 1980s. Their tumultuous marriage and everyday violence that was normalized within the family gave me an opaque understanding of what constitutes love and what constitutes abuse while I was growing up. Sent to an all-girls boarding school in the hills early on provided a much-needed escape. I moved to New Delhi for higher studies as a teenager, and soon began to realize that daily harassment on roads and public buses, ragging on college campuses, catcalling by anonymous men and rape threats by stalkers was considered normal behavior; something women who grew up in the city learnt to navigate from early childhood. Depending on which part of the city you lived in, the extent of the abuse varied. Your caste background, economic conditions and political affiliations determined that. Law and order were tools reserved for those who had access to power. Since I was fair-skinned' and 'photogenic', I chanced upon jobs in the burgeoning beauty industry that was beginning to thrive in the early 2000s.

The underbelly of the modeling scene in New Delhi, where I worked for a few years, provided me with enough ammunition and confidence I needed to make the big move to Mumbai - the city of dreams but also of nightmares. Navigating exploitative model coordinators, photographers and older lecherous men in the seedy lanes of Malviya Nagar, I learnt the art of disguise, playing deaf and dumb when required, with one singular goal in mind - survival. Despite my parents' disapproval, I moved to Mumbai with my younger sister and some meagre savings when she got admission to St. Xavier's College, hoping to protect us from the casteist, feudal, north Indian way of life only to soon discover my youthful ignorance. My life in Mumbai started with me finding an apartment in Lokhandwala with the help of a model I'd met. After sending my pictures to agencies and production houses, I soon began to get jobs in print and advertising. That model's career was on its way down and one day, after a few drinks, he ended up getting violent and tried to molest my sister. When she opened to me, I went to his studio, broke whatever I could, gave him a few slaps, screamed expletives and told him to never show his face again. That episode shook both my sister and me and I blamed myself for not being able to ensure her safety. Things started looking up in 2005 when I participated in the Miss India beauty pageant. I won a crown, traveled all over the country, represented India at an international beauty pageant, and was treated like a state guest in Uttarakhand where my father worked. I even had a garden named after me by the state that had recently seceded from Uttar Pradesh and needed its own role models.

The Times group, organizers of the Miss India pageant, made sure they got their money's worth by working us around the clock. Along with the other winners, I flew around for sponsor visits, press meets, fashion shows and hosted a reality show on television. Work flowed in; I endorsed various brands, my face was on billboards and covers of magazines. I now had a social life, dated a young aspiring actor from Juhu, signed a film contract and began to feel at home in Mumbai. Other than my sister, I also supported a younger cousin that came to live with me and dreamed of becoming a singer in the Hindi film industry.

My big 'Bollywood' debut ran into roadblocks when Raj Kanwar, a filmmaker who'd signed a 10-film contract with me, did not start work on his films nor did he allow me to work on any other films that I was offered.

He said: *'Nayi heroine band mutthi ki tarah hoti hai'* (A new actress is like a closed fist), *'Ek baar khul jaaye, toh jaage uski kismet'*. (Once opened, then it's her destiny.)

A year later, John Matthew Mathan, a respected filmmaker and Bhushan Kumar, a film producer and owner of a music label, approached me for a film they were making with then-popular singer Himesh Reshammiya in the lead. When I told them about my contract, Bhushan Kumar came up with a plan. He set up a meeting with Raj Kanwar and Shahid Kapoor, a young promising actor then, on the pretext of developing a project together. Raj Kanwar's previous film 'Humko Deewana Kar Gaye' had tanked at the box office and he was very excited at the prospect. Bhushan Kumar asked Kanwar to release me from his contract as a favor so I could be cast in his other film, since, after all, they were 'one big family'. Bhushan Kumar called me to his office to sign 'A New Love Ishtory' where he gave me an envelope as a signing amount for the film. It contained two 500 Rupee notes (less than 14$). I got a text from him later that night- 'I would love to know you more. Let's get together sometime.' I wrote back saying- 'Absolutely! Let's go on a double date. You bring your wife. I'll bring my boyfriend.' He never wrote to me again. The film took years to make and Bhushan pulled the finance once Reshammiya's films proved duds at the box office. I was compelled to shoot a couple of songs without director John Matthew Mathan's involvement just to quickly wrap up the film. I was neither paid nor called for the dubbing. The incomplete and incohesive final cut was sold straight to a TV channel, with another woman's voice. The cast and crew were never informed. By then, new beauty pageant winners and fresh faces had appeared on the scene and it seemed like my big Bollywood debut was not going to happen. The newly made friendships, sisterhoods and allegiances in the industry began to falter, and my relationship with the young actor from Juhu who was making his Bollywood debut ended.

In 2009, I signed a small indie film titled 'Miss Lovely' with an all new cast and crew. I was required on the set for not more than 15 days. An actor named Nawazuddin Siddiqui who liked to call himself 'Nowaz' was signed for one of the lead roles. I'd never heard of him so I wasn't sure whether he could act at all. During one of my interactions on the sets with Nowaz, he gave me a CD that had a short film on it called 'Bypass' which also starred actor Irrfan Khan, his senior from National School of Drama who was helping him get acting jobs. I was amazed by his performance and screen presence. The Nowaz on the set was nothing like the Nowaz on screen. Since I'd barely noticed him on the set before, I was intrigued. The next time I met him, he sensed my curiosity and invited me to his house for lunch. His frugal apartment and grandiose generosity warmed my heart. We talked about his life and I found him real, after all the superficial 'filmy' interactions I'd had in the past years.

One morning, when I was home and he had been shooting all night, Nowaz sent me a text saying he was near my building. I invited him over and asked him to come and have breakfast with me. When I opened the door, he grabbed me. I tried to push but he wouldn't let go. After a little coercion, I finally gave in. I wasn't sure what to make of this relationship. He told me it was his dream to have a Miss India or an actress wife, just like Paresh Rawal and Manoj Bajpayee. I found his little confession funny but endearing. I was drawn to the stories from his life. I introduced him to my sister and friends. But he was very insecure around them and preferred to spend time with me alone. He often complained about how he was judged on his looks, skin color and that he wasn't fluent in English. I tried to help him deal with his insecurities, but he was stuck in a state of victimization. In the next couple of months, I began to discover one lie after another. Nowaz had engaged multiple women, giving each one a different story; one of them even called me from his phone and started yelling at me. I also found out about a woman he'd married in Haldwani, whose family had sued him for making dowry demands. I told him to clean up his mess, be honest with himself and everyone around him also that I did not want to see him again.

I signed a Kannada film and continued modeling to pay the bills. My sister finished college, started working and found love. She was planning her wedding around the time I met a guy named Mayank Singh Singhvi at a friend's birthday party. He was an investment banker and had nothing to do with film, which to me, was like a breath of fresh air. Within two months of meeting me, Mayank tattooed my name on his chest and told me that he was in love with me. I didn't feel the same way about him. But he managed to get into my social circle and develop a bond with my family and friends who insisted I 'settle down'. In 2011, on my 29. birthday, he gave me a ring and asked me to marry him. Mayank, as I found out later, was a sociopath, and I broke off my engagement at the end of 2011. His ego was bruised, and his anger was uncontrollable. Using casteist slurs, he got abusive and physically violent. I went to a friend's house to protect myself and left Mumbai soon after with a broken spirit. Mayank created a false narrative about me after I left that many of my friends chose to believe, which hurt even more. I moved to Dehradun where my father lived, did vipassana and spent time on my own to heal. 'Miss Lovely' got into the Cannes Film Festival in 2012. I felt vindicated and enjoyed the attention of the international press. I posed, preened, finally saw myself on the big screen and returned a changed woman.

Nawaz and I met at Cannes after three years. We hadn't spoken to each other since 2009. He was apologetic for his past behavior, told me he'd worked on his issues, dissolved his first marriage and married a second time. I started laughing. He started crying, confessing he and his second wife were living separately and it was even more complicated since he now had a daughter who he missed dearly. I looked at him with compassion and told him that he could call me if he needed to talk. There was one caveat though - He must never lie to me again. 2012 was the year he got his first brush with 'fame'. He wasn't used to public life or much attention. He would call me every day not knowing how to deal with it and I tried to guide him through the madness. I was living in Dehradun that time and had applied for a film appreciation course at FTII in Pune. I didn't take up any film offers I was getting because I wanted to study post my Cannes experience and was not inclined to return to my previous 'filmy' life. I tried reconnecting with my family. My mother who had been living separately from my father for years was struggling with mental health and my father was about to retire from government service. Nawaz had family in Dehradun who I had been introduced to. I was very fond of his brother Faizy and his wife. We all even celebrated Eid together once. In 2013, Nawaz was offered a film by Buddhadeb Dasgupta titled 'Anwar ka ajab kissa' and he called me to ask me if I would do a small role in that film. I would only be required to shoot for 3 days. I gladly agreed and went to Shimultata where the shoot was scheduled. He tried to re-engage me sexually, begging me to be with him but I refused, saying I was happy to be his friend and nothing else. After coming back from the shoot, I didn't take his calls and maintained my distance.

I met Nawaz again in 2014 at the 'Miss Lovely' India release. This time he came in a SUV, with an entourage as the 'star' of the film. He was constantly throwing tantrums, upset with the way the promotions were being handled. He complained that the director should've just made a painting at home if he didn't care much about box-office. He was very awkward around me, so I tried to overcompensate by praising him in media interactions and indulged him to make him feel secure. One evening, after a promotional event in Ahmedabad, he tried to grab me again. I just walked away. *'Anwar ka ajab kissa'* didn't get a theatrical release and I heard from various sources that Nawaz had started telling people that I was a terrible actress. I didn't get too many films offers after that.

In 2017, Nawazuddin Siddiqui wrote a memoir called 'An ordinary life', with writer Rituparna Chatterjee, which was published by Penguin Random House. Under the title 'Relationships', he wrote a completely fabricated account of our relationship without my knowledge or consent. Before the book launch, publicists leaked sensational excerpts to garner interest in the book. A senior theatre and television actress Sunita Rajwar who had known Nawaz since her NSD days confirmed his 'extraordinary lies' and filed a case. He offered a token social media apology withdrawing the book. I ordered the book online a week later and it was delivered to my house.

Director Anurag Kashyap, Nawaz's mentor and close collaborator who chose to turn a blind eye towards sexual harassment within his own company, continues to support Nawaz and his story. Writer Rituparna Chatterjee with her completely unethical, defamatory and poorly researched book is not apologetic either. I tried to seek legal help and spoke to a lawyer. His advice to me was to 'meditate' and forget about the whole thing unless I wanted to get on every news channel and have a media trial. Another lawyer from New Delhi took it upon himself to file a complaint against the actor with the National Commission of Women. News channels and publications regurgitated the sensational content from the book along with images from different phases of my life adding further fabricated layers to the story. This public scandal was one of the biggest controversies of 2017. Penguin Random House took no responsibility and remained silent.

Filmmakers, Writers, Publishers, Journalists, Lawyers -nobody can take a high moral ground. They were all complicit in this collective public shaming.

Nawazuddin Siddiqui after playing the role of 'Manto' became the harbinger of truth. He was invited by JNU and various literary festivals as a guest where he played the role of truth-teller effortlessly. His fan following on social media multiplied; GQ magazine then awarded him 'Actor of the year'. Netflix started a second season of 'Sacred Games' with him in the lead. Nawaz's repeated stance that he wrote the memoir while he was preparing for the role of Saadat Hasan Manto makes for the perfect irony.

In June this year, I received a call from a woman who introduced herself as Mayank Singhvi's wife; the same man I was briefly engaged to, in 2011. She wanted to know my reasons for calling off the engagement. I told her my story. She confided in me that she'd been abused from the first week of their marriage and was trying to get out. We stayed in touch forming a kind of sisterhood. A few days later she was found dead in her marital home under mysterious circumstances. Mayank Singhvi was taken into judicial custody.

Violence against women may be a common feature faced by all women in India, but there is no denying the fact that certain kinds of violence are customarily reserved solely for Dalit women. More so for those who assert themselves and reject caste and patriarchal domination. While crimes against upper caste women are taken seriously and elicit more empathy, violation of rights of Dalit women and the injustice meted out to us has an excruciating long history. Statistics show that crimes against Dalits have risen by 746% in the last one decade. A Dalit atrocity is committed every 15 minutes and six Dalit women are raped every day. Most cases are neither registered nor acted upon and the perpetrators go scot-free. Power is an everyday, socialized and embodied phenomenon. In the case of Nawaz and I, it is easy to see how power dynamics changed through the years and with that, also the narrative. Nawaz being an aspirational, sexually repressed Indian man whose toxic male entitlement grew with his success, is hardly surprising. What is interesting to note is that despite not identifying as a Hindu, he carries deep caste prejudices since he chose to protect the honor of his 'Brahmin' wife after their names came up in the CDR scam while on the other hand, he felt very comfortable painting me as a seductress wearing faux for in his book, who he could sexually exploit, for public imagination.

The director of 'Miss Lovely', Ashim Ahluwalia, who I had known through the years, had been a friend and a voice of reason. I always shared my dating disasters and Mumbai misadventures with him, and he usually helped me put things into perspective. Ashim's marriage with one of the producers of Miss Lovely ended and he began seeking me out as his emotional anchor. We were there for each other through difficult times and he encouraged me to return to films.

Patriarchy has no gender. Nor does abuse. We can't forget the role of mothers and wives who are equally responsible in covering or enabling their sons' and husbands' crimes. Women in power like Nandita Das and Kavita

Krishnan have all shown professional and political allegiance with predators and enabled them through their silence or solidarity. Lending their voices to 'survivors' of the #Me-too movement now only comes across as fraudulent. It's time to realize that the pompous, neoliberal, savarna feminism is not going to liberate anyone. Unless the Savarna feminists do not dismantle the same power structures from which they have benefitted, women in this country will continue to be gaslit, exploited and maligned; their dreams thwarted, voices silenced, bodies assaulted, and histories erased.

The selective outrage of the supposed 'liberals' and 'Indian leftists' benefits only their convenience, and we most note that it finally took a Dalit student, Raya Sarkar in academia and a beauty pageant winner, Tanushree Dutta, to burst the Bollywood bubble while they silently looked on for years. *Last but not the least*, filmmaker Sajid Khan made a few predictions when a close friend of ours was opening her second restaurant - 'This place will shut down within a year, mark my words.' To his actress girlfriend he said, 'She won't survive a day without me in Bollywood'. 'And, this one', looking at me straight, 'will soon commit suicide.' My restaurateur friend is opening her fourth restaurant. It is difficult to get a table at the other three. The actress' career skyrocketed after she dumped the filmmaker and I, have managed to stay alive."

Rediff. News came out with an article, *'#MeToo fallout in Bollywood'* on 22nd October 2018. "Will Nana Patekar's role be deleted from Housefull 4? Will Subhash Kapoor lose the Jolly LLB franchise? Is- Anu Malik's career in limbo? Subhash K Jha mulls over these questions. It could be a replay of what transpired after Kevin Spacey was accused of sexual offences, Nana Patekar could find his role removed from the underproduction comedy franchise Housefull 4. When Tanushree Dutta's revelations placed Nana at the centre of the controversy, he was shooting Housefull 4. After the outraged protests, Patekar may find his role written out of the film. Says a source close to Housefull 4, "In Hollywood, they scrapped Kevin Spacey's role from *'All the Money in The World'* and replaced him with Christopher Plummer overnight. Some such surgical operation is a possibility in this case. Instead of replacing Nana, they may cut his role from the film." While Sajid Nadiadwala, who co-produces Housefull 4 and Super 30, refrained - directs -- as well as Housefull 4 entirely. "There is *Not a single woman who does not have a #MeToo story"*, said actress Renuka Shahane. Director Subhash Kapoor, accused of sexual misconduct, lost the biopic he was meant to direct for Aamir Khan and Bhushan Kumar, *'Mogul'*, based on the late music baron Gulshan Kumar's life. "Fox Star, who produced the *Jolly LLB* series, have zero tolerance for sexual offences," says a source. Akshay Kumar, who plays the lead, has made it clear that he won't work with anyone linked to sexual offences. "Housefull 4 Director Sajid Khan has been accused of sexual misconduct and had to be fired on" Akshay says-so. Subhash Kapoor will have to go too." Anu Malik is dropped from *Indian Idol*. Anu Malik has been removed as a judge on Sony Entertainment Television's *Indian Idol* where he has been a judge on the show right from its inception. Sources at Sony say the composer was "absolutely sure" of his position on *Indian Idol*. 'There is no *Indian Idol* without Anu Malik,' he is said to have told some colleagues. With Anu out of *Indian Idol*, he has nothing to fall back on to keep his career going. His songs were recently used in *Sui Dhaaga*, but will big banners, or even small, still come to him with offers?"

Rediffcom. News came out with a related article the same day *'Men are* trembling *now'*. "'Predators will always try, but I'm sure there will be less. We need one or two big examples like this.' Olga tells *Rediff. com's* Archana Masih about how the work environment has changed for women journalists since she began her career 52 years ago, about the sexual harassment charges against MJ Akbar, her editor at two publications, and where the #MeToo movement is headed.

How the work environment has changed for women journalists: When I began in journalism, it was a man's world. There are more women than men in journalism today. I was the *first* reporter to be taken in by the *Ananda Bazar Patrika*. They had women doing food columns, but when I joined, Ananda Bazar had never had any woman reporter. My interview was not even like an interview. I remember being told 'See how they take to you', but they accepted me from the first day. Within a month of my joining I was sent on an assignment to Sri Lanka. There was a small bureau in Mumbai. I went, sat in my place and started to work. It was just me, the manager and one more person who looked after advertising.

I started to report whatever there was. Whenever men came from the Calcutta office (where the Ananda Bazar Patrika group is headquartered), they always looked sideways to see who this creature was. I was one of those wearing tight skirts and heels. A female on the staff was a novelty over there. When you are young you are very confident, you think you can do anything. I was accepted even by colleagues at other newspapers. They used to say that they treat women badly and do not take them seriously but from day one, I was taken very seriously. In fact, I owe a lot to male colleagues from other newspapers who really helped me.

If junior reporters ever complained to her about sexual harassment: No. No junior came to complain to me. I don't know how we never knew about (MJ) Akbar. Women did not complain about it. (Olga worked with Akbar twice, at the Mumbai bureau of *Sunday* magazine and then at *The Asian Age* when Akbar was the editor based in Calcutta and New Delhi). I was quite shocked to know that all this was going on. One knew that Akbar had a glad eye like a lot of men have, but never to this extent that one is reading. I was very surprised. He educated you in journalism. He told you what to do with your story, how to start it, etc. He ha-d a hot temper and I owe a lot to him but whatever he is today, I am shocked about him. In Mumbai, I knew he would call people to his room, but I never heard that anyone had complained about it. Akbar joined *Sunday* as the youngest editor at 27. He changed the look of the magazine and it became a must-read for everybody. It was so popular. Wherever I went, people knew me because of the magazine. No other paper or magazine had such an impact. Then he employed me in the Asian Age. He was always in Delhi. He then became a politician. He had such a respected journalism career. It is sad how he has squandered everything."

On 23rd October 2018, *Rediff.com News* published awe-inspiring, 'Dear sexual predator'.

Dear sexual predator,

'I don't care how accomplished you are, and I don't care about your career which has burst into pretty flames.' 'I do care about all the women you've abused and scarred and made life hell for,' says Mitali Saran. I know it's wrong, but I think about you all the time. What are you wearing? I like to imagine you in your hair shirt, under your cloak of shame with a thick lining of regret. It's haawt. I'm very worried for you because the impossible has happened: Twitter is even angrier! It's the worst. Your deepest fears have come true -- the headlines have been taken over by hordes of angry, possibly hairy feminists with no sense of humor.

Why can't they just relax and take a joke, right? (A good banging would help them, but they're too boring and ugly and frigid to get laid.) They should get some sense knocked into them by the more understanding ladies, the ones who talk feminism and walk bro code, who agree with you that 'Men are like that' and 'If she's going to be a tease, she's got it coming' and 'Why did it take her so long to speak up' and 'She enjoyed the perks of the attention'. Maybe they could re-educate the less understanding ladies who go on about consent in every moment and sovereignty over one's body. It's just mayhem out there -- those vindictive women are breaking every rule in the big book of patriarchy, which is their big fancy word for 'society'.

Can you imagine publicly, sometimes anonymously, sharing old texts, or anecdotes about your behavior -- totally normal man behavior! They're being so negative. What's the fuss about a little feel or a little sexting or a little tongue or a little penetration, especially if she's awake? Some of them should be grateful that anyone is looking at them at all.

Most importantly, what about due process? Isn't presumption of innocence the cornerstone of justice? Last year when women in academia compiled a list of men accused of sexually harassing or assaulting people (known as #LoSHA), many ladies came through, insisting that one can't accuse people of harassment or assault without hard evidence. (Luckily, some hard evidence works like that perfect murder weapon, the ice dagger. Hyuk, hyuk!) This year, most of them agree that the same tactics are legitimate. Talk about rocking the boat and upsetting the applecart, both of which are owned, filled, and managed by people like you. Talk about tying up the farmer and setting fire to the farm. I mean, are these law-abiding citizens, or guerrillas rejecting conventional rules of engagement on the grounds that the power equation doesn't allow for it? Instead of smacking them down, companies are double checking to see if previous complaints were properly investigated, which, by the way, makes it look as if they are aware that 'due process' doesn't work.

Whose side are they on? I mean, can 500 million bros be wrong? Women used to be cute when they were angry -- now they're scary aft. Star editors, journalists, celebrity consultants, actors, directors, lyricists, comedians, leading lights in the NGO sector. Is nobody safe in the world, run smoothly and comfortably for so long? *I'm so worried about your future.* Ha, just kidding! I don't care: what you're wearing; what you're feeling; how accomplished you are; about your career which has burst into pretty flames; or about your reputation -- I hope it never recovers enough for you to forget what it looks like right now. I do care about those of your family members who are appalled by your behavior -- you've dumped a world of pain into their lives too. And I do care about all the women you've abused and scarred and made life hell for. *Do you feel bad about that? Yeah, me too.*" [Courtesy: *Business Standard*]

On 24th October, another viewpoint appeared on *Rediff.com News* as, *'Why #MeToo needs all our support'*. '"#MeToo is not to be dismissed as 'shoot and scoot' but seen as the uncovering of dark truths about seemingly sophisticated and powerful personalities, or at least as one providing catharsis to a survivor,' notes Utkarsh Mishra. My hesitant contemplation of penning my thoughts about the #MeToo movement in India transformed into a firm, burning desire over the past week. Not the least because the unforeseen support lent by about 20 women journalists -- including a former boss and an ex-colleague of mine -- to Priya Ramani in her legal fight forced a hitherto stubborn Union minister to step down. But the fire was lit by a column by a veteran woman journalist in the Indian Express that, I must say, was spectacularly stupid. Frankly, the Express should have treated the column the same way it chose to publish censored information during the Emergency. But this time, by blacking out the text; that way, it would have conveyed to the reader the magnitude of its sheer nonsensicality. Digressing from her perennial conflicts with India's 'socialism' and welfare schemes like MNREGA, this time the columnist attacked the #MeToo movement for being 'too elite'.

Social media is a double-edged sword. While the platform serves as a healthy tool to spread positivity and inspire the world, unfortunately, some use it to spread hate and negativity. Celebrities, particularly celebrity mums are often the soft target of trolls. From what they wear and eat to what they do in their 'me time', celebrity lives are subject to scrutiny and almost always becomes the point of discussion and debate. Presenting a listicle of dreadful incidents of violence and abuse against rural women whose videos she saw on social media, she asked how this #MeToo campaign would help those poor victims. In her pursuit to deride the movement, she put all phrases like 'sexual harassment', 'abuse', 'brave women' and 'predators' in quotes. Because, apparently, it is not sexual harassment for a young woman to have herself grabbed from behind by a man older than her father and have his tongue shoved down her throat. And if you belong to that privileged fraternity of women who go out to work on their own terms and earn enough to support an upper middle- class lifestyle then, hey, you can't be harassed.

Added to this column were *WhatsApp* messages and Facebook posts by friends and family members -- sadly, all women -- critical of the movement, accompanied by the usual questions: Why did they wait all these years? Why didn't they file a complaint then? Why did they continue to work at the same place? Every touch is not harassment etc. The major point that the veteran woman journalist and other women questioning the movement are missing is that this movement facilitated the uncovering of a vicious reality which even those women considered to be 'empowered' live out daily. Rather than dismiss it as mere pretensions, those genuinely concerned would ask if this is what the 'empowered' women face and if this is what the seemingly gentlemen types do, then imagine the horrors the not-so-privileged women of our society would be going through.

The movement puts a question mark on the very notion that education and the strength to earn their own living 'empowers' women. It says that even if you escape one set of predators in your home or neighborhood or village, you will certainly be introduced to another in your fancy offices or elegant university campuses. Often the latter happens to be shrewder and slyer. It is grossly unfair to dismiss the #MeToo movement as 'grumbling by elite women who got what they wanted at that time but have a problem with it now'. I also intend to address a few other doubts and questions that I have encountered about this movement.

Why didn't they raise their voices then? *Firstly,* most such incidents involve a young woman just starting out on her career and a man enjoying unbridled power in an organization. Speaking up becomes a bit more difficult in such a case. Moreover, such incidents shock a helpless victim tremendously, repressing her reflexes, as not even in her wildest dream would she have anticipated a physical assault by her middle-aged boss at her workplace while being asked to assist in regular work. (Thanks to the #MeToo movement, though, now one will not rule out such a possibility.) *Secondly,* when a powerful person having greater reach in an organization attacks you, who would you trust to lodge a complaint with? In several cases, the complaints of survivors were not taken seriously even by their female bosses, who did their best to shield the predator instead. *Thirdly,* I don't think there were Internal Complaints Committees at that time, which were recommended by the Supreme Court in the Vishakha guidelines in 1997 and mandated by Sexual Harassment of Women at Workplace (Prevention, Prohibition and Redressal) Act, 2013. The options, therefore, were very limited. *Lastly,* it is not only due to the fear of losing one's job that one avoided taking up the issue, but also due to the fear of escalation of harassment in case the complaint went in vain. *Sadly, it only emboldened the predators.*

However, the #MeToo campaign can change all these. On one hand, by creating a favorable environment for the survivors where their complaints are taken seriously and, on the other, by presenting the perpetrators with a disincentive that they can be named and shamed.

***Legal options*:** Often the women who are joining this wave are criticized for not resorting to legal remedies at the time of the harassment. Even if one musters up courage to embroil oneself in the rigors of a court case, the options, as mentioned earlier, were very limited those days. 'Sexual harassment' or 'outraging a woman's modesty' were loosely defined terms in the Indian Penal Code and there was no separate Act dealing with sexual harassment at the workplace. It was only after the Bhanwari Devi case in 1997 that the Supreme Court issued the Vishakha guidelines, and sexual harassment was clearly defined. But the most powerful legal weapon against such crimes was made available only in 2013 -- in the aftermath of the horrific Delhi gang rape of December 16, 2012 -- in the form of Sexual Harassment of Women at Workplace (Prevention, Prohibition and Redressal) Act, 2013. Also, the Criminal Law Amendment Act of 2013 substantially modified Section 354 of the IPC, dealing with 'outraging modesty', and listing online stalking, forcing a woman to talk against her wish etc. as criminal offences.

In criminal trials, the burden of proof lies on the prosecution. And it could be very difficult to prove if one was 'touched inappropriately', especially in a closed room with no witnesses. The only possible disincentive for such men to desist from this sort of behavior could be the fear that they can be outed. And that's what the #Me campaign does. But there are some who have the gall to go to court alleging defamation even in the face of a concerted campaign calling out their predatory behavior. It requires a movement like #MeToo to take on such people. It is very difficult for an individual to do that, especially someone who just starting out in her career.

Why did they continue to work in the same organization? Excuse me! Why should I derail my career because of the sleazy behavior of some maniac? A safe environment at workplaces is not a privilege to be given but a right of every employee. And the one who is disturbing such an atmosphere needs to go, not the person at the receiving end. This argument also reflects that mentality of our society where a family's answer to a complaint of eve-teasing by their daughter is to stop her from going to school, college or work. Many girls, and women, therefore, prefer not to tell their family about the daily harassment they face lest they be confined to their homes.

All bad behavior is not harassment True. But even inappropriate behavior not amounting to physical harassment can give the victim a lot of anxiety. I've seen many commenting that 'You see, if someone backs off after your snub, then you shouldn't consider it harassment'. Technically true, but why be so shameless to elicit a blunt response from someone, can't you read the signals and stop acting like a moron? But some who don't do that because in their own parallel universe they think that enough persuasion is going to get them what they want. And sometimes their big masculine ago is also hurt by a terse response so they begin maligning the girl. Women have all the right to not expect their male colleagues make repeated attempts at wooing them, and they shouldn't be blamed for freaking out if that is what they encounter all the time.

And finally, the men: A lot of concern has been raised about the misuse of this movement. After all, one anonymous complaint can cost a person his job and reputation. But this very movement has also presented us with the example of Varun Grover to allay such fears. His detailed response and willingness to be investigated by any committee the 'victim's choosing' has convinced most of his followers of his innocence. However, there is no denying that the amended Section 354 can be misused, just like IPC 498A or the amended SC/ST Atrocities (Prevention) Act. When concerns are raised about the misuse of draconian anti-terror laws, then experts advise us to live with this 'necessary evil' in order to contain a larger problem. Something of that sort can be also said about concerns regarding #MeToo. Nevertheless, the need to place safeguards arises from the very coarseness of such movements. And, therefore, the nature of this movement must be preserved. It is not to be dismissed as a 'shoot and scoot' but seen as the uncovering of dark truths about seemingly sophisticated and powerful personalities, or at least as one providing catharsis to a survivor. *Is that such a bad thing*? [*Utkarsh Mishra/Rediff.com*]

On 27th October 2018, *Rediff.com News* published, '*Durga, Shakti and #MeToo*'. "'This year, it may be pertinent to look at some of the myths that invoke her warrior form, where she manifests herself as Shakti, the underlying strength in all humanity,' says Arundhuti Dasgupta. It is that time of the year when the goddess is worshipped in several parts of the country. But this year, it may be pertinent to look at some of the myths that invoke her warrior form, where she manifests herself as Shakti, the underlying strength in all humanity. #MeToo, anyone? The goddess in India, as in Ancient Egypt and Greece, appears before us in many forms. So, she is the prosperity-endowing Lakshmi as much as she is the bloodthirsty Kali or Chandi.

In many myths, especially older ones, the goddess appears as a dual divinity. She is both a generative and destructive force and, in this form, draws from the archetype of the earth mother who can be both nurturing and calamitous. For instance, the Greek goddess Artemis is the goddess of childbirth and death and disease (for females). Joseph Campbell (Primitive Mythology) says 'We find the imagery of the mother associated almost equally with beatitude and danger, birth and death, the inexhaustible nourishing breast and the tearing claws of the ogress'.

Durga and Kali are examples of the above in India; Hathor in Egypt and Gaia, the Greek earth goddess, would fit the same frame. Durga is both a mother goddess, who comes visiting her family on earth every year, and ruthless killer of demons on the battlefield. Among the most enduring myths around her is the slaying of the buffalo demon, Mahishasura, which also earns her the epithet of Mahishasuramardini. Her story appears in several texts, but the most detailed version of the battle is in the Devi Mahatmya. In this version, Durga was sent to the battlefield by the entire pantheon of gods to defeat Mahisha, who wanted to be king of the heavens. A boon from creator god Brahma had granted him conditional immortality; no man or god could kill him; death would come only by a woman's hand. But when Durga appeared on the battlefield, the demon, instead of fighting her with the full force of his vast army, began a courtship dance. He sent his generals and aides to woo the goddess on his behalf and when all failed, stepped out to win the goddess with his riches, his powerful persona and undying love for her. But Durga rejected him and in his anger, he attacked her, bringing about his end.

This myth offers many meanings. It has been used to show how absolute power leads to arrogance and destruction. Durga has also become a metaphor for military success. In the Ramayana as told in the Kalika Purana (not the Valmiki version), Durga comes to Rama's aid on the battlefield and after Ravana was killed, the gods led by Brahma held a special worship for her. Across the ancient world, the power of goddesses is the subject of many narratives, but so is the underlying acceptance of the fact that the woman (goddess or not) is to be won by a man or god.

In Scandinavian mythology, Freyr is the god of fertility and plenty and an all-powerful figure. He was smitten by the underworld giant Gerd who did not reciprocate his feelings. Freyr offered Gerd all the riches at his disposal and when that failed threatened her with the sword. But she still didn't relent until a friend of the gods and giants, Skirmir, stepped in and convinced her to give in to the god or else the giants would be wiped out. One rule for the gods and another for the giants and demons, discrimination was woven into the social fabric from the start. In many societies, the nature of the goddess changed as men took control of the social structure as priests, bards and kings. Durga, for instance, was merged with the more benign form of Parvati, mother to a brood of goddesses and gods. In Indonesia, a poem composed sometime in the 14th century laments the fall of Uma, the wife of Bhatara Guru who was unfaithful to her husband. She is cursed by her husband and turns into a demoness called Durga with huge flaring nostrils and patchy skin who is forced to live in the graveyard for 12 years till she is exorcised of her sins by Shiva. For a society that was keen to punish adulterous women, this myth served as an effective warning. Maybe it is time to flip the old myths and find some new meanings and metaphors to help us navigate modern times." [Source: *Business Standard*]

On 29th October 2018, *Rediff.com News* published, "*#MeToo will change the narrative forever*'. "'#MeToo is a giant stride towards protesting sexual/verbal assault.' 'It is very important for us, as a society, to 'listen', to introspect and to understand that this is part of 'change' towards a safer society.' 'Hushing it up will only encourage the perpetrators who will begin to feel that they are invincible.' *In 2017, when the MeToo movement gained momentum in the West, a group of Indian artistes had declared that India was ready for its #TimesUp moment.* Four actresses -- Rima Kallingal, Remya Nambisan, Geetu Mohandas and the actress who was abducted and molested in early 2017 -- quit the Association of Malayalam Movie Artists in June 2017 to protest the reinstatement of accused actor Dileep in AMMA. The Women in Cinema Collective was started by a group of female artistes and directors in 2017 to protect the interests of female actors and crew members and fight for equal opportunities (external link) and provide a safe working environment in the industry. While WCC has a strong support of followers both online and offline, it has lately been the target of trolls and hate on social media. "Due process by law is an important part of the #MeToo movement. Calling out itself is a big step, but most women are using this because they believe there was no 'due process' available," actress and director Revathi, president, Women in Cinema Collective, tells Rediff.com's Divya Nair. At the WCC media meet, you mentioned an incident that occurred 25 years ago (Revathi said a 17-year-old girl had knocked at her door and how she and her grandmother calmed the minor through the night. Revathi later clarified that no sexual assault happened). Do you think people are overreacting that you brought up the incident now? It was an incident that disturbed me. How can anyone knock on a woman's door and scare her? If we ask around, I am sure, we will find many such instances where one would have endured that fear and kept quiet about it. I shared that instance at the press meet only because I feel strongly that henceforth no one should ever have the impertinence to force someone into submission and in case that happens, we should have someone we can call, someone in the film unit we can trust. This is where the role of ICC (internal complaints committee) is important with committee members who are committed to the cause. I have been a conscientious person who has raised my voice for several causes. Some people have misunderstood the context in which I spoke about the incident and are digressing by pointing fingers at me.

You have worked across the entertainment industry. Have you faced any such untoward incidents in your career? Where there are men and women at work, there is always some harmless flirting.

Only when one crosses 'the line' it gets uncomfortable. In most people's lives, there will be a couple in instances where someone crosses the comfort line. It has happened to me too, but I was able to speak up and stop it before anything untoward happened. My parents have taught me to speak up and never endure anything that I am not comfortable with. That has given me the fortitude to oppose whenever faced with such situations. Family support is very important, be it for a girl or a boy, to encounter and protest any kind of harassment or assault.

Why do you think the #MeToo movement took so long to come to India? I believe that such movements happen when we are all ready to face it. It takes a lot of courage to speak about such intimate things, as each girl who speaks might be hurting her immediate family, friends and her own self. Also, we, as a society are always scrutinizing the women and ready to point fingers at them, even if it wasn't her fault. A woman is always asked to keep quiet no matter what, by parents, teachers, brothers, even husbands. #MeToo is a giant stride towards openly protesting sexual/verbal assault and it is very important for us, as a society, to 'listen', to introspect and to understand that this is part of 'change' towards a safer society. Hushing it up will only encourage the perpetrators who will begin to feel that they are invincible.

A section of the audience alleges that the WCC is targeting actor Dileep or rather, one incidence. Do you agree? Actor Dileep's arrest shocked everyone in the industry and outside, as for the first time an actor filed a FIR and the enquiry led to one of our own members in the industry. The abduction incident triggered in the formation of this collective and it is our foremost objective to procure justice for 'her'. The WCC is not interested in targeting any individual but is working as a watch dog in this case. It is also essential to have a redressal mechanism in the industry and we have neglected this. Rather, we seem to have brushed it aside for far too long simply by shutting one's eyes to the 'happenings.' Every step that the WCC has taken until now, is towards a safer and equal workspace in our industry.

What exactly is the WCC's stand right now? What do you expect AMMA to do to make things right? How can they take stringent and fair action? The WCC, then and now, raises our collective voice when there is injustice done to a woman in our industry. AMMA did not follow their existing bylaws when deciding in this 'extraordinary situation'. We, Padma Priya, Parvathy and me as members tried our best to give them an informed solution. The effort was made to help the association make the right decision which would then lay an archetype for the future. Now, as a step towards progressing to where the rest of the film industries are moving -- AMMA needs to revamp their byelaws, to be more inclusive and take steps towards the safety of their women members. A redressal cell, where the complaints, however small, are officially registered, is essential. In the end it is not just byelaws and laws that can create a safe working environment, it is the attitude and sensitivity of the executive members, who are the office bearers that makes the difference and bring about changes. They need to get out of the 'boys club' attitude and become a gender sensitive group.

Did you ever feel threatened while supporting the WCC? I am one of the founding members of the WCC and I believe in 'equal space', 'equal opportunities' and a 'safe working place' in our industry. How can I feel threatened? When an artist/crew member approaches the WCC to help them file/report a case of sexual harassment, how does the WCC help the victim? We are still evolving and are hoping to create all the necessary support in the immediate future. At present, we are an advocacy group that raises awareness about issues in our industry and finding solutions. This is a path that has never been tread so we are hoping to create the necessary redressal mechanisms within our industry. The process had already begun.

What happens when the person accused is powerful and tries to intimidate the victim to drop the case? How does the WCC help? We stand by her as we are doing with our colleague at present.

Are you surprised by some/any of the names that have come up for allegations? No. I am not surprised but saddened by some names.

Do trolls and social media hate bother you? I am not very active in social media, so I don't get affected by them.

Do you feel the #MeToo movement will bring positive change? #MeToo movement, will change the narrative forever. The courage that some women have shown is laudable and it's heartening to see that more women are standing by them. Social media as a platform has changed communication and helps an individual to reach out to the world personally. Most perpetrators fear their image getting tarnished, so such people will think twice before attempting any kind of assault -- verbally or sexually, in future. As people are named, the law too will get stringent towards sexual assault/harassment. Society at large, will become aware of the existence of such situations and educate the future generation to safeguard themselves.

Will naming and shaming alone help? Or you think the accused (if proven) should be given tough punishment? Due process by law is an important part of the #MeToo movement. Calling out itself is a big step, but most women are using this because they believe there was no 'due process' available.

In our country, justice takes years, sometimes decades. Justice delayed is justice denied. This needs to change. Sexual harassment/rape cases must go to trial in the shortest period. Only then will more women have the courage to speak up. When they speak up and justice is done, no parent or person in our society will tell victims to keep quiet. Feeling empowered to speak up. is the first step towards a safer society.

What advice/message do you have for readers who are scared to speak up against harassment? When people are ready, they will speak up. One cannot force or instigate anyone to speak up. But in the mood of #MeToo, if anyone wants to speak up, I am sure there will be many who will support and walk along with them. Personally, I feel the person who wants to speak up should meet a counsellor to be sure that they are ready as the repercussions can be distressing.

What advice would you give young actors/artists? How can they prevent themselves from being harassed or abused at work? One should have the courage to speak up and say 'NO', and the other needs to understand that a 'NO means NO'. I don't need to give any more advice/message to this generation as they have the biggest tool in their hands: The smart phone. They know best how to use it. So, use it to help yourself and for your own benefit. [*Divya Nair/Rediff.com*]

On 31st October 2018, *Rediffmail.com News* article: '*Phase Two of #MeToo begins*'." MJ Akbar underestimated the level of pent-up anger and commitment among these women,' a young lawyer tells Sunil Sethi. 'Memory,' said Oscar Wilde, '*is the diary we all carry about with us.*' In many painful accounts that women have exhumed from their working lives at the hands of men, the roiling of long-buried humiliations are now known as a 'trigger'. News portals at the frontline of the #MeToo campaign carry warnings that the disturbing content may 'trigger' other memories. In a radical redefinition of sexual harassment our daily lexicon, too, has radically changed. A male aggressor is no longer a 'groper', 'lecher', 'pouncer' or 'old rogue', but 'predator'.

Victims are 'survivors'. With the resignation of former editor and BJP minister MJ Akbar, Phase One of #MeToo has ended in a decisive victory for the growing lineup of women journalists who called him out. Whether he voluntarily stepped down or was asked to be immaterial; as the first political casualty and most high-profile of public figures outed, his resignation is a major step forward for the movement. But he is by no means contrite or apologetic.

Phase Two of #MeToo has moved quickly from the newsroom to the courtroom following Mr. Akbar's criminal complaint against Priya Ramani whose tweet opened the floodgates. Having churned the world of academics, entertainment and the media, it is now causing ripples in the legal fraternity -- not only as a test case but because of its unusual inversion. In a curious role reversal, Akbar, the accused, is now the complainant, and the accuser, Ms. Ramani, is the new accused. Akbar's defamation employs a long string of adverbs ('willfully, deliberately, intentionally, maliciously', etc.) to denounce her -- and how socially damaging and hurtful to his personal image and career built with toil. Ms. Ramani will be in the dock to defend herself.

Comparisons are odious but, were a parallel to be drawn, it would be the long drawn out, and ultimately tragic, case of Oscar Wilde vs the Marquess of Queensbury, a watershed mark in legal and literary history. It all began a bit like Ms. Ramani's terse tweet of October 8. On February 18, 1895, Queensbury (whose son was Wilde's lover) left his calling card at Wilde's London club. It simply read, 'Oscar Wilde is a sodomite.' Wilde sued for defamation; in the sensational battle that ensued, Queensbury's lawyers produced a series of men, some quite young, with whom Wilde had had homosexual liaisons. Homosexuality then being a crime, they succeeded in portraying him as a depraved old man luring young men into acts 'of gross indecency'. Public opinion swerved so sharply that Wilde, the most celebrated and admired writer of his time, pleadingly had to remind the court that 'I am the prosecutor'.

To the question why MJ Akbar's action is only against Ms. Ramani, whose allegation is mild compared to the far more damning testimonies of the others (and they number as many as 20), the answer is that if he sued all, he would be subjected to cross-examination 20 times, with fresh arguments and evidence. Ms. Ramani, of course, can summon all the others in her 'defenses of the truth'. Perhaps the most harrowing account is by Ghazala Wahab of her days at The Asian Age, an ugly cat-and-mouse game of molesting and emotional blackmail inside the editor's cabin. Akbar's defense is that it was a 'tiny cubicle patched together by plywood and glass'. No, says Ms. Wahab, by 1997 he had moved into a large, book-lined virtually soundproof chamber when her troubles began. Among Oscar Wilde's most-quoted epigrams is 'I can resist everything except temptation'. Akbar's victims, like Wilde's, were often young and vulnerable and from small towns.

Like the literary leviathan's, his undeniable brilliance, power and professional reputation were magnetic. When the shades fell from their eyes, some of the women left or gave him a wide berth. Despite his notoriety, older women colleagues were either unsuspecting or helpless. 'I never realized MJ had his eyes on her (Ghazala)... What happened to her was horrific... She is not the type to make up a single word... I somehow believed that an arrogant man like him would not pursue someone who rebuffed him,' says senior journalist Seema Guha, who also worked at the paper. Many like her will rise to take a stand on whose truth prevails. No one is betting on how long, or how far, the legal fight will go. But if an injunction last year by Baba Ramdev to ban his biography by journalist Priyanka Pathak-Narain is any indication, it could move swiftly. The case has already reached the Supreme Court. Given the huge stirring of public interest in M J Akbar vs Priya Ramani and support for #MeToo, it should be speedy. "Akbar has underestimated the level of pent-up anger and commitment among these women. It is not a sudden meltdown," says a young lawyer. Wilde, whose birthday it was some days ago, died broken and penniless at the age of 46. He had the last word, though. 'The truth,' he said, 'is rarely pure and never simple.'"

[*Sunil Sethi*/Source: *Business Standard*]

On 15th November 2018, Sonam Kapoor opened on the problems she had with sexual predators in Bollywood on *MSN Entertainment*, 'Sonam K Ahuja finally opens up on #MeToo: I admit that I have been part of the problem' by Pramod Gaikwad. "Last month, Sonam Kapoor had decided to take a break from Twitter after facing severe backlash when she had labelled a man on *Twitter* 'harasser' without a reason. She was accused of playing woman card to quickly dismiss an argument then. People had called her a 'fake feminist' after she disregarded Kangana Ranaut's sexual harassment allegations against Vikas Bahl. *The Veere Di Wedding* actress was also heavily criticized and trolled for tweeting 'Good on you AIB' soon after the comedy group All India Bakchod (AIB) had issued a statement following multiple sexual harassment allegations against stand-up comedian Utsav Chakraborty. She happens to be a good friend of Tanmay Bhat, co-founder of All India Bakchod group and had supported the comedy group earlier when they had faced massive flak for their AIB Roast episodes on YouTube in 2015.

And now after maintaining a stoic silence for over a month on the matter, Sonam has finally given her two cents on the MeToo movement in India. She admitted that she has been a part of the problem but now has pledged to stop working with proven sexual predators from now onwards.

"*I've been part of movies which I know are a part of the problem.* I own up to them now. I admit that I have been part of the problem. Often, we do things unknowingly, but when we know better, we should own up to it. That's how we grow from it. There's also fear of losing assignments and jobs you've worked hard to get, but today, after the courage Tanushree Dutta has exhibited, let there not be any open secrets in any industry anymore. I pledge to never endorse or work with individuals proven to be predatory and guilty," Sonam wrote in her article published in *Thrive Global*.

Sonam lauded the courage of women who risked their identities to name their perpetrators and shame them in public and urged people to believe in survivors. "While people must be treated as innocent until proven guilty, we need to remember that women are taking on incredible personal risk and trauma to tell their stories. We owe them, at the least, our trust and support," she said. Stressing upon bringing a shift in the mindset as a society, Sonam said, "What we need is an entire mental reboot. A shift in mindset which acknowledges that sons and daughters should not be treated differently. That you don't have to give your daughter away. Most likely, she'll walk the road herself and will, often, turn around to come AND care for you when you're old." She also talked about the importance of consent and ditch the entitlement. She further said that if people like her who have earned fame should always speak up and take sides as not doing so may put you on the side of the person who is wrong. I believe that people in every industry—not just Bollywood—need to speak up. People in positions like mine should speak up. While I understand that it's not everyone's job to preach change, it's pivotal that you do. Your fame has earned you this platform and you cannot wash your hands off the responsibility that comes with it. If you are silent and don't take sides then you are, I am afraid, on the side of the person who is wrong. Always take sides," she said. Urging people to stop sexist jokes, Sonam said, "As Indians, we tend to laugh at inappropriate jokes out of politeness. It's not funny, it has never been funny. Roasts, for example, are not funny. It's not okay to make sexist, homophobic, racist jokes in an environment which is rife with sexism and discrimination."

She also expressed her displeasure of being labelled and urged people to end it and reject the perpetrators. During the ongoing #MeToo movement in India, many women have come out and shared their experiences of assault or inappropriate behavior. We look at some celebrities, including Twinkle Khanna (L) and Neha Dhupia, who have showed their support in the movement.

Concluding her article with her final word of caution, Sonam said, " Each one of us, as a supporter of the #MeToo movement, must be with survivors regardless of their gender. It's the bracketing of this movement as men v/s women that can weaken the powerful punches survivors have landed on our superficially inclusive workplaces. In a society where women are complicit in perpetuating misogyny, it shouldn't be about women v/s men. It should be about survivors and perpetrators, about making the society less misogynist, entitled and changing how we think."

On 27th November 2018, *The Indian Express* published, '*Male actors think they will look younger if they romance young actresses: Waheeda Rehman*', by Priyanka Sharma. "They would tell me, especially Dev (Anand), 'You don't know Waheeda. Public wants to see us.' (And I would tell him), 'Yeah, see you and me also.' He would reply, 'No. What happens is that a man stays young forever.' I would ask him that who said that. This is a problem that has existed since the beginning and it continues even today.

A 60-year-old or 52-year-old is being a romantic hero and for a girl, after 25, it's said, 'It's enough.' They (male actors) think, 'We will look as young as the age of the actresses we work with.' There's an insecurity," she said. It was also the most logical thing for Waheeda to fight with her producers over the huge pay disparity. "Pay disparity was same during our times as well and it used to make me angry. But the producers would tell me, 'More girls go to the theaters to watch films and they want to follow the men, not women!'"

Waheeda Rehman also talked about the status of women in the industry five decades ago and how it has changed today. Sharing her take on the ongoing MeToo movement, the actor said she never had an unpleasant experience on a film set nor did she see something happening with women around. "I think in those days they were scared to misbehave with the leading lady because there was a big chance that the lady would say, 'I am walking out of the movie or throw him out.' So, it was a risky thing for them to do."

The actor said the #MeToo stories in the industry that broke last month shocked her as they had names of people who she thought were decent. She said, "Yes, I was very shocked and very pained actually that I thought they were decent people, how could this happen, why should this happen? It's very sad actually. It affects the family, the children. It's very sad." She said because the society empowers women much more than it did five decades ago, women should not fear calling out their perpetrators. "Men have to behave themselves and women have to be very alert. And whatever happens. report immediately. Don't wait for long because society is with you. We are with you. Your parents are with you. What more do you want? You shouldn't be scared. Report and sort, it out." Apart from that, Waheeda also believes the increasing presence of women on a film set is also one of the essentials for a safe environment. The actor said, "If there are more women on sets, then you will feel more secure and that person will be more sympathetic towards you. *The industry is more equal for women today.* There was a gap of 16 years in my career. When I returned, I saw a lot of girls on the set and I wondered what were they doing there? They are now art directors, assistant directors, directors and it's very good," she said.

AFTERWORD

One must have noted throughout the book that we are a country not necessarily united, and full of diversities. So, there is no unity in diversity. There are many paradoxes and prejudices, sharp differences of opinion, countless divergent views mired with innumerable controversies but not always truthful to our motherland. The most repeatedly played controversy and blackmail for a dozen years from 2002 to 2014 has been the willful false purposeful maligning of BJP strongman and the then Gujarat CM Narendra Modi who won the assembly elections with nearly two-thirds majority during three successive elections. Congress – INC in its first avatar and now Congress (I) – has been thoroughly corrupt. It was never a Nationalistic party is a well-known observation to dispassionate observers. But it can be so wicked, only a few could fathom. Ajay Angre's piece on *India Opines* and titled, '*Who Was Responsible for The Political Assassination of Narendra Modi??*' blows the lid off the dirty, murky and shameful politics played by this unethical non-democratic autocratic family-held private limited company rather than a political outfit. Angre wrote: "*I am now convinced after the Ishrat Jahan Fake Encounter Exposure. Isharat Fake Encounter Scam* orchestrated with the planned motive to nail Narendra Modi by Congress and all the Human Rights Activists hired by corrupt Congress who were sadistically enjoying the politically motivated propaganda with their corrupt media friends in TV Debates for as long as 10 long years to fix Narendra Modi before National Elections are total frauds.

I am convinced *Now* that they are more than NGOs and HRA, they operate as political lobbies as and when their services are required by political parties and foreign Agencies funding them. I am shocked to watch the way Human Rights Activists are still trying to defend their earlier fake positions saying their concern is more about the Human Rights violations by the then Gujarat Police, CM of Gujarat and Home minister of that state. Even after it is now clear from the Government official records sought through RTI query by *TIMES NOW* Reporter, the then UPA

Home Minister P. Chidambaram wrote the fabricated story about the *'Innocence'* of Ishrat Jehan as Fake Encounter. They also call it a Murder by the Gujarat State leadership that is former CM Narendra Modi and HM Amit Shah. But what evidence all of them had to claim that she was innocent?? The then CBI and IB Reports.

Every one of these *Sold* Human Rights Activists is hell-bent to prove that Narendra Modi and Amit Shah killed an innocent civilian, a young college going girl. And all the political opponents of Modi took the clue to build their National Election Campaign around it to prove Modi is a killer of an innocent girl called Ishrat Jehan and it only proves how much he hates Muslim community. This was their Vote-Bank Politics which the voters rejected and gave their verdict in favor of Narendra Modi with their huge mandate to lead India. They failed to prove all their allegations against Narendra Modi because all their charges were politically motivated, lies, and false.

But none of them *Ever* applied for the RTI query from the government records on the Ishrat case to find out where the actual truth lies?? Because all of them were hired by Congress to carry out a vicious political propaganda against Modi with the help of their corrupt paid media friends, so that before National elections he can be fixed politically and eliminated from the electoral race the Prince of Gandhi family was facing.

None of these paid Congress agents ever thought of getting down to the bottom of the truth before taking up their positions?? Why?? What were the compulsions?? Were their political motives and compulsions to spread the "Lies" to "FIX" Narendra Modi?? Of course, it was clear, this political lobby of so-called Human Rights Activists were working with the Congress High Command to help camouflage the truth about Ishrat Jahan. All of them like John Dayal, Tushar Gandhi, Vrinda Grover, Kavitha Krishnamurthy, Medha Patkar and many others, who were involved in misleading the people of India at large with the "Political Lie", were constantly trying to hammer the message to people with their false convictions just because they were hired to spread the political lies.

<u>Can you call them human rights activists who do not even bother for a minute to think</u>? With their propaganda and innocent person, is PM Modi going to be politically assassinated?? The serious charges all of them were making in the TV Debates with their convictions ignoring the truth too is a very serious crime of abetting for falsely framing an innocent for political motives who was mentally tortured day and night and all of them, the

so-called Human Right Activists were, directly and indirectly, involved in sending an innocent person to gallows.

How in this political case, the Human Rights of an innocent person is protected by John Dayal, Tushar Gandhi, Vrinda Grover, Kavitha Krishnamurthy and like others? They were all trying to prove without any knowledge and just went by some false fabricated reports prepared by the then Home ministry with political motives which are now being exposed to these so-called activists who were blind, taking the fabricated reports against an innocent person? Today, after the truth is exposed of the Congress-manufactured Ishrat Fake Encounter Political Scam, these Activists are treading cautiously and saying she might have been a terrorist, but police had no rights to kill an innocent person till proven guilty. What a foolish, irrational baseless logic!

Let the policemen get killed by the criminals but the criminals or terrorists should not be killed. They also mean we care a damn for the human rights of the Cops and all those getting killed or maimed or disabled in terror attacks. That is how these Human Rights Activists Think. I was shocked to listen to some of the pseudo-intellectuals of this country like Senior Journalist Kumar Ketkar saying I don't trust IB, CBI or any intelligence agency of this country. I am convinced, Ishrat was an innocent victim killed by the Gujarat Police. Is this man a Senior journalist?? Or, a Paid Journalist?? Even Tushar Gandhi, great grandson of Mahatma Gandhi who stood always by the Truth and only Truth says she was an innocent killed in the fake encounter?? On what basis? One can always say I cannot comment because I was not IB or CBI or Part of police investigation exercise. That is acceptable, but today the Human Rights Activists are passing judgements on any alleged accused before even the judiciary convicts the accused. On what basis he or any Human Right Activist can make any statement on Ishrat Jehan when they are not a part of intelligence agencies or police investigations?? And when they are cornered with their false positioning, then they take an easy escape route saying, it is for the court to decide and it is acceptable to us.

Then dear human right activists, *'Why do you open your mouths where you have no business'*?? And surprisingly, you change your positions swiftly when 2002 Gujarat riots or Dadri killing is debated. Then you quickly change your political positioning and say, Of course It is very clear, Narendra Modi was the mastermind behind killings of the Muslims in

2002 Gujrat riots, fascist Narendra Modi and hardcore *Hindutva wadi* RSS was responsible for Dadri mob lynching.

Why this hypocrisy? *Why double standards*? And when you are questioned about Malda and Purnia communal Riots where the fanatics and extremists of the Muslim community targeted Hindus…. Don't you see Human Rights Violations? But *you* choose to keep quiet. When you are questioned about the rights of Kashmiri Pandits living as Refugees in their own country…. You don't want to fight for their Human Rights. Again, you choose to keep quiet.

When You are questioned about 1984 Sikh Genocide when innocent Sikh men, women, and Children were burnt alive, brutally killed by Congressmen and their sponsored Goons… You do not want to fight for their Rights. Isn't it because Congress was involved in 1984 Delhi Riots?? Then, *who are YOU really fighting for??? Where your political agenda is served? Where you get hired for the set political targets like Narendra Modi, BJP, RSS?? Who really are you fighting for*?

And how is that, you do not do your homework? Get correct information through RTI queries?? Do your own investigations impartially when you take up the issues, especially when the issues are politically charged and motivated and driven with the political objectives serving political agendas??? *Time has come to expose all these so called fake human right activists.*

Who are they working for? Which political parties? Who is hiring them? And why are they funded by the foreign agencies? And by unknown entities in millions of dollars which these so- called human right activists do not like to disclose??

Wake-up India! You are under attack not from the outsiders but from the insiders who are like (green) snakes in the grass. You can't see them really. But they are poisonous snakes and dangerous. You better watch your back. [By Ajay Angre Modi]

Autocracy was at its peak and within-party democracy touched its nadir on 24th May 2016 when the West Bengal PCC chairman Adhir Choudhury asked the newly elected MLAs to sign a 100-rupee two-page stamp paper agreeing to abide by four points: *First,* "I do swear my unqualified allegiance to Congress (I) led by Hon'ble Smt. Sonia Gandhi Ji as president and Rahul Gandhi Ji as vice president. *Second,* "I, as a member of the legislative assembly will not get involved in any anti-party activity. Even if I do not agree with any party policy and/or party decision.

I will not make any negative comment thereon and/or I shall not take any negative action to the detriment of the party. In such a scenario, I shall resign from my post as MLA before making such comment and/or taking such action." *Third* point refers to MLAs "abiding by party guidelines and follow guidelines framed by CLP leader and the chief whip in the floor of assembly. *Fourth* confirms that the first three are "true to my knowledge." Privately, some of the MLAs feared that such a move would dilute the democratic nature of the party, if it existed at all!

Were and are we ever secular? Was secularism thrust upon us by way of Constitutional amendment by a Muslim PM as the founding fathers never felt the necessity of it in the original Constitution? What remains of the Constitution after practically two amendments per year on an average? These questions are not easy to be settled. One view on secularism was presented by an illustrated public servant in a memorial lecture scheduled for 4th April 2016 that for some reasons was cancelled. Here it is: Late BG Deshmukh Memorial Lecture 2016 by Dr. Madhav Godbole at Mantralaya in Mumbai. 'IS INDIA A SECULAR NATION?'

Introduction: At the outset, I must say how happy I am to have this opportunity to address this august gathering in the memory of Late BG Deshmukh, one of the most illustrious civil servants of India. I had the privilege of working closely with him in the State and the Centre. It was because of him that, as principal finance secretary, I could initiate and vigorously implement zero-base budgeting in the state and earned, what some of the detractors believed, the ignominious, but what I am ever proud of, nick-name of "Mr. No". I am glad to know that his "glorious" tradition of finance secretary being the 'punching bag' has continued in Maharashtra to this day! If only all states had more "Mr. Nos", the state governments would have done yeomen service by enhancing the rate of growth of the states and ensuring more productive public expenditures. B.G., as he used to be fondly and reverentially known, was brutally frank and open in tendering his advice to his colleagues and political executives. He achieved the rare distinction of occupying the three highest and most coveted positions in the civil service of chief secretary of a state, cabinet secretary and principal secretary to the PM. He personified the best in the "endangered species" of the civil service.

I am going to speak today on whether India is a secular nation. I have deliberately framed the question so as not to restrict it to 'India as a secular state'. For, I believe, it is not enough if the Indian state is secular, which it is not. It is equally, if not more, important that we are a secular society, a secular nation. I believe this question needs to be asked, reflected upon and answered truthfully.[1] My latest book, 'Secularism, *India at Cross-Roads*', on this subject is being brought out by Rupa & Co., New Delhi, shortly. It is perhaps the first book totally devoted to operationalization of secularism and comprehensively looks at the constitutional, statutory, policy and administrative issues in the light of the experience of the working of secularism gained over the last 66 years since the adoption of the Constitution. [some portions of the speech have been italicized for emphasis]

The Backdrop: At the outset it must be stated that I am a firm believer in the concept of secularism. It is my conviction that India's survival as a multi-religious, multi-lingual, multi-racial, multi-cultural society will depend on how successful it is in working its secularism. Presently, religious minorities constitute about 20% of India's population, with Muslims accounting for 14.2%. According to some estimates, in a few years, this percentage is likely to stabilize at a little over 25, with Muslims accounting for 20%. With extremist and radical external forces such as Islamic State of Iraq and Syria (ISIS) and Inter-Services Intelligence (ISI) of Pakistan, to name just two, bent on disturbing the peace and tranquility in the country, it will be fool-hardy to neglect the welfare of minorities. No society can prosper or be at peace with itself if one-fourths of its population feels neglected, deprived and unwanted.

There is a great deal of talk in the country about the appeasement of minorities in general and Muslims in particular but socio-economic indicators of Muslims brought out by Justice Sachar Committee bring out convincingly how this so-called "vote-bank" of some political parties has remained at the margin all these years. It is shocking to see that Parliament did not have time to discuss the findings of this report as also the major recommendations of Justice Ranganath Mishra Commission report. Both these high-level expert groups were appointed by the then United Progressive Alliance (UPA) government. Many in this distinguished gathering are aware of the predecessor-successor complex which is so common in civil services. Unfortunately, studies of expert committees and commissions too have been afflicted by this virus. Secularism was expected to bring about the integration of the diverse elements of Indian society. But it is a travesty that the majority community as well as the minorities are dissatisfied with it. In fact, the concept of secularism has lost all credibility.

It must be stated that India would not have been either a parliamentary democracy or a 'secular' nation, to whatever degree it is, without the firm commitment of Nehru and Patel to these precepts. The Indian Constitution is one of the most explicitly 'secular' Constitutions in the world though the founding fathers of the Constitution could not agree on calling it secular for fears that it would be perceived as anti-religious or irreligious in the Western sense of the term. It was felt that by calling it secular, the Constitution would be denuded of the ethical and moral underpinning of the religious precepts which are so necessary for the governance of the country. This deficiency was made good during the Emergency in 1976 by the 42nd Amendment by the inclusion of the word 'secular' in the Preamble of the Constitution.

It is disconcerting to see that, in recent times, serious questions are being raised about India's secularism. It is for the first time since independence that the *Hindu Rashtra* ideology is being talked about so openly, defiantly and persistently. It is interesting to note that Jawaharlal Nehru had made his position clear on *Hindu Rashtra* way back on 6th September 1951: "It may sound very nice to some people to hear it said that we will create a *Hindu Rashtra*, etc... Hindus are in a majority in this country and whatever they wish will be done. But the moment you talk *of Hindu Rashtra* you speak in a language which no other country except one can comprehend and that country is Pakistan because they are familiar with this concept. They can immediately justify their creation of an Islamic nation by pointing out to the world that we are doing something similar. *Hindu Rashtra* can only mean one thing and that is to leave the modern way and get into a narrow, old fashioned way of thinking, and fragment India into pieces. Those who are not Hindus will be reduced in status. You may say patronizingly that you will look after the Muslims or Christians or others as in Pakistan they say that they will look after the Hindus. Do you think any race or individual will accept for long the claim that they are looked after while we sit above them?" Gopal S. and Iyengar Uma, ed., The Essential Writings of Jawaharlal Nehru, vol. I, Oxford University Press, New Delhi, 2003, p. 186.

If the Supreme Court had not categorically declared in SR Bommai vs. Union of India ((1994) SCC 1) that secularism is a part of the basic structure of the Constitution and Parliament has no powers to dilute it in any way, concerted efforts would have been made by some political parties to amend the Constitution to dilute its secular tenets. In retrospect, it is fortunate that the proposal of the Janata government contained in the 44th Amendment Bill, 1978, for effecting amendment of the Constitution by holding a referendum on certain important matters such as its secular or democratic character, abridging or taking away fundamental rights, prejudicing or impeding free and fair elections on the basis of adult suffrage, and compromising the independence of the judiciary, did not find acceptance in the Rajya Sabha. Otherwise, attempts would even have been made to rally public opinion in favor of doing away with the secular characteristics of the Constitution and I would not be surprised if, in the present polarized political atmosphere in the country, it would have found a majority support. The Supreme Court itself has expressed apprehensions in this regard: "India till now is a secular country…we do not know for how long it will remain a secular country." (*Indian Express*, February 10, 2015: 1)

Against this background, it is necessary to examine what needs to be done to safeguard secularism from political turmoil and vicissitudes and to ensure that it will continue to be an important ingredient of the basic structure of the Constitution. In this context, it will be appropriate to recall what Jefferson, the statesman who played a great part in the making of the American Constitution, had stated: "We may consider each generation as a distinct nation, with [a] right, by the will of the majority, to bind themselves, but none to bind the succeeding generation, more than the inhabitants of another country." I hope proposals made hereafter would be looked at in this light.

Secularism-Constitutional Precepts and Reality: A series of articles in the Constitution underline the precepts of secularism. These include: article 14--equality before law; article 15--prohibition of discrimination on grounds of religion, race, caste, sex or place of birth; article 16--equality of opportunity in matters of public employment which, inter alia, lays down that no citizen shall, on grounds of religion, race, caste etc. shall be ineligible for, or discriminated against in respect of employment or office under the state; article 19--protection of certain rights regarding freedom of speech and expression, to assemble peaceably and without arms, to form associations or unions, to move freely throughout the territory of India, to reside and settle in any part of the territory of India, and to practice any profession, or to carry on any occupation, trade or business; article 21--protection of life and personal property; article 25--freedom of conscience and free profession, practice and propagation of religion; article 26--freedom to manage religious affairs; article 27--freedom as to payment of taxes for promotion of any particular religion; article 28--freedom as to attendance at religious instruction or religious worship in certain educational institutions; article 29--protection of interests of minorities; and article 30--right of minorities to establish and administer educational institutions. Reference must also be made to the two provisions in the directive principles of state policy which have considerable significance in sustaining secularism in the country. These are article 44-uniform civil code for the citizens, and article 48--organization of agriculture and animal husbandry which has been invoked for banning cow slaughter in several states. Particular attention may also be invited to article 51A on fundamental duties which, in clause (e), lays down the duty to promote harmony and the spirit of common brotherhood amongst all people of India transcending religious, linguistic and regional or sectional diversities; and to renounce practices derogatory to the dignity of women; and clause (f) to value and preserve the rich heritage of our composite culture.

The reality is however quite disappointing. The majority community as also the minorities are totally disillusioned with the working of secularism. Instead of being the cementing force, secularism has led to alienation of all communities. This is borne out by series of failures in important areas. These include grievance of Hindus that rules, regulations and restrictions are being prescribed only for their religious institutions; non-implementation of the uniform civil code; passage of Muslim Women's Divorce Act to appease the radical, orthodox and conservative Muslim elements, totaling disregarding the liberal and reformist Muslim view; propagation of religion by Muslims and Christians leading to large-scale conversions, particularly in the tribal areas and of persons below the poverty line, and unjustified protection given to minority educational institutions.

Equally disconcerting are some other signposts which raise serious doubts about how secular India is! *Most important of these are non-separation of religion from politics*, wanton demolition of the Babri Masjid, anti-Sikh riots in Delhi and other places in 1984, horrific riots in Mumbai in December 1992 and January 1993, and burning of Hindu pilgrims including women and children at Godhra station, unbelievable atrocities in riots in Godhra and other cities in Gujarat 2002, continued widespread communalism and communal violence in several parts of the country which led to 8,449 communal incidents resulting in 7,229 deaths and 47,321 persons injured in a brief span of 1954 to 1985, and banning of cow slaughter leading to curtailment of freedom of persons about what to eat and restricting their freedom to carry on any profession and trade.

Due to constraints of time and space, I shall briefly deal with only a few of these features. What is striking is the total lack of political will on the part of all political parties to address these critical issues, thereby raising serious doubts about their real commitment to secularism, whatever may be the rhetoric indulged in by them for public consumption. There are two very strong views in the country regarding enactment of a uniform civil code. It needs to be noted that while an impression was created by the speeches of Vallabhbhai Patel, Jawaharlal Nehru and others in the Constituent Assembly that Muslims had agreed to go along with the provision for uniform civil code, careful reading of the debates clearly shows that all Muslim members, without an exception, were stoutly opposed to making a provision for a uniform civil code even in the directive principles of state policy and had in fact pressed for deleting it altogether. There has been no change in the stand of the Muslims since then.

Evidently no political party, including the BJP, will be able to get such a bill passed in the Parliament. In my soon-to-be released book on secularism I have elaborately brought out the strong opposition of Hindus which had to be resisted while enacting the Hindu Code and how there was a persistent cry of Hindu religion being in danger. Even prominent leaders of the Congress party itself, like Rajendra Prasad, who was the President of the Constituent Assembly and the President of India later, were stoutly opposed to the reforms in Hindu law. We, as a nation, should be eternally grateful to Jawaharlal Nehru for standing firm and having the relevant enactments passed. It is, however, unfortunate that Nehru did not show similar courage in initiating enactment of a uniform civil code. If reforms in Muslim personal law had been pursued, the social and religious ethos of the country would have undergone significant changes by now. Having lost the golden opportunity at that time, it will be impossible to enact a uniform civil code now, irrespective of the exhortations of the Supreme Court, unless there is a strong reformist and liberal move from within the Muslim community. Sadly, all political parties are remiss in encouraging modern, scientific, enlightened, progressive and liberal leadership among the Muslims. While enactment of a uniform civil code will thus have to inevitably wait, separation of religion from politics is of such urgency that no time should be wasted in bringing this about. It is interesting to note that the Constituent Assembly (Legislative) had passed an explicit resolution on the subject as far back as 3rd April 1948. In fact, it was perhaps the first major resolution passed by the Assembly. The resolution moved by Ananthasayanam Ayyangar read as under:

Whereas it is essential for the proper functioning of democracy and the growth of national unity and solidarity that communalism should be eliminated from Indian life, this Assembly is of opinion that no communal organization which by its constitution or by the exercise of discretionary power vested in any of its officers or organs, admits to or excludes from its membership persons on grounds of religion, race and caste, or any of them, should be permitted to engage in any activities other than those essential for the bona fide religious and cultural needs of the community, and that all steps, legislative and administrative, necessary to prevent such activities should be taken.

Nehru had welcomed the resolution and assured that the government "wished to do everything in their power to achieve the objective which lies behind this resolution... The only alternative is civil conflict. We have seen as a matter of fact how far communalism in politics has led us; all of us remember the grave dangers through which we have passed and the terrible consequences we have seen..." The resolution slightly amended to permit any activities other than those essential for the bona fide religious, cultural, social and educational needs of the community was passed by the Constituent Assembly.[3]Government of India, Ministry of Information and Broadcasting, Independence and After--A Collection of the More Important Speeches of Jawaharlal Nehru from September 1946 to May 1949, New Delhi, 1949, pp. 4751. But though Nehru was PM for 17 years, he failed to take any action on the resolution. The only other time when any political party enjoyed 2/3rd majority in the Lok Sabha, to be able to see through such a constitutional amendment, was when Indira Gandhi and Rajiv Gandhi were in power. But they too did not find it politically expedient to act on the resolution. It was only after the demolition of the Babri Masjid, when the secular credentials of the Congress party were being seriously questioned in India and abroad, that PV Narasimha Rao government brought the Constitution (80th Amendment) Bill and a bill for amendment of the Representation of People Act before Parliament in 1993 to bring about separation of religion from politics. However, no effort was made by the government to take other political parties into confidence and to build a national consensus and create pressure of public opinion on the subject. The bills were so shoddily piloted in Parliament as to raise serious doubts whether the government wanted them to be passed at all or whether it was meant to be just a window-dressing exercise. As a result, the bills failed to receive adequate support and had to be withdrawn. Though over two decades have elapsed since then and though the Congress or UPA led by that party was in power for most of this period, no effort was made to revive the proposal. *This once again brings out the hollowness of the commitment of so-called secular parties to secularism.* With the BJP in power at the Centre since 2014, it will be futile to expect any action in foreseeable future. But, unless this issue is addressed seriously, India's secular credentials will continue to be questioned.

'The Ayodhya Debacle' in my memoirs Unfinished Innings published by Orient Longman way back in 1996.[4]Madhav Godbole, Unfinished Innings--Recollections and Reflections of a Civil Servant, Orient Longman, New Delhi, 1996. I have also dealt at length in my article in the Economic and Political Weekly,[5]Madhav Godbole, 'Ayodhya and India's Mahabharat: Constitutional Issues and Proprieties', Economic and Political Weekly, 27 May 2006, with the untenable defense given by PV Narasimha Rao in his book Ayodhya[6]Madhav Godbole, The Judiciary and Governance in India, Rupa & Co., New Delhi, 2008, p. 69, December 1992 published by Penguin/Viking, posthumously, in 2006, in which Rao has claimed that he was unable to take any action due to the restrictive provisions of the Constitution and that he was made a scape-goat by Congress party. This must be the only case of its kind in history in which the PM has alleged of being made a scapegoat!! Otherwise, it is the well accepted prerogative of PMs to find a scapegoat for each of their lapses!

The Ayodhya debacle has several other firsts to its credit. PM Rao's assurance of "rebuilding the mosque" given immediately after its demolition on 6 December 1992 has remained on paper. Kalyan Singh, who was the chief minister of U.P. at the time and who had given assurances to the National Integration Council, the government of India and the Supreme Court to fully safeguard the Babri Masjid, has been elevated as a Governor by the NDA government. Earlier, the Supreme Court, before which he was hauled up for contempt of court, gave punishment of imprisonment till the rising of the court and a token fine of INR 2,000! The judicial commission of inquiry under the chairmanship of Justice M. Liberhahn, set up within a week of the demolition of the mosque, created a world record by taking 17 years to complete the inquiry and effectively found no one guilty! The CBI cases against the perpetrators of the crime are still languishing though 22 years have elapsed. It is this callousness and connivance which goes to show how sham is India's commitment to secularism. On this background to call secularism a part of the basic structure of the Constitution makes no sense.

Equally disconcerting is the perpetrators of crimes in the widespread communal riots have been casually and leniently handled by the respective state governments. Despite appointing dozens of committees and commissions to identify those responsible in the anti-Sikh riots in Delhi, hardly any action has been taken against the leaders of the Congress party who are alleged to have instigated the riots. These riots took place under the benign leadership of the central government and were therefore shocking. The riots in Mumbai in December 1992 and January 1993 is another can of worms. Justice Srikrishna Commission has commented on them at great length. But the political parties and persons responsible have been permitted to go scot-free. The usual adage of the law taking its own course has been held to ridicule. The Godhra riots were qualitatively different in that it was the state-sponsored violence against the minorities. The National Human Rights Commission and the Supreme Court have done a yeomen service in upholding the rule of law but the main issue of the urgency of reorganization of police administration which has been highlighted by the judicial commissions as also the citizens' commissions again and again has been over-looked. Even the directions of the Supreme Court issued as far back as 2006 in a public interest litigation have remained on paper. What kind of a robust and vigilant democracy are we if even the orders of the highest court in the country are not to be implemented?

Finally, the question to be asked is whether banning cow slaughter is in keeping with the concept of secularism. The SC upholding the constitutional validity of these enactments by a majority decision of 6 to 1 on 26th October 2005 ((2005) 8 SCC 534) has closed all options, at least for the present. It proves the adage that the SC is supreme only because there is no appeal over its decision. As one of its judges had said, "If there were an appellate court over us, probably a majority of our judgments would be upset." It would also be worth recalling what Justice Brennan, a judge of the US Supreme Court, had said, "The Supreme Court [of United States] is not final because it is infallible; the court is infallible because it is final."[6]Madhav Godbole, The Judiciary and Governance in India, Rupa & Co., New Delhi, 2008, p. 69.

In a secular state, religion is expected to be a purely personal and private matter and is not supposed to have anything to do with the governance of the country. The Supreme Court had observed in the Bommai case that if religion is not separated from politics, religion of the ruling party tends to become the state religion. This seems to be coming true. The BJP and its affiliate parties have given to the prevention of cow slaughter sanctity of Hindu religious precept. But this is hardly justified. Further, the fundamental right of persons to practice any profession or to carry on any occupation, trade or business contained in article 19 (1) (g) of the Constitution has been over-ridden by article 48, one of the directive principles of state policy. In the scheme of the Constitution, directive principles are not supposed to over-ride the fundamental rights. But it has now become a sacrilege to even raise such questions. Economic justification for enforcing cow slaughter is also highly questionable. It is unfortunate that though Nehru was staunchly opposed to prevention of cow slaughter, he did not oppose the inclusion of this provision in the Constitution. In fact, the discussion in the Constituent Assembly shows that a political decision to incorporate this provision was taken in the Congress Party meeting and it was merely formalized in the Constituent Assembly by putting forth spacious and unconvincing arguments. This is yet another instance of the ambivalence of the Constitution on secularism.

<u>Constitution Making-- Inevitably an Exercise in Give and Take</u>: The gigantic, complex and highly emotive exercise of uniting and integrating this continental sized country, including, apart from British India, more than 550 princely states, and comprising multiplicity of religions, languages, cultures, customs, traditions, political and social divisions was attempted for the first time in the history of India and credit must be given to the founding fathers of the Constitution for carrying all these diverse elements with them and unanimously agreeing on such an epoch-making Constitution. Though the Congress party alone had an overwhelming presence all over the country, due to Mahatma Gandhi's foresight, eminent persons representing different viewpoints were elected to the Constituent Assembly with the support of the Congress party. One of them Dr. BR Ambedkar, who was also made the chairman of the drafting committee. Understandably, the Constitution was a compromise document. This is particularly evident in the provisions pertaining to secularism.

Nehru and Patel were particularly keen on doing away with the communal electorates and the reservation of seats in legislatures based on the strength of religious communities. Once this objective was achieved with the concurrence of the minorities, the Congress party was prepared to concede the other demands of minorities as a compromise. As a result, provisions were made in the Constitution to include right to propagation of religion as a fundamental right, at the instance of Muslims and Christians on the ground that propagation was a part of their religion. The right of minorities to establish and administer educational institutions was also similarly recognized as a fundamental right despite reservations expressed by several members including Jayaprakash Narayan and Rajkumari Amrit Kaur.

Operationalizing Secularism: As stated earlier, India's future is intrinsically tied up with secularism. To make a real success of it, time has come to seriously examine its working during the last 66 years since the adoption of the Constitution. There are no political compulsions any longer. I have made an objective and dispassionate attempt to look at the relevant issues in the discussion hereinafter. Since the proposals are aimed at strengthening secularism, they are not adversely affected by the injunction of the Supreme Court on non-amendability of the provisions pertaining to secularism.

Define the word 'secular': It is best to start the exercise with the basics. As stated earlier, the founding fathers of the Constitution had reservations about the word 'secular'. But, as the Constituent Assembly debates bring out, there was no doubt in anyone's mind that India was giving itself a secular Constitution. But, the definition of the word 'secular' was never debated or agreed upon. Even Nehru seemed ambivalent about the true meaning of secularism though he was responsible for firmly advocating it: "It is perhaps not very easy even to find a good word [presumably in Hindi] for 'secular'. Some people think that it means something opposed to religion. That obviously is not correct. What it means is that it is a state which honors all faiths equally and gives them equal opportunities; that, as a state, it does not allow itself to be attached to one faith or religion, which then becomes the state religion."[7] Gopal S., Jawaharlal Nehru--An Anthology, Oxford University Press, Delhi, 1980, page 330. Banning of cow slaughter is clear proof that Hindu religion is being made into a state religion!

In 1976, when the word 'secular' was included in the Preamble via the 42nd Amendment, this question was evaded, and no definition was provided. After the massive defeat of the Congress party in Lok Sabha elections in 1977, the question arose of reconsideration of *this highly controversial amendment*, which effectively had rewritten the Constitution on many crucial points. The Forty-fourth amendment bill introduced by the Janata government in 1978 contained definition of the word 'secular' as equal respect for all religions. However, this was objected to by the Congress party which still had a majority in the Rajya Sabha (as has been the position in 2014-16) and therefore this clause was dropped. Again, an effort was made in 1993 to include the same definition in the Constitution (Eightieth) Amendment bill on separation of religion from politics but, as stated earlier, this bill itself fell through. As a result, as of now, there is no definition of this term. One must fall back on the diverse ways in which the word has been described. In governmental parlance, it is understood as *"sarva dharma samabhava"*-- treating all religions equally or equal respect for all religions. The Hindi translations of the word namely, *"Dharmanirapeksha"* or *"panthanirapeksa"* or *"nidharmee"* too have been rightly questioned. Another definition put forth is that government should be equidistant from all religions. Serious questions have been raised about the validity of these definitions. For example, Late Justice RA Jahagirdar has, in his erudite articles in The Radical Humanist[8] Jahagirdar R.A., 'Secularism Revisited', The Radical Humanist, February 2015 (p. 24) and March 2015 (pp. 356). 9 Kashyap Subhash C., History of the Parliament of India, vol. 4, Shipra Publications, Delhi, 1997, p. 91, emphasized how these definitions are untenable. The Supreme Court has been interpreting the word 'secular' in different ways. At one extreme was its interpretation in the Bommai case when it declared that there must be a wall between the state and the religion, and a political party must not be linked to any religion, as otherwise, the religion of such a party is perceived as a state religion. Reference must also be made to the statement of HR Gokhale, law minister, during the Emergency. While piloting the Forty-second Amendment Bill in the Lok Sabha, Gokhale was highly critical of the concept of 'basic structure' devised by the Supreme Court. He said: "First of all I do not agree, with much respect to the Supreme Court, that there is something like the basic features which could not be amended...What is not defined cannot exist and it is incapable of defining it."[9]Kashyap Subhash C., History of the Parliament of India, vol. 4, Shipra Publications, Delhi, 1997, p. 91. If the same logic is extended to secularism, since the word 'secular' has not been defined, does it mean that India is not secular? Since secularism has been declared by the Supreme Court as a part of the basic structure of the Constitution, governments, both at the Centre and in the states, must be made accountable for implementing it. But, how can the state be held accountable unless the meaning of the term 'secular' is clear? It is high time a national debate is started on the subject to arrive at a political and societal consensus and to include the definition in the Constitution.

Define the word 'minority': I shall now turn to the word 'minority'. The concept of secularism is based on recognition and protection of minorities. The two cannot be separated. One would have therefore expected that the founding fathers of the Constitution would first define the term minorities. Unfortunately, this was never done. The Constitution merely takes off from where the British had left it, which was in fact the very epitome of the British policy of 'divide and rule'. For want of a clear definition, the Supreme Court has adopted the highly questionable criterion of numerical strength. As a result, a community will be treated as a minority till its population exceeds 50% of the total. This will make a mockery of the concept of minority. In the India context, apart from other considerations, this is highly relevant. Muslims are already 14% of the population. According to some estimates, their population is expected to stabilize at about 20% in the next few years. Even if this estimate turns out to be an under-estimate, as some would like to believe, it may stabilize at 25-30%. Should it be recognized as a minority? What should be the cut-off? This issue needs to be debated. It is no doubt an extremely sensitive and divisive issue but, as a mature democracy, India must debate it rationally and objectively, keeping the political baggage aside.

Creation of a Commission on Secularism: The Supreme Court has done a great service to the country by declaring that secularism is a part of the basic structure of the Constitution. However, it is on paper and no steps have been taken so far to translate it into reality, except for it becoming a part of political rhetoric. Some of the other features of basic structure recognized by the Supreme Court, are parliamentary democracy, independence of judiciary, freedom of press, etc. For each one of these, over the years institutional and legal framework has been established to make sure that they are carefully nurtured and safeguarded. For example, the Election Commission of India has been sufficiently empowered to ensure that there are free and fair elections in the country and electoral malpractices are put down with a heavy hand. Parliament of India is vigilant about safeguarding its independence, privileges and supremacy. The judiciary, after its shocking experience of being undermined during the Emergency in 1975-77, has been vigilant in guarding its turf. In fact, since then, Indian Judiciary has emerged as the world's most powerful judiciary with even matters pertaining to appointments of high court and

Supreme Court judges coming entirely under the Supreme Court. This is the only case of its kind in the world. In 2015, the Supreme Court has declared unconstitutional the law unanimously passed by Parliament to appoint a National Judicial Commission for the purpose. The Supreme Court and the Election Commission have emerged as the most respected institutions in the country, enjoying highest credibility. This is no mean achievement.

Against this background it is unfortunate that no steps have been taken by the government to ensure proper implementation of secularism and to give it credibility. In fact, secularism has lost all credibility since it has become a plaything in the hands of political parties, irrespective of which hues and colors they belong. At the same time, it needs to be emphasized that secularism will decide how India would emerge over the years. In the decade of the 1980s, we have seen how fringe and extremist elements in the miniscule religious minority of Sikhs, comprising just about 1.5 percent of India's total population, held the country to ransom for nearly a decade and led to shocking alienation of common Sikhs, not just in India but also those residing abroad.

By comparison, the Muslim population in India is already a little over 14%. As stated earlier, it is projected to stabilize around 20% in the next few years. Most Muslims in India are highly tolerant and peace-loving, but there are fringe and extremist elements which cannot be overlooked. Particularly with the external forces such as ISIS, al-Qaeda and ISI, it would be in India's interest to ensure that home grown terrorist forces are not permitted to emerge. But this is only the negative side of it. It is necessary that the issue should be addressed in a positive manner to bring the Muslims in the mainstream of society. In this context, the atmosphere in the country since the beginning of 2015 is of serious concern. The issues pertaining to secularism emerge in diverse sectors of society. These relate to attempts at rewriting history, communalization of academic and research institutions, rewriting of textbooks, circumscribing artistic freedom and so on. At present these issues can be agitated primarily before the higher judiciary as Parliament has mostly become dysfunctional. Whatever is raised in Parliament inevitably becomes highly politicized and is looked upon on as party loyalties and strategies.

The experience of agitating issues pertaining to secularism by way of public interest litigation (PIL) has also been far from happy. Strictly PIL is supposed to be a non-adversarial litigation. It is expected that both parties would look at the issues constructively to find a workable and acceptable solution to the problem at hand. However, experience has been quite the contrary. Practically in every case the government has taken an adversarial position and contested even reasonable proposals put forth by the petitioners. *Secondly*, as brought out in my book, *'The Judiciary and Governance in India'* (2008), the process of admission of a PIL is somewhat opaque and the outcome hardly predictable. *Thirdly*, it takes unduly long time to get the final decision of the court. For example, in the PIL pertaining to appointment of a Lokpal, due to the resistance of successive governments, the case was heard by the Supreme Court on 29 occasions and was finally closed on 12th September 2003 as 'none is ready with the matter to make submissions'.

PIL pertaining to non-implementation of the recommendations of the National Police Commission regarding modalities for appointments, etc. of police officers, took over 12 years for the SC to give a final decision. The same was the position in PILs pertaining to Haj subsidy, proliferation of Sharia courts as a parallel judicial system, *Ram Janm Bhoomi-Babri Masjid* dispute and so on. In this light, taking recourse to PIL does not appear to be an alternative to setting up of any independent institution for deciding matters pertaining to secularism.

Clearly, the time has come to create a new institution, namely, a Commission on Secularism (COS) for ensuring adherence to the constitutional mandate on secularism. I had propounded this idea while discussing the lessons of Partition in my book The Holocaust of Indian Partition--An Inquest (2006). To be effective, such a commission must be appointed by an amendment of the Constitution and should be presided over by a former chief justice of India, with five other members drawn from among former judges of the Supreme Court, chief justices of the high courts, eminent jurists, and other public figures of highest integrity and reputation. The term of the members should be five years or attainment of the age of 72 years, whichever is earlier. The commission should be covered by the provisions of the Contempt of Court Act.

The selection of the chairman and members of the COS should be transparently apolitical. The selection committee may comprise the vice president of India, the prime minister, the speaker, the chief justice of India, union home minister and the leaders of opposition in the Lok Sabha and the Rajya Sabha. Such a commission will be able to take a holistic view on all matters pertaining to secularism and even intervene in matters coming up before the high courts and the Supreme Court. Reference may be made in this context to the very laudable role played by the National Human Right Commission (NHRC) which had intervened in the cases pertaining to Godhra pogrom before the Supreme Court and has become an important moral voice to reckon with. At the time when there are only a few national leaders of stature left in the country with any moral authority and credibility who command universal public respect, the commission on secularism will be ideally suited to fill the vacuum.

The COS will be best equipped to create public awareness on secularism. Its open hearings will provide an opportunity to all political parties, intellectuals, religious leaders, non-government organizations, and concerned citizens to argue their points of view, either in person or through an advocate, in a free and fair manner. Keeping in view the basic purpose of setting up the COS, it is suggested that the hearings of the commission should also be televised. It is only through such a public discourse that the values of secularism enshrined in the Constitution can be translated.

The commission should have the responsibility to pronounce judgments on all declarations, actions and programs of political parties, public institutions, state and central governments, electronic and print media, and others, so far as their impact on secularism is concerned. The commission may take cognizance of such actions *Suo moto* or on an application from any individual or organization. The decision of the commission should be binding on all concerned, unless it is set aside or modified by the Supreme Court. Thus, inevitably the powers and authority of COS will have to be much wider than those of National Human Rights Commission, whose recommendations are not binding on the government. It may be relevant in this context to recall that the often-violent agitations for ban on cow slaughter subsided, when the matter went before the high courts and later the Supreme Court, irrespective of the merits of their decisions. Similarly, the highly emotive and explosive issues pertaining to implementation of secular policies need to be depoliticized by entrusting them to a constitutional commission on secularism. It may be recalled that Turkey's ruling Justice and Development Party (AKP) faced a serious battle for survival in 2007 when the country's constitutional court reviewed a case to ban the party for its alleged anti-secular activities in violation of the Turkish Constitution.

The reports of all commissions and bodies set up by the government are required to be submitted by them to the government which in turn submits them to Parliament. Often, there is considerable delay in the process and the government chooses the time politically most convenient and opportune for the purpose. Looking to the special position proposed to be accorded to the COS, it is suggested that the annual or any special reports of the commission may be submitted by the commission directly to Parliament and the government, and released simultaneously to the media and the public.

Secularism is a precious fundamental right of each citizen and the COS would ensure that it becomes a reality. I am aware that such a step will be resisted by vested interests, but if pressure of public opinion is built up, its establishment would make a significant difference to the way India is governed. The question which remains is whether there will be statesmanship and political will to support this far-reaching and over-due political reform. A national campaign needs to be launched to prevail upon all political parties to initiate and support steps for a constitutional amendment to set up a commission on secularism.

Separation of Religion from Politics: The serious problem of communalism and communal violence was brought out earlier. It is interesting to see from the fortnightly letter of Nehru to chief ministers as far back as 3rd September 1954 that the nature or the intensity of the communal problem has not changed even after passage of 62 years since then, underlining the importance once again of separation of religion from politics. Nehru had written: "there are some Muslims in some centers who might be prone to mischief. There are one or two Muslim organizations that have been carrying on objectionable activities… The Hindu communal organizations are aggressive, and they can play on the religious or other feelings of the majority community… Agitations like the anti-cow slaughter are also used for this purpose. I have no doubt that many people who participate in this agitation are influenced by political or like motives and not so much by religious ones. The RSS utilizes this for its own purposes."[10]Gopal S. and Iyengar Uma, ed., The essential Writings of Jawaharlal Nehru, vol. I, Oxford University Press, New Delhi, 2003, pp. 190-1.

Earlier, Jawaharlal Nehru had reiterated in his fortnightly letter to the chief ministers on 5th February 1948: "There is a strong opinion in the country, with which I sympathize, that no political-religious organization or rather no organization confined to a particular religious group and aiming at political ends, should be allowed to function. We have suffered enough from this type of communalism whether it is Muslim or Hindu or Sikh...I do not want, of course, to suppress any legitimate political activity. But the combination of political activity with a religious group is a dangerous one as we know from experience. You will have to give thought to this matter as to what should be done."[11]Parthasarathy G., ed., Jawaharlal Nehru--Letters to Chief Ministers 1947-1964, Jawaharlal Nehru Memorial Fund, New Delhi, 1985, p.60.

Unfortunately, *these remained only pious wishes and, during his long tenure of 17 years as PM, Nehru miserably failed to take any further action.* I firmly believe that unless this issue is addressed with enough political resolve to carry through a suitable constitution amendment, it will be futile to talk about India as a secular nation. On the basis of the past experience and to meet the concerns expressed by some political parties during the debate on the Constitution (Eightieth) Amendment Bill in 1993 regarding the likely misuse of such an enactment, I would suggest that the amendment bill should be confined only to deregistration of a political party which has religious links and restraining such political party from contesting elections at any level in the country. A political consensus needs to be built up among political parties for the purpose. If any political parties are not prepared to join in the consensus, a strong public opinion will have to be created nationally to isolate them and to go ahead with the constitution amendment, disregarding their opposition. Some persons may consider this a tall order but there is no getting away from such a surgical operation, if the nation is to be saved!

Right to Propagation of Religion: Apart from giving freedom of conscience and permitting free profession and practice of religion, article 25 gives freedom of propagation of religion. There was considerable controversy about giving this right, and that too as a fundamental right. Several members in the Constituent Assembly had spoken against giving such a right but their objections were overruled on the spacious plea that it was necessary to give this right in accordance with the compromise which was arrived at with the Muslims and the Christians who had argued that propagation was a duty cast on them by their religion. The recommendations of the '*Niyogi Committee on Activities of the Christian Missionaries*' on the subject underline how serious has been the problem of conversion, particularly in the tribal areas.[12]Niyogi Committee Report on Christian Missionary Activities, 1956, http://en. wikipedia.org/wiki.

There are several decisions of the high courts and the Supreme Court according to which the right to propagation is not a right to conversion.

The activities of Muslims and Christian missionaries in some parts of the country have led to serious law and order problems. The *ghar-wapsi* (returning home) movement undertaken by the Hindu organizations has also led to communal tensions and agitations in various places. It is high time this problem is nipped in the bud by amending article 25 to delete the word 'propagation' therefrom.

Doing *Away with Protection to Minority Educational Institutions*: Articles 25 to 29 of the Constitution are really the crux of secularism, except for the word 'propagation' as discussed earlier. Article 30 (1) which gives right to minorities to establish and administer educational institutions is, in one sense, an appendage and need not have been there at all. But this too was inserted, particularly at the instance of the Christians and Anglo-Indians who had several educational institutions. There was considerable opposition to this article in the Constituent Assembly, but the Congress party wanted to be generous to the minorities, disregarding the likely long-term implications of encouraging separate identities and undermining spread of secular education. There is no justification to continue this right. If at all, it could be retained for the linguistic minorities. But considering the rapid spread of English as a medium of instruction all over the country, including in the rural areas, due to the forces of globalization and spread of information technology. it is no longer necessary to give this right even to linguistic minorities.

Deleting Provision for Prohibition of Cow Slaughter: Article 48, though a part of the directive principles, has now been elevated in public discourse to the level of a fundamental right. The marginal note of this article is innocuously worded as 'organization of agriculture and animal husbandry'. However, the sting is really in the sentence which asks the state to prohibit the slaughter of cows and calves and other milch and draught cattle. The basic question is whether such a total ban on slaughter of cows and their progeny is justified on any grounds at all except that of the religious sentiments of the Hindus. But there is no universal demand for a total ban by all Hindus. Most importantly, such a ban is not in keeping with secularism.

Particularly in the drought-hit areas in several states such as Maharashtra, it is causing large-scale distress to farmers. As I have stated earlier, Indian Constitution is a mix of several compromises, particularly in so far as its proclaimed secular ideology is concerned. Particularly after the BJP government came to power in the Centre in 2014, the demand for banning cow slaughter has gained strength. Effectively 'ban the beef' has become the national motto and another potent instrument in the hands of extremist elements to disturb the peace, tranquility and communal harmony in the country. Jawaharlal Nehru had stoutly opposed the demand for banning cow slaughter during his term and had even staked his prime minister-ship thereon. Thereafter the stand of the Congress party has changed completely and now it seems to be as much in favor of the total ban as the BJP and the Shiv Sena. It is time to consider seriously whether India can sustain its claim as a secular nation by resorting to such populist measures. I am firmly of the view that all well-meaning people in the country should come forward to strongly oppose the present moves on the subject.

Two Basic Electoral Reforms

Making Voting Compulsory: Secularism in India has remained at the margin mainly because people have not looked at it as their fundamental right. In fact, it is considered an important ingredient of vote-bank politics. Unless all eligible voters participate in the elections, the accountability of the political parties cannot be established fully. The government of Gujarat had taken the initiative in the matter by enacting a law for making voting compulsory for elections to village panchayats. The Governor had reserved the bill for approval of the President. In many instances in the past, the central government has looked at several proposals received from the state governments in a partisan manner. This bill was one of them and was kept pending by UPA government for a long time. A Private Members' Bill had also been introduced in Parliament during the UPA regime to make voting compulsory, but it was not supported by the government.

Voting has been made compulsory at least in 30 democracies round the world. They include, among others, Argentina, Australia, Austria, Belgium, Bolivia, Brazil, Costa Rica, Cyprus, Fiji, Greece, Luxembourg, Peru, Singapore, Switzerland and Uruguay. Compulsory voting was introduced in Australia in 1924 when the voter turnout was just about 58% in 1922 elections. Now Australia consistently boasts of a voter turnout of over 90%. Compulsory voting in Belgium went back to 1893. Currently voter turnout in Belgium is the same. *[Godbole Madhav, Good Governance Never on India's Radar*, Rupa & Co., New Delhi, 2014, pp. 174-5, 248-9.]

As can be seen, the results achieved are quite striking. The objections raised to making voting compulsory are hardly convincing. For example, it is argued that a person cannot be forced to vote if he does not want to. The law can provide that a person would have the option to go to the polling station and mark his preference on the ballot paper in a separate box showing his disinclination to vote. Another objection which has been raised is that it would be administratively impossible to deal with hundreds and thousands of cases where people default and do not vote. Even this objection is not sustainable as such cases can even be dealt with by post by conveying to the person that he would have to pay the prescribed fine for contravention of the law for compulsory voting. Even announcing on a notice board, in the case of village panchayats, and in newspapers, in other cases, names of persons who have not voted, could serve the purpose of shaming the persons. Particularly in a case like India where the day of voting is declared a public holiday, there is no justification to not vote. In the final analysis question is whether absentee democracy is what we are aiming at. If all minorities, for example, make it a point to go and vote, their political leverage will increase by leaps and bounds, and their voice cannot be ignored by the political parties any longer. When the voting age was reduced by Rajiv Gandhi government from 21 years to 18 years, doubts were raised about its advisability, but we have seen what difference it has made to the political life in the country. Similarly, now voting needs to be made compulsory for the elections to the local bodies, state legislatures and Parliament.

Making 50 %+1 Vote Necessary to Win: The first-past-the-post system adopted in India since the British times, though simple to administer, suffers from some important deficiencies. It is seen that in most cases the winning candidate gets negligible votes, at times just 20 to 30 percent of the total, which is a mockery of representative democracy. In the elections to UP Assembly held in 2007, 96.53% of the winners polled less than 50% of the votes cast. The corresponding figures were 89.71% in Bihar (2005), 88.89% in Bihar (2006), 81.63% in Tamil Nadu (2006), 93.84% in Jharkhand (2005) and so on. In the Lok Sabha elections in 2004, the corresponding percentage was 59.85. [Gopalaswami N., Political Parties and Elections: Some Issues, Journal of Constitutional and Parliamentary Studies, vol. 41, #3-4, New Delhi, July-December 2007, p. 196.

The National Commission to Review the Working of the Constitution (NCRWC) has also invited attention to this matter and has stated: "The multiplicity of political parties combined with our Westminster-based first-past-the post system results in most legislators and parliamentarians getting elected on a minority vote. In other words, they usually win by obtaining less than 50% of the votes cast, i.e. with more votes cast against them than in their favor. There are states where 85 to 90% legislators have won on a minority vote. At the national level, the proportion of MPs who have won on a minority vote is over 67% at an average for the last three Lok Sabha elections. In extreme cases, some candidates have won even with 13% of the votes polled. But more importantly in this system often the winning candidate confines his propaganda to his own caste, creed, language or religious group. Particularly in a country like India which is a multi-religious, multi-racial, multi-linguistic and multi-ethnic society a system must be devised which would make it as representative of this diverse community as possible. This can be done only by laying down that a winning candidate must get minimum 50% plus 1 vote. To be able to achieve this, a candidate would necessarily have to appeal to a broad spectrum of his constituency. This will be especially important for minorities since they are often neglected and overlooked in the present election campaigns.

At times, it is argued that this will prolong the election process and would be administratively impossible to implement. However, this is clearly not based on any in-depth understanding of the issues. With the adoption of the electronic voting system it should not be difficult to hold a second round of voting among the two top candidates who had received the maximum votes. The Election Commission has also favored this suggestion and has said that it sees no difficulty in its implementation. The NCRWC had also recognized "the beneficial potential of this system for a more representative democracy". The commission has recommended that the government and the Election Commission of India should examine this issue in all its aspects, consult various political parties and other interests that might consider themselves affected by this change and evaluate the acceptability and benefits of this system. The Commission recommended a careful and full examination of this issue.[15]Government of India, Review of the Working of the Constitution, Report of the National Commission to Review the Working of the Constitution, vol. II, Book 1, New Delhi, 2002, pp. 91-2.

If secularism is to be strengthened in the country, I strongly believe that this electoral reform is necessary and needs to be implemented as soon as possible. According to the Nepal's Ambassador to India, Deep Kumar Upadhyay, Nepal's newly promulgated Constitution is the most progressive in South Asia with its provisions of 33% reservation for women. It also has both first-past-the-post system as well as proportional representation. This combination of the two ensures that minorities' representation is taken care of. (Indian Express, September 24, 2015: 1)

Centre-State Relations and Bogey of Federalism: During the last few years several critical issues facing the country have got bogged down due to the fears expressed by the states about the federalism getting adversely affected. This cry for 'federalism in danger' is as dangerous as the cry of 'religion in danger'. This has affected policies in various areas such as enacting a model law for *Lokayuktas*, enactment of a central legislation for the Central Bureau of Investigation, reorganization of the railway police protection force, setting up of a federal police agency and so on. When the Constitution was prepared, the problems of law and order, terrorism, Naxalism, organized crime, and crime with international ramifications were not serious enough and, therefore, the subjects 'public order' and 'police' were put in the State List. Ideally, both these should have been put in the Concurrent List, as is the case in several Western democracies. As a result, states have been objecting to the role of central government in these matters. But this has not prevented the states from relying on the deployment of central para-military forces, when the occasion demanded. But restricting the role of the central government has led to cases such as Ayodhya debacle, Godhra riots and major communal riots in several states. Time has therefore come to take a serious view on amendment of the Constitution. Federalism will be relevant only if the country survives!

These issues are particularly relevant if communal violence and communal riots are to be dealt with effectively. The experience so far shows that unless the central government is enabled to take an active role in the matter, merely making available to states central para-military forces and intelligence inputs from central agencies will not be adequate.

Restructuring Police Departments: Experience has shown that weaknesses and inadequacies of police have been largely responsible for starting or escalating communal violence. The root cause of this is the politicization and communalization of police in various states. Several judicial commissions of inquiry appointed on major communal riots have strongly brought out this point. Reference must be made in this context to the decision of the Supreme Court in the public interest litigation on non-implementation of the recommendations of the national police commission. The final decision of the court came only in September 2006, nearly 12 years after the filing of the PILs. Though inordinately delayed, the Supreme Court laid down guidelines for reorganization of the police departments in the states and the Centre. Though nearly a decade has elapsed since the decision of the Supreme Court, most major state governments have not implemented the court orders. For example, the data collected by the Bureau of Police Research and Development (BPR&D) for the year 2013 shows that almost 80% of Superintendents of Police (SPs) in districts across the country got transferred within two years of their tenure in a district. Over 50% got transferred in less than a year. According to the data, UP has been the worst offender in terms of transferring officers before their two-year tenure is complete. Even Officers senior to SPs have not been spared. As per the data, in 2013, 114 range DIGs faced transfers within a year of their tenure. As many as 48 were transferred within two years. (i.e. November 29, 2015: 7) For some strange reason, the Supreme Court has been reluctant to haul up the defaulting states for contempt of court.

Another matter of serious concern is the politicization and communalization of police. In this connection special mention must be made of the statements of LK Advani who had spearheaded the Babri Masjid agitation. He has written in his autobiography, '*My Country My Life*': "I recall vividly an experience *en-route* from Ayodhya to Lucknow [on December 6, 1992 after demolition of the Babri Masjid]. Despite strict security all along the 135 km journey, I could see people engaged in celebrations everywhere. Within half an hour of our departure from Ayodhya, our car was stopped by the police. On seeing that the car carried Pramod Mahajan and me, a senior officer of the UP government walked up to us [and] said, '*Mr. Advani, Koch bacha to nahin no? Bilkul saaf kar diya na?*' (I hope nothing of the structure is surviving and that it has been totally raised to the ground.) I am recounting this incident only to highlight the general mood of the populace, including employees and officials of the state government, after the tragic development in Ayodhya—that of jubilation." Advani L.K., My Country, My Life, Rupa & Co., New Delhi, 2008, p. 402. 18 Government of India, Ministry of Home Affairs, Eighth and Concluding Report of the National Police Commission, New Delhi, 1981, p. 52.

The National Police Commission in its eighth and concluding report submitted in May 1981 had made one significant recommendation. An officer who has functioned as the DGP /IGP, after his retirement from service, shall not be eligible for any employment under the government of India or under the state government or in any public undertaking in which GOI or the state government have a financial interest. Government of India, Ministry of Home Affairs, Eighth and Concluding Report of the National Police Commission, New Delhi, 1981, p. 52. This is equally relevant for the senior Indian Administrative Service officers. This very critical recommendation ought to have been acted upon expeditiously. There have been any number of instances where senior police [and IAS] officers who had obliged the political party in power during the communal riots have been handsomely rewarded. One can cite dozens of instances to support this. I would suggest that even now it is not too late to accept this recommendation. I would like to suggest only one amplification thereof, namely, such officers will not also be given political party tickets to contest elections during a cooling-off period of three years.

To create confidence amongst the minorities that they will be treated fairly, justly and their life and property will be safeguarded, all efforts must be made to deal with the communal bias in the police. The precepts of secularism, safeguarding the interests of the minorities and importance of human rights are some of the subjects which need to be included in the syllabus of police training institutions. In the refresher courses organized for field police officers and constabulary, actual case studies of communal riots, findings of official inquiries or judicial commissions of inquiries must be placed before them for discussion. Knowledgeable representatives of minority communities could be invited for interaction with the police personnel in the training sessions. Unfortunately, this important aspect has been totally lost sight of.

It is also necessary to give enough representation to minorities in the police services. In this context, the example of the Rapid Action Force of the central government which is often deployed during communal riots is noteworthy. Conscious efforts have been made by the central government to give representation to minorities in this force. This example needs to be replicated in the states. The indication of how the winds are blowing since the coming to power of the BJP government at the Centre in 2014 is the recent instruction issued by the home ministry to the NCRB not to publish the data on Muslims in police. The publication of such data first began 16 years ago. It is for the first time that such a ban has been imposed. (*Indian Express*, November 30, 2015: 1) Such efforts are counter-productive for the success of secularism. The NCRB report for 2013 showed that there were 108,000 Muslim police who accounted for 6.27% of the total strength of 1,731,000 police in the country compared to 7.55% in 2007. Public pressure must be brought on the government to revise this decision to ensure that data on Muslims in police will be published each year.

Rule of Law and Reality: Even if police departments are restructured as above and other changes suggested herein are affected, unless rule of law is established in the country, nothing substantial can be achieved. This is particularly true in dealing with an important and sensitive subject like secularism. Reference must be made to the important provisions of sections 153-A and 153-B of Indian Penal Code (IPC) which have largely remained on paper. The 'majesty of law' about which a common citizen hears time and again is supposed to have laid down that 'howsoever high you maybe, the law is above you'. This is certainly not true so far as the high and mighty in public life are concerned.

Full powers need to be given to the senior police officers to directly prosecute persons infringing these provisions, without the necessity of obtaining the approval of the state government. Experience has shown that the state governments look at this question entirely from a political point of view and withhold the approval for prosecution or even reject the proposal altogether. It is seen that cases filed under these sections are often withdrawn later at the behest of the government for political ends. If secularism is to be translated into reality, communalism will have to be put down with a firm hand. And this would be possible only by ensuring that the above provisions of IPC are made effective. The National Commission to Review the Working of the Constitution has also said that "effective implementation of laws is lacking. This deserves the highest degree of attention" (p. 87). Toward this end, as recommended by the second administrative reforms commission (SARC), the provision contained in section 196 CrPC requiring prior sanction of union or state government or the district magistrate for initiating prosecution for offences under sections 153A, 153B, 295A (deliberate and malicious acts, intended to outrage religious feelings of any class by insulting its religion or religious beliefs). and section 505 (statements conducing to public mischief) sub-sections (1)(c) (with intent to incite, or which is likely to incite, any class or community of persons to commit any offence against any other class or community), (2) (statements creating or promoting enmity, hatred or ill-will between classes) and (3) (offences under subsection (2) committed in place of worship, etc.) of IPC, be deleted. It has also rightly suggested that the punishment for communal offences be enhanced, and special courts should be set up for speedy disposal of the cases. I fully agree with the recommendation of SARC that a separate law to deal with communal violence is not required. The UPA government's proposal in this regard had led to bitter confrontation between the states and the Centre and the political parties which were in opposition then. Strengthening of the provisions of the IPC and CrPC will be adequate to deal with the situation.

Last 69 years since Independence have seen not only repeated incidents of communal violence, as brought out above, but regrettably some of these riots had literally turned into massacres. To recall, a few of these were: Jabalpur riot in 1961, Ahmedabad riot in 1969, anti-Sikh riots in Delhi in 1984, Mumbai riots in 1992-93 and Godhra riots in 2002. Against this background it is necessary to make a special provision to deal with genocides such as these. The law should provide to make such offences cognizable and non-bailable and much stricter punishment extending up to life imprisonment. Fear of law must be inculcated unambiguously, and anti-social elements which generally take advantage of these situations and the government functionaries who either connive at them or even support them must also be dealt with severely.

Unusual times call for unusual solutions. Experience has shown that hardly any worthwhile action has been taken so far against government functionaries who were handling these situations and had failed miserably. Time has come to examine whether the provisions of the law of torts should be extended to all those remiss in handling the genocides. Class action suits need to be initiated in such cases as it would be impossible for the individual victims to file cases against the concerned powerful politicians and police functionaries. It is only by applying the provisions of the law of torts that they would become seriously aware of their responsibilities.

Another legislation which has wholly remained on paper is the Religious Institutions (Prevention of Misuse) Act, 1988. Rajiv Gandhi government must be given credit for enacting this legislation, but it has remained only as a showpiece. It was seen during the Punjab agitation that there was a large-scale misuse of Gurudwaras by the terrorists for preaching their ideology. In Jammu and Kashmir, the separatists have been using Friday Namaz gatherings to launch their ideological offensive against the central government and its organizations. Hardly any action has been taken in these cases. Same is true of the Places of Worship (Special Provisions) Act, 1991 which too has not been acted upon.

It is equally frustrating to see that communal speeches made by candidates have not been adequately dealt with under the provisions of the Representation of People Act, 1951. In this context, the observation of the Supreme Court in one of the cases is significant. The Court had said: so long as communal political parties are not banned from participating in political life of the country, there is very little that the courts can do to restrain. Reference must also be made to the recommendation of the 'National Commission to Review the Working of the Constitution' in this regard. The commission has recommended: "Any election campaigning based on caste or religion and any attempt to spread caste and communal hatred during elections should be punishable with mandatory imprisonment. If such acts are done at the instance of the candidate or his election agents, these would be punishable with disqualification." (p. 87) Unfortunately, no action has been taken by the government on this recommendation.

Adoption of Inquisitorial System: The experience of investigation of crimes in communal riots has raised serious questions, whether it be anti-Sikh riots in Delhi or riots in Mumbai or Godhra or any other major communal riots in the country. There is a widely prevalent view that such cases are not investigated properly, and the police often act under political pressure or in a communal manner favoring one community or the other. It would be recalled that in some cases even a plea was made to the high courts and Supreme Court that a special investigation team (SIT) may be appointed by the court and the investigation may also be carried out under the supervision of the court. Such petitions were agreed to by the Supreme Court in Godhra cases but obviously this cannot be done in every case considering the workload of the high courts and Supreme Court. It is therefore time to consider whether in cases involving serious communal riots, the French model of *'police judiciare'* should be adopted.

Justice Malimath 'committee on reforms of criminal justice system' has noted that: The inquisitorial system is certainly efficient in the sense that the investigation is supervised by the judicial magistrate which results in a high rate of conviction. The committee on balance felt that a fair trial and with fairness to the accused, are better protected in the adversarial system. However, the committee felt that some of the good features of the inquisitorial system can be adopted to strengthen the adversarial system and to make it more effective. This includes the duty of the court to search for truth, to assign a pro-active role to the judges, to give directions to the investigating officers and prosecution agencies in the matter of investigation and leading evidence with the object of seeking the truth and focusing on justice to victims. Government of India, Ministry of Home Affairs, Report of the Committee on Reforms of Criminal Justice System (Justice VS Malimath Committee), vol. I, New Delhi, 2003, pp. 265-6. BK Nehru, former civil servant, diplomat and Governor, in his book '*Thoughts On Our Present Discontents*' has invited attention to the fact that: "In a country where telling lies in a court of law is not regarded as immoral, and where the police are unfortunately not always above manufacturing evidence and extorting confession, a system of this kind [inquisitorial] would, ... be definitely more suitable to our needs than our present procedures. As a result of a thorough magisterial investigation already made, the onus to prove his innocence lies heavily on the accused. This will shock our lawyers who have inherited Anglo-Saxon prejudices along with their system, but there is reason to believe that there are fewer miscarriages of justice under the continental system and much greater enforcement of the law than is prevalent in India today". Nehru BK, Thoughts on Our Present Discontents, Allied Publishers, Delhi, 1986, pp. 111-2.

The Law Commission in its seventy seventh report submitted in 1978, had recommended that "Although we have adopted the accusatorial system the trial judge should not play an altogether passive role, but must take greater interest and elicit such information as may be helpful in finding the truth".[23]Government of India, Ministry of Law and Justice, Law Commission of India, 77th Report on Delays and Arrears in Trial Courts, New Delhi, 1978, p. 157.

Despite these valid arguments there are many legal luminaries who are strongly opposed to any change-over from the existing system. I had in my book 'The Judiciary and Governance in India' (2008) examined these facets in the light of experience in many cases. I had stated: "This touching faith in the present state of Indian criminal justice system is difficult to understand. Even a cursory look at the data regarding the conviction rate should be instructive in this regard. In 1968 the conviction rate was 70 percent. In 1999 it came down to below 40% and in 2003 it was 35 percent. In 2006 it was estimated to be below 30%. According to the then chief justice of Bombay High Court Justice MB Shah, the conviction rate was just 5%." I had suggested that a trial should be given to the inquisitorial system on a pilot basis in selected districts. (Godbole 2008: 440-4) This has assumed new urgency in the context of increasing threats to secularism. In all major cases with a bearing on secularism in recent years, it has come to light that the police investigations and convictions leave much to be desired. This has created a great sense of insecurity among the victims of these riots who mostly belonged to minorities. I, therefore, believe that the time has come to take a decision that at least in cases of serious communal riots, to begin with, inquisitorial system should be adopted. This one single step will go a long way in reassuring the minorities that the government is serious about making a reality of secularism.

<u>*To Sum Up*</u>: The above analysis shows that a great deal remains to be done if secularism is to become a way of life in India. This will be possible only if there is a real political, social and intellectual commitment to it and, the state and central governments, the political parties, the civil society and the media strive for it. I am thankful to the Maharashtra Regional Branch of the Indian Institute of Public Administration headed by Shri Swadheen Kshatriya for giving me this valuable opportunity to share my thoughts with you." [Dr. Madhav Godbole is former union home secretary and secretary justice]

<u>We must be united first.</u> Then and only then we can tackle the problems/issues whether they are external, natural or internal. That is the only way we can get over our ignominious past and move forward with development for one and all irrespective of our caste, creed, political affiliation, regional or religious preferences or any other prejudices we may be harboring. We have to always keep in our mind what the youngest ever American President, John F Kennedy once said: *"The country comes first. We have to do whatever we can for our country without expecting what the country can do for me."* This, for we Hindustanis, is Now or NEVER!

<u>What is the status of women in India</u>? On the face of it, it appears inferior to that of men. Women, all over the world, have been treated unequally and kept suppressed. Even in the USA, women got their voting rights only in 1921 i.e. 132 years after the country started its independence existence. Our founding fathers gave voting rights to everyone above 21 years of age which has been reduced to 18 only half a century subsequently. India is not an exception on the question of equality to females. In fact, ours has been more male dominated than many other countries. This is paradoxical considering our ancestors appeared to have given more prominence to women since no *Yagna* was complete if the better half of the person wanting that was not present. On 17th December 2015, *Rediff.*

com News tried to answer that in its own way via an article, *'Participation of women in decision-making roles in India'*. "Women are now entering high-level decision-making positions in the world. The Universal Declaration of Human Rights recognizes the right of every person to take part in the government of his or her country. *Equal access of men and women to power, decision-making and leadership at all levels is a necessary precondition for the proper functioning of democracy.* Our *Rediff labs* team analyzed 2014 data from the Ministry of Statistics and Program Implementation on the participation of women in decision making at administrative levels in India in three different sectors.

Women judges in high courts. There were only 2 women judges out of 30 judges in the Supreme Court and there were only 58 women judges out of 609 judges in different High Courts. The highest percentages of women judges are present in high courts of Delhi, Chandigarh, Chennai, and Mumbai and no women judge in a total of 6 high courts in India.

Women in Politics: Female participation in elections has gone up from 56% in 15th General Elections in 2009 to 66% in the latest 16th in 2014. In the states, women share is only 8% in assemblies. The percentage is calculated as the number of women MLAs elected and the total number of seats for that state. The state assembles with highest percentage of women MLAs are Haryana, Rajasthan, West Bengal and Bihar.

Women in Civil Service. Among the All-India and Central Group 'A' Services, 30% females are in Indian Economic Service and only 12% in Indian Trade Service. The percentage of women in different services: Indian Forest Service 28; Indian Audit & Account Service 24; Indian Postal Service 21; Indian Information Service 21; Indian Foreign Service 19; Indian Statistical Service 15; Indian Administrative Service 14; and Indian Trade Service 11." [These data are from Ministry of Statistics and Program Implementation].

Therefore, notwithstanding, the statutory provisions in our Constitution, equality between the two sexes does not exist in practice despite statutory provisions, for example 30% legislatures must be women, and so on. There is quite a lot of discrimination in different walks of life, contrary to the express enunciation. All this is happening despite women have clearly outclassed and outmaneuvered men even in male-dominated fields.

Equality in the law among the various religions is a must if we want to follow the spirit and letter of our constitution unless we decide to write it afresh! Uniform civil code is an integral requirement to bring about this much-needed ingredient in any society. Moreover, we must rectify the colossal wrongs done by 'Muslim' Nehru and his dynasty if we must usher in a real secularism. Fortunately, we have a prime minister, Narendra Modi, who for the first time is bold enough and fully committed to take even unconventional measures for the betterment of we Hindustanis! The well-known thinker '*Madhu Kishwar's open letter to PM Modi on how to break the UCC stalemate*', on 27th August 2017 in *Economic Times* is a must for everyone concerned.

Dear Prime Minister Modi,

You have hailed the judgment of the Hon'ble Supreme Court on triple talaq as "historic" for granting equality to Muslim women and for "being a powerful measure for women empowerment." This despite the convoluted and tortured 272-page verdict of CJI, JS Khehar pronounced that "Triple Talaq is a constitutionally valid mode of divorce being intrinsic to Islamic personal law and hence part of fundamental rights". Interestingly, three other justices didn't see this interpretation worth supporting. It's a sad commentary on our secular democracy that a full bench of the Supreme Court, which doesn't have to go begging for Muslim votes, couldn't muster the courage to take a firm view against abhorrent practices that even Islamic, theocratic countries have banned. The fact that the mighty SC judges couldn't make up their mind on the validity of triple talaq within Sharia, leave alone its constitutional validity, shows how ill-equipped our secular courts are to don the mantle of qazis, mullahs and maulvis.

It defies comprehension why those who defend the divine sanctity of the Muslim personal law have willingly submitted to adjudication by India's secular courts where non-Muslim judges unfamiliar with the intricacies of Islamic law and zero knowledge of Arabic decide matters ostensibly based on Sharia and Koran. It is akin to having IAS officers delivering Friday sermons or leading Eid prayers.

As with much else, you have inherited this political mess from Congress government led by ultra-secular Nehru who, in the 1950s, doggedly pushed through half-baked reforms to create a Uniform Civil Code (UCC) *only* for Hindus. This, despite Ambedkar and several other leading lights of the Congress insisting that India needed to live up to its promise of being a secular state and hence honor the Directive Principle enshrined in Article 44 of the Indian Constitution, which clearly mandates that "the state shall endeavor to secure for all citizens a Uniform Civil Code throughout the the territory of India". But Nehru bestowed to Muslim personal law a status far above India's Constitution and gave us a messed-up version of a Hindu Civil Code, which has had to be amended again and again, with many new laws added in recent decades for protection of Hindu women's rights in the family.

Do Only Muslims Follow Personal Laws? Most people rooting for the enactment of UCC are under the mistaken impression that only Muslims and Christians follow their customary laws. The reality is that even Hindus generally follow the customary practices prevalent among their respective castes, sects and communities. For instance, despite amendments in the Hindu Succession Act that give women equal inheritance rights, daughters in countless Hindu families don't get any share in parental property. Instead, parents seek to "compensate" daughters by giving them dowry at the time of marriage, which has been declared illegal by the Dowry Prohibition Act.

Similarly, most Hindu communities continue to avoid *intra-gotra* marriages because they uphold this belief with passion that people belonging to the same gotra share a brother-sister bond. In their moral universe, a sagotra marriage is as good as incest even though there is no bar on sagotra marriages under the Hindu Marriage Act.

Likewise, the custom of marrying within one's caste and community continues among Hindus, Muslims and Christians alike, even though Hindu, Christian, or Muslim law doesn't require people to marry within their caste. Tribal customary laws are lethally weighted against women without anyone daring to touch them because the issue is seen to be politically volatile.

Breaking the Stalemate: The only way to break the stalemate on UCC is to undo the damage done by the Nehru-led government, which forced India's secular courts to decide on family disputes based on laws claiming religious sanction. The solution is much simpler than made out to be: The following proposal made by me in 1985 at the time of *Shah Bano controversy* has the potential to break the stalemate on UCC even today, that too without coercing Muslims and Christians into reform. It also enables the government to follow the Directive Principle of our Constitution that mandates that "the state shall endeavor to secure for the citizens Uniform Civil Code throughout the territory of India":

The secular courts of our country should stop adjudicating disputes based on personal laws of any community — be it Hindu, Muslim,

Christian or Parsi. Let's junk all the laws containing a communal tag, including Hindu Civil Code.

- The state should confine itself to adjudicating cases only under the already existing secular laws such as the Indian Marriage Act, Indian Divorce Act, Indian Succession Act, and Indian Wards & Guardianship Act. This will cancel out the need to enact a new Uniform Civil Code.
- The existing "Indian" laws should be applicable to all citizens that decide to approach the secular courts, irrespective of their caste, creed, gender or religion. However, these laws may need to be carefully reviewed and improved to make them truly egalitarian and gender-just.
- Those who wish to continue with the customary practices of their community, claiming religious or customary sanctity, should be free to do so, provided they don't expect secular courts of India to adjudicate and enforce their personal laws.
- The onus of ensuring compliance with what passes under the guise of the Muslim, Christian, Sikh, or Hindu customary law should rest with the consensually accepted leaders of that community instead of putting it on India's secular law courts.
- However, if even one party to a family dispute feels wronged or dissatisfied with the verdict of the authority adjudicating customary law, that aggrieved person should have the right to approach the Indian courts where the dispute should be adjudicated only within the framework of secular laws & constitutional principles.
- An alternative to a UCC would be to junk all laws with a communal tag — including the Hindu Civil Code — and adopt existing Indian family laws
- A growing number of Muslim women are filing cases under the Dowry Prohibition Act as well as the law against domestic violence, even though these laws don't draw legitimacy from the Quran or the Sharia. This is because these laws don't have the word "Hindu" attached to them.

<u>*Laws Apply Only When People Seek its Protection*</u>: Those who think this amounts to giving a free hand to regressive elements within each community should remember that family laws enacted by the state,

including provisions of the Indian Penal Code, come into play only when someone invokes their protection through the police and law courts. For example, beating up one's wife is a punishable offence. But if a battered wife chooses not to seek redress, the best of laws cannot be of help to her. Similarly, Muslim women who accept second or third marriages of their husbands are not going to benefit even if the arbitrary triple talaq is declared illegal.

Now concrete evidence is there that when better options are available, women don't hesitate to avail of them. Today, a growing number of Muslim women are filing cases under the Dowry Prohibition Act as well as the law against domestic violence, even though these laws don't draw legitimacy from Koran or Sharia. Neither the AIMPLB nor any maulvi has dared prohibit Muslim women from doing so. This is because these laws don't have the word "Hindu" attached.

The spontaneous, voluntary use of secular laws by affected women of all religions have had the salutary effect of bringing Hindu, Muslim, Christian, Sikh, Buddhist, tribal, non-tribal women on a common platform to fight for what are problems for women of all communities. Therefore, if we are serious about a Uniform Civil Code, let's do away with laws with a communal tag and let the two systems compete based on voluntary compliance. Dumping the Hindu Civil Code will also take the wind out if sails of all those who allege that UCC is a ploy to Hinduize Muslims and Christians. [*ET CONTRIBUTORS*]

On 2nd September 2018, *Rediff.com News* published an article, '*Why 2019 won't be like 2004 for the BJP*'. '"Vajpayee was predictable in his ways. Modi is a schemer, possessed of a shrewdness that can be rewarding in the chaotic world of politics. 'His political journey gives reason to believe that 2019 will be another milestone in his private project,' notes Vikram Johri. Reactions to former PM Vajpayee's death reconfirmed the huge popularity the leader enjoyed not just among the BJP cadre but a vast swathe of the political leadership. His funeral procession through Delhi was reminiscent of the sort of public grief usually associated with the passing of South Indian thespians. Tears flowed freely at the subsequent *Shraddhanjali Sabha* organized by the government. Op-eds written in the aftermath of Vajpayee's death have focused on his political and economic legacy, the first characterized by his large-heartedness, most notably on Kashmir, and the second by his determination to take forward the reforms unleashed by PV Narasimha Rao nearly a decade before Vajpayee's term as the PM.

From telecom to IT, highways to electricity, it was repeatedly pointed out that we are reaping the fruits of the seeds sown by him. The dichotomy of his immense popularity and good governance on the one hand and the BJP's drubbing in the 2004 polls cannot be overstressed. 'India Shining', the ad campaign his government unleashed in the run-up to the 2004 polls, has since become the advertising equivalent of 'the road to hell...' Even Vajpayee's fiercest critics must have been dumbstruck by that loss, given the long, hard road he and LK Advani, his deputy in the party and government, took to bring the BJP to the fore. That loss will not easily be forgotten in the BJP, which is quick to point out that the subsequent UPA dispensation diluted the promise of the NDA years.

The prospect of defeat, despite an acknowledged track record in government, must particularly roil PM Modi and BJP President Amit Shah as they look to avoid that outcome next year. Modi is arguably as popular as Vajpayee, but his popularity is of a decidedly different hue. Vajpayee was known and celebrated for his expansiveness. Both Mamata Banerjee and Mehbooba Mufti, who are unlikely to say kind things about Modi, heaped praise on Vajpayee after his death. Vajpayee the poet was indistinguishable from Vajpayee the politician, a factor that may have contributed to the inertia that led to the 2004 outcome.

Modi's popularity has a more deliberate sheen. Unlike Vajpayee, he gives the impression of carving out a mandate in his favor. One example of this is his willingness to go after others in the political class. In popular perception, the cases against Lalu Prasad as well as P Chidambaram and his son could not have proceeded without his go-ahead Modi is also careful not to give the impression that his government is only working for the rich, an unfortunate correlation for any leader who seeks to reform economic policies. The rural push undertaken by his government, including *Jan Dhan*, housing and the provision of LPG, is one part of that story. Another instance of Modi's doggedness is the army's renewed push in Kashmir to smoke out Pakistan-funded terrorists. The government's going after the likes of Vijay Mallya and the exercise of demonetization feed into a larger narrative of an administration keen to reform a plutocratic system. The most crucial point of difference between the two leaders, however, may lie in their worldviews. Modi is willing to raise questions -- such as the need to reform Muslim law -- that Vajpayee avoided. Aware of his reputation and that of his party, he is cautiously tackling issues around minority rights that have long vexed the Indian polity.

Finally, Modi and Shah run an electoral machine unrivalled in the history of Indian politics. While Modi's popularity has some role to play in the string of victories the BJP has enjoyed since 2014, Shah's micromanagement must share the credit. Obsessed with numbers, the duo has been making inroads into traditionally BJP-averse areas like Bengal and Kerala to make up for any seats the party may lose in the Hindi heartland. Vajpayee was too retiring a man to lose sleep over *panna pramukhs*. *It is for these reasons that Modi is likelier to return to power next year than Vajpayee was in 2004.* Vajpayee was a multidimensional man who was nevertheless predictable in his ways. Modi is a schemer, possessed of a shrewdness that can be rewarding in the chaotic world of politics. His political journey thus far gives reason to believe that 2019 will be another milestone in his private project. [Source: *Business Standard*:]

On 25th December 2014, Modi made an unscheduled impromptu halt to then Pakistan Premier Nawaz Sharif's residence at Lahore to enforce his will to improve Indo-Pak relations. Nawaz could not move forward due to army's intentions in keeping alive terrorism as the state policy. In an apparent thaw in talks, Pakistan has conveyed to India its decision to open the Kartarpur Corridor for the Sikh pilgrims on Guru Nanak's 550th birth anniversary, Foreign Minister Shah Mahmood Qureshi said Thursday, the 22nd November 2018. Although the present PM Imran Khan is a creation of Pakistani army, the implications of this unusual step need to be studied carefully! Is it really a thaw as Imran is continuously making statements to improve Indo-Pak relations? But his army must first stop pushing its trained terrorists across LoC!

Earlier on 31st August, *Rediff.com News* published, *'Chanting Ambedkar's name makes Dalit leaders cross over to BJP'*. 'The BJP stems from the RSS that craves, notwithstanding its myriad camouflages, to re-establish their supremacist regime. They believe in everything that India had in its ancient 'Vedic' past, including the caste system. 'Dr Anand Teltumbde was one of the intellectuals and civil rights activists whose homes were raided by the Pune police on Tuesday, August 28. Professor Detumble was in Mumbai when a Pune police team searched his home in Panaji and his response to the raid was published.

Earlier this month, Dr Teltumbde published his latest book, *'Republic of Caste: Thinking Equality in the Time of Neoliberal Hindutva'*. In the book, he explains how the condition of Dalits has remained more or less the same post-Independence, how various political parties were able to co-opt them from time to time, and how the masses were betrayed by Dalit leaders who benefitted from the concern of the ruling classes for their votes. "I have not seen any Dalit leader in his lap ever voicing any criticism against Modi!" Dr Teltumbde told *Rediff.com's* Syed Firdaus Ashraf in an interview conducted a couple of weeks before the police raid on his home.

If they open their mouths in protest, they are labelled as Maoists. You write that Dr Ambedkar disowned the Constitution saying he was used as a hack. Ambedkar was initially opposed to a Constituent Assembly, but when it was convened, he was very desperate to get into it because he was anxious to see whatever safeguards he won for Dalits are continued in the Constitution. There was no way he could enter it, however, as his party had won just two seats in the provincial assemblies. He managed to get elected from the Khulna-Jessore constituency in East Bengal with the help of Jogendranath Mandal, a Dalit leader in united Bengal. Soon, however, his membership got annulled due to the Partition of India, vide the Mountbatten Plan of June 1947. Mysteriously, the Congress that treated him as anathema decided to shelve its plan and get him elected from the Bombay assembly before the next session of the Constituent Assembly was convened. There is no documentary evidence to uncover this mystery but given the dislike of Nehru for Ambedkar and the neutrality of Patel, it could not have been other than Gandhi who was capable of this. Because, as an emerging icon of the lower strata of the country, only Ambedkar could provide the Constitution the much-needed security. He was accordingly made chairman of the most important committee, the drafting committee, and later projected as the chief architect of the Constitution. No doubt he did much of piloting and correcting the draft (which was already made) of the Constitution single-handedly, but the Constituent Assembly debate clearly reveals his specific contribution. When Dalits zealously attribute the making of the Constitution to him, they do not understand that they accuse him of its infirmities. Ambedkar spoke out that his main purpose behind getting into the Constituent Assembly was to safeguard the Dalit interests.

Initially, he was sanguine about his accomplishment but within two years he was completely disillusioned to disown it in the strongest possible words. When we ask why he allowed self to be abused, we forget the context in which he worked and the making of the man. Ambedkar was a pragmatist who believed in maximizing the utility of given circumstances.

The Congress kept Dalits with them for very long, till the 1990s. How did the shift to the BJP occur? Yes, during the early years, Congress had a near monopoly over Dalit, Adivasi and minority votes, alongside the upper caste votes. RSS, which proclaimed it as a cultural organization, floated a political party, Bhartiya Jan Sangh. But could not have much impact. It was only after (Madhukar Dattatray) Deoras becoming its *sarsanghchalak* that new strategies were forged to expand the constituency. RSS silently entered the forested regions and began working among the tribals to gradually Hinduize them. Deoras realized the importance of Dr Ambedkar as well as the Dalits. He silently included Ambedkar in the RSS's *pratahsmaraniya* (one who should be remembered each morning). In 1983, RSS floated a new special purpose vehicle, the *Samajik Samarstha Manch*, to woo middle class urban Dalits. They did not meet with much success but persisted with it for decades. They brought out a huge amount of literature subtly saffronizing Ambedkar. 'The entire process is conducted as though I was a dreaded Dalits who came to treat Ambedkar as a symbol of their pride and prestige, took pride in acknowledgement of the Brahminic organization. This infirmity of Dalits is used by the political parties to the hilt.

Dr Ambedkar fell prey to Gandhi as far as signing the Poona Pact was concerned, but which he regretted later, if I am not mistaken. Yes, he was blackmailed by Gandhi into signing the Poona Pact that would annul the communal award allotting separate electorates to the Dalits and give them double the reserved seats in exchange. It was difficult for him to resist any more in the face of falling health of Gandhi. Surprisingly, Ambedkar's reaction to it was happiness. He said if that was what Gandhi wanted, he would have happily given him. *But soon he realized the import of signing it and regretted it.* Dalit leaders in the BJP and their allies like Ram Vilas Paswan are upset that the National Green Tribunal is now headed by Justice AK Goel who as Supreme Court judge delivered the order to 'dilute' the SC/ST Atrocities Act. He is called a weather cock to assess political weather. He holds a record for remaining a central minister whichever party comes to power. He, like many Dalit leaders, must justify his existence to the voters uttering some platitudes. If they do not take up issues like the 'dilution' of the SC/ST Atrocities Act and reservation for Dalits in promotions, then their legitimacy comes into question. Their legitimacy with the ruling circle is that they are the leaders of Dalits. They maintain this bogey.

Don't you feel that YB Chavan getting Dalits into the Congress, thus bringing them into the national discourse, was good for India as a country? Ultimately you have. Don't you feel that Y B Chavan getting Dalits into the Congress, thus bringing them into the national discourse, was good for India as a country? Ultimately you must get everyone together for our country to work. This sounds like advocating *samarasata*, social harmony, of the RSS. It is like saying what is the harm for Muslims to say that they are Islamic Hindus or Christians as Christi Hindus.

Right now, all Dalit parties are rising against Modi over the SC/ST Act issue. What, according to them, has been done to the Act? As a matter of fact, none of the Dalit parties is seriously concerned with the SC/ST Act. If they have woken up to its dilution in the recent judgment of the Supreme Court, it is due to the concerns being raised among Dalits. Given this development, they make a noise to display their concern for Dalits. Don't you feel that YB Chavan getting Dalits into the Congress, thus bringing them into the national discourse, was good for India as a country? Ultimately you get everyone together for our country to work. This sounds like advocating *samarasata*, social harmony, of the RSS. It is like saying what is the harm for Muslims to say that they are Islamic Hindus or Christians as Christi Hindus.

Can that be done? Muslims, Christians, Dalits, Adivasis are significant communities in India and there is no other way than recognizing them as such. The national interest rests not on hammering homogeneity but acknowledging and recognizing diversity. The RSS is grossly mistaken; it must recognize that each of its acts is a destruction of the legacy of India, that they so loudly claim."

www.ingramcontent.com/pod-product-compliance
Lightning Source LLC
LaVergne TN
LVHW091527060526
838200LV00036B/516